John D. Martin

Representations of Jews in Late Medieval and Early Modern German Literature

PETER LANG

Oxford · Bern · Berlin · Bruxelles · Frankfurt am Main · New York · Wien

Bibliographic information published by Die Deutsche Bibliothek
Die Deutsche Bibliothek lists this publication in the Deutsche Nationalbibliografie;
detailed bibliographic data is available on the Internet at ‹http://dnb.ddb.de›.

British Library and Library of Congress Cataloguing-in-Publication Data:
A catalogue record for this book is available from *The British Library,* Great Britain,
and from *The Library of Congress,* USA

Cover photo by Henry Maitek, Cologne, of eruve matzo plate (1770),
Alsatian Museum, Strasbourg
Cover design: Thomas Jaberg, Peter Lang AG

ISSN 1079-2384
ISBN 3-03910-068-8
US-ISBN 0-8204-6884-3

Printed in Germany

Contents

Chapter One:
The State of Contemporary Research

In the concluding remarks to his essay, "Der Talmudjude. Vom mittelalterlichen Ursprung eines neuzeitlichen Themas," Alexander Patschovsky observes:

> Ein Menschenbild aus solcherart gedeuteter Quelle trug naturgemäss nicht nur sinistre Züge. Überhaupt muss man sich hüten, das christliche Judenbild des späten Mittelalters als bloss negativ anzusehen. Es gibt durchaus Spuren, die in eine andere Richtung weisen, die zu sammeln und zu ordnen [sind], aber einer eigenen Betrachtung bedürfen; ich muss es hier bei dieser Andeutung belassen. Aber es ist ganz klar: So positive Gegenströmungen es auch gab – das negative, zum Monströsen sich verfestigende Bild beherrschte die Szene, war schier übermächtig.[1]

The title of the essay addresses one of the key issues in the current discussion of the images of Jews in medieval Christian thought. Just how strong are the connections between medieval and modern anti-Jewish hostility? If, as Patschovsky's title implies, the origins of a particular modern anti-Jewish stereotype are located in ideas from the Middle Ages, how did these same ideas shape Jewish-Christian relations in medieval and modern Europe? Exactly what were the counter-streams to the dominant view that he identifies as sheerly overpowering and what effects did these counter-streams have on relations between Jews and Christians? These are complex questions for historians and literary scholars alike, but the treatment they have received in recent scholarship has not always reflected the complexity of Jewish–Christian relations in the European Middle Ages.

Before addressing the attempts of historians and literary critics to describe Jewish–Christian relations in medieval German-speaking Europe, it seems helpful to provide the reader with a broad, general overview of the chief historical events, focusing on the thirteenth through the fifteenth centuries. The beginning of the thirteenth century continued a long period in which central European Jews lived with their Christian neighbors in peace. The massacres of the First Crusade in 1096 were more than a century past. Though the *Sicut Iudeis* letters from the Apostolic See gradually codified the legal status of Jews as generally inferior to that of free Christians, those same letters, along with imperial edicts, also provided the Jews of central Europe with a degree of legal protection that in some ways exceede d that of the Christian freeman.[2] The fact that the Jews had belonged, in the early Middle Ages, by virtue of their superior literacy and international connections to the higher social classes in the Holy Roman Empire contributed significantly to their ability to maintain their traditional legal protections into the High Middle Ages.[3] Throughout the thirteenth and fourteenth centuries, conditions for Jews were generally favorable in the Empire, especially so within the lands of the Austrian dukes, with Vienna in particular harboring a thriving Jewish community.[4] During the Rintfleisch pogroms of 1298, ritual murder accusations in the late 1290s and early 1300s, and during the sporadic accusations of host desecration in the same period, the Habsburgs secured for the Jews in Austria both ducal and imperial protection by force of arms.[5] Only in the second half of the fourteenth century did the condition of Jews in the Habsburg territories worsen significantly. The Jews of Vienna were spared the violent pogroms associated with the well-poisoning accusation in connection with the plague outbreaks of 1348–50; however, they fell victim to the twin accusations of host desecration and complicity with the Hussites in 1420. These patently false accusations led to a mass extermination of Jews in Austria in 1421, completely destroying the Jewish community in Vienna and ending in a few weeks what had been decades of peaceful, if often strained, Jewish–Christian coexistence.[6]

Elsewhere in medieval, German-speaking Europe, though, the end of the thirteenth century and beginning of the fourteenth marked the end of a period of peace and growth and the beginning of a long period in which persecutions became more frequent and lasted longer than they had before. It is true that, occasionally, years and even decades passed in which nearly frictionless coexistence was the norm.[7] It is, however, also true that late medieval German-speaking Europe never again produced anything approaching the long span of

2

peaceful Jewish–Christian coexistence in the seven centuries between the Christianization of the Roman Empire and the First Crusade.[8]

The most extensive and organized mob actions against Jews in German-speaking medieval Europe come at the end of the thirteenth century. In 1298 a man, reportedly a disgruntled butcher, initiated a series of attacks on Jewish communities in the cities of the Holy Roman Empire. "König Rintfleisch," as he came to be known, led an army of peasants and workmen in slaughtering perhaps as many as 10,000 people in the Rhine region.[9] After the Rintfleisch pogroms, not even forty full years would pass before southwestern German-speaking Europe was again the scene of widespread anti-Jewish violence. In the year 1336, a dispossessed Franconian nobleman, Arnold von Uissingheim, who came to be known as "König Armleder," initiated another wave of regional pogroms.[10] Though von Uissingheim himself was captured and executed in 1337,[11] organized mobs, some of which were led by Johannes Zimberli, continued to attack Jews of central German cities through 1338.[12] The years of the plague, 1348–50, produced another outbreak of widespread violence against Jews, after which such violence tapers off until the 1380s, when pogroms and attacks once again begin to increase to the point that in German-speaking Europe not a single decade between the 1380s and 1570s is completely free of anti-Jewish violence.[13]

In the course of the fifteenth century, there were other pogroms and expulsions beyond the German and Austrian pogroms described above. However, throughout the fifteenth century, Christians in German-speaking Europe also came to the defense of their imperiled Jewish neighbors, and Holy Roman Emperors enforced imperial decrees protecting Jews at a time when the Empire's fiscal gains from the Jewish community were diminishing.[14] The same late fifteenth century that heard the anti-Jewish preaching of Petrus Nigri heard also the more tolerant preaching of Nicolas of Cusa. The late fifteenth and early sixteenth centuries also witnessed the reigns of Friedrich II, Friedrich III, and Maximilian I, all of whom were accused by their political enemies of being too friendly to the Jews, that is, of protecting them against the hostile intentions of their Christian neighbors.[15] This evidence of persisting attitudes of religious and social tolerance, even in the face of widespread anti-Jewish violence, suggests that the relations between Jews and Christians were more complex than a simple 'oppressed/oppressor' diad.

In recent decades historians and literary scholars who study medieval and early modern Jewish–Christian relations in Western Europe have developed a number of theses concerning the relationship between Christian ideas about Jews and the treatment of Jews in medieval Christian society. In attempting to explain the events of the late thirteenth through the late fourteenth centuries, historians have devoted much attention to changes in the philosophical and theological bases of medieval Christian life that occurred in the twelfth and thirteenth centuries. These changes are said to set the tone for the treatment of Jews by Christians in Christian Europe throughout the late Middle Ages and the early modern period. Jakob Katz, writing in 1961, noted that legal protections of Jews, including a large degree of religious freedom, trade rights, judicial autonomy, and even the right to bear arms, were preserved in Germany well into the thirteenth century, the century that ended with the "Rintfleisch" pogroms. The preservation of Jewish legal privileges continued through this period in spite of the fact that Christian theology saw Jews as covenant breakers.[16]

Though Katz recognized that the thirteenth century saw deleterious changes in the social status of Jews, he did not speculate about its possible causes. Recent influential works in the study of Jewish–Christian relations in medieval Europe, such as R. I. Moore's *Formation of a Persecuting Society*,[17] Anna Sapir-Abulafia's *Jews and Christians in the Twelfth Century Renaissance*,[18] Jeremy Cohen's *The Friars and the Jews*,[19] and Robert Chazan's monograph on thirteenth-century missions to Jews,[20] have all pinpointed a shift in emphasis from faith to reason in Christian thought and a growth in the blood libel as the most influential and most destructive of these changes. More will be said about these two changes below. Others, such as Markus Wenninger, point to economic factors as playing the deciding role in the decline of the status of Jews in Christian Europe in the late Middle Ages. According to Wenninger, the theological objections to Judaism may have provided the intellectual justification for the treatment of Jews in medieval Christian Europe, but in reality these objections only served to mask the true motives of anti-Jewish

4

laws and actions: greed and class envy. Fear of economic competition, coupled with resentment of real or imagined material advantages of Jews, was the true driving force behind the rise in anti-Jewish animus.[21]

Unlike Wenninger, most historians accept that theological and philosophical developments taking place in the twelfth and thirteenth centuries began a progressive, irreversible dehumanization and demonization of Jews in the minds of West-European Christians. Sapir-Abulafia, Cohen, and Chazan regard the increased emphasis on the role of reason in matters of faith as the driving force behind the increasing dehumanization of Jews through the Middle Ages. The idea that reason, as the most God-like of human faculties, played the deciding role in religious faith, translated, according to these authors, into the idea that those who did not accept the true faith were by nature somehow less than human and could therefore be treated accordingly.[22] The historian Amos Funkenstein identified the origins of this idea in his 1968 essay "Changes in the Patterns of Christian Anti-Jewish Polemics in the Twelfth Century." Adducing his evidence from the works of Anselm of Canterbury, Peter the Venerable, Peter Abelard, Thomas Aquinas, and their Jewish respondents, Funkenstein argued that rationalist thought played the deciding role in the thirteenth-century attacks on rabbinical Judaism and prompted the legal degradation of the status of Jews in Europe. The factors that made this new rationalist bent in Christian theology dangerous, he argues, were the conflation of faith with reason and the conflation of cognitive error with moral corruption.[23] Chazan and Sapir-Abulafia make the increased emphasis on the role of reason the core of their arguments, whereas it is but one component of Cohen's argument.

The second of these influential and destructive changes in Christian attitudes toward Jews, the growth of the blood libel, has likewise been the focus of much scholarship in recent decades. R. I. Moore, John McCulloh,[24] and others have explored the origins of the ritual murder accusation and its use in justifications for acts of anti-Jewish violence in medieval Europe. Miri Rubin, in her monograph *Corpus Christi*,[25] similarly focuses on the origins of the accusation, specifically on the role of changes in Eucharistic theology in promoting it. She argues that the changes in the doctrine of transubstantiation that took place in the thirteenth and fourteenth centuries, specifically the change from a metaphorical, mystical understanding of the Eucharist to a belief in the literal presence of Christ's blood and body in the wine and the bread, fueled the growth of the blood libel. Eucharistic dramas, aimed at convincing the populace of the miraculous nature of the Eucharist, also served the purpose of promoting anti-Jewish stereotypes by dramatizing the Jewish rejection of this new doctrine in ever more grotesque ways.[26] She revisits the role of the host desecration accusation in promoting anti-Jewish sentiment in her more recent monograph *Gentile Tales*. In this book, she documents the use of the accusation to arouse the rage of mobs, as well as the skepticism with which the accusation was received by some chroniclers, and yet adopted as a justification for murder and robbery after the fact.[27] The idea that Jews, because of their collective rejection of Jesus, were less rational and, therefore, morally suspect, made the blood libel accusation plausible. Its success in provoking anti-Jewish violence guaranteed its continued use.

The argument that the blood libel functioned primarily as a legal and moral justification for violence against Jews also plays a significant role in R. Po-Chia Hsia's 1988 monograph *The Myth of Ritual Murder*.[28] In the monograph Hsia argues that the stories of bleeding hosts tortured and Christian children martyred at the hands of bloodthirsty Jews, after they had served the purpose of promoting the political and financial ends of local clerics or magistrates in Endingen, Trent, Freiburg, and other cities of the Holy Roman Empire, served also to perpetuate the belief in the bloodthirstiness of Jews. Hsia outlines his principal ideas about the blood libel's influence on pages 5–11 of his introduction. His discussion of persecutions in Endingen[29] and Passau[30] best exemplifies his key argument: that one of the main functions of ritual murder and host desecration stories was their own perpetuation. In both Endingen and Passau, indeed, in every case he discusses, the ritual murder accusation was able to succeed, when it did succeed, because of the "common knowledge" that Jews sacrifice Christian children. This accusation was born in other, earlier accusations of ritual murder. The accusations led to trials that left court records afterward. These records in their turn provided the material for ballads, plays, and poems, all of which provided evidence for further ritual murder accusations.[31]

The growth of these two ideas – that Jews were somehow less possessed of the rational faculty and that they sought the blood of Christians for use in their religious rites – can be interpreted as the deliberate invention of an ideological figure needed to "stitch up" inconsistencies in a belief system.[32] The question then arises: What inconsistencies in the belief system were these ideas intended to address? Was it an inconsistency in the behavior of the Jews of Europe in the medieval Christian worldview or an inconsistency in the behavior of medieval Christians themselves toward their Jewish neighbors? The persistence of Jews in their religion was perceived in the Middle Ages as both an ongoing challenge to and affirmation of Christian truth.[33] This was a tension present already in the New Testament, and Augustine's elaboration of the concept of Jewish witness – the idea that Jews as Jews must be preserved as living witnesses to the truth and authenticity of the Torah and the Prophets – did not insure that the tolerance it called for would benefit Jews in a Christian society.[34] At the time of the First Crusade, Jewish communities throughout the Holy Roman Empire had been subjected to rapacious attacks by bloodthirsty mobs, and yet some of these same Jewish communities had been defended by the co-religionists of their attackers.[35] For the medieval Christian, then, the question became: who was acting in a way truly consistent with the will of God, those who killed the Jews who resisted conversion or those who protected them? In the centuries following the murders of 1096, the question became relevant anew with each public outburst of anti-Jewish violence. The rampaging mobs led by "König Rintfleisch" and "König Armleder" were put down by armies of men who belonged to the same supra-regional church as the mobs themselves. Similarly, local priests and civic authorities who exploited the blood libel found themselves openly opposed by the popes. Gregory the Tenth, writing in the 1270's, was quite vehement in his condemnation of the accusation, stating that no Christians who brought the charge before a court were to be believed and noting that the charge only seemed to appear when princes were in want of money.[36] The conflict between local church and civic authorities, who promoted the blood libel for their own purposes, and the orthodox position of Jewish innocence further highlights the variation in attitudes toward Jews within medieval Christendom.

The development of two ideas, that Jews were less possessed of divinely-imparted reason and possessed of a vengeful thirst for Christian blood served quite well the psychological purposes of those who plundered and killed Jews. The ideas provided them with a needed justification for violent acts that were, in light of accepted teachings about the place of Jews in Christian society, unjustifiable. These two ideas allowed morally unacceptable personal motives, such as greed, or political ones to be concealed beneath a veneer of moral rectitude, freeing ostensibly Christian persons from the guilt of shedding innocent blood.[37] Jews could be seen not as a living testimony to the truth and authenticity of scripture, but as idolaters in a "demonically inspired cult of secrets," to borrow Funkenstein's turn of phrase.[38] Throughout the Middle Ages, the Augustinian doctrine of the *bellum justum*, which had provided a basis for the waging of war on fellow Christians and unbelievers alike, collided with Augustinian and biblical teachings about the role of the Jews. The latter made the tortured moral logic of the justification for anti-Jewish violence necessary, while the former made it possible.

An assumption that has long guided research in this field, predating the above-mentioned monographs but shared by them, is that one sees only a decline in generally peaceful social relations between Jews and Christians in the rhetoric of literary and non-literary texts of late medieval Europe. It has long been held that the decline in peaceful relations seen in the twelfth and thirteenth centuries becomes the normal condition in the centuries that follow, with no change or variation. Though research in medieval European Jewish history has, in recent years, weakened the hold of the "lachrymose" view of medieval Jewish history in scholarship, the view that the medieval period in Christian Europe was bleak and punctuated by horrific violence remains influential.[39] The bleak view of medieval Jewish history certainly guided Joshua Trachtenberg's 1943 monograph *The Devil and the Jews*.[40] This book has been highly influential in shaping modern perceptions of medieval Jewish–Christian relations, to the point that every one of the recent monographs cited in the preceding

8

two pages refers to it as an authoritative account of medieval Christian thinking about Jews as expressed in the popular culture of that time. Trachtenberg argued that medieval Christian Europe, specifically Germany, developed through and promoted in literature a degraded and dehumanized conception of the Jews that remained unchanging and unchallenged for centuries. A brief quotation from the conclusion of *The Devil and the Jews* is instructive on this point:

> Protestant reform made no difference as far as the Jew was concerned: its attitude toward him remained fixed in medieval tradition. The era of rationalism and liberalism made no difference – it passed the masses by unnoticed. Not until medieval habits of thought – and the social conditions in which they flourish – have been uprooted will there be a difference.[41]

That Trachtenberg equates medieval thinking with antipathy and hostility toward Jews is a necessary product of his own view of history. Trachtenberg and other writers who share a teleological view of history and who see the growth of religious tolerance as an inevitable and necessary component of human progress have emphasized the strongest expressions of anti-Jewish thought in theological writings as well as popular literary forms of the late Middle Ages. Citing a specific example from late medieval German literature, Trachtenberg maintains:

> The German Lenten play *Herzog von Burgund*, by Hans Folz [fifteenth century], also based on the Antichrist theme, omits the reference to the Antichrist's Jewish parentage but places the eager adherence of Jews to him in sharp relief by playing up their contemporaneous situation, referring especially to the recent expulsion of Jewish communities along the Rhine and the Danube. The Jews are his protagonists on the stage, extolling before their Christian audience the "new order" that he is about to inaugurate, which will be dominated by their own *Jüdischheit*, for, they exult, as the *Entchrist*, his mission is "to put an end to the Christians."
>
> The effect of these plays upon the passions of the mob may be gauged from the action of the Frankfort City Council, in 1469, establishing special regulations for the protection of the Jewish quarter during the period when such a play was being presented.[42]

The above is not Trachtenberg's only comment on the image of Jews in medieval German literature, but it is a telling one. We must keep in mind that he was writing in 1943. Three guiding assumptions inform his work: that modern hostility toward and hatred of Jews in Germany (and Europe as a whole) was a direct product of "medieval" thinking; that the conception of Jews in medieval Germany became and then remained exclusively diabolical; and that this conception had a direct influence on the minds of medieval and modern Germans.

For the sake of accuracy, it should be pointed out that Trachtenberg was not the first to assume the equivalence of modern, racially-determined anti-Jewish attitudes, the phenomenon we know as anti-Semitism, and medieval anti-Jewish hostility, as the title of Wilhelm Grau's *Antisemitismus im späten Mittelalter: Das Ende der Regensburger Judengemeinde: 1450–1519*, written in 1934, clearly demonstrates.[43] Trachtenberg, however, wrote in English, reached a wider audience, and influenced two generations of scholars. Among historians writing on the matter of Jews in medieval Germany, citing Trachtenberg or at least accepting his assumptions about the image of Jews in medieval German thought, has become well-nigh obligatory. Among prominent scholars and historians who deal with the place of Jews in medieval German society, Cecil Roth, Norman Cohn, Amos Funkenstein, Robert Chazan, R. I. Moore, Gavin Langmuir, and R. Po-Chia Hsia all either quote him directly or build some of his assumptions about the role of the Jew in the minds of Christians in medieval German-speaking Europe into their own work. Funkenstein is quite explicit in repeating Trachtenberg's equation of medieval and modern attitudes, asserting that "a clear line leads from the [medieval] blood libel to the *Protocols of the Elders of Zion.*"[44] Two of Trachtenberg's theses, that of the increase in vilification of Jews in medieval literature and that of the influence of literature on public behavior, were repeated in a 1991 essay:

> If the fourth century witnesses a major development from evangelical to patristic anti-Jewish propaganda, and from archetypical diabolical metaphors to an organized theological system of vilification with its own enriched dehumanizing lexicon, the eleventh century shows their integration into the daily life and mentalities of Christianized Europe, their increased dissemination through the popularizing mass media (sermons, theatre, visual arts), and their efficacity in a mythical-demagogic manipulation of human illusions and fears. The importance of the millennium phenomenon and the related First Crusade for understanding the transformation of anti-Jewish propaganda can hardly be understated.[45]

Here the author, writing some 48 years after Trachtenberg, only repeats Trachtenberg's assertion about the uncontested power of the diabolical image of the Jews in the Middle Ages in another form.

Trachtenberg and those who wrote later but shared his ideas seem to emphasize dehumanized images of Jews in medieval literature to achieve specific ideological ends. It seems on one level, they define the Nazi regime as an atavistic expression of "medieval" ideas, exonerating the Enlightenment and post-Enlightenment ideas that unquestionably informed Nazi ideology from any guilt in bringing about the Holocaust. On another, they promote an extremely negative view of medieval Christian culture, discrediting it through association with the monstrous atrocities of the National Socialist regime.[46] The "link" between "medieval" ideas about Jews and modern anti-Semitism played a role in the marketing of a collection of conference proceedings that appeared in 1991.[47] The cover of the collection, entitled *Juden im Mittelalter*, bore the following brief description, "Bei dieser Tagung ging es um … Greuelpropaganda, mittelalterliche Judenverfolgung, Ritualmordlegenden, etc.: Auschwitz beginnt nicht erst 1941!" Logically, if we accept that Auschwitz didn't begin in 1941, it becomes more difficult to attribute unquestionable culpability to those who lived in 1941 and either actively or passively contributed to its horrors. The modern scholar's link between Nazi ideology's "medieval" ideas about Jews may, in fact, be a kind of *Vergangenheitsbewältigung*.

Trachtenberg, then, established a scholarly orthodoxy concerning the image of Jews in the medieval Christian − specifically the medieval German mind − and this orthodoxy has remained largely intact and influential into and beyond the 1990s. He regarded ritual murder tales, stories of tortured Eucharists, anti-Jewish theological treatises, and Passion plays as components of a single, unvaryingly monstrous "medieval" image of the Jew. Though there is considerable disagreement among the historians mentioned above as to the exact causes and reasons for the observed changes in the Jews' status and the rhetoric about them, there is agreement that the changes were wholly negative and that medieval literature played a decisive role in affecting them. Trachtenberg's view of medieval literature is also held by historians and scholars who study the Holocaust, such as John

Weiss[48] and Daniel Goldhagen.[49] Though neither author refers to a single authentic medieval source, both of them uncritically accept that the monstrous image of the Jew reigned unchecked and unquestioned in the medieval Christian mind. Writing in 1996, Goldhagen cites Trachtenberg as the authoritative source for a reliable characterization of literary treatments of Jews in medieval German-speaking Europe.[50] An unnuanced, simplistic, and deeply antagonistic attitude toward the Christian culture of medieval Germany strongly influences scholarship not only in the field of medieval studies, but in studies attempting to explain the persistence of anti-Jewish attitudes in the twentieth century as well. A quotation from Norman Cohn, whose late 1967 monograph was updated and reissued in 1996, neatly encapsulates the view of medieval depictions of Jews hitherto discussed:

> From the time of the first crusade onwards, Jews were presented as children of the Devil, agents employed by Satan for the express purpose of combating Christianity and harming Christians. It was in the twelfth century that they were first accused of murdering Christian children, of torturing the consecrated wafer, and of poisoning the wells. It is true that popes and bishops frequently and emphatically condemned these fabrications, but the lower clergy continued to propagate them, and they came to be generally believed. But above all it was said that Jews worshipped the Devil, who rewarded them collectively by making them masters of black magic; so that however helpless individual Jews might seem, Jewry possessed limitless powers for evil....
>
> If Judaism, with its profound sense of election and elaborate system of taboos tended in any case to make Jews into a people apart, Christian preaching and teaching ensured that they would be treated not simply as strangers but as most dangerous enemies. During the Middle Ages, Jews were almost wholly without legal rights and were frequently massacred by the mob.[51]

The persuasiveness of Cohn's assertions is undermined by a number of factual errors that he makes in his generalization about the attitudes toward Jews in medieval Christian society. The most glaring of these is the assertion that the twelfth century saw the rise of the blood libel, the accusation of host desecration, and the accusation of well poisoning. In fact, not even the first of these that has its origins in the twelfth century, the blood libel having its origins in the pre-Christian world, while the latter accusations originate in the late thirteenth and mid-fourteenth centuries respectively.[52] His assertions that medieval

Jews were largely without legal rights is also undermined by the work of Jakob Katz and others who noted that the legally privileged status of Jews was a major source of resentment toward them. The decline in status that Katz, Sapir-Abulafia, and Moore all comment on could not have occurred had the Jews possessed no legal advantages for kings to contest and emperors to sustain or revoke. Furthermore, if one returns to the chronology of anti-Jewish violence in the introduction of this chapter, what is remarkable about the first six hundred years of the Middle Ages is not the frequency of anti-Jewish violence, but rather its infrequency. The accusations against Jews and the acts of violence to which Cohn refers are, with the exception of the pogroms connected to the First Crusade, products of the late Middle Ages, if not the Renaissance.

Other prominent historians of late medieval and early modern German-speaking Europe, such as Frantisek Graus and Heiko Oberman, have pointed out that the equation of medieval and modern anti-Jewish attitudes, such as that seen in Funkenstein's "clear line" from the medieval blood libel to the *Protocols of the Elders of Zion*, does violence to both history and language. In this, they follow the thinking of Hannah Arendt. Arendt pointed out that racial thinking of the sort familiar to those who lived in the twentieth century originated only in the late eighteenth and early nineteenth centuries, after the Napoleonic wars. Specifically, she identifies the reaction of the European colonizers to certain barbaric practices of indigenous Africans, Asians, and Pacific Islanders as the driving force in the rise of modern racist thought. Modern racism arose, she argued, out of a psychological need that the "civilized" Europeans had to distance themselves from the Asian, Pacific, and African "barbarians" by defining the latter groups out of the human species. Racism as we now know it was therefore alien to any period prior to the late eighteenth or early nineteenth century.[53] Writing a few years after Arendt, French scholar Léon Poliakov acknowledges the modern origin of racial anti-Semitism, seriously questions the validity of using the term to describe pre-modern anti-Jewish attitudes, but ultimately falls back on the term as a blanket descriptor for all expressions of Jew-hatred.[54]

In a similar vein, Graus disputed the use of the term "medieval Anti-Semitism." In his essay on the development of the traditions about Jews in late medieval and early modern Europe, he criticized both the use of the term "mittelalterlich" to describe the common negative stereotypes about Jews in European civilization and the overgeneralization of the term "Antisemitismus" to describe the attitudes toward Jews in pre-modern society. The former was, in his estimation, an anachronistic back-projection of ideas that were developed in the time between the sixteenth and eighteenth centuries, and the latter an imprecise and unhelpful use of terminology.[55] Indeed, anyone making even a cursory survey of medieval legal sources cannot help but note the fact that "Jewishness" was defined in purely religious terms in German-speaking Europe in the Middle Ages, without any reference to ethnicity or racial physical characteristics.[56] This is not to say that the medieval European had no awareness of ethnic difference between Jews and non-Jews, but that the awareness of ethnic difference did not have the determining influence that it has in modern anti-Jewish hostility. The dominant influences were religious tension and what can only be called class envy, the latter being largely a matter of skewed perceptions of power relations brought on by the enforcement of imperial protections.

By way of contrast, the anti-Semitism of the late eighteenth century onward was marked not by rejection of the Jewish religion itself, but by a pronounced emphasis on the immutability of congenital racial characteristics. In the development of anti-Jewish bigotry, Jewishness was seen from the end of the eighteenth century onward as an unalterable "taint" which change in religion did not remove, and adherence to Judaism or any other belief in the supernatural as another "symptom" of the mental inferiority of the race.[57] This is not the medieval Christian attitude toward Jews. Oberman warned of an "Entleerung der Begriffe" if we insist on seeing the anti-Jewish attitudes of the Middle Ages as being identical in essence with those of the nineteenth and twentieth centuries. Writing some years later, Johannes Heil delivered a useful summary of the scholarship on the "definition problem," concluding that modern "Antisemitismus" is differentiated from "Antijudaismus" by a belief in the immutability and undesirability of "Judensein" that leaves open no possibility of positively evaluated change or historically situated purpose.[58]

14

In his essay "The Origins of Anti-Semitism: Ancient Evidence and Modern Interpretations," Nicholas de Lange also pleaded for the term to be "reserved and restricted to its proper use," since doing otherwise "serves almost any other interest than the pursuit of historical objectivity."[59] Likewise, historians such as Sapir-Abulafia have advanced theses calling for a sharp differentiation between anti-Judaism, that is, religiously motivated antipathy toward observers of the traditional Jewish religion, and anti-Semitism, that is, racially motivated hostility toward persons of Jewish ancestry, regardless of their religion. In his monograph, *Toward a Definition of Antisemitism*, Langmuir seems to waver between two opinions, seeing the need for such distinctions on one hand,[60] and yet asserting that medieval and National Socialist hostilities toward Jews were "the same in kind."[61] Writing two years later, he goes on to assert not only a need to distinguish between anti-Judaism and anti-Semitism, but a need to differentiate between attitudes among Christians in order to account for the available data on Jewish–Christian relations in the Middle Ages:

> If we examine Christianity empirically and not through the lens of theological categories, it is clear that hatred of Jews is not a necessary result of belief in the divinity of Jesus of Nazareth. Neither is it an expression of something that never existed, *the* Christian faith or *the* universal church [Langmuir's italics]. Christian hostility toward Jews has been an expression of the faiths of individual Christians, and because their faiths have varied, so, too, have their attitudes toward Jews.[62]

A detailed study of how Christian attitudes toward Jews varied over time, how individual Christian theologians and Christendom as a whole both modified and developed their perceptions of Jews and Judaism over time appeared nine years after Langmuir's remarks in Jeremy Cohen's monograph *Living Letters of the Law. Ideas of the Jew in Medieval Christianity*.[63] Reminiscent of Zizek's comments on the use of ideological figures to resolve inconsistencies in belief systems, Cohen posits the development of a "doctrinally-crafted hermeneutic Jew," whose primary function was to reflect Christian thinking about the proper place of Jews in an ordered Christian society.[64] Writing with specific reference to Christian religious polemics against Jewish rejection of Christianity, Cohen elaborates the concept in his introduction:

Throughout this process of self-definition and propagation, Christianity never dispensed with its hermeneutically crafted Jew. From the first stages of its development, the Jew *served a purpose* [Cohen's italics] – or a mélange of purposes – in the new religion, purposes that rendered *Adversus Iudaeos* a basic medium for Christian self-expression, whose applications far exceeded direct confrontations between Christians and Jews. Simply put, the Jew had a particular role to play in a divinely ordained historical drama. His role stemmed from his failure to embrace Christianity when Jesus, his own kinsman, came to redeem him and his people before all others. This failure, in turn, had a hermeneutical basis: it derived from a deficient reading of the biblical covenant that God had revealed to him, an inability to discern the fulfillment of the Old Testament in the New.[65]

The "hermeneutic Jew" developed in late Antiquity would be adapted in the course of the Middle Ages to address the changing position of Jews in Christian society and the changing position of Christendom itself as it became the dominant culture in Europe and met the military, theological, and cultural challenge posed by the Islamic conquest of Spain and the Holy Land. Where Augustine saw a legitimate place for Jews as Jews in Christian society, viewing Jews as witnesses to the truth of scripture,[66] Isidore of Seville saw no such legitimate place for Jews in Christian society unless they became Christians, viewing Jews as a threat to the integrity of a wholly Catholic Spain.[67] Later medieval developments of the hermeneutic Jew would contain variations on these extremes, with variations near to one position or the other sometimes appearing in the works of the same author. Bernard of Clairvaux, at various turns, refers to the Jews as both "carnal and irrational" in their understanding of Scripture and as people who could and did profess true love for God, making his conception of the Jew one of the most complex in the Middle Ages.[68] Because of its flexibility and breadth, the theoretical model of the "hermeneutic Jew" will be revisited below.

The breadth in adapted forms that the hermeneutic Jew took as the Middle Ages advanced accords well with Langmuir's earlier observations. Langmuir's conclusions about the variations in Christian faith and corresponding variations in Christian attitudes toward Jews are also supported by the findings of Robert Lerner in his monograph, *The Feast of Saint Abraham*.[69] Lerner's book treats a strand of Christian Millennialism influenced by the theology of the Franciscan friar Joachim de Fiore who, after having experienced a vision in the Holy

Land, wrote and preached a vision of the future in which Jews and Christians would live in irenic coexistence in a Messianic kingdom.[70] Joachim de Fiore wrote and founded monasteries in the late twelfth century and, in spite of the prevailing anti-Jewish attitudes of his culture, his ideas continued to have influence well into the late fourteenth century.

Of particular relevance for the present discussion is Lerner's account of Friedrich von Braunschweig (Frederick of Brunswick in Lerner's text), a Franciscan whose writings and preaching on the place of Jews in Salvation History derived more or less directly from Joachim de Fiore's teachings. Belonging to the prophets of Saxony, a group of Franciscans who preached extensively on the biblical prophetic vision of the future, Friedrich seems to have attracted a considerable following and to have had strong connections with the Jewish communities in Saxony.[71] In his teaching on the Millennial kingdom, Friedrich preached that the Jews would be instrumental in the defeat of the coming Anti-Christ and that they would be exalted, enjoying a thousand years of blessings.[72] Opponents of his teaching, particularly of its philo-Judaic aspect, eventually silenced him, having him arrested and imprisoned in Speyer. He had gone to the city to preach, quite possibly because Speyer was home to a thriving Jewish community.[73]

Certainly, Langmuir's observation helps account for the fact that Christians were both the assailants and defenders of Jews in instances of medieval anti-Jewish violence, from the First Crusade, to the career and arrest of Friedrich von Braunschweig, to the expulsions from Spain and Portugal at the end of the fifteenth century. Langmuir's observation about the Christian belief in the Messianity of Jesus does not resolve the conflict in his discussion of medieval and modern anti-Jewish attitudes. The question that arises for Langmuir and all who doubt the necessity of making the distinction in terminology that Oberman and Graus call for, then, is this: if all antipathy toward Jews is in essence the same, then why did the Nazis see the need for such measures as the Nuremberg laws, which defined Jewishness in specifically racial terms? Indeed, if the "medieval" ideas about Jews were still so strong an influence on German thought in the early twentieth century, why rely, as Hitler most assuredly did, on

17

nineteenth-century philosophers and writers such as Nietzsche, Gobineau, H.S. Chamberlain, and Darwin to provide the philosophical basis for National Socialist racial ideology?[74]

Another difficulty arises for those who read every condemnation of Jews as an expression of anti-Semitism; namely, that if we do so, we find ourselves in the untenable position of having to label the Prophets of Israel some of the arch-anti-Semites of all time.[75] In sum, the term anti-Semitism has in modern parlance a racially loaded character that has no parallel in the lexicon of medieval Germany. Though it is concerned primarily with events in the medieval kingdom of Aragon, a brief quotation from David Nirenberg's recent monograph is applicable to the problem of connecting medieval to modern anti-Jewish attitudes:

> We need no longer insist on continuities of meaning in claims about minorities wherever we find continuities in form, since we can see how the meanings of existing forms are altered by the work that they are asked to do, and by the uses to which they are put. This means that we can be more critical than we have previously been about attempts to link medieval and modern mentalities, medieval ritual murder accusations and modern genocide. The problem of periodization is central in this attempt to disrupt a now almost orthodox view of the steady march of European intolerance across the centuries.
>
> Historians have assembled that view in large part by stringing together episodes of large-scale violence against minorities. In Jewish historiography, for example, scholars have drawn a line of mounting intolerance from the Rhineland massacres of the First Crusade, through the expulsions and massacres of the thirteenth, fourteenth, and fifteenth centuries, through German ritual murder trials and Russian pogroms, to *Kristallnacht* and the concentration camps... The more we restore to those outbreaks of violence their own peculiarities, the less easy it is to assimilate them to our own concerns, as homogeneity and teleology are replaced by difference and contingency.[76]

The views of Oberman, Graus, and Nirenberg will be subscribed to throughout this monograph, since their approach is one that at once respects the alterity of the Middle Ages and does the least violence to both history and language. Nirenberg's remarks about "difference and contigency" in attitudes about Jews apply to the development of such attitudes in the course of the Middle Ages, as well as to essential differences between medieval and modern attitudes. Modern anti-Semitism does, as Suha Arafat's 1999 statements clearly demonstrate, occasionally use some of the same rhetorical weapons as those that were part of the medieval European arsenal of anti-Jewish accusations.[77] However, the fact that proponents of modern anti-Semitism have availed themselves of the same rhetorical weapons as proponents of medieval anti-Jewish hostility has no bearing whatsoever on the essential difference between the two phenomena. The modern term anti-Semitism possesses racial and political overtones that make it impossible to apply the term with any accuracy to medieval anti-Jewish attitudes in German-speaking Europe.

In accepting the call to differentiate between medieval and modern anti-Jewish attitudes, this book will necessarily place itself at odds with the prevailing opinion in scholarship focused on the depiction of Jews in medieval German literature. Scholars in the field of medieval German literature have, on the whole, agreed with the conclusions of the historians who equate medieval and modern anti-Jewish attitudes. Concomitant with the equation of medieval and modern anti-Jewish hostility is the uncritical acceptance of the proposition that only the decline in Jewish–Christian relations in medieval German-speaking Europe is reflected in medieval German literature. Touber and Lomitzer refer to the medieval brand of anti-Jewish hostility as Antisemitism in their works, as do Natascha Bremer and A. C. Gow in their monographs, which will be discussed at greater length below.[78] Though some contributors to a 1991 volume of essays on the topic "Juden im Mittelalter" did differentiate between anti-Semitism and anti-Judaism, not all did, and neither did the publishers themselves. Though Winfried Frey was careful to differentiate between anti-Semitism and anti-Judaism in the essay that he contributed to the volume, he nevertheless entitled the essay "Gottesmörder und Menschenfeinde: Zum Judenbild der deutschen Literatur des Mittelalters," as if the two words used in his title encompassed all images of Jews to be found in all of medieval German literature.[79] It was this volume's cover that bore the statement linking medieval literature and culture to Auschwitz, mentioned above.[80] It is possible that the decision to place this statement – "Auschwitz beginnt nicht erst 1941" – on the cover may have been more influenced by the desire to make the medieval topic seem more accessible to the modern German reading audience than by the editors' intellectual views on the nature

19

of medieval and modern antipathy toward Jews. It is just as possible that the decision did reflect the editors' true views. In any case, the statement is typical of the unnuanced approach of many academics who deal with this difficult topic. More will be said concerning the anti-Judaism or anti-Semitism question as individual scholarly works are addressed below.

Since Trachtenberg, literary scholars have attributed to medieval literature, specifically to medieval religious drama, a large role in promoting anti-Jewish attitudes and provoking anti-Jewish violence. In this attribution, they conform to the prevailing opinion among historians, discussed above. Two significant monographs on the subject bear mention here. The first of these is Natascha Bremer's *Das Bild der Juden in den Passionsspielen und der bildenden Kunst des deutschen Mittelalters*,[81] the second Edith Wenzel's *"Do worden die Judden alle geschant." Rolle und Funktion der Juden in spätmittelalterlichen Spielen*.[82] A third work dealing with the image of Jews in medieval German literature, A. C. Gow's *The Red Jews: Antisemitism in an Apocalyptic Age, 1200–1600*,[83] does not limit itself to covering religious drama, but follows one specific image of Jews through its expression in a variety of literary genres. These three monographs and the literature supporting them will be discussed in the following pages. The review will demonstrate the degree to which these monographs have contributed to the currently dominant picture of medieval Christian thinking about Jews and the tenability of their conclusions.

Bremer's monograph begins with a thorough review of historical research on the status of Jews in medieval Christian Europe. Drawing heavily on the work of historians such as Bernhard Blumenkranz, Solomon Grayzel, and Guido Kisch, she argues that, from the First Crusade onward, there is a continuous decline in the status of Jews in Europe that proceeds inexorably and irreversibly into the early modern period.[84] It is only the decline that is reflected in the images of Jews in Christian art and drama. Over time, she asserts, the image of Jews in the medieval Christian mind becomes ever more demonic, inhuman, and phantasmagoric.[85] Furthermore, she argues that the image of Jews in art and liturgical drama not only reflected popular thinking about the place of Jews in Christian society, but shaped it as

20

well. What law codes and doctrinal statements from the Christian Church authorities decreed, the Passion plays justified by providing the appropriate images of Jews. Bremer, then, sees the depictions of suffering in the Passion plays as analogous to the productive cough of a tubercular, both symptom of and means of spreading a disease – in this case, hatred of Jews.

Key to their fulfilling this latter function, the perpetuation of anti-Jewish sentiment in the populace, was the conflation of the historical time of the Gospels with the contemporary milieu.[86] In addressing the conflation of history and contemporary reality, Bremer argues that this conflation is of great significance in revealing the rising hatred of Jews in medieval German society:

> Bezeichnend für die drei ältesten Spiele[87] ist es, dass sie den Zuschauer belehren und an die Erlösung erinnern wollten und vor allem seinen Glauben stärken sollten. Es gibt wenige Erweiterungen durch den Verfasser. Der Ton der Spiele ist ernst und würdig, und sie sind auch in den Szenen der Geißelung und der Dornenkrönung sehr zurückhaltend im Gegensatz zu den Prügel- und Spottorgien der jüngeren Spiele....[88] Auch die Darstellung der Juden entspricht der didaktischen Funktion dieser Spiele. Obwohl sie unmißverständlich als die am Tod Christi Schuldigen gezeigt werden, fehlt in diesen Spielen die grenzenlose Verachtung und die böse Karikatur der jüngeren Spiele. Ihre Rolle ist im Sinne der kirchlichen Dogmas gestaltet: ihre Ablehnung des Messias und der Verrat sind die Ursache ihrer Verdammung. Die Spiele versuchen nicht, einen Bezug auf die Gegenwart herzustellen (mit Ausnahme der Ständesatire im Wiener Passionsspiel und die Rolle des Rufus im St. Galler Passionsspiel).[89]

According to Bremer, then, the great danger to German Jews of the later Middle Ages was that the Passion plays had gradually become more and more concrete in their projection of Gospel events onto contemporary reality. Simultaneous with this growing conflation of Salvation History and contemporary reality was a growing luridness in the depiction of Christ's sufferings in both drama and the visual arts. With the increased emphasis on the sufferings of Jesus in late medieval art came an increased vividness in the portrayal of the animosity and cruelty of his Jewish accusers.[90] These factors together directed the vicarious outrage at the behavior of the stage "Jews" onto the actual Jews who lived next to the participants in and audiences of these and other Passion plays.[91]

As Bremer sketches it out, this development takes more than three hundred years to reach a culmination, to produce the unvaryingly diabolical and inhuman picture of Jews that dominated the medieval Christian mind unopposed. To illustrate the development, she chooses as her starting and ending points the twelfth-century Latin *Ludus de Antichristo* and the late fifteenth-century German *Alsfelder Passionsspiel*, respectively. In the *Ludus de Antichristo*, the Jews, led by the allegorical figure *Synagoga*, are depicted as the unwilling dupes of the Antichrist, who recoil in horror when they discover that they have been deceived. They convert immediately on discovering the deception, and they are subsequently martyred for Christ. In the *Alsfelder Passionsspiel*, the Jews are depicted as the willing accomplices of the Devil, intent on destroying Christians.[92]

Strictly speaking, the *Ludus de Antichristo* does not belong in the tradition of *Passionsspiele* as such, but to the tradition of *Antichristspiele*. It does, however, deal with biblical material and presents us with one of Bremer's most interesting observations. As seen in the quotation above, Bremer sees the function of the earliest *Passionsspiele* as one of religious education. This being the case, they relied heavily on the biblical texts of the Passion to determine their content:

> Die drei ältesten überlieferten Passionsspiele, das Benediktbeurer, Wiener, und St. Galler Passionspiel, lehnen sich noch eng an die Bibel an…. In den beiden ersten Spielen ist die Rolle der Juden noch stark von der Bibel abhängig, und es gibt keine Neuschöpfungen oder Auslegungen der Judenszenen seitens der Verfasser…. Die Juden halten sich am Anfang des Spiels im Hintergrund und treten erst kurz vor der Gefangennahme stärker in Erscheinung. Ihre angebliche Verstocktheit und ihre strikte Weigerung, Jesus als den Messias anzuerkennen, werden auch hier unmißverständlich gezeigt, aber in diesen Spielen fehlt die Karikatur, die böse Satire, die Judenhetze und die gezielt eingesetzte Judenfeindlichkeit der jüngeren Spiele. Es ist kaum ein Bezug auf die Gegenwart genommen, mit Ausnahme der Ständesatire im Wiener Passionsspiel und der Rolle des Rufus in dem St. Galler Passionsspiel.[93]

The purpose of the plays, their intended audience, along with theological trends and moral attitudes toward the Jews, played a determinative role in the way that the Jews were depicted in dramas. As long as the focus of the plays was on the Passion itself, and not on contemporary social conditions, Jews were not subjected to harshly

22

negative stereotyping. As the Passion plays began to become more popular entertainment than religious instruction, the door opened for the inclusion of more "modern" attitudes. That is to say, as long as the plays were written by clergy and for religious purposes, the anti-Jewish element was restrained. This was in spite of the fact that the Passion plays, by the nature of their subject matter, could lend themselves easily to an ever more lurid, inhuman image of Jews. Likewise, *Antichristspiele,* because of the nature of their subject matter, were bound to depict Jews negatively in some degree. The same is true of the *Endinger Judenspiel,* based as it is on a ritual murder trial.[94] Together with the subject matter of these various plays, developments in Christian thought about the place of Jews in society, explain, in Bremer's thinking, the worsening image of Jews in medieval German drama.

There are some problems with Bremer's conclusions. First, her data sample is extremely small and stems without exception from the very late Middle Ages and early modern period. Her "ältere Spiele" – the Passion plays of Benediktbeu, Vienna, and St. Gall – are all from the fourteenth century, while her later plays – the Frankfurt and Alsfeld Passion plays – are from the 1490s, with the Alsfeld Passion play being perhaps later still. The *Frankfurter Dirigierrolle* she groups with the later plays, though the most reliable studies date it contemporaneous with or possibly earlier than the earliest version and certainly earlier than the earliest surviving manuscript of the St. Gall Passion play.[95] Furthermore, she is forced to draw in material not strictly belonging to the vernacular Passion play tradition, specifically the twelfth-century Latin *Ludus de Antichristo,* in order to extend her chronology back far enough to predate the time of the great decline in the social status of Jews, which she sees reflected in the images of Jews that we have in these plays. The Passion plays in question were all, without exception, produced after the period that she identifies as the turning point in medieval Christian European attitudes toward Jews, the beginning of the fourteenth century.[96] Therefore, they are all products of the same "anti-Semitic" age, and yet contain wide variations in their depictions of Jews.

While Bremer deals, in her treatment of literature,[97] with a period of nearly two hundred years and focuses almost exclusively on the

Passion plays, Edith Wenzel deals with a much shorter period and a broader range of dramatic forms. In her monograph *"Do worden die Judden alle geschant." Rolle und Funktion der Juden in spätmittel-alterlichen Spielen*, she treats the late medieval and early modern Passion plays, specifically those from Frankfurt and Alsfeld, and also the carnival plays of Nuremberger writer and barber Hans Folz. Like Bremer, Wenzel identifies the late Middle Ages as a period when the depiction of Jews took a marked turn for the worse:

> Daß die zur Stereotypie tendierende Darstellung der Juden in den Spielen kein Spiegelbild der jüdischen Lebensbedingungen sein kann oder sein will, dürfte selbstverständlich sein. Diese Darstellungen basieren vielmehr auf einem Konglomerat aus literarisch tradierten Mustern, religionsgeschichtlich bedingten Vorstellungen und diffusen, affektiv geladenen Erwartungs- und Verhaltens-dispositionen, die vor allem im 15. Jahrhundert zu einem ausgeprägt negativen Fremdenstereotyp geführt haben.[98]

Though she argues that the various factors influencing the degrading way Jews were depicted in late medieval drama are first fully articulated only in the fifteenth century, she also asserts that the depiction of Jews in the fourteenth-century *Frankfurter Dirigierrolle* represents an unprecedented breakthrough in negative stereotyping of Jews.[99] In view of the fact that one of the other two extant Passion plays of the fourteenth century predating the *Frankfurter Dirigier-rolle*, the *Wiener Passionsspiel*, does not mention the Jews even once, this last assertion seems a safe one.[100] However, the question remains: if the factors that produced the increased demonization of Jews in medieval German religious drama were not in place until the fifteenth century, what accounts for the vileness of the image of Jews in a play from the fourteenth?

The major change that she identifies in the fifteenth century is best exemplified by the contrast between the image of Jews from the *Frankfurter Dirigierrolle* of pre-1350 and their image in the *Frank-furter Passionsspiel* from 1493. The change is the introduction into the plays of anti-Jewish elements that were not of a religious nature. This is a development that she addresses in her discussion of the relationship of the two texts:

Das literarische Judenbild hat sich im Zeitraum von der Mitte des 14. Jahrhunderts bis zum Ende des 15. Jahrhundets soweit verändert, dass Ergänzungen mit Hilfe des älteren Textes schon aus diesem Grunde fragwürdig erscheinen müssen. Deutlich lässt sich dies an einem Vergleich der beiden Disputationsszenen in der Frankfurter Dirigierrolle und im Alsfelder Passionsspiel ablesen. Gerade die Judenszenen boten dem spätmittelalterlichen Bearbeiter die Möglichkeit, den Grundbestand des Passionsspiels zu erweitern und zu aktualisieren; dazu stand im 15. Jahrhundert bereits ein reiches Arsenal an literarischen Judenbildern zur Verfügung, die nicht länger auf die religiösen Vorbehalte gegen die Juden beschränkt waren, sondern immer stärker die sozialen und wirtschaftlichen Beschuldigungen miteinbezogen.[101]

There are a number of interesting points in this passage. Here she makes the subtle assertion that the *Grundbestand* of the Passion plays contained an element of anti-Jewish hostility that only needed to be built on by later writers. Treating as they did the arrest, trial, and execution of Jesus at the behest of the Jewish religious authorities, the plays necessarily had to depict some degree of Jewish hostility toward the first Christians. The writers of the individual plays were free to develop this element of the plays as little as they wanted, as in the Vienna or St. Gall Passion plays, or as much as they wanted, as in the Frankfurt and Alsfeld plays. Though she mentions the interweaving of theological disputation scenes in the Frankfurt and Alsfeld plays, she does not explore the idea that this element of the plays, too, may have played some role in the way Jews are depicted in them. Her remarks on this particular aspect of these Passion plays are limited to their effects on the structure of the plays, not to the effect that depicting theological debate has on the characterization of the Jewish participants. Wenzel sees the disputation, especially that of the Alsfelder Passion play, as alien to the plots, providing only additional context for the confrontation with the Jewish leaders.[102]

Finally, throughout her discussion of the Frankfurt and Alsfeld plays, she repeatedly states that the increase in demonizing, subhuman stereotypes of Jews in the Passion plays is an outgrowth of an increase in economically motivated anti-Jewish animus.[103] However, she also asserts that the religious element is always the basis for the anti-Jewish sentiment, the foundation on which all of the other negative stereotypes are based.[104] Further, she sees this religiously derived hostility as so pervasive that it overwhelms whatever impulses toward positive depictions of Jews may in fact be present in the plays.[105] Her identification of the religiously-derived antipathy and what can be called class envy that were the main engines in medieval anti-Jewish thinking as "Antisemitismus" sets her firmly against Oberman, Graus, Nirenberg, and other scholars who recognize that terminological clarity is needed in order to achieve any semblance of historical accuracy.[106] The strong emphasis on these two factors, the economic and religious animus, in all the dramatic texts she examines leads her to the conclusion that the image of Jews in all medieval drama was exclusively, monolithically negative and without any positive counter-image.[107]

Here it is necessary to conclude the overview of recent literary scholarship with the work of A. C. Gow. In contrast to the studies of Bremer and Wenzel, A. C. Gow's monograph *The Red Jews: Anti-Semitism in an Apocalyptic Age 1200–1600* ranges over a broad variety of literary forms and genres. His interest lies in documenting a specific stereotyped image of Jews in all of its manifestations in late medieval and early modern German literature. Specifically, he traces the "Red Jews" motif through its appearances in chronicles, plays, and poems during the period 1200–1600. He describes the construction of these "Red Jews" as a conflation of three legendary and religious traditions: that of the lost tribes of Israel; that of the barbaric, cannibalistic tribes that Alexander the Great walled up in the Caucasus; and that of Gog and Magog from the Revelation of St. John. The "Red Jews" were constructed from these disparate elements to serve in literature as the ultimate enemies of Christendom. At no point in his work does Gow distinguish between medieval and modern anti-Jewish attitudes. Neither does he see a need to distinguish between anti-Judaism and anti-Semitism. Indeed, he does not even entertain the possibility that such a distinction may be necessary or helpful, but accepts the demonstrably flawed premise that the two are essentially identical. With that assumed, Gow argues that the apocalyptic fears that grip Europe repeatedly in these four centuries are so connected to anti-Semitism, and therefore the legend of the "Red Jews," that it is necessary to study both if a "coherent and accurate picture of both is to emerge."[108]

As thorough as Gow's study is, it is not without difficulties. The methodological problem of equating medieval and early modern anti-Jewish attitudes with "Anti-Semitism" has already been discussed at some length, and so will not be rehearsed here. Another difficulty in Gow's work is that it, like Bremer's and Wenzel's, has problems matching the chronology of anti-Jewish violence with the growth of anti-Jewish imagery. The problem here lies not so much in a discrepancy between the emergence of this specific image of Jews as inhuman cannibals and an increase in the frequency of pogroms, but with the ubiquity of the image in times when pogroms were few and far between. Gow documents the appearance of the "Red Jews" in diverse sources beginning as early as 1165 and continuing into the sixteenth century.[109] He fails, however, to make a strong case for a causal link between the popularity of the image of the Jew as sadistic cannibal who thirsts for Christian blood and specific actions taken against the Jews. Nowhere does he attempt to account for the passage of years, even decades without anti-Jewish violence in the very cities where stories of the "Red Jews" were widely disseminated. In the concluding pages of the monograph, he is forced to concede that it is not possible to prove that these vernacular sources provide an accurate summation of popular beliefs about Jews, a concession which undermines his stronger statements about the "inextricable" connections between apocalyptic fear and "anti-Semitism." The following excerpt from his conclusion illustrates the difficulty:

> Throughout this study, I have distinguished between Latin sources that refer to the Ten Tribes, to Gog and Magog, or to both, and vernacular ("Germanic") sources that spread the legend of the Red Jews. It would be nice to be able to *prove* that vernacular sources dating from the thirteenth and fourteenth centuries reflect popular belief. Yet they were written by courtly poets or literate urbanites for a restricted audience.... Vernacular letters in Germany had a relatively young but already quite independent tradition, which made room for this creatively hateful version of the Jews' role at the end of time. Although it is impossible to determine with certainty whether or not the majority of the population believed in the imminent advent of the Red Jews, courtly vernacular poems and early German exegetical works cannot but have helped spread the legend among the broader strata of society. The results of this development started to appear as early as 1349, when the Zurich year-book accuses European Jews of having received the

foul plague-poison from the Red Jews – from which we can assume a fairly widespread knowledge of this red peril.[110]

If one reads this monograph with an eye on the chronology of the pogroms and expulsions of Jews, one is likely to come away with the impression that neither the "anti-Semitism" nor the "Apocalypticism" that Gow identifies as "inextricably intertwined" had as much influence on public behavior as local politics and personal greed.[111] Jews were killed in or expelled from many cities of the Holy Roman Empire during the years of plague in the mid-fourteenth century.[112] In the late fifteenth century, a new, smaller wave of trials, executions, and expulsions was provoked by a series of ritual murder accusations.[113] The fact that there were trials, as grossly unjust as those trials were, tells us something about the way that medieval legal authorities thought about Jews. They did not dispose of Jews with impunity – indeed, the grants of imperial and papal protection made such treatment of the Jews politically dangerous.[114] Some moral and legal justification had to be fabricated in order to authorize the use of violence.

The attempts to protect the Jews even amid violent persecution as well as the elapsed time between waves of widespread violent persecution are perhaps the biggest difficulties to accepting Gow's argument. Unlike Bremer and Wenzel, he chose to study a specific image of the Jew in the works of medieval Christian authors. This being the case, his study is not open to criticisms that attack it for ignoring contradictory evidence present in the very texts he uses. Where Bremer and Wenzel err in arguing that there is but one image of Jews in the Passion plays, Gow errs in over-generalizing the findings about the "Red Jews." He over-generalizes in such a way that they become, to his mind, the arch-typical image of Jews in the mind of medieval Christian Germans. If this image of the Jew had indeed been archetypical in the mind of the populace of medieval Germany, one is forced to ask why years and decades elapsed between pogroms. One is also forced to ask why the Papal See and imperial throne attempted to provide medieval German Jews with any degree of legal protection whatsoever. Finally, if this was the image of Jews that dominated the mind of the medieval Christian in Germany, one is forced to ask: how, given the state of power relations at that time, did any German Jews survive the Middle Ages? Either this image did not have the power to provoke the kind of Jew-hatred that Gow sees in this period, or there were other ways of thinking about Jews present in the culture, other mental images that provided a counterweight to this one.

The problem here is not that Gow argues that this legend was "creatively hateful" in its depiction of Jews, nor that it can be shown to have had an effect on the way at least one chronicler thought about Jews. The problem lies rather in his eagerness to see this image of Jew as monstrous cannibal as an expression of ubiquitous and unanimous hatred of Jews in late medieval and early modern Germany. Returning to the observations of Jakob Katz for a moment, friendly relations between Jews and Christians remained common throughout the Middle Ages.[115] Had the image of Jews in the minds of medieval Germans been so completely demonic, such amicable relations would have been impossible. Clearly they were not; therefore the sole image of Jews in the minds of the Christian populace of late medieval Germany could not have been the diabolical and inhuman one that Gow, Wenzel, and Bremer propose. The facts of daily life in medieval Germany make it difficult to defend the thesis that such conceptions of Jews as inhuman monsters exerted an unchallenged and un-questioned influence over the minds of medieval Christians in the period that these authors treat. Nevertheless, the proposition that just such an image of the Jew exerted just such an influence is one of the guiding ideas shared by all three monographs.

Evidence for the presence of morally neutral and occasional morally positive depictions of Jews in medieval European culture was presented in a series of lectures given by art historian Bernhard Blumenkranz in 1963, lectures that were published in 1965.[116] In his discussion of artworks depicting events from the New Testament, Blumenkranz notes that the overwhelming tendency of the time was to present the Jews in the most damning light possible. Artists frequently went so far as to contradict the record of events as found in the Gospel narratives, giving the Jewish authorities an active role in the Cruci-fixion itself, the role played by the Roman executioners.[117] Counter to this tendency, however, are a number of illuminated manuscripts and

29

altarpieces whose creators depicted key figures from the New Testament or Apocrypha as Jews. Though they may not be as common as
artworks that depict Jews in a hostile light, there are medieval works
of art in which Saint Joachim, Saint Joseph, Saint Simeon, and even
Jesus and his disciples were clearly depicted as Jews. Among these
images, a Jewish Saint Joseph is cited as particularly common.[118]
What these artworks do for our grasp of the image of Jews in the
medieval Christian mind is to remind us that medieval Christians were
aware of the Jewishness of their own religion.

Common to the respective monographs of these three scholars is
the thesis that literature provides valuable insight into the thoughts
that drive a society. The next chapters, which examine how the
literary expressions of the Jewish–Christian theological conflict reflect
popular medieval thinking about this clash of worldviews, will re-
examine medieval German literature in order to expand the current
scholarly understanding of medieval German depictions of Jews. The
goal of this re-examination is to illuminate facets of medieval
Christianity's literary imagining of the Jew that demonstrate complexity and sympathy. Recalling the "mélange of purposes" that
Cohen's "hermeneutic Jew" served, we see that German medieval
literature presents us with a variety of representations of Jews, each
adapted to address some theological or social question, or simply to
promote a given way of thinking about Jews. What we have in literary
depictions of Jews is not so much one "hermeneutic Jew" adapted to
serve a variety of purposes, but a variety of literary Jews created in
response to hermeneutic needs of Christendom at various times and
places. The essential hermeneutic need answered by all literary
depictions of Jews was the need to explain the continued Jewish
rejection of Jesus and their continued presence in Christian society.
How were these facts to be explained and how were the Jews
themselves to be understood? All of the literary figures in some
degree correlate to the differing theological responses to these
questions. The more positive depictions of Jews that Bremer sees in
the earlier Passion plays correlate to the Augustinian conception of the
Jew as living witness to the authenticity of the prophets, while the
later "diabolical" Jews – the willing servants of evil – correlate to the
conceptions of Isidore or Agobard. The echoes of the conflicted,

30

eschatological Jew of Gregory the Great – at times the servant of the Anti-Christ, at times his victim along with Christians[119] – resound in the *Ludus de Antichristo* and reverberate harshly in Hans Folz's *Ein Spil von dem Herzogen von Burgund.* The voice of the rationally persuadable Jew of Anselm, Gilbert Crispin, and Peter Abelard is heard again in the various treatments of the Silvester legend, alongside the irrational and unpersuable Jew of Guibert of Nogent.[120] There is something of simplification in all of these examples, as all of the medieval theologians named above described Jews in different ways in different works – or even in different passages taken from the same work. The key concepts for understanding the depiction of Jews in medieval German literature are those of adaptability and contingency in the Christian imagining of the Jew throughout the Middle Ages. At no time was there a single "literary Jew," rather a constellation of Jewish figures who spoke to different aspects of Christian thought about the place of Jews in the world.

Chapters two through four will deal specifically with the representations of Jews and Jewish–Christian theological disputes in the Easter and Passion plays, devoting special attention to Bremer's thesis that these plays reflect a gradual worsening of Jewish–Christian relations in later medieval Europe. Chapter five will treat the legend of Saint Silvester, perhaps the most influential work of medieval hagiography in shaping medieval perceptions of Jews. Chapter six will deal with the varied representations of Jews in the works of Hans Folz and in popular hagiographical literature, and will by necessity touch on the depiction of Jews in a variety of literary forms. The works of central import will be the late medieval legendaries and collections of saints' lives, such as *Der Heiligen Leben* and the *Legenda Aurea*, but the treatment of hagiographic narratives in other forms, such as the *Reimpaarspruch* or the *Fastnachtspiel*, will also be necessary. By dealing with works of different genres, I intend to explore the effects of genre on the variation in thinking about Jews. Chapter seven will deal with the image of Jews in popular fable and didactic literature of the late Middle Ages. The primary focus will be on the vast body of medieval texts transmitting the Aesopic fables, since this body of texts as it was used in the Middle Ages can reveal to us how the medieval mind interpreted the Jew as a symbol. The didactic literature similarly reveals how medieval writers and redactors fit Jews into their own view of the world. It so provides modern readers with insight into the medieval moral vision of the cosmos. In the course of these seven chapters, we shall see that the monstrous image of Jews was never the sole image of Jews in any of these major genres of medieval German literature. As the hermeneutic Jew of medieval theology was adapted to serve a variety of purposes, so, too, the literary Jew took a variety of forms in popular literature, and, hence, in the popular imagination, each revealing another aspect of the complex and ambivalent picture of Jews in that imagination.

The choice of the group of texts to be explored in the following pages has been influenced by two factors. The first is the significance of the Jewish figures or the importance of the Jews as a topic of discussion in the texts. The second is the accessibility of the text to a popular audience in medieval German-speaking Europe. That is to say, rare, exceptional cases of positive depictions of Jews will not be examined, but rather the representations of Jews in some of the most widely disseminated and extensively preserved texts of the German Middle Ages. There exist literally hundreds of medieval German texts that make cursory mention of Jews and their place in Christian society, and it would be impractical to attempt to deal with all of them here. Some of these texts are *Minnelieder,* some narrative poems, some romances and epics with Jewish figures in minor roles (e.g., Wolfram's *Willehalm*),[121] and yet others medieval sermons that deal with the place of Jews in Christian society. While reference to the last group of texts will be made where deemed necessary for the sake of comprehensiveness, the focus of this study is neither homiletic literature nor the teachings of the church contained therein. This study is intended to be thorough but cannot possibly be exhaustive, even within the chronological limitations I have set for myself. This being the case, it seems wisest to limit discussion to the texts that received the highest degree of contemporary audience exposure, and which have been the focus of the most scholarly attention in the past few decades. It is these last texts that have been key in shaping the views of scholars on the topic at hand, and they must of necessity be addressed.

Chapter Two: The *Saint Gall Passion Play* and the *Frankfurter Dirigierrolle*

The deeper conflict over the nature of Passion playing remains unresolved. For more than a century, meanwhile, outsiders have condemned the play as anti-Semitic. But the criticisms have intensified since the 1960s. The script's depiction of Jews as hateful and vengeful Christ-Killers had been given new emphasis when nineteenth-century revisers eliminated Lucifer and a host of devils who had previously been Jesus's main adversaries. As a play that traces its roots to medieval morality drama evolved into a more naturalistic revenge play, the motive and role of the Jewish leaders in seeking Jesus's death gradually expanded.[1]

This quotation, taken from an article written for the popular press by a scholar of the Oberammergau Passion play, provides a starting point for the discussion of the medieval Passion plays in this chapter. In addition to demonstrating the contemporary relevance of the topic of medieval Passion plays by connecting the Oberammergau Passion Play to its less famous antecedents, Shapiro's scholarship on the development of the Oberammergau Passion also supports one of the theses argued in the preceding chapter, namely, that the element of racialist thinking in stereotypes and caricatures of Jews is a recent development, historically speaking, and one not at home in the Middle Ages. To this observation, one should add only the qualification that the modern Oberammergau Passion Play did not "evolve" into a play that depicted the vengefulness and hatefulness of the Jews as innate, racially determined characteristics. Rather, it was developed into such a play by persons motivated to create such a depiction of Jews. The Passion play of Oberammergau did not become what it became by random change and selection pressure.

In the previous chapter, it was argued that contemporary literary scholars and critics have erred in asserting that the image of Jews in medieval German literature was wholly given to demonization, caricature, and dehumanization. The chief reasons for this error were faulty assumptions about the nature of medieval anti-Jewish attitudes and a limited selection of texts. This chapter will examine medieval texts for evidence of the more differentiated view of medieval German images of Jews. It will begin with an overview of the history of Passion and Easter plays. From there it will move on to discuss the images of Jews in these Passion and Easter plays, texts that are used to promote the reigning orthodox view of medieval German depictions of Jews. Some of these very works contain images of Jews that do not conform to the demonic or subhuman stereotype, but instead present evidence that medieval Christian authors writing in German could and did imagine Jews in roles other than those of "Christ-killer," "sorcerer," or "usurer." In examining the plays, it is only logical to follow the sequence of the Gospels, therefore the sequence of the liturgical calendar, and examine the Passion plays followed by the Easter plays.

Though the origins of the German-language Passion and Easter plays are geographically uncertain, the Rhine region in the West seems the most probable location for the earliest versions of these drama types. The plays reached their apparent height of development and popularity in different times in different locations, with no one locality having a particularly long or well-recorded history of their performance prior to the fourteenth century.[2] In the scholarship of the past century, attempts have been made to reconstruct a developmental history of the Passion plays. It has been clear, however, for some decades now that there was no gradual "evolution" of the plays from the simple to the complex. As Rolf Bergman pointed out, the earlier Passion plays are, in many cases, more extensively developed in both length and formal complexity than the later ones.[3] The idea that there was a development of German-language plays first from Latin liturgical dramas and then from macaronic Latin–German texts has also proven untenable, as Wolfgang Michael has explained:

> Die Entstehung des Dramas in der Volkssprache ist nicht leicht zu erklären. Da die meisten Zuhörer kein Latein verstanden, da also, meinte man, sie den Vorführungen nicht folgen konnten, so habe sich, sozusagen als Interlinear-glossen, deutscher Text eingeschlichen; der deutsche Text habe schließlich überwogen; und das Lateinische sei einzig in den Ur- und Kernszenen wie der Visitatio als letztes Denkmal des liturgischen Dramas stehengeblieben. Eine hübsche These. Leider paßt sie nicht zu den Tatsachen. Wir haben zwar einen

Text, wo das Deutsche das Lateinische begleitet wie ausführliche Untertitel in einem fremdsprachigen Film: Das *Trierer Osterspiel*. Hier also wäre die angebliche Zwischenstufe dokumentiert. Doch dieses eine Beispiel wurde erst im 15. oder frühstens 14. Jahrhundert niedergeschrieben. Dagegen stammt das erste deutsche Osterspiel, das *Osterspiel von Muri*, aus der Mitte des 13. Jahrhunderts, und der Text ist nahezu ausnahmslos Deutsch.[4]

On the face of it, it would seem that Michael's assertions are at odds with those of Helmut de Boor, who argued that it was possible to trace the developments of religious drama in late medieval Germany in a series of broad strokes. What keeps Michael's assertions from flatly contradicting those of de Boor is that the few facts about the gradual development of the Passion and Easter plays that de Boor establishes with acceptable certainty are themselves vague. He writes that the Passion and Easter plays became more popular in the course of the fifteenth century, with the Passion plays eventually becoming the more dominant of the two forms. They reached an apex of popularity in the early sixteenth century, and generally declined thereafter. In de Boor's own words:

Im 13. Jh. verlagerte sich in den geistlichen Spielen das Hauptgewicht vom Oster- und Weihnachtsgeschehen auf die Darstellung des Erlösungswerks Christi in der Karwoche. Seine dramatische Ausgestaltung im Geiste der Scholastik und Mystik ist die Arbeit der folgenden zwei Jahrhunderte. Man ging von den Osterspielen über zu den *Passionsspielen*. Unter dem Einfluss der Passions- oder Leidenstheologie wird die Leidensgeschichte Christi zum Hauptthema. Seit der zweiten Hälfte des 14. Jhs. dringt in allen Teilen des deutschen Sprachraumes das Passionsspiel empor und breitet sich in rascher Folge aus. Nicht alles, was unter diesem Namen geht, ist Leiden-Christi-Spiel im engeren Sinn. Manchmal wird auch die biblische Vorgeschichte, die das Erlösungswerk nötig machte, vorgeführt.[5]

Throughout the Middle Ages, the primary focus of the religious dramas was educational, with the combination of spoken and sung texts accompanying gesture and dance to convey the message.[6] The plays were frequently performed in public locales, each of which was suited to the scene for which it provided context (e.g., *mercator* scenes at the marketplace). The players were craftsmen, artisans, and students, in contrast to the earlier periods in the history of German drama, in which the clergy had been the sole source of both the production staff and the cast.[7] De Boor still sees the development of the late medieval religious drama as a telos, following broad but clear lines of artistic progress that mirrored social progress. Michael's work takes issue with the idea that the changes in the late medieval religious drama are to be construed as part of a teleological continuum, going from less complex and more Latin dependent to more complex and fully independent of Latin. Where de Boor posited a scheme of progress from a Latin tradition to an independent German one, Michael argues from the dates of the primary texts, that the two existed parallel to each other from a very early date. The Latin texts served, according to Michael, as models for the German, but only in a loosely construed sense of the term.[8]

The St. Gall Passion play of the early fourteenth century provides important evidence for Michael's revision of previous scholarly opinion about the development of the Passion and Easter plays in the late Middle Ages. The paleographical evidence for dating the St. Gall Passion play to the first half of the fourteenth century is detailed in Rudolf Schützeichel's *Das mittelrheinische Passionsspiel der St. Galler Handschrift 919*.[9] In addition to having a spoken text that is wholly in the vernacular, the work is the earliest Passion play that has come down to us preserved in its entirety.[10] It is only fitting, therefore, that it should be the first play dealt with in this chapter. Continuing in chronological order, the Passion plays treated in the following three chapters are: the Frankfurt *Dirigierrolle*, the Tirolian Passion plays, the Benediktbeu Passion play, the Vienna Passion play, the Frankfurt Passion play, and the Alsfeld Passion play. Especial attention will be given to those Passion plays that Bremer and Wenzel treat most extensively: the St. Gall, Frankfurt, and Alsfeld plays.

Both Bremer and Wenzel refer to the St. Gall Passion play, the former using it to buttress her argument that the demonization of Jews in medieval drama gradually worsened with time. She emphasizes this aspect of her study most extensively when discussing the differences between the older (fourteenth-century)[11] Passion plays and the younger (fifteenth-century plays).[12] The chronological difficulty with this aspect of her argument was dealt with in the first chapter, and will not be recapitulated in detail here except to say the following: It is clear that any demonization of the Jews in the very earliest extant vernacular Passion play makes the "gradual worsening" hypothesis problematic, if not untenable. As we shall see, the aggressive and cruel Rufus in the St. Gall Passion play is no less a "demonized" Jewish figure than similar figures seen in much later Passion plays. The difficulty for the "gradual worsening" hypothesis further increases in light of the evidence of an early date for the Frankfurt *Dirigierrolle*, a fourteenth-century Passion play that will be discussed at greater length below.[13]

Futhermore, if we see some mix of varied types of Jewish figures in this earliest vernacular Passion play, the argument that medieval German literature consistently degraded and demonized the Jews and offered no significant countervailing images of them is suspect. In light of the theological considerations that informed both the Christian and Jewish communities in medieval Europe, we must also be cautious with our use of the terms "demonizing" and "dehumanizing" with respect to medieval statements about the Jewish rejection of Jesus. As has been trenchantly observed by Jakob Katz, the nature of Christianity and of Judaism requires each to evaluate some theological claims of the other negatively.[14] This being the case, it is a dubious claim to assert that depictions of the Jewish rejection of Christianity by their nature constitute a form of literary demonization of the Jews, though modern critics have done so.[15] Because both Bremer and Wenzel are adamant in asserting that the depictions of Jews in the Passion plays are representative of depictions of Jews in medieval German literature as a whole, any counter-evidence to their assertions that can be adduced from the Passion plays has implications for the scholarly evaluation of medieval German literature as a whole. If it can be demonstrated that these plays contain a differentiated image of the Jews, then any generalizations about the "demonization of Jews" that pervades all of medieval German literature must be abandoned as indefensible.

In the pages that follow we shall examine the texts of the medieval German Passion plays in greater detail, adducing from them evidence challenging the totalizing statements about the form and function of depictions of Jews in medieval German literature that have been dominant in scholarship for the past seventy years. In this examination, we will focus on the vernacular plays used by Bremer and Wenzel: the St. Gall Passion play, the Frankfurt *Dirigierrolle*, the

Frankfurt Passion play, and the Alsfeld Passion play. In order to provide a more secure basis for conclusions about the depiction of Jews in Passion plays, however, the body of texts examined here will include texts that neither Bremer nor Wenzel discussed in their research.[16] The presentation of texts will begin with the early fourteenth-century St. Gall Passion play and will continue in chronological order, as best that order has been ascertained by scholars from the available evidence.

The St. Gall Passion play begins with a declaration of the play's educational intent voiced by the figure of St. Augustine. Augustine is, as a point of fact, a stock figure in Passion and Easter plays, frequently playing the role of *Expositor Ludi*, or even, as we shall later see, that of theological interlocutor, directly engaging the Jewish figures in the plays in theological disputations. Here his role is the former. He states the purpose of the play, which is to present the key events of the life of Christ:

> Hore, heilge cristenheit,
> Dir wirt noch hude vorgeleit,
> Wie aller der werlte schopper
> mit zeichen offenbere,
> dar zuo mit heilger lere
> und auch bit grozer sere
> gewandelt hat vf ertrich
> und wart gemartelt dorch dich.[17] (St.G.P., 1–9)

The explicit purpose of the play is to provide religious instruction to the audience, with particular emphasis on the theology of the atonement, as the phrase "gemartelt dorch dich" indicates.

The play moves from the initial scene in which Christ transforms water into wine at the marriage feast of Cana to the baptism of Jesus by John the Baptist. The baptism scene is the first in which we see a confrontation between the followers of Jesus and Jewish religious authorities:

> Tunc iudei intrant ad iohannem dicentes:
> > Gent ir zwene dorthin dan,
> > und bident ienen man,
> > daz er vns wolle machen kunt,
> > wer er sie, zuo dirre stunt

Tunc duo venientes ad iohannem:
> Vil guder man, wir biden dich,
> daz duo vns sages werlich,
> ob du sist elyas.
> Liber fruont, nuo sage vns daz.[18] (St.G.P., 52–60)

In their first appearance in this Passion play, the Jewish religious authorities are curious about the message of John the Baptist, and inquire whether he might be the prophet Elijah, who, according to Jewish tradition, was to return before the advent of the Messiah. Upon learning that John is not Elijah, they ask whether or not he is the Messiah (61–4). Once he has explained to them that he is neither Elijah nor the Messiah, John explains that he is the "voice crying in the wilderness" of Isaiah 40:3–5, a forerunner of the Messiah (65–85). Their response to his self-identification is to ask for baptism themselves:

Tunc nuncii:
> Sit wir zuo godes riche
> nahen sicherliche
> mit dem daufe, so kere her,
> vnd deufe vns alle zuo diser ger.[19] (St.G.P., 86–9)

The scene is taken, as Bremer correctly pointed out, almost verbatim from the Gospel of John.[20]

In the Passion play, two men who are clearly identified as Jews approach John the Baptist and ask to know the truth about him and about the Christ. By introducing the Jewish figures in the play with this scene, the fourteenth-century dramatist chose as his first scene of the Gospel narrative a scene in which Jews appear as people who eagerly seek the kingdom of God. More specifically, the characters in this scene are representatives of the Jewish religious elite, and they are depicted as seeking the truth about God, not as venal or irrationally hateful creatures. It is clear from this scene alone that the play did not present its audience with an image of religious Jews as a unified body of "Christ-killers." Rather, the Jewish community is shown, in this scene, as God-seekers, some of whom decided to follow Christ, while others opposed him.

A closer examination of two figures from the St. Gall Passion, Rufus and Malchus, raises serious questions about two of Bremer's and Wenzel's central theses: that of the unrelentingly negative character of the depictions and that of the gradual worsening in the depictions of Jews. The figures in question challenge the two theses in different ways. Rufus presents us with a stereotype of the ruthless, cruel, Christ-hating Jews that Wenzel and Bremer assert only developed later, while Malchus presents us with a Jewish figure who is sympathetic to Jesus, even to the point of coming to Jesus's defense. Though the play does scrupulously follow the biblical accounts of Jesus's ministry, it also embellishes and emends the biblical text where the compiler deemed it necessary to do so for the sake of dramatic impact. Rufus and Malchus, however, are the only named Jewish religious leaders who speak substantive dialogue that is not taken word for word from the New Testament. As such, it is through them that the creator of the St. Gall Passion Play had the greatest opportunity to develop Jewish figures freely, departing from roles prescribed by the Gospel accounts. Even with this freedom, adherence to the biblical text is strong and consistent. An example of the play's reliance on the biblical text is seen in Rufus's first confrontation with Jesus in the scene between Jesus and the adulterous woman in the Gospel of John:

> Tunc iudeis ducentibus mulierem rufus dicat unus "Magister":
>> Gib uns dinen rat.
>> Dise frauwe ir e gebrochen hat.
>> Moyses e, nach der wir leben
>> hat uns solich gebot gegeben,
>> daz man die huren steine.
>> Der selben ist sie eine.
> Tunc Iesus inclinans se in terram scribat et cantet, "Si quis sine peccato" etc et dicat:
>> Wer ane sunde ist und ane meyne
>> der werfe an dise fraue einen stein.[21] (St.G.P., 222–9)

The New Testament text reads:

Early in the morning he came again to the Temple; all the people came to him, and he sat down and taught them. The scribes and the Pharisees brought a woman who had been caught in adultery, and placing her in the midst they said to him,

"Teacher, this woman has been caught in the act of adultery. Now in the law Moses commanded us to stone such. What do you say about her?" This they said to test him, that they might have some charge to bring against him. Jesus bent down and wrote with his finger on the ground. And as they continued to ask him, he stood up and said to them, "Let him who is without sin among you be the first to throw a stone at her." (John 7:53–8:7)

This first appearance of Rufus sets the tone for all of his later inter- actions with Jesus in the play. According to Bremer, Rufus embodies here a judgmental and merciless character type that is associated with one faction of the Jewish religious authorities in the play, and he voices most of the uncredited verbal attacks on Jesus recorded in the Gospel of John. Commenting on his role in the play, she writes:

Die wichtigste Rolle in GP kommt Rufus (auf Latein "rothaarig") zu, der als Vertreter der Juden fungiert (rufus nomine Judeorum, n.V.996). Daß der Vertreter der Juden rothaarig ist, hängt mit der Farbensymbolik im Mittelalter zusammen. Hier ist Rot in seiner negativen Symbolik benutzt (als Farbe der Hölle) und hat die gleiche Bedeutung wie bei Judas (s.S.199). Somit ist der Bezug zu den Teufeln und der Hölle hergestellt, und die Juden werden als Komplizen des Bösen gekennzeichnet.... Rufus tritt vor und verkündet den Willen der Juden und treibt die Handlung voran: als die Juden die Ehebrecherin vorführen, ist Rufus der Wortführer; an der Gefangennahme beteiligt er sich als Sprecher; bei allen Verhören – durch Annas, Kaiphas, Pilatus, Herodes – tritt er als Ankläger auf....[22]

In emphasizing the role of the color symbolism in the character of Rufus and his role as the accuser first of the adulterous woman and later of Jesus, Bremer ignores several aspects of this text that are of import for our interpretation of the Jewish figures in the play. The dramatist follows his model from the Gospel of John in that he does not in any way criticize the Jews for their reliance on the Law of Moses. Neither in the Gospel account nor in the treatment of the scene in the Passion play does Jesus condemn the Jews for following the Torah. Instead, Jesus turns the decision to implement the law into a moment of moral self-examination for the men who would execute the adulteress, forcing them to ask themselves if they truly have the moral authority to carry out the execution. Significantly, none of them fails this test. They relent, demonstrating the qualities of mercy and honest self-knowledge. It is also significant that the dramatist did not deign to include John's comment on the motives of the Jewish religious leaders: that they merely arranged the confrontation in order to test Jesus. Had his intent been to underscore the malice and corruption of the Jewish religious authorities, it seems that he would not have left this comment out.

The question whether we, as modern readers attempting to understand the medieval reception of a text, can associate the Jews in the St. Gall Passion play with evil is further complicated in the scene that depicts the healing of the blind man at the synagogue, as recounted in the ninth chapter of the Gospel of John. Though neither Rufus nor Malchus appears in this scene, the division in the first-century Jewish religious community that the two represent in this play is evident. The passage is lengthy, but it bears rehearsing here, underscoring the diversity in the depiction of Jews that is central to the more general discussion of the image of Jews in medieval drama. Following Jesus's instructions, the blind man washes his eyes and is given sight (340–43). When the crowd of Jews sees this miracle, they respond variously. Some question whether the man actually is the blind man whom they knew previously or merely a man resembling him, while others affirm his identity (344–53). When questioned both by the crowd and the Pharisees, the man reassures them of his identity and affirms that Jesus did give him sight, though he was born blind (354–69). When pressed on the point by the Pharisee Cayphas, he repeats his earlier assertion, in this exchange:

Respondens cecus cantet "Ille homo" ut supra et dicat "Der mensche" ut prius.
Iterum cayphas dicat:
    Der mensch ist nicht von gode,
    der wider godes gebode
    dir nach diner sage
    half an eime vierdage.
Respondet alter meier iudeus:
    So zwiueln ich dar an sunder,
    dut ein sunder solich wunder.
Tunc annas ad cecum dicat:
    Waz wilt du abir von deme iehen,
    der dich gemahte sehen?
Respondens cecus:
    Er ist ein prophete vor war.
    Dar vor han ich in offenbar.

Iterum annas ad servum suum:
    Ich gleuben der rede nit,
    die dirre von ime selber gith.
    Rufe sime vatter her zuo stunt.
    Der dut vns die warheit kont.[23] (St.G.P., 370–83)

This passage is taken almost verbatim from the Gospel of John:

> And as he (Jesus) said this, he spat on the ground and made clay of the spittle and anointed the man's eyes saying to him, "Go, wash in the pool of Siloam," (which means Sent). So he went and washed and came back seeing. The neighbors and those who had seen him before as a beggar, said, "Is this not the man who used to sit and beg?" Some said, "It is he"; others said, "No, but he is like him." He said, "I am the man." They said to him, "Then how were your eyes opened?" He answered, "The man called Jesus made clay and anointed my eyes and said to me, 'Go to Siloam and wash'; so I went and washed and received my sight." They said to him, "Where is he?" He said, "I do not know." They brought to the Pharisees the man who had formerly been blind. Now it was the Sabbath day when Jesus made the clay and opened his eyes. The Pharisees again asked him how he had received his sight. And he said to them, "He put clay on my eyes, and I washed, and I see." Some of the Pharisees said, "This man is not from God, for he does not keep the Sabbath." But others said, "How can a man who is a sinner do such signs?" There was a division among them. (John 9:6–16)

The episode dramatized here illustrates the inter-Jewish nature of the conflict about Jesus that the play depicts. All of the characters in the scene are identified as Jews, yet their opinions about Jesus differ. Rather than anachronistically depicting a conflict between Gentile Christians and Jews, the play depicts conflict among Jews about the nature and person of Jesus. In this scene, Caiaphas ("Cayphas" in the text) and Annas express the open hostility toward Jesus on the part of Jewish religious authorities. The blind man, the older bystander, and the blind man's father confess varying degrees of belief in Jesus's nature as a prophet. This latter reaction to Jesus will find its most consistent and dramatically significant representative in the person of Malchus, as we shall see below.

In contrast to Rufus, Malchus serves as the voice of a more open attitude toward Jesus. Though the name Malchus is taken from the Gospel of John,[24] the role of the character is significantly greater in the Passion play than in the biblical account. The Malchus of the St. Gall Passion play voices many of the sentiments sympathetic to Jesus that are, in the Gospel accounts, voiced by Jewish religious leaders who are left unnamed. Malchus's first significant dialogue occurs at the beginning of the scene depicting the resurrection of Lazarus. Initially, he questions how Jesus, who had healed a blind man, could allow a friend to die of sickness:

> Tunc dicat Malchus:
> > Horent, ir iuden alle,
> > wie vch min rat gevalle.
> > Der einen blinden machet gesehen,
> > wie mohte dem das leit ie geschehen,
> > daz sin lieber front irsturbe.
> > die wil ez ime so groz leit irworbe?[25] (St.G.P., 518–23)

Comparing the above passage with the text from the Gospel of John demonstrates the transformation of Malchus from a character identified only once in the Gospel narrative into one who interacts with Jesus at various key points in his career:

> Jesus wept. So the Jews said, "See how he loved him!" But some of them said, "Could not he who opened the eyes of the blind man have kept this man from dying?" (John 11:35–7)

It is significant that Malchus does not doubt that Jesus did, in fact, give the blind man his sight. The question that he poses relates only to the apparent conflict between Jesus's ability to work one miracle and his inability to prevent his friend's painful death. After Jesus restores Lazarus to life, Malchus makes the following statement:

> Deinde currat malchus ad Iudeos dicens:
> > Horent, ir herren, wunder groz.
> > Lazarus was unser genoz.
> > Den sach ich sicherlichen dot.
> > Der selbe, als ime Iesus gebot,
> > Erstunt an dem vierden dage.
> > Bit warheit ich daz sage.
> > Daz bringet die werlet gar in den sin,
> > Daz sie gleubent all an in.
> > Die rede bedrahten in korzer frist.
> > Sie gleubent alle, daz er si crist.[26] (St.G.P., 538–47)

44

In this scene, he affirms the reality of Jesus's miraculous raising of Lazarus from the dead, yet he also agrees with Caiaphas's judgment that Jesus be put to death for the sake of the nation:

> Respondens cayphas cantet "Expedit nobis" [et] dicat:
>> Ir herren, horent minen rat,
>> daz beide nuoz vnd warheit hat.
>> Ez ist weger, einer sterbe,
>> dan alle die werlet virderbe.
> Respondet malchus:
>> Herre bischof, ir hant wisen muot.
>> Der rat dunket mich vil guot.[27] (St.G.P. 563–7)

Here the action of the play follows the Gospel account closely, as a reading of the parallel passage from John demonstrates:

> Many of the Jews therefore, who had come with Mary and had seen what he did, believed in him; but some of them went to the Pharisees and told them what Jesus had done. So the chief Priests and the Pharisees gathered the council and said, "What are we to do? For this man performs many signs. If we let him go on thus, everyone will believe in him and the Romans will come and destroy both our holy place and our nation." But one of them, Caiaphas, who was high priest that year, said to them, "You know nothing at all; you do not understand that it is expedient for you that one man should die for the people, and that the the whole nation should not perish." (John 12:45–50)

The contradictory nature of these two intellectual positions, seen in the same character, further emphasizes the inter-Jewish conflict over the person of Jesus and adds an additional layer of complexity to the image of Jews in the St. Gall Passion Play. Later, in the scene of Jesus's capture in the garden of Gethsemane, Malchus himself becomes the beneficiary of Jesus's healing. When the crowd of temple guards and religious leaders comes to apprehend Jesus, Peter attempts to defend him, attacking Malchus as described in the passage from John's Gospel quoted above. Malchus cries out in pain and humiliation at the loss of his ear (727–32). Jesus admonishes Peter to put away his sword, calms and then heals Malchus (733–48). Out of gratitude for the healing, Malchus says:

Iterum Iudeus ad Iesum:
    Iesus ist ein vil guder man.
    Er kan wol seczen oren an.
    Als lebe ich, des bin ich gemeit,
    Ich gedun ime nummer kein leit.[28] (St.G.P., 749–52)

Malchus's speech on Jesus's behalf differentiates him from the stock image of the Jew as implacable enemy of Jesus, inasmuch as he acknowledges Jesus as "ein vil guder man," and refuses to do him further harm. His development from vacillating opponent of Jesus to thankful beneficiary of Jesus's healing differentiates him from the relentlessly hostile stock character that scholars such as Frey and Miklautsch posit as the "typical" Jewish characters of medieval German literature. His presence, as that of the emissaries sent to John the Baptist in the first scene of the drama proper, reveals a much more differentiated approach to the Jewish reaction to Jesus in this drama. Even in the confrontation with the Pharisees regarding the adulterous woman, the dramatist followed the Gospel narrative and did not depict Jesus as condemning Jews for obeying the Torah. Instead the audience saw Jewish religious leaders who, when they were questioned about their own moral authority, possessed sufficient honesty and moral integrity to season justice with mercy.

By way of contrast, Rufus is depicted as a relentless and implac-able enemy and as such does conform to the stereotype posited by Frey, Miklautsch, and others. Rufus responds to Malchus's defense of Jesus with the words, "Du must vor unsern meister gan, / wie vil du gudes habes gedan" ("you must appear before our leaders, regardless of how much good you've done" 757–8). Along with the figures of Caiaphas and Annas, Rufus forms the core of the Jewish leadership that is hostile to Jesus in two scenes discussed above. Later, during the scene of Jesus's interrogation by the Jewish High Priest, Rufus acts as the chief witness for the prosecution. Annas, addressing Jesus as "duo wunderere" ("you sorcerer"), first asks Jesus to explain his teaching; replying, Jesus says that those questioning him are already aware of his teaching, since he has always taught publicly (796–801). On hearing this reply, Rufus accuses Jesus of impiety in his response:

Tunc rufus dat ei alapam dicens
>Daz duo nummer werdes vro.
>Wie entwortes duo eime vorsten so?

Annas dicat ad Iudeos
>Weiz vwer keiner [ein] missedat,
>die dirre man begangen hat?
>Die sal er vns hie sagen,
>daz wir sie von ime clagen.

Respondet rufus
>Ich wil bezuogen hie vorwar,
>daz er geredet hat vffenbar.

Et cantet "Solvite templum hoc" et dicat
>Ich wil bezuogen hie vorwar,
>daz er hat geredet vffenbar,
>das man den tempel breche nider.
>So wolt er in machen wider
>in drin dagen ganz als e.
>Noch danne sprach er rede me.
>Er sprach, er were godes suon.
>Nuo wartent, waz wollent ir herzuo duon?[29] (St.G.P., 802–17)

In this scene, as in the trial scenes that follow, the words of several accusers of Jesus, who are left unnamed in the Gospel accounts, are given to Rufus. This aspect of the character is particularly clear in the accusation of Jesus before Pilate:

Tunc rufus dicat ad pylatum:
>Pylate, wir bringen einen man,
>der wol bit zaubernisse kan.
>Dar umme, wilt du gerechte han,
>so duo ime den dot an.

Tunc dicat Pylatus:
>Waz hat er vbels gedan,
>daz er sal zuo buze stan?

Respondens rufus dicat:
>Sin vbel werg, sin vbel gedang
>vns dar zu getwungen hant,
>daz wir in haben herbrath.
>Wir hedens anders nit gedath.

Respondet pylatus:
>Ir sollent mich baz virnemen lan,
>war an er habe missedan.

Respondet rufus:
> Er hat virboden vberal,
> daz nieman dem keyser sal
> vorbaz sine sture geben.
> Dar vmme hat er virwirket sin leben.
> Er nimmet sich auch des riches an.
> Den keiser also smehen kan.[30] (St.G.P., 870–87)

Later, in the scene of Jesus's torture at the hands of the Roman soldiers, Rufus is depicted as offering the torturers money to increase the pain that they inflict:

Rufus:
> Wuzent uf mine Iudescheit,
> ich gelonen uch wol der arbeit.
> Ir sollent zwenzig marg han
> wollent irn bit flize understan.[31] (St.G.P., 910–14)

His offer comes after Pilate has demonstrated a cruelty of his own by enjoining the soldiers to inflict pain on Jesus the likes of which he has never before experienced (904–09). Through the invocation of Rufus's "Iudescheit" as guarantor of his promised reward for their cruelty, the dramatist associates Jewishness with cruelty, presenting the audience with an image of the Jew as cruel torturer of Christ. Noteworthy is the fact that this interaction between Rufus and the guards has no parallel in the Gospel accounts. It is clearly an invention of the dramatist, intended to heighten the cruelty seen in the character. Rufus's function as an embodiment of the Jewish rejection of Jesus continues through the scene of Jesus's trial before Pilate, the trial before Herod, and the scene of the Crucifixion itself. In the conclusion of the first trial, Rufus and Pilate exchange the following words:

Tunc dicat Pylatus:
> Nuo sehent vwern kunig an.
> Den vinden ich kein schult han.
> So ist er auch gar sere geschlagen.
> Dar vmme mohtent ir wol gedagen.
Respondent Iudei "Regem non habemus"
Et dicat rufus:
> Dem keiser biden wir ere.
> Keines kunges viriehen [wir] mere.

Iterum pylatus:
> Waz duon wir danne disme man,
> der nie keine sunde hat gedan?

Respondent Iudei "Crucifige, crucifige eum"

Et dicat rufus:
> Duo salt in cruzigen alzuo hant.
> Wan er hat diz groze lant
> virirret von galylea biz her.
> Sicherlich, daz arnet er.[32] (St.G.P., 920–31)

The dramatist is careful to emphasize Pilate's unwillingness to execute Jesus and his being distinct from the Jews. In doing so he also emphasizes the Jewishness of Jesus, as Pilate refers to Jesus as "vwern kunig" – your king – the king of Jews and not of Romans, thereby defining himself as a non-Jew and Jesus as a Jew. Rufus accuses Jesus of deceiving the whole nation – that is, Jesus's own Jewish nation – and therefore deserving death. From the trial before Pilate, the scene then moves to the trial before Herod. Standing before Herod, Rufus continues his role as spokesman for the Jewish religious authorities:

Dicat herodes:
> Willekomme, ir herren alle.
> Sagent mir, waz vch gevalle.

Respondens rufus:
> Herre, do bringen wir dir einen man,
> der alle die werlet virleiden kan.
> Der ist von dime lande.
> Pylatum duhte schande,
> rehte[n] vber in zuo dirre vrist.
> [Wan] du hie geweltig bist.[33] (St.G.P., 940–7)

Here Rufus repeats the accusation that Jesus is a deceiver and a threat to Roman rule, an accusation that he and Caiaphas repeat a third time in the second appearance before Pilate. In this piece of dialogue, Rufus responds to the warnings from Pilate's wife, a detail based not on the Gospel of John but on that of Matthew (1035–8):

Respondet rufus:
> Herre, des alten wibes drauom
> salt duo nit nemem grozen gauom.
> Duo salt ez vor die warheit han,
> lestu Iesum dir ingan,

der keyser zornet es wider dich.
Wan [er] redet an daz rich.
Swer sich des kunnigriches nimme[t] an,
des keysers vnfruontschaft muoz er han.
Respondet pylatus:
Wollent ir nit do von wenken,
ich solle vwern kunig irhenken,
dez hant ir vmmer schande,
swo man ez saget in dem lande.
Iduei cantent "Regem non habemus"
Et dicat kayphas
Wir han anders kunges nit,
als vnser zunge hie virgith,
was des keysers sunder wan.
Do von salt duo disen henken lan,
wilt du des keysers hulde han.[34] (St.G.P., 1035–55)

Following this exchange comes the last attempt of Pilate to distance himself from the execution of Christ and the statement of the Jewish leaders that the moral responsibility for the execution should fall on them and their children (1059–67). Likewise, Pilate distances himself from the Jews while emphasizing the Jewishness of Jesus with the words "vwern kunig." From there the play moves on to the scene of the Crucifixion, in which Rufus speaks the following to Jesus as he is being taken to the cross:

Stig vf, man muoz dich henken.
Des math duo nit intwenken.
Duo hast vns leides vil gedan,
daz wir dich hie ingelten lan.
Duo breidete dine lere
vil dicke vf vnser vnere.
Daz sagen ich dir zuo swere.[35] (St.G.P., 1084–90)

The central thought conveyed here is that the Jewish religious authorities sought Jesus's death for the sake of their own injured pride.

The image of the Jew seen in Rufus is, in essence, no less a vilification or demonization than that seen in the "diabolical" Jews of the *Alsfelder Passionsspiel*, the play that both Bremer and Wenzel identify as the acme of demonization of Jews in medieval drama.[36] Rufus's reaction to Jesus contrasts starkly with those of the emissaries seen at the beginning of the play and with that of Malchus, though all of these characters are depicted as members of the same Jewish community. Their concurrence in this play renders dubious any simplistic claims about the image of Jews in the Passion plays of medieval Germany. The presence of so cruel a figure as Rufus in this earliest of extant vernacular Passion plays clearly demonstrates that the "diabolical" image of the later medieval plays is not such an innovation, while that of Malchus demonstrates that dramatists of medieval German-speaking Europe could and did depict Jews in a sympathetic light. Though Rufus has no counterpart in Scripture per se while Malchus does, we also must keep in mind that both of these figures are representations of Jews whose roles in the Passion play are largely original with the dramatist(s) who compiled the St. Gall play's text, with each of them embodying differing conceptions of the Jew. The two figures represent opposing ends of a spectrum in the depiction of Jews in the St. Gall Passion, while the various other Jewish figures, such as the emissaries and the onlookers at the tomb of Lazarus, represent other possibilities along that spectrum. Already in this earliest extant vernacular Passion play, we have a broad variation in the representation of Jews.

While the St. Gall Passion play of the early fourteenth century provides modern researchers ample material for analyzing its representation of Jews, the same cannot be said of the Frankfurt *Dirigierrolle*, a text also originating in the first half of the fourteenth century. The dating of the Frankfurt *Dirigierrolle* has proven to be more difficult than that of the St. Gall Passion play, with some scholars positing dates as late as 1360, others dates as early as 1315. Richard Froning, and other scholars following him, date the play to the time after 1350, attributing it to one Baldemar von Peterweil, a canon in Frankfurt's St. Bartholomew's church.[37] The difficulty of dating this play can be attributed in part to the desire of some scholars to see the *Dirigierrolle* as dependent on the St. Gall Passion play and the desire of others to place it chronologically in the time after the plague pogroms of 1349–50.[38] The viability of both of these premises has been compromised by recent scholarship. The apparent connections between the two plays can be better explained by their common source in the Gospels, while the paleographical and archival evidence argues for a date before 1349, most probably between 1315 and 1345.[39] The significant differences in structure and content between the two plays also undermine the later date and the suggestion that the *Dirigierrolle* might be dependent on the St. Gall play. One significant difference in content between the two is in the depiction of the Jews in the *Dirigierrolle*, as the following explication will make clear.

In marked contrast to the St. Gall Passion play, the Frankfurt *Dirigierrolle* begins with a confrontation between the Hebrew Prophets and a group of contemporary fourteenth-century Jews in which the figure of Saint Augustine serves as moderator. The role of St. Augustine as the representative of Christian apologetics in the mission to the Jews likely had its origin, however indirectly, in a popular pseudo-Augustinian tract known as *Altercatione Ecclesiae et Synogogae*. The qualifiers "however indirectly" must be used to describe the relationship between the pseudo-Augustinian tract and the Passion plays for the reason that the argumentation of the tract and the use of Augustine as a stock apologist had become so widespread in the late Middle Ages that it was possible for a dramatist to make use of both arguments and the literary figure without having seen the original text.[40] The tract, which originated in the fifth century, had a long and nebulous history before becoming a source for the Christian–Jewish confrontations in the Passion plays.[41]

Before the first confrontation from the *Dirigierrolle* is cited, it should be noted that the entire text consists of dialog prompts, giving modern researchers sparse evidence of the full scope of the play's treatment of its subject matter. Nevertheless, the limited evidence that we do have is sufficient to allow us to draw some valid conclusions about the image of Jews conveyed in the play. The initial confrontation between the Hebrew Prophets and the modern Jews reads as follows:

> Hoc clamore finito Augustinus proponat sermonem qui sequitur:
>> Ir hershaf, stillit uwern shal!
> David rex respondeat ei:
>> Ich heizin David godes kneht.

Isac Judeus respondeat ei:
    Swig a David.
Augustinus ad Solomonem
Salomon dicat.
Bandir Iudeus respondeat.
Item Augustinus ad Danielem:
    Diz horet alle godis kint!
Daniel surgat et dicat:
    Post septuaginta ebdomata –
et dicat:
    Nu hort, was ich uch sagen sol.
Ioseph Iudeus respondeat:
    Swig a dor! waz claffis du? [42] (1–10)

Forming a prologue for the Passion itself, the confrontation between Augustine, the prophets, and the modern Jews continues to line 22. This brief passage from the prologue is typical for the depiction of Jews in the Frankfurt *Dirigierrolle* as a whole; they are depicted as being vociferously hostile to the Messianic prophecies applied to Christ, here presented by unambiguously Jewish figures. The abusive verbiage, such as "swig a" and "was claffis du," clearly indicates that the dramatist aims to depict Jews as enemies of divine revelation, even from the mouths of their own prophets, and as persons not so much interested in theological engagement as insulting the representatives of Christianity, including Jesus himself.[43] Typical of the depiction of the Jews' hostility toward Jesus is a scene that is based on John 8:12–59 but gives the Jewish figures modern (that is, fourteenth-century German) names:

Item Kalman Iudeus respondeat:
Nu sage mir, duo dummer man –
Ihesus dicat:
    Seht, der heylige Abraham –
Item Mannes Iudeus respondeat:
    Wie ist die rede so gestalt!
Item Ihesus:
    Ja, ich sage uch [vor war] –
Item Mannes:
    Warzuo ist dise rede guot?
Hic Iudei querant lapides quasi Ihesum velint lapidare, et dicat Ihesus:
    Guote werg han ich getan – [44] (F.D. 78–85)

As Wenzel points out, this passage deviates significantly from its biblical source in a way that serves only to emphasize the hostility of the Jews toward Jesus and, by inference, toward those who apply the Messianic prophecies to him.[45]

The contrast between the initial image of Jews in the St. Gall Passion play and that in the Frankfurt *Dirigierrolle* is stark. In the former, the initial meeting between John the Baptist and the representatives of the Jewish religious authorities is non-confrontational, even amicable. In the latter, modern-day Jews, not Jews of Jesus's time, are shown at the outset as people who reject the revealed truth of God as spoken from the mouths of their own prophets. Their hostility to Christological readings of the biblical Psalms and prophetic writings is put on display in the opening scene of the performance, with no Jewish figure willing to even hear out the Christological readings of the passages from their own Scriptures. Whereas the opening scene of the St. Gall Passion play presented its audience with first-century Jews who struggled to learn the truth, the corresponding scene in the Frankfurt *Dirigierrolle* presented its audience with Jews who reject their own sacred texts.

Throughout the text of the Frankfurt *Dirigierrolle*, the Jewish leaders are presented as uniformly hostile in their rejection of Jesus. The *Dirigierrolle* offers little nuance in its depiction of Jews in their confrontations with Jesus, offering in these scenes no counterweight to the hostile and, in the eyes of a Christian audience, blasphemous Jewish opponents of Jesus. Unlike the St. Gall Passion play, there is little emphasis on the Jewish origin of Jesus and his disciples, nor is there emphasis on the inter-Jewish nature of the original conflict between followers of Christ and Jewish religious authorities. There is no sympathetic figure among the Jewish leaders present at the resurrection of Lazarus, and the scene of Lazarus's raising from the dead is followed immediately by a scene in which the Jewish leaders plot to kill Jesus.[46] Though we have only dialogue prompts from which to adduce evidence in this text, the preponderance of that evidence suggests that the dominant image of the Jews presented here is that of a group united in their hostility toward Jesus and his followers. In fact, the few figures appearing in the Frankfurt *Dirigier-rolle* who are clearly identified as being both sympathetic toward

Jesus and Jewish – the "pueri Ebreorum," Simon the Pharisee, Nicodemus, and Joseph of Arimathea – are all relegated to minor roles.[47] As the expansion of the role of Malchus revealed something of the conception of the Jews held by the compiler of the St. Gall Passion play, it seems that the truncating of the biblical roles of Joseph and Nicodemus here reveals an unwillingness to put sympathetic Jewish figures on stage.

The concluding scene involves a disputation, moderated by St. Augustine, between the figures *Ecclesia* and *Synagoga*. Attested in the plastic arts from the ninth century on, the motif of the Church as successor of the Synagogue, *Ecclesia* as a reigning queen and *Synagoga* as her deposed, often blindfolded predecessor, was here brought to life on the stage.[48] Though the exact content of this disputation cannot be deduced from the extant evidence, it is clear that the figure *Synagoga*, symbolically representing both rejection of Christ inherent in the official theology of rabbinical Judaism and the authoritarian hierarchy that enforced this theology, remains openly hostile to Christ.[49] In the conversion of a group of Jews from *Synagoga*'s entourage at the end of the play, with Augustine saying to them "Des hymelriches sit ir wert!" ("you are worthy of heaven!" 369), we see a willingness to see Jews as eligible for Christian salvation, not as irredeemably lost.

Finally, two Passion plays often neglected by modern scholars bear mention here. In discussing them even briefly, we gain a firmer grasp of the range of the roles given Jews in the Passion plays. The earlier of the two plays, the Benediktbeu Passion play, originated near the turn of the fourteenth century, the text appearing at the end of the *Carmina Burana* manuscript.[50] The text is composed in a mixture of Latin and German, with German dialogue frequently recapitulating Latin dialogue that was written to be sung, prompting one editor, Froning, to refer to it as a "religious opera" of little dramaturgical finesse.[51] The play begins with the scene in which Jesus heals the blind man, a scene that is given nothing like the extensive development found in the fourteenth-century Passion plays discussed above. In the scene immediately following the healing of the blind man, the drama treats Jesus's encounter with the tax collector Zaccheus.[52] In both the Gospel text and the Passion play, the message conveyed by this encounter is revealed only in the final words Jesus speaks: "Quia hodie huic domui salus facta est, eo quod et tu sis filius Abrahe."[53] In both the Gospel account and the play, the encounter emphasizes the reach of God's mercy – extending even to the corrupt tax collector who served the Roman conquerors – and the judeocentric nature of Jesus's mission.

The Benediktbeu Passion play's treatment of the anointing of Jesus by the sinful woman at the house of Simon the Pharisee may also have some bearing on the depiction of Jews, and specifically the depiction of Jewish religious authorities, in medieval religious drama. Related in the Gospel of Luke,[54] the encounter, like the encounter with Zaccheus, emphasizes the message of forgiveness for past sin through the mercy of God. Curiously, this encounter also emphasizes Jesus's own Jewishness through his host, Simon the Pharisee, who addresses him as "Rabbi" (15). Even more curious is the apparent conflation of the characters Simon the Pharisee and Simon Peter that occurs between verses 105 and 115:

> Item statim (Jesus speaking to his host):
> > Symon, habeo tibi aliquid dicere!
> Symon Petrus
> > Magister, dic!
> Dicit Jesus:
> > Debitores habuit quidam creditorum
> > Duos, quibus credidit spe denariorum:
> > Hic quingentos debuit, alter quinquagenos;
> > Sed eosdem penitus fecerat egenos;
> > Cum nequirent reddere, totum relaxavit;
> > Quis eorum igitur ipsum plus amarit?
> Symon respondet:
> > Estimo, quod ille plus, cui plus donavit.
> Iesus dicat:
> > Tua sic sententia recte iudicavit.[55] (B.P. 105–15)

The conflation of the two figures may be due simply to error. However, it is also possible that the dramatist did know that he was dealing with two figures named Simon, one a Pharisee and the other a disciple of Christ, and deliberately shifted the moment of moral insight in this encounter to the disciple in order to further emphasize the moral obtuseness of the Pharisees as a group. If so, it would

56

represent a substantial departure from the Gospel text, and a contrast with the Zaccheus scene described above. Speaking against this possible interpretation, however, is the omission of Jesus's concluding remarks from the Gospel account, in which he condemns Simon's less than exemplary practice of hospitality.

Seen as a whole, the Benediktbeu Passion play deviates little from the Gospel texts, limiting its dialogue to brief quotes from the Passion narratives. This being the case, the role of the Pharisees as Jesus's accusers comes to the fore only in the trial and execution scenes, which occupy the last third of the text (170–273). At the end of the play, Joseph of Arimathea, who in the Gospels is clearly identified as a member of the Jewish religious elite, comes to take Jesus's body for burial (274–81).

The exchange between Simon the Pharisee and Jesus taken from the Gospel of Luke serves as the dramatic high point of the early fourteenth-century Vienna Passion play. The Vienna Passion Play is preserved in a fragmentary manuscript of the early fourteenth century, though there are linguistic anomalies that suggest that the text itself originated in the late thirteenth century.[56] A scant 532 lines long, it begins with a scene depicting the temptation of Eve by the Devil, and ends mid-way through the Last Supper, with Jesus's words to Judas, "Swem ich den bizzen regche drâte, / der wil mich an dirre stunt verrâte" ("the one to whom I now give this morsel, he will betray me this very hour" 531–2.).[57] Unlike the somewhat younger Benediktbeu Passion – and, again contradicting the assertion that the Passion plays followed some path of development from the less complex to the more complex – the Vienna Passion play develops the scene extensively, so that it occupies verses 349 to 506, approximately 20% of the extant fragmentary text. The Vienna Passion play does not omit Jesus's charge against Simon: that Simon himself neglected the most elementary duties of hospitality and so behaved in a much less thoughtful and considerate way than the "sinful woman" whose very contact with Jesus raised Simon's suspicions of Jesus's authenticity as a prophet (456–60). Jesus's charge against Simon and the unfavorable comparison to the repentant woman is pronounced first in Latin (485–90) and then in German:

Ditz wîp hât mit iren zeheren gewaschen mîne fûze,
Unt hôt sie wol tausent stunt gechusset also sueze,
Unt hât mit gûter salben daz haupt mir bestrichen:
Dez unt ander gûter werch bin ich von dir beswichen.
Dô von sag ich dir nû daz unt wil ir dô mit lônen:
Ir suln ir sunde vergeben sîn unt haben von himel die crône.[58] (V.P., 491–6)

The emphasis in this encounter is on mercy and forgiveness, with Simon's failing being, as in the Benediktbeu Passion, a lack of personal moral insight.

Of the fourteenth-century Passion plays, it is clear that the only one in which the Jewish figures are accorded much dramatic development at all is the St. Gall play. Unsurprisingly, this is also the play that contains the widest range in its depiction of Jews. In the St. Gall play, we see Jews as seekers after divine truth in the figures of the two emissaries, as relentless opponents of Jesus in the figure of Rufus, and as thankful beneficiaries of Jesus's healing ministry in the figure of Malchus. In the Frankfurt *Dirigierrolle*, the image of Jews is far more one-dimensional: we see them as hostile opponents of Jesus and little else. The meager evidence provided by the Benediktbeu and Vienna plays shows only little interest in depicting the conflict between Jesus and his opponents among the Jewish religious leaders. The Benediktbeu play includes only a few sparse details that are necessary for an accurate re-telling of the Gospel Passion narrative. The dramatic treatment of the encounter between Jesus and Simon in both plays provides little material for those seeking insight into the medieval Christian conception of the Jew. In the fifteenth century, the treatment of Jews in Passion plays would continue to be varied but would also, as we shall see below, produce one work that would come to represent the nadir of demonization of Jews in medieval religious drama.

Chapter Three:
The Tirol, Halle and Frankfurt Passion Plays

The largest single group of medieval Passion plays that has been preserved is a group of seven plays from the late fifteenth century. Six of these are closely related, sharing large portions of text and considerable structural similarities: the Sterzing (St), American (A), Bozen (B), Pfarrkirch (Pf), and Brixen (Br) Passion Plays, together with a fragmentary manuscript (M). A seventh play, the Passion play of Halle (H), contains enough common text to be considered part of this group, but differs from them to such a significant degree that it must be treated as a separate work. Collectively known as the Tirol Passion plays, after their region of origin, they were first committed to writing in the period between 1460 and 1500.[1] The texts of the first six of these plays differ from each other in orthography and occasional minor textual omissions or additions. In the Tiroler Passion play we are dealing not with one but three individually realized dramas in six whole or fragmentary versions. All begin with a council of the Jews, in which the leaders among the Pharisees expound their grievances against Jesus and discuss their plans to arrest and kill him (lines 1–1192). The second play begins with the trial of Jesus before the Pharisees and Pilate and concludes with the Crucifixion (1193–2837). The third of the plays begins with a meeting of angels who tell of the Resurrection and concludes with an attempt by the Roman soldiers and the Jewish religious authorities to "persuade" the audience that Jesus did not rise from the grave (2838–3951).

In the last of the three plays, only the Pfarrkirch, American, Bozen, and parts of the Brixen texts have been preserved. The preserved text of the Sterzing Passion ends with the second of the three plays.[2] Especially close are the affinities between the Sterzing and Pfarrkirch Passion plays, with the affinities between these two and the Halle Passion play being sufficient to support the hypothesis that they derive from a common source, a now-lost Passion play of Tirol (T).[3] The text that St, Pf, B, Br, A, and M share indicates that the source text consisted of three discrete plays: the first treating the events of the Passion up to Jesus's trial before the Sanhedrin; the second, his trials before Pilate and Herod, the Crucifixion, and Jesus's burial; and the third Jesus's Resurrection and post Resurrection appearance to the Apostles.[4]

Although it belongs to the group of Passion plays from Tirol and even shares a common source with them, the Passion play of Halle is sufficiently distinct from the other plays of the group in its structure to warrant separate treatment. Though it shares with them a tripartite structure, the scenes chosen for the Halle play differ from those chosen for the others. The differences between them are therefore differences of form and content, and are extensive. As we shall see, the differences between the Halle Passion play and the others of this group (St, Pf, B, Br, A, M) are relevant to the current consideration of the image of Jews in late medieval German literature. Specifically, its choice of scenes, treatment of certain Jewish characters, and emphasis on specific aspects of Christianity's origins set it apart from the other plays. Like the six other plays, it is a product of the late fifteenth century. This being the case, the differences between them with respect to the treatment of Jewish characters and the emphasis on the Jewish origins of Christianity are relevant here. In the next several pages, the focus of this discussion will be on the six Tirolian Passion plays, then on the Passion play of Halle.

Like the St. Gall Passion play, the Tirol Passion plays begin with the presentation of the subject matter, a statement of the plays' intended function as a means of religious instruction.[5] Following immediately on this scene, comes a scene treating the aftermath of Jesus's driving the moneychangers from the temple courts. In this scene, the Jewish religious leaders differ in their reaction to Jesus's deeds. Here Annas responds to the report of Jesus's activities:

> Annas respondit:
>> Für war das ist ain pöse phlicht,
>> Der dise sach nit für sicht!
>> Darumb, ir herren, wil ich ewch sagen,
>> Als ir das volk all hye hört klagen,

Von Ihesu, der sich nennet Crist,
Der doch ain verkerer ist,
Des volkes und der rechten ee;
Er tuet uns allen sammen wee
Mit seiner newen lere.[6] (T.P. 126–34)

After Annas and a character referred to as "Rabi Samuel" have voiced their condemnations of Jesus, concluding that Jesus deserves to be killed (146–53), Annas asks Nicodemus for his advice and receives an unexpected response:

Annas dicit ad Nicodemum:
    Nycodemus, was rattest dw
    Uns zw dissen sachen nun?
Nicodemus dicit:
    Was rattes welt ir, das ich thue?
    Ich kan nicht ratten dar tzw:
    Wan dye ler, dye er hat
    Und dye werckt, dye er begat,
    Sind dye an in von got kummen,
    Man sicht es an allen enden:
    Seine wunder tzw lenden
    Schnelle un in kurtzer frist,
    Ob es von got kummen ist;
    Darumb lebet sunder ane not.
    Ich rat nicht auf seinen tot:
    Sein ler und sein leben sindt schlecht
    Und in allen dingen gerecht.
Annas ad Nicodemum:
    Phui dich, dw pösser trugner!
    Dein hertz ist aller eren lär!
    Flewch pald von unserem rat
    Schnelliklich und auch trat.
Nicodemus recedit[7] (T.P. 154–72)

The verbal exchange between Annas and Nicodemus sets the tone for two further exchanges in this scene: the exchange between Annas and Joseph of Arimathea (173–96) and that between Annas and Zedonius (197–210). In each case, the conflict arises when a figure clearly identified as a Jew – in the case of Nicodemus and Joseph, as members of the religious elite among the Jews – defends Jesus from the accusation of being a deceiver and misleader of the people. In each case, it is the belief that Jesus was sent by God that prompts Annas, the representative of the Jewish religious authorities, to drive each of Jesus's successive defenders out of the Jewish congregation. Nicodemus and Joseph defend Jesus on the basis of their knowledge of his works and teaching, while Zedonius's reason is somewhat more personal in nature:

Annas querit a Zedonio
    Zedonius, was rattest dw
    Uns zw dyssen sachen nu?
Zedonius respondit:
    Was sol ich ratten an des todt,
    Der mir gesechende augen pot,
    Da ich plindt wardt geporen
    Und het mein gesicht verloren?
    Das wisset alle ane spot:
    Er ist mein herr und mein got!
    Das wil ich reden offen war.
    Wer anderst spricht, der sagt nit war.
Annas dicit Zedonio:
    Fleuch von hinnen pald!
    Das dein ungelück wald!
    Wiltu sein nicht enperen,
    So müss wir dich anderst leren.[8] (T.P. 126–91)

The common text of the Tirol Passion plays begins with a scene of conflict within the Jewish religious leadership, conflict which centers on the teaching and identity of Jesus. Three times in rapid succession, the audience sees the following: Those among the Jewish religious community who defend Jesus are quickly ostracized by their fellows. The inter-Jewish nature of the conflict between early followers of Jesus and the religious authorities of his day is emphasized clearly and unmistakably. By depicting the initial conflict between followers of Jesus and the Jewish religious leaders as an inter-Jewish doctrinal conflict, this group of texts remains true to the Gospel records in substance, while expanding and elaborating on the Gospel accounts. An example of this is seen in the expansion of Nicodemus's response to the accusations against Jesus, which takes but one verse in the

Gospel of John.[9] Jesus's confrontation with the money lenders in the Temple is described in dramatic, even belligerent terms (76–105), while the man born blind and given sight by Jesus is given both a name, Zedonius, and a voice in the initial confrontation between Jesus's Jewish opponents and his Jewish supporters. Much like the St. Gall Passion play, the Tirol Passion plays present in their opening scene a Jewish community that is divided on the question of Jesus's Messiahship.

The opening scenes of both texts emphasize the Jewish origins of Christianity. The text of the Tirol Passion plays, however, presents only the events immediately preceding the capture, trial, and crucifixion of Jesus. This being the case, it must, of necessity, present a view of the Jewish religious authorities that emphasizes their opposition to Jesus's teachings and claims about himself. In the presentation of the conflict between Jesus and the Jewish religious authorities, however, the compilers of the Tirol Passion plays evince an acute consciousness of Jesus's place as a Jew among Jews. The question of Jesus's identity as Messiah, a question that has no logical coherence outside of the context of the fulfilment of Jewish prophecy, is emphasized here to a greater degree than in the St. Gall Passion play. With little elaboration of the Gospel accounts, the text clarifies the point of conflict to an unmistakable degree in the scene of Jesus's trial before the Sanhedrin:

> Cayphas dicit salvatori:
> > Hörest nit, was die zw hant
> > Auff dich getzewgent all sambt?
> > Grosse und jammerliche geschicht!
> > Warum verantwurst dw dich nicht?
> Salvator tacet.
> Cayphas clamat alta voce: "Adjuro te per deum vivum, ut dicas nobis, sy tu es Cristus, filius dei!" Et dicit:
> > Ich beschwer dich anne spot,
> > Pey dem lebenttigen got,
> > Ob dw seist Cristus, gottes sun:
> > Das lass uns all hie wissen nun.
> Salvator dicit ad Caypham: "Sy vobis dixero, non creditis michi; si autem interrogavero, non respondebitis michi neque dimitetis. Verruntamen dico vobis: Vos videbitis filium hominis sedentem ad dextris et venientem in nubibis celi."

Salvator dicit:

> Sag ich euch nu die warhait,
> So gelawbt ir mir zw kainer tzeit;
> Wegunt ich aber euch zw fragen,
> So welt ir mir kain antwurt sagen:
> So lat ir mich nit ledig für war.
> Aber ir werdt sechen mit der engel schar
> Des menschen sun euch werden schein
> Tzw der gerechten hant des vatters sein,
> Da in wirt untter schaiden ain wolck
> Ob sammung aller welde volk.[10] (T.P. 1063–80)

Caiaphas presses his questioning further, eliciting an even clearer claim to Messiahship from Jesus, to which he responds by calling Jesus a blasphemer and condemning him to death (1064–92). The confrontation between Jesus and the Sanhedrin continues after this exchange, with the other leaders of the group condemning and mocking Jesus. Annas brings the condemnation of Jesus to its conclusion, convincing his fellow religious leaders to take Jesus to Pilate (1147–60). The first section of the play concludes as it begins, with emphasis on both the Jewish origins of Christianity and the rejection of Christ by the Jewish religious leaders of his day. Jesus and his followers – Nicodemus and Joseph as well as the disciples – are depicted as Jews in this play, as the content of Caiaphas's accusations makes clear in both the opening and closing scene of the first play. The accusations of apostasy and blasphemy against Jesus and his followers have no logical coherence unless the audience understands that Jesus and his followers are themselves Jews, "Jews" here defined unequivocally as adherents to the faith of Abraham and Moses, and not simply members of a particular Semitic ethnic group.

The conflict between followers and opponents of Jesus among the Jewish religious leadership is revisited in the second play, which focuses on the Crucifixion. Following Jesus's death, Joseph of Arimathea reappears on stage, joining Nicodemus:

> Tunc Joseph cum servo suo venit ad Nicodemum et dicit:
> Ich pit dich Nicodem, edler man,
> Das dw mir hewt wellest peystan,

> Das wir Jhesum, den hoch werden,
> Bestatten zw der erden.
Nicodemus ad Joseph:
>> Joseph, lieber frewnt mein,
>> Ich wil dir geren hilflich sein;
>> Was mir darumb laides beschicht,
>> Des wil ich alles achten nicht:
>> So süll wir noch sein unverzagt
>> An im in allen seinen nötten,
>> Und sol man uns darumb tötten;
>> Wan der herr Jhesu Cryst
>> Unser got un erlösser ist.[11] (T.P. 2589–2601)

The conflict between those Jews who accept and those who reject the Messianic claims of Jesus is underscored throughout this scene. In an exchange with Pilate, Joseph refers to "der juden neyd" (the Jews' envy) as the source of the contempt and rejection that Jesus suffered (2658–65). In like manner, Nicodemus refers to "der pösen juden list" ("the slyness of the evil Jews") as the motivation for the cruelty in Jesus's execution (2688–94). Both of these characters have been clearly identified throughout the play as Jews, quite particularly as members of the Jewish leadership. Their condemnation of their fellow Jews here underscores the inter-Jewish nature of the conflict over Jesus and dramatizes for the audience the theological basis of the Jew–Christian division. The basis for that division is unmistakably identified as the acceptance or rejection of the Messianic claims of Jesus, a point further emphasized in the following exchange between Caiaphas, Annas, and Joseph. Annas and Caiaphas demand to know why Joseph has buried Jesus against their express orders, and Joseph responds by saying that he is convinced both of Jesus's Messiahship and the venal motives behind the decision to have him executed (2778–2801). Annas then responds:

Annas dicit:
>> Joseph, so hör ich wol,
>> Das dich die jüdischhait halten sol
>> Als ainen, der sein jünger ist;
>> Da von wirt in kurtzer fryst
>> Dein leib und auch dein leben
>> Mit grimen in den todt geben.

Joseph dicit:
> Ich verlaugen meines gottes nicht,
> Was mir von euch darumb beschicht!

Cayphas dicit ad Joseph:
> So muestu unser gefangen sein
> Und muest leyden von uns des todes peyn,
> Seyt ich ye an dir spür;
> Kumbt die österlich zeyt herfür,
> Dw muest darumb sterben
> Und lästerlich verderben.[12] (T.P. 2778–2815)

Here the conflict reaches its conclusion with the rejection of and threat of lethal violence against Christ-following Jews by Christ-rejecting Jews.

The common text of St, Pf, Br, B, A, and M focuses on the conflict between the Jewish religious elites and the Christ-following Jews (Joseph, Nicodemus, et al.) to a much greater degree than does that of the Halle Passion play. Where the group of six plays begins the Passion narrative (as opposed to the Easter narrative) with a heated confrontation between Jewish leaders who believe Jesus is Messiah and those who do not, the Halle Passion play begins with a council of devils in Hell. It is the devils who are plotting to rid themselves of Jesus:

Primus diabolus ad Luciper:
> Herr Luciper, pis gueter ding!
> Die sach die wird noch woll ring,
> Bait nur ain klaine weill:
> Wier wellen schiessn scharffe pfeyll,
> Die muessen die juden durch tringen:
> Sy muessen unser liedl singen
> Und uns totten diesen man.
> Darumb pis nu zbeyfls an:
> Die sach die wirt pald woll sten.
> Wol auff all, wir muessen gen!
> Die juden wollen habn ain rath,
> Der gleich uber in gatt:
> Das wirt ain guter anfang;
> Darumb wol auff, saumpt euch nit lang![13] (H.P. 130–43)

This devils' council contextualizes the scene that follows it: the confrontation between the Jewish religious leadership, represented by Caiaphas and Annas, and the Jews who follow Jesus, represented by Joseph, Nicodemus, and Zedonius. It is the devils of Hell who plot Jesus's demise in the Halle Passion, shooting their sharp arrows into the Jewish religious leaders in order to bring about the outcome that they desire. The impulse to kill Jesus is therefore depicted as something alien to the Jewish leadership, a foreign element introduced to their thinking by a malevolent supernatural power. The Jews are depicted here as the dupes of a group of devils, not their willing agents in bringing about Jesus's demise. The idea that Jews are best understood as victims of a supernatural malevolence and are not themselves the originators of their opposition to Christ is developed more fully in the Alsfeld Passion play. That Jews are depicted as victims of diabolic forces and not their witting accomplices derives from medieval conceptions of sin and has implications for our understanding the medieval reception of the Jewish figures as they appear in the Passion plays. A full discussion of these matters will follow in the treatment of the Alsfeld Passion play.

Also significant is the depiction of the Last Supper in the Halle Passion play. In accord with the Gospel accounts, the Halle Passion emphasizes the fact that the Last Supper was a Passover Seder in an unmistakable fashion, yet at the same time gives a Christian tone to the event through the use of the word "osterlamp" (Easter lamb):

Hospes ad servum
    Knecht, kum pald zu mir,
    Richt alle ding (schaff ich mit dier),
    Schau, das es alles sey her pey,
    Was dan der juden gbonhet sey,
    So man das osterlamb essn will.
    Dreitzehen sind ir: ist nit zu vill.
Servus ad hospitem:
    Herr, grust nu deine gest;
    Ich will warlichn thuen das pest![14] (H.P. 481–9)

After the host has welcomed Jesus and his disciples and offered them the water, basin, and towels necessary to wash their hands in accord-

ance with Jewish custom (490–3), the Jewish nature of their celebration is directly affirmed again:

> Deinde servus portet baculos vel etiam calceos et dicat:
> > Her, dy stäb sind da und als damit,
> > Wie es dan ist der juden sit,
> > So man das osterlamp essn thuet;
> > Das lamb wirt auch sicher guet.
> Hospes ad Jhesum:
> > Her maister, es ist zeit,
> > Das ir euch all zue richtn seit
> > Das osterlamp zu essen drat,
> > Wie Moises das gepoten hat:
> > Schurczt euch auf und legt euch an;
> > Ich wils fudern, so meyst ich khan.[15] (H.P. 494–503)

The master then asks the servant to bring in the lamb (504–05). As he
does so, the servant delivers the following lines of dialogue:

> Servus portat agnum dicens:
> > Got gesegn euch das essn
> > Und well unser nimmer mer vergessen!
> > Das lamp ist berait nach dem alten testament,
> > Recht woll gepraten und nit verprent.
> > Eildt pehendt und est von stat,
> > Wie dan Moises gepoten hat.[16] (H.P. 506–12)

The host repeatedly expresses concern that the meal be carried out
in accord with Jewish ritual law, using phrases such as "wie es dan ist
der juden sit," and "wie Moises dan geboten hat," that clearly indicate
that his guests, Jesus and his disciples, are Jews. It also demonstrates
that their Jewishness is something that is evaluated positively. The
repeated urging to eat the lamb quickly reveals knowledge of the
Passover ritual's origins, while the repeated use of the word "osterlamp" shows a conflation of Christian and Jewish terminology. The
emphasis on the observance of the Mosaic Covenant in the Last
Supper implicitly acknowledges that the Christian sacrament of
Communion, a ritual commemoration of the event depicted in this
scene, has its origins in the celebration of this most sacred of Jewish
observances. The Halle Passion play expresses this point in a way that

the texts of the other Tirol Passion plays do not. The corresponding text from the Tirol Passion play reads:

Deinde, cum venerint ad portantem aquam
Petrus dicit:
>   Guetter man, dir sey bekannt:
>   Unser maister hat uns gesant,
>   Uns zwen, zw dem herren dein;
>   Wo ist sein haus? Das thue uns schein.
Homo portans lagenam aque dicit:
>   Ich weys ewch auff das rechte spor:
>   Get mir nach, ich gee ewch vor
>   Und tzayg ewch zw disser fryst,
>   Wo meines herren haws ist.
Et sic vadunt ad hospitem, qui dicit:
>   Seidt willikom, ir herren guet,
>   Saget an: Was ist ewch zu muet?
Johannes dicit:
>   Herr, das thue wir dir pekant:
>   Unser maister hat uns gesant,
>   Uns tzwen, zw dir und spricht,
>   Er well des osterlampes phlicht
>   Pey dir heint hynnen essen;
>   Das er und auch sein junger gemein
>   Dye hochtzeyt wellen pey dir sein.[17] (T.P. 298–314)

As seen in this passage, the common text of St, Pf, B, Br, A, and M includes no references to the fact that the Last Supper was a Passover Seder, an observation of "der juden sit," carried out "wie Moises geboten hat." The use of the word "osterlamp" further establishes a Christian context free of reference to the Jewish origins of Christianity in the Tiroler Passion plays except for the Halle text. What is made explicit in the Halle Passion play – the Jewish origin of a Christian sacrament – is not even mentioned in the others of the Tirol group, except for the following brief passages. The first contains Jesus's blessing the bread:

Iterum salvator ad discipulos:
>   Ich wil ewch geben ein newe ee,
>   Das osterlamp sol nicht me;

Für war ich sag ewch, das
Es ain betzaichung was
Der newen e und anderst nicht.
Hin für man niessen sicht
Mich für das lamp in prottes schein:
Ich pin das lamp, das der sünden pein
Aller welt auff im trayt.... (T.P. 398–406)

In the second of these passages, he blesses the wine:

Consimiliter accipiens calicem benedicit et dicit ad discipulos:
Trinckt! Das tranck vil freyden pirt:
Das ist mein pluet, das für ewch wirt
Vergossen und für all menschait.
Dye alt ee is hin gelaydt;
Das ist der kelch der newen ee.[18] (T.P. 416–20)

The only reference to the Mosaic Covenant in this text is to its supercession through the new covenant of Christ. While the common text of St, Pf, B, Br, A, and M emphasizes the Jewish origins of Christianity through figures such as Joseph, Nicodemus, and Zedonius, it does not emphasize the Jewish identity of Christ and the disciples in the Last Supper, nor does it emphasize the Jewishness of that observance. The Halle Passion play, as seen above, emphasizes both the Jewishness of Jesus and his disciples and the continuity between the "new law" and the "old law," as the Mosaic covenant is seen from a Christian perspective, with unmistakable clarity. The common text of the other Tirolian Passion plays emphasizes only the discontinuity between the "alt ee" and the "new ee."

It should be noted that all of the Passion plays from Tirol, both the closely related group of six and the Halle Passion play, emphasize the Jewish origins of Christianity, though in different ways. By transforming Joseph of Arimathea and Nicodemus, who are two minor figures among the Jewish religious elite in the New Testament narratives, into key figures in the Passion narrative, both plays present their audiences with Jewish figures who were allies of Jesus. The Halle Passion even emphasizs the Jewishness of Jesus and his disciples, repeatedly stating that their first observance of what would become the Christian sacrament of Communion was, in fact, the celebration of a Jewish religious rite. With their focus on the first-century inter-Jewish conflict about Jesus, the Tirol Passion plays present a conflicting and contradictory image of Jews and their relationship to Jesus, depicting them neither as irredeemably evil nor as necessary foes of the Christian message.

Further, the emphasis on the Jewish origins of Christianity is multi-valent in its signification. It can convey the message that Christianity supersedes Judaism, but this of itself does not necessarily imply a condemnation of Jews. Instructing a gentile Christian audience that the Christian message was originally intended for and came from the Jews, these plays can also convey the message that Christianity is best understood as a continuation of Judaism. It is also possible that the conflict between the Christ-accepting and Christ-rejecting Jews would lead an audience to see the Jewish religion, though not the Jews as a people, as an essentially flawed, outdated religion.

One message that the representation of Jews in these plays certainly does not convey is a message that the Christian Gospel offers no hope to the Jews and that Jews have no proper place in Christian society. This list of interpretive possibilities is not exhaustive, but it does give insight into the range of possible interpretations of the Jews in the Tirol Passion plays. When one considers the events surrounding the pogroms of the fourteenth and fifteenth centuries, particularly the fact that some Christians attacked while others defended their Jewish neighbors, the multiplicity of interpretive possibilities also offers us an explanation for public behavior superior to that offered by the thesis that medieval German literature always villified and demonized the Jews. To determine if the same multiplicity of interpretive possibilities existed in other late medieval German Passion plays, we will now turn to the Frankfurt Passion play of 1493.

Approximately 150 years younger than the *Frankfurter Dirigier-rolle*, the Frankfurt Passion play follows the outline provided by its predecessor closely enough for some scholars to postulate that the former was the source for the latter.[19] The Frankfurt Passion play is, unlike the earlier work, a fully developed dramatic work, not a mere collection of dialogue prompts and stage directions. Like many of the other Passion plays (Tirol, Alsfeld), the Frankfurt play from 1493 consists of different sections – in this case two – that were performed on separate days. The first day of the play begins with Augustine, the Prophets, and other biblical figures presenting Messianic passages of the Torah, Psalms, and Prophets to an unreceptive audience of modern (late fifteenth-century) Jews (1–332), and ends with Jesus's capture in the garden of Gethsemane (2253–2423). The second day's play begins with Jesus's interrogation before the Sanhedrin (2423–75) and ends with John, Mary, Joseph, and Nicodemus laying Jesus's body in the grave (4381–4408). The tone of the confrontation between the Prophets and representatives of modern Judaism that begins the play is exemplified in the following excerpt:

> Daniel dicit:
>> Nu horet, was ich uch sagen sol!
>> Diß wort sult ir vornemen wol:
>> "Der war heilant Crist,
>> der uns zu droste kunfftig ist,
>> sal sin benediet leben
>> vor uns setzen und geben
>> in den bitterlichen dot:
>> suß wil er dragen unser not!"
> Joseph rabi:
>> Swiga, dor! Was claffestu?
>> Du were uff hude so frue!
>> Wer dinen warten neme gaum
>> Und dir beschiede diesn draum,
>> Den du hast vorgeleit,
>> Siech, der beginck ein arbeit,
>> Die dir gar notze were!
>> Doch lern besser mere:
>> Lijhe phennig uff phant, als ich!
>> Das mag rich machen dich!
>> So mag dir baße gelingen,
>> Dan ob du soltest singen
>> Allen diesen langen mey
>> "Baruch otta adoney!"[20] (F.P. 139–60)

Wenzel and Bremer both assert that this scene establishes a strict and immediate divison between irredeemable Jews and the redeemed or redeemable non-Jews. Addressing this point, Wenzel writes:

Eine weitere und bedeutsamere Dimension gewinnt diese Darstellung, wenn die beiden Gruppen [Jews and Christians] im Sinne des theologischen Weltverständnisses als Vertreter der göttlichen und der weltlichen Sphäre verstanden werden…. Sprache, Argumente und Gestik der Propheten sind charakterisiert durch die Aura der unveränderlichen Heilswelt, die Juden hingegen stellen sich selbst in ihrer irdischen Befangenheit dar. Ihr Interesse ist einseitig ausgerichtet auf die diesseitige Welt, ihre Argumente gegen die Heilslehre gründen auf der vergänglichen Macht des Reichtums, ihre Sprache, von Beleidigungen und Schimpfworten geprägt, ist die Sprache, die dem Weltlichen verhaftet ist. Die Kluft zwischen Heiligen und Verdammten – zwischen "Heilswelt und sæculum" – wird dem Publikum im Vorspiel sinnfällig vor Augen geführt.[21]

Bremer in particular argues that the pronoun "ir" is repeatedly used by non-Jewish characters to emphasize the otherness of the Jews, their place outside the reach of Christian salvation.[22] That the scene emphasizes the rejection of Jesus by the Jews and also depicts the Jews as greedy and impious is beyond question, as illustrated by Rabbi Joseph's hostility toward the prophet Daniel and mockery of his own liturgical song above. Beyond this, though, the Frankfurt Passion play introduces a new, decidedly non-theological dimension to the depiction of Jesus's Jewish opponents: The depiction of "Jewish greed" as a fundamental defining characteristics.[23] What remains open to question, though, is whether the play does, in fact, depict all Jews as callous Christ-haters and enemies of the good that Jesus embodies. The play's reliance on New Testament texts as sources leaves open the possibility that the Jewish figures of Nicodemus, Joseph, the blind man (Zedonius in the Tirol plays), and Malchus will play the roles by now familiar from the earlier Passion plays. If it can be demonstrated that these figures do play substantial roles in the Frankfurt Passion play of 1493, then the argument that the play's depiction of Jews expresses late medieval anti-Jewish hostility and only that cannot be maintained. An examination of the roles of these figures is therefore in order.

In the discussion of the St. Gall Passion play, it became clear that the character Malchus was the voice of the Jew who moved from hostility toward Jesus to acceptance of him and his teaching. In contrast to the Malchus of the St. Gall play, the Malchus of the Frankfurt Passion play first appears as an opponent of Jesus and remains such for the duration of the play. The following dialogue is typical of his tone throughout his confrontations with Jesus:

> Malchus dicit judeis:
>> Horet, ir judden, nuwe mere,
>> Waß hait getain der trogener;
>> Sprach hait he den stummen geben!
>> Er ist ein schlack, als muß ich leben![24] (F.P. 648–51)

Later, he shows no gratitude in return for Jesus's healing his wounded ear, repeating his earlier characterization of Jesus as a sorcerer:

> Salvator tollens auriculum reponens Malcho.
> Malchus dicit Iudeis:
>> Ir Iudden horit, was ich uch sagen:
>> Ein ore wart mir abgeslagen,
>> Das name der zeuberer,
>> Ihesus der gauckeler,
>> Und satzt mirs widder an,
>> Als abe iß nie keme von dan,
>> Als ir alle schawet hie!
>> Sehet, wo geschah das ye?[25] (F.P. 2391–98)

Though he does affirm the reality of the miracle, something that a Christian audience would find positive, the Malchus of the *Frankfurter Passionsspiel* is, nevertheless, among the majority of Jewish religious leaders who join in condemning Christ as a deceiver, while Nicodemus becomes the one figure among the Jewish leaders who speaks out on Jesus's behalf against the majority:

> Nicodemus dicit:
>> A Gotschalg, du salt die ridde lan!
>> Jhesus ist ein guder man!
>> Siner wandelung ist he gar gut:
>> Kein zauberer soliche zeuchen dut![26] (F.P. 1757–60)

This first defense he gives in the confrontation between Jesus and his hostile interlocutors, the Pharisees. Himself a Pharisee, Nicodemus later defends Jesus at his trial:

Nicodemus dicit Cayphe:

> Ir herren, saget, umb was
> ir findet und sprechet das,
> das Jhesus sij ein kebisch kint?
> Fromer lude doch viel hie sint,
> den iss allen kund ist,
> das Ihesus mutter, den man nent Crist,
> hat ein vatter in der ee:
> Darumb dut mir dise ride we,
> und der lugen ungelimpf,
> wan solichs ist ein boser schymph![27] (F.P. 2743–52)

It should be noted here that the accusations against which Nicodemus defends Jesus come directly from the Talmud and other Jewish sources, and as such contribute not to the representation of Jewish "blindness" or inability to perceive the truth, but to a realistic depiction of rabbinical teachings about Jesus.[28] The fact that both groups, medieval Jews and Christians, saw the conflict as centering on the Christian truth claims about the person of Jesus thoroughly undermines any attempt to portray the medieval Jewish–Christian conflict as essentially racial in motivation rather than religious. The heart of the conflict, in the eyes of the Christian dramatist as well as the Christian and Jewish theologians, lay in the acceptance or rejection of Jesus's Messianic claims. Nicodemus's defense of Jesus against his colleagues follows the account in the Gospel of St. John in considerable detail – though the dramatist does elaborate on the accusations levelled against Jesus by including the charge of bastardry. The source passage from St. John's Gospel comes from the account of Jesus's confrontations with other Jewish teachers and religious authorities during Passover celebrations in Jerusalem. It reads as follows:

> Then the officers came to the chief priests and Pharisees, who said to them, "Why have you not brought him?" The officers answered, "No man ever spoke like this man!" Then the Pharisees answered them, "Are you also deceived? Have any of the rulers or the Pharisees believed in him? But this crowd is accursed and does not know the law." Nicodemus (he who came to Jesus by night, being one of them) said to them, "Does our law judge a man before hearing him and knowing what he is doing?" They answered and said to him, "Are you also from Galilee? Look into it and you will see that no prophet has arisen from Galilee!"[29]

Nicodemus's appeal in the Gospel text is paralleled in the Frankfurt Passion play by the appeal to judge Jesus by his deeds. Nicodemus's role as one of Jesus's few Jewish defenders is given further emphasis in the dramatization by the decision to turn him into the defender of Jesus's parentage as well. The division among the first-century Jews on the question of Jesus's Messiahship is here faithfully rendered, so that assertions that Jews are, in these plays, always depicted as enemies of Christ and Christians seem overstated.[30] It seems, however, safe to say that the reliance on the Gospel accounts in Passion plays such as the Frankfurt Passion offered the medieval audience a sympathetic Jewish character with whom they could identify. Likewise, the praise Jesus receives from the Jewish crowd at his entry into Jerusalem, a scene that also parallels Gospel accounts, offered the medieval audience an image of Jews as people who welcomed Christ into Jerusalem:

> Lieberdrut parvus Judeus dicit:
> > Crist, Davidis sone, dir sy geseyt
> > lob und ere an underscheit!
> > Gegrusset sistu, Davidis sone,
> > hie un in dem hymmelthron!
> > Du bist der war heilant,
> > der uns zu droste ist gesant:
> > gebenediet sistu manigfalt!
> > Alles folg du erlosen salt
> > mit dinen gotlichen handen
> > von des falschen tufels banden!
> Pueri cantant secundum versum:
> > Israhel es tu rex Davidis–
> Et tercius puer dicit:
> > Du bist ein konig von Israhel,
> > geborn an Davidis stam an fel!
> > Du salt uns allen wilkomen sin
> > in dem namen got des vatters din![31] (F.P. 1825–38)

Scenes such as this one, with characters clearly identified as Jews shown to be allies of Christ and the disciples, allowed medieval audiences to see Jews as potential allies rather than as a unified group bent on the destruction of Christianity.

The play also follows the narrative of John's Gospel in its treatment of Joseph of Arimathea, a fellow Pharisee who joins Nicodemus in requesting permission to remove Jesus's body from the cross:

> Interim Ioseph ab Arimathia veniat ad Pilatum postulans corpus Jhesu et dicit:
>> Pylate her, ich bitten dich,
>> das du wollest geweren mich!
>> Jhesus der herre ist todt,
>> irgangen ist itzunt sin not:
>> des lass mich en neman herabe,
>> das man ene bestad zu dem grabe!
>> Irfulle hude myn begir,
>> so wil ich ummer dancken dir![32] (F.P. 4307–14)

For the purpose of comparison, the account from the Gospel of St. John follows:

> After this, Joseph of Arimathea, being a disciple of Jesus but secretly for fear of the Jews, asked Pilate that he might take away the body of Jesus; and Pilate gave him permission. So he came and took the body of Jesus. And Nicodemus, who first came to Jesus by night, came also, bringing a mixture of myrrh and aloes weighing about a hundred pounds. Then they took the body of Jesus and bound it in strips of linen with spices as is the custom of the Jews to bury.[33]

Note that because the play perforce uses direct discourse rather than an indirect report, greater immediacy and pathos are brought to Joseph and Nicodemus's care for the body of the crucified Christ. Note also that Joseph, a Jewish leader, refers to Jesus as "der herre," that is, the Lord. What emerges – both from the Johannine Gospel and the acknowledgment of the Jewishness of these disciples in the Frankfurt Passion play – is not an image of a unanimously hate-obsessed, greedy, self-righteous Jewish religious leadership, but of a religious leadership that is divided in its reaction to Christ's teachings about himself and about the nature of man and God. The play conveys this varied depiction of the Jews even though it is the play that introduces the "usurer" stereotype of the Jew to the Passion play corpus.

The presence of Jewish leaders among the followers and defenders of Jesus undercuts the view that the play is built only on the stark conflict between Jews and Christians, which Wenzel describes as "Der Dualismus zwischen der Welt des Bösen und des Guten, zwischen den Juden und Rechtgläubigen," inspired by the confrontations between Jesus and "the Jews" in the Gospel of John.[34] Jews, specifically the Jewish leaders Nicodemus and Joseph, are among the believers in Christ, the "Rechtgläubigen" in this context. The historical origin of Christianity among Jews is brought to the stage in this particular Passion play, necessitating a sympathetic portrayal of certain Jewish figures and an emphasis on Christ's own Jewishness. The former is seen in the characters of Nicodemus and Joseph, the latter in the praise of Jesus as "David's son" and "the king of Israel," seen above. Though Wenzel does note that Joseph and Nicodemus are identified as members of the Jewish religious leadership who are sympathetic to Jesus, she does not afford the characters any import in revealing either the author's or the audience's conception of the Jews.[35] Instead, her writing is informed by the presumption that the only aspects of the portrayal of Jews in the Frankfurter Passion play that could have had any effect on the audience or could reveal anything of the dramatist's own convictions about Jews are those emphasizing the "aggressive disbelief" and the "greed of the Jews."[36] In view of the fact that the two Jewish leaders are pivotal figures in the Passion narrative and are themselves extremely popular figures in medieval literature, it seems that their role as Jews who defend Jesus and see to his burial could not help but have a benign influence on the audience's conception of Jews.[37]

The identification of Joseph and Nicodemus as Jews is clear in the texts above, as is the identification of Jesus as Jew, though this latter identification is subtler. The confrontations between Jesus and the Jewish religious authorities, such as those found in 748–809, have no coherence apart from the assumption that Jesus himself is a Jewish teacher and therefore has authority to speak in disputations concerning the Mosaic law. Likewise, the use of the epithets "David's son" and "King of Israel" have no coherence outside of a Jewish context. From the inclusion of Nicodemus and Joseph and the identification of Jesus as a Jew in the play, it is clear that the point of contention – in the mind of the medieval Christian author of the Frankfurt Passion play – was not ethnic continuity and that Jewish resistance to the Christian

Gospel was not conceived of as a symptom of an inherited race-based defect. The play depicts Jesus and his followers as Jews who meet opposition from other Jews, and in that respect it provides a more varied image of Jews than that which Wenzel posits: a monolithically negative image without any counterpart, or, in her own words: "Das negative Stereotyp von Juden entbehrt jeglicher positiven Gegenpole."[38] In the figures of Joseph and Nicodemus as in the emphasis on Jesus's own place as a Jew fulfilling God's promises made to Jews, the play not only reminds its audience that Jews were their potential coreligionists, but also that "Salvation is from the Jews." Likewise, Bremer's remarks on the Frankfurt Passion fail to account for the manifest diversity in the play's depiction of first-century reactions to Jesus in the Jewish faith community. Instead, she flatly asserts that the Jews in the Frankfurt Passion play are always depicted as enemies of Christ who are beyond redemption, which is clearly not the case. In contrast to the earlier plays, the inclusion of additional biblical scenes in the *Frankfurter Passionsspiel* has a provocative function:

> Die neu eingefügten Szenen aus der Bibel, wie das kanaanäische Weib, die Samariterin, der römische Hauptmann, zeigen den Unterschied zwischen den Juden und Heiden: die Heiden, obwohl unwissend und in Unkenntnis der Alten Schrift, bekehren sich spontan zu Jesus, weil sie in ihm den Messias erkennen; die Juden bleiben, trotz aller Prophezeiungen, die in ihrer Schrift geschrieben stehen, stur und lehnen Jesus ab[39]

Though the Frankfurt play does exceed its predecessors in anti-Jewish vitriol, it is false to assert that all Jews appearing in the play are enemies of Christ, just as it is false to suggest, as Bermer does in the above passage, that all pagan figures in the play convert. The contrast between Jews and pagans that she posits does not exist in the text in the clarity and to the degree she describes.

Chapter Four: The Alsfeld Passion Play

The last of the vernacular Passion plays to be considered here is the Alsfeld Passion play, a product of the very late fifteenth or very early sixteenth century.[1] The difficulty in dating the play's origins precisely arises in part because the manuscript, though dated to 1501, is written in two hands and contains large portions of text drawn from earlier fifteenth-century sources, including the *Frankfurter Dirigierrolle,* the Frankfurt Passion Play, the *Trierer Marienklage,* and a fragment known as the Friedberg Text.[2] As one might expect, given that the Frankfurt plays served as a proximate source and that all Passion plays ultimately share the Gospels as their common source, the Alsfeld play has much in common with the Frankfurt plays. One of the many commonalities, as we shall see below, is that it, like they, contains Jewish figures who defend Jesus, and does not present in its Jewish figures a ceaseless parade of Christ-haters.

The one substantial difference between the hostile Jews of the Frankfurt Passion play and the hostile Jews of the Alsfeld Passion play is the direct connection of the Jews with the Devil in the Alsfeld play, a phenomenon that Wenzel refers to as the "Verteufelung" of the Jews.[3] The Jews in the other Passion plays oppose Christ, to be sure, but their motives remain humanly comprehensible ones: pride, jealousy, zeal for the law and traditions of their forefathers, and fear. In contrast, the majority of Jews in the Alfeld Passion play, as Wenzel rightly points out, are driven by a diabolic animus. Her comments on this aspect of the play summarize her treatment of the play as a whole:

> Das Alsfelder Passionsspiel zeigt in seinem Teufelsvorspiel eine weitere Entwick-
> lungsstufe in der Darstellung und Deutung der Juden im Rahmen des geistlichen
> Spiels: Während die Frankfurter Dirigierrolle noch eine Bekehrung der Juden und
> damit auch deren Erlösung auf der Bühne exemplarisch vorführte, sind die
> Möglichkeiten zur Bekehrung und Erlösung im Alsfelder Passionsspiel von
> vornherein ausgeschlossen. Die Juden sind nicht mehr Teil des göttlichen Heils-
> planes, zu dem sie grundsätzlich auch dann noch gehören, wenn sie Christus töten
> lassen, sondern Teil des bösen Prinzips. An die Stelle des Aufrufes zur Bekehrung

treten die Anklagen der Juden und die Aufforderung zur Rache, weil sie allein die Schuld am Tode Christi trügen.... Die Juden sind somit in dieser Welt beheimatete Handlanger der höllischen Mächte – sie sind in letzter Konsequenz keine Kinder Gottes, sondern die Marionetten des Teufels.[4]

What is problematic about this statement is that it fails to account for the presence and the impact of figures such as Joseph, Nicodemus, and other Jews who are shown to be something other than "Marionetten des Teufels." Wenzel is right to point out that the animus toward Christ in this play is depicted as coming directly from the Devil; however, she overstates her case when she argues that the Jews are shown as willing accomplices.[5] The very texts that she cites in support of her reading of the play, verses 183–90, 234–41, 330–3, and 285–305, make clear that the Jews are to be seen as the victims of a diabolical deception, and not the willing perpetrators of such a deception. Here the Alsfeld Passion play echoes that of Halle, discussed earlier, which opens with a council of devils who are plotting to deceive the Jews into rejecting Christ. That the dramatist depicted the Jews as people who were deceived by a supernatural diabolical power into seeking Christ's death and were not willing accomplices of the Devil is seen in the following passage. The speaker is a devil called "Raffenzan":

> Ich byns geheyssen Raffenzan:
> Alle boßheyt heben ich gern an,
> Myn hercz ist falscher list vol!
> Das hon ich bewyßet an den Judden wol:
> Den hon ich geradden allzyt,
> Das sie solden tragen haß und nyt
> Uff Jhesum den frommen mentschen!
> Daruff was alle myn gedencken!
> Ich hon auch gestifftet under en,
> Das sie en nit woln horen adder sehen
> Und vorsmehen en als eyn untedigen man,
> Und hie doch nie keyn sunde gewann
> Adder nie keyn ubbel yn sym herczen hot gedocht!
> Her Luciper, das hon ich als volnbracht![6] (A.P. 282–95)

The words of a second devil, Binckenbangk, further emphasize that the Jews were to be seen as dupes, and not deceivers:

Ich han gefaren die wernt alle umb
Die wyde und auch die krumme:
Darin hon ich viel arges zubracht
Beyde tage und nacht!
Das wel ich alles losßen stan
Und das nu eyn frommekeyt wisßen lan!
Eyn from mentsche, Jhesus gnant,
Dem ward nie keyn sunde bekant,
Das hon die Judden gefangen eyn haß:
(umb syn gerechtigkeit geschach das!)
Das hon ich geradden en allen![7] (A.P. 324–34)

The animus against Christ is unquestionably motivated by devils. The Jews, however, are not shown to seek these devils out or even to accept their advice knowingly. The diabolical animus is alien to them, imposed from the outside, and not generated from within; that is to say, it is not depicted as an essential, indelible characteristic of Jews.

That the Jews' opposition to Christ is generated by a host of devils and is extrinsic to them is best understood in light of medieval doctrines of sin and free will, discussed at some length and in detail by Jeffrey Burton Russel in his monograph *Lucifer: The Devil in the Middle Ages*.[8] While medieval theologians did acknowledge an innate corruption in human will, there was considerable debate on the nature of this corruption and its implications for human moral culpability and the question of salvation.[9] The theological view that predominated in the Middle Ages was one that acknowledged human volition but also allowed that volition could be and often was subjected to outside diabolical influence. Commenting on the relationship of theology to the depiction of evil in the arts, Russel writes:

> The Devil went through several movements of decline and revival in the central and late Middle Ages. The fading Lucifer in the theology of the twelfth and thirteenth centuries was matched by the growth of a literature based on secular concerns such as feudalism and courtly love, and later by the growth of humanism, which attributed evil to human motivations more than the machinations of demons.... On the other hand, the Devil of the desert fathers, Gregory, and Aelfric remained alive in homiletic literature and in the poetry and drama that drew on homiletics, liturgy, and theology. The triumph of free-will nominalism in the fourteenth and fifteenth centuries and the terrifying famines and plagues of the same period made the Devil an intensely threatening figure in much of later medieval art and literature.[10]

83

The medieval understanding of free will and the role of the Devil as tempter and deceiver therefore must be taken into account when we consider these medieval depictions of Jews as the victims of "the machinations of demons," as in the Alsfeld Passion play. In depicting the Jews as unwitting and therefore unwilling accomplices of the Devil, the Alsfeld Passion follows a strand of medieval theology and thinking about Jews (and other unbelievers) that treats them as humans who are not truly, willfully evil, but tragically deceived. As such, it conforms to the medieval conception of the Devil's role in generating sin of all kinds.

A well-known literary treatment of this medieval concept of the Devil comes from Hartmann von Aue's *Gregorius*. In this version of the Gregorius peccator legend, the incestuous seduction of sister by brother that results in the conception of the title character is repeatedly attributed to a deception perpetrated by the Devil himself. Establishing the Devil's motives in leading Gregorius's parents to commit the incest that brings him into the world, Hartmann writes:

> Dô dise wünne und den gemach
> der werlte vîent ersach,
> der durch hôchvart und durch nît,
> versigelt in der hellen lît
> ir beiden êren in verdrôz
> (wan si dûhte in alze grôz).[11] (301–08)

Having established the motive, Hartmann then elaborates concerning the methods that "der werlte vîent," who "durch hôchvart und durch nît / versigelt in der helle lît" ("because of arrogance and envy lies sealed in hell," 305–06), employs in his assault on the soul of the "jungherre":

> Daz eine was diu minne
> diu im verriet die sinne,
> daz ander sîner swester schœne,
> daz dritte stiuvels hœne,
> daz vierde was sîn kintheit
> diu ûf in mit dem tiuvel streit
> unz daz er in dar ûf brâhte
> daz er benamen gedâhte

mit sîner swester slâfen.
wâfen, herre, wâfen
über des hellenhundes list,
daz er uns so geværic ist![12] (323–34)

Just as Gregorius is the victim of the Devil's malice and cunning deception, so the Jews in the Alsfelder Passion play are presented as victims of diabolical mendacity. The council of devils has taken pains to make sure that the Jews would be lead astray, inciting them to hate Jesus. By placing the devils on the stage and giving such dramatic emphasis to their role in deceiving the Jews, the medieval dramatist indicates that the Jews otherwise would not have acted as they did against Jesus.

The depiction of Jews as victims of the Devil's malicious wiles, seen in the Alsfeld Passion play as in Gregorius, contrasts with another authentically medieval view of Jews, Moslems, and heretics. In that view, forcefully advanced by Peter the Venerable in the twelfth century, the three groups are regarded as willing participants in Lucifer's war against God.[13] The unknown author(s) of the Alsfeld Passion play here present a literary Jew akin to the Jew as understood by Peter Abelard. In his struggle to reconcile Jewish unbelief in the face of Christian witness and argument with the moral teachings of Judaism and their continued role in Salvation History, Abelard attributed to the Jews a deficiency of faith as well as reason, rather than deliberate malice.[14] Because their unbelief was due to a deficiency in their ability to interpret Scripture correctly rather than malice, Abelard argued, Jews were not culpable for sins stemming from their unbelief, though the unbelief itself still bars them from salvation.[15] Here, as in the Halle Passion play above, it is a satanic deception that mitigates the culpability of the stage Jews rather than the hermeneutic deficiency that Abelard identified. Nevertheless, it is clear that the Jews are not presented in the Alsfeld Passion play as willing tools of evil.

Furthermore, the animus in Jewish opposition to Christ is never depicted as unanimous. As in the Frankfurt and St. Gall Passion plays, there are in the Alsfeld Passion play Jews who openly declare Jesus as Messiah, as the following two quotations illustrate. They are both taken from the scene in which Jesus's triumphant entry into Jerusalem is dramatized:

> Interim ducunt azinum ad Jhesum et manebit Jhesus in eodem loco, donec Judei occurrunt ei. Tunc quartus Judeus scilicet Bifus dicit in loco suo scilicet Jherusalem:
>> Nu horet, er herren, was ich uch sage!
>> Ich was nu an eym tage
>> da Jhesus groiss zeichen thed,
>> zu Bethanien yn der stad:
>> er hiess von dem tode uffstan
>> Lazarum eynen toden man
>> und liess en widder genesen!
>> Das mocht von nicht gewessen
>> dan von dem waren godes degen!
>> Hie hat yn der selben erden gelegen
>> wol vier ganczer tage!
>> Vor war ich uch das sage:
>> ich gleub an en, do ich dit sach,
>> want mer myn synn das vor ware sprach,
>> das hie ist der ware Crist,
>> den wer heyssen Messias![16] (A.P. 2532–48)

The second passage:

> Quintus Judeus scilicet Lendikile dicit:
>> Vor war, er herren, ich sagen uch das:
>> hie ist der war Messias!
>> Ich wel uch das vor ware jehen:
>> hie macht eyn blynden sehen,
>> der do blynt wart geborn!
>> Got hot en zu eym sone usserkorn![17] (A.P. 2557–63)

These two characters are joined by other members of the Jewish crowd, some named, some unnamed, in hailing Jesus as Messiah.[18] This scene, however, is followed immediately by a series of confrontations between Jesus and the Jewish religious elites, who are led by *Synagoga*.[19] By bringing the conflict between Jewish factions that supported and those that opposed Jesus to the stage, the medieval dramatist not only yielded to historical accuracy, but also, if inadvertently, rendered a picture of Jews in which some figures would appear sympathetic to a Christian audience. That two of the characters who hail Jesus as Messiah, Bifus and Lendenkile, are the same characters who accompany the figure of *Synagoga* in other scenes of confrontation with Jesus and who mock him during the Crucifixion could not have escaped the audience. Though Wenzel dismisses their apparently vacillating attitude toward Jesus as a sign of the dramatist's lack of finesse that is without any import for our interpretation of the play, it should be noted that the change in the attitude of the Jewish crowd reflects the accounts of all four Gospels.[20] What we have in the depiction of inter-Jewish conflict and vacillation on the matter of Jesus's Messiahship is an attempt at historical and theological verisimilitude that has the effect of producing a conflicted image of the Jews as sometimes friends, sometimes bitter enemies of Jesus.

Also common to the Frankfurt and Alsfeld plays is the inclusion of the figures Nicodemus and Joseph, who function on one level as reminders of the Jewish origins of the Christian church and on another level as reminders of the willingness of some contemporary Jews to acknowledge Jesus as Messiah. In the Alsfeld Passion play as in the Frankfurt Passion play, Nicodemus defends Jesus against the charge of bastardry. Here, as in the Frankfurt Passion, the accusation occurs in the context of Jesus's trial before Pilate:

> Nicodemus respondit:
>> Ir herren, saget umb was
>> er sprechet und fyndet das,
>> das Jhesus were eyn kebes-kynt!
>> Frommer lude hie noch viel synt,
>> den das alle kuntlich ist,
>> das Jhesus mutter, den man nennet Crist,
>> hat eyn vatter zu der ee![21] (A.P. 3704–10)

It should be noted again that the accusation of bastardry, present in both of these Passion plays, is extra-biblical, having its origin in Jewish anti-Christian religious polemic. That the compilers of both of these plays saw fit to include the accusation and a refutation of it by a Jewish religious leader who is sympathetic to Jesus suggests two things: that they were familiar with the Jewish polemic and that they saw Jews as potentially receptive to the Christian salvation message, not as always and only enemies of Christendom.

Later, after the scene of the Crucifixion, Joseph is the person who, after conferring with Mary and John the Apostle, approaches Pilate to request the body of Jesus:

> Et sic vadunt ad Pilatum centurio et Joseph. Joseph dicit ad Pilatum:
> > Pilate, herre, ich kommen zu dir
> > Und bidden dich, das du nicht vorsagest mer
> > Jhesum, der do hanget doit
> > Und oberwonden hoit syn noit!
> > Den gibe mer von dem crucze herabe
> > Und loiß mich en yn die erde begraben!
> > Des bidden ich dich jammerlich:
> > Pilate, des gewere mich!
> Pilatus respondit Joseph:
> > Her Joseph edel von Armathie,
> > Eyn Judde fromme und frye:
> > Der bede, die du gebedden hoist,
> > Darumb wel ich nemmen rait
> > Zu den rittern, die hie stan,
> > Die alirst von em gan!
> > Hot hie vorlorn gar syn leben,
> > so wel ich dir en gern geben![22] (A.P. 6541–56)

It is significant for any interpretation of the play's treatment of Jews that Pilate refers to Joseph as "eyn Judde from and frye." It is also significant for our understanding of the play that two Roman soldiers, not the Jews, resist Joseph's wish to bury Jesus, intending to heap additional shame on Christ (6575–7). Two other soldiers suggest that Pilate grant Joseph's request (6579–84), which Pilate then does. Nicodemus then joins Joseph and aids him in removing the body and preparing it for burial (6591–6620). Joseph's role in this matter is a detail that is in accordance with the record of the Gospels of Matthew, Mark, and Luke, not only the Gospel of John, which Wenzel names as the model for the play.[23] In the synoptic Gospels, however, only Joseph is mentioned in the burial account. Nicodemus's role is mentioned only in John.[24]

The play clearly identifies these men as both Jews and followers of Jesus. The medieval German audience seeing this play performed would then have seen figures identified as Jews both persecuting and defending Jesus and his disciples. The community of Jews seen on the stage of the *Alsfelder Passionsspiel* is one that is at odds with itself over the identity of Jesus, up to and even after the point of his trial and execution. Wenzel acknowledges this ambivalence, but she argues that it plays a minor role, if any, in our understanding of the text's conception of the Jews:

> Auf den ersten Blick könnte man diese Passage [the triumphal entry into Jerusalem, v. 2514–2655] des Alsfelder Passionspiels als eine Art "Bekehrungs-szene" deuten, die das ansonsten verfolgte Prinzip der negativen Judendarstellung durchbricht. Die zahlreichen Widersprüchlichkeiten und Unklarheiten verweisen jedoch eher auf eine ungeschickte Textveränderung, die keiner konsequenten Linie folgt und daher eher als Unvermögen des Textinterpolators denn als bewußte Neugestaltung aufzufassen ist.[25]

This judgment seems inaccurate when considered in light of the faithfulness of the play to its source materials in the Gospels. The lack of clarity and the apparent contradictions in the play's treatment of the Jews can and should rightly be attributed to the conflicted, contra-dictory, and decidedly ambiguous image of Jews as a people that is found in the Gospels, documents which, and this fact cannot be over-emphasized, were written by first-century Jews.

Commenting on the disputation scene in the Alsfeld Passion play, the scene that she takes as emblematic for the depiction of Jews in the play as a whole, Wenzel writes:

> Die Juden sind aus dem Erlösungsprozeß ausgeschlossen, und in der Disputation wird die Begründung dafür geliefert. Weil sie sich wider besseres Wissen dem wahren Glauben verweigern, grenzen sie sich aus der Schar der Ungläubigen – und damit der potentiell Gläubigen aus….[26]

What the scene of the council of devils reveals, though, is that the Jews, in the mind of the compiler of the Alsfeld Passion play, did not deny the true faith against their own better knowledge, but out of a diabolically inflicted ignorance of Jesus's true identity. The Jews in the Alsfeld Passion play were therefore robbed of the opportunity to make any kind of informed decision.

In the same vein, the influential roles that are given to Joseph and Nicodemus in the play, as well as the presence of other Jewish figures who accept Jesus as Messiah substantially weaken the argument that the compiler(s) of the play – or the audience – saw the Jews as forever shut out of the possibility of Redemption. The presence of the same figures undercuts the assertion that the conflict between the two faiths, symbolized by *Ecclesia* and *Synagoga* was seen as unresolvable. In order for those assertions to obtain, the audience would have had to remain completely unaware of or unaffected by the figures discussed above. What Wenzel is arguing, in essence, is this: the audience would have been more emotionally affected by the scenes of Judas's betrayal or the confrontations between Jesus and the hostile members of the Sanhedrin than by the scene in which two Jewish leaders, Nicodemus and Joseph, see to the burial of a young rabbi from Nazareth, returning his corpse to Mary and John (6699–6792).

What seems just as likely, is that the latter scenes cannot be ascribed any less emotional power than the former. Therefore, the ambivalent image of the Jewish relationship to Jesus – his rejection by many, acceptance by few of his own people – reminded the audience of the ongoing theological tension between the two deeply religious communities. The demonization of the Jews, even in the *Alsfelder Passionsspiel*, is less than total and unequivocal. The existence and influence of neutral or even positive images of Jews in the collective mind of medieval German audiences would go far in explaining why, in spite of the presence and influence of such relentlessly cruel, Christ-and-Christian-hating Jewish figures as the Rufus of the St. Gall Passion play, years and even decades elapsed between mass incidents of anti-Jewish violence. Two countervailing images of Jews at least were at work in the mental world of medieval Christians in German-speaking Europe, producing highly varied responses to Jews in the real world.

Another noteworthy aspect of these plays is the fact that the Frankfurt and Alsfeld Passion plays, with their substantially different images of Jews, are, at most, separated by a mere eight years, with the former text stemming from 1493, the latter from sometime around 1501. This limits the amount of time for changes in the Christian public's attitudes toward Jews, such as the increase in economically

90

motivated hostility.[27] One possible explanation for the difference lies in expression of local attitudes. It could be that anti-Jewish resentment was more pronounced in Alsfeld than in Frankfurt, though this proposition is impossible to prove. Indeed, it cannot be confirmed or disconfirmed on the basis of our available evidence, literary texts, and chronicles. We simply have too few of them to provide a good data sample for measuring and comparing the degree of anti-Jewish sentiment in the two cities.

Another possible explanation for the variation in attitudes toward Jews seen in the Passion plays is that such variation is inherent both in the Passion narrative and in the long tradition of medieval Christian theology. It is from these two sources, the New Testament and centuries-old theological debates about the role of the Jews in Salvation History, that the medieval ideas about the place of Jews in Christian society were developed. That the wide spectrum of ideas about Jews that these sources – everything from the Gospels to the fifteenth-century works of Petrus Nigri and Nicholas Cusanus – provide should be reflected in the content of the Passion plays should surprise no one.[28] It seems clear that the variation in the treatment of the Jews in biblical (New Testament) and extra-biblical source matter remains the only explanation to explore if we wish to account for the variation in attitudes that we see in these plays. Bremer, though she argued in her conclusion that there is an anti-Jewish intolerance inherent to Christianity that accounts for the extremely negative images of Jews in the Passion plays,[29] is forced by the data to concede that the plays which hold fast to the biblical narrative remain tame in their treatment of Jews.[30]

Like Bremer, Wenzel identifies the Gospel of John as the source of the anti-Jewish attitudes, but she also argues that the Passion plays adopt a more conciliatory tone toward the Jews only so long as they follow the text of the Gospels closely. She observes just such a close dependence on the Gospels in the Alsfeld Passion play, noting that "die Schärfe der Vorwürfe und Beleidigungen von Seiten der Juden ist im Alsfelder Passionsspiel im Vergleich zum Frankfurter Passionsspiel zurückgenommen."[31] How these two contradictory positions are to be reconciled – one seeing the Gospels as the source of the "anti-Semitism" in the Passion plays, the other seeing those same documents as the sources of a more conciliatory attitude – is a point that neither author adequately addresses. Wenzel instead issues blanket statements about the negative "Judenbild" common to all medieval German literature and dismisses the Jewish characters who do not fit the mold of literary "demonization" or "dehumanization" of the Jews as unimportant or clumsy.[32]

The obvious resolution, as indicated above, is to admit that the ambivalence derives from the Gospels and other theological sources and that these sources themselves contain no unified, unnuanced, or "anti-Semitic" image of Jews. Indeed, a scholar must question the assumption that the polemical statements in the New Testament are anti-Semitic or anti-Judaic in nature. Writing on the relationship between the New Testament and the Hebrew prophetic writings, Craig Evans observes that the following terms were used by Jewish Prophets to describe Israel: "a sinful nation," "the offspring of evildoers," "a rebellious people," "offspring of an adulterer and a harlot," and "children of transgression."[33] Elaborating on the prophetic declarations of God's rejection of Israel in Isaiah 2:6, Jeremiah 14:19, and Hosea 4:6, Evans writes:

> There are no statements in the New Testament that approximate these angry expressions. Unlike Isaiah and Jeremiah, Jesus commanded his disciples to forgive (Matt. 6:14–15). Unlike Jeremiah, Jesus teaches his disciples to pray for their enemies (Matt. 5:44).… Never does Jesus or any of the writers of the New Testament say that Israel has been rejected. Indeed, Paul proclaims the precise opposite – Romans 11:1.[34]

Evans further observes:

> Unfortunately, later generations of Christians, by this time predominantly non-Jewish, misunderstood (innocently in some instances, maliciously in others) the hermeneutic of prophetic critcism. No longer understood as a challenge from within the community of faith, it was understood as condemnation of a particular people outside of the faith.[35]

Evans's observations raise an important point. In those cases where the Passion plays closely rely on Scripture, they are forced by this reliance on Scripture to restore the original inter-Jewish context of Jesus's words and deeds. When this context is restored on stage before an audience, it necessarily confronts the audience with Jewish figures who must be interpreted *in bonam partem*. This being the case, writers who find "anti-Semitism" in the New Testament, or in documents based closely on it, do so on the basis of anachronistic and logically unsound assumptions.[36] Dealing with the Crucifixion of Jesus as they do, the nature of the Passion plays afforded the medieval dramatists opportunities to depict the Jewish leaders of the New Testament as cruel, unjust, and corrupt. However, adherence to the New Testament text actually limited the one-sidedness of such depictions, and provided a check to their severity. It was the texts that departed furthest from the Gospel accounts, as discussed above, that offered the most degraded and villainous Jewish figures to their public.[37]

In contrast, the Easter plays, by their nature, had little in their material to provide any check to the depiction of Jews as enemies of Christ. Treating as they do the Resurrection of Jesus, Easter plays offer little opportunity to depict the Jewish leaders as anything other than opponents of Christ who seek to deny or conceal the reality of his Resurrection. However, the subject matter of the Easter plays also limits the degree to which Jewish leaders can be depicted as cruel or ruthless. Where the Passion plays are rife with scenes of direct confrontation between Jewish leaders and Jesus, as well as scenes that lend themselves to the dramatization of physical cruelty, the Jews of the Easter play are relegated by and large to background roles. In some Easter plays, they do not appear on stage at all, but are referred to by characters such as Mary and Mary Magdelene. Exactly how the different emphasis of the Easter plays affected the stage depiction of the Jewish authorities shall become clear below.

Though the focus of the present discussion is on the literary tradition in the German language, it is necessary to make note of the fact that Latin Easter plays were among the earliest Easter plays produced in German-speaking medieval Europe, and that wholly Latin Easter plays continued to be produced for centuries alongside mixed-language and vernacular Easter plays. The *Klosterneuburger Oster-spiel* from the period around 1200, the *Prager Osterspiel* from the late thirteenth or early fourteenth century, and the *Engelberger Osterspiel* from 1372 all share a number of traits apart from being exclusively Latin texts.[38] All of them are very brief, the *Prager Osterspiel* consisting of one scene; all adhere strictly to the biblical text; and none contains any lengthy diatribes against the Jews. The reason for this concentration is that the plays were originally conceived of as works of religious instruction as much as drama, and therefore followed closely the texts of the Scriptures from which they were drawn.[39] Their concentration on small sections of the Resurrection narrative has a necessarily limiting effect on the way that the plays depict the Jewish reception of Jesus. The *Prager* and *Engelberger* Easter plays treat only the meeting between the risen Jesus and the three Marys, while the *Klosterneuburger* play treats a number of episodes from biblical and extra-biblical sources. Among them are Pilate's sending the guards to the tomb at the request of the Jewish authorities, the Harrowing of Hell, the initial disbelief of the Apostles, and the meeting with the three Marys. The Jewish rejection of Jesus forms a background element and not, as shall be the case in other Easter plays, the basis for an exercise in anti-Jewish hostility.

The earliest of the mixed German-Latin or wholly German Easter plays to be handed down to us is *Das Osterspiel von Muri*,[40] which is preserved in a single manuscript of early thirteenth-century provenance. It is divided into individual scenes, treating Pilate's meeting with Caiphas, the placement of the grave watch, the Harrowing of Hell, the Resurrection, the conspiracy to conceal the Resurrection, and Jesus's post-Resurrection meetings with his apostles and disciples. The play departs substantially from the source texts, the Gospel narratives, in that it strongly suggests that the Jewish authorities are alone responsible for Jesus's execution. Two brief texts from the play demonstrate the emphasis on the responsibility of the Jewish leaders for Jesus's death and their hostility to the Resurrection. In the first, the Jews speak to the soldier assigned to watch Jesus's grave:

> Ir drige sullent ligen hie,
> so ligen and der sitvn die,
> so ligen dise dorte,
> vnd die an ienme orte!
> Wachent wol und slafent nicht,
> so wird vich dc vich ist virphlicht.
> Wend abir ir nicht bihalten dc,

so mvessen wir vich sin gihaz:
da von so hvetent sere!⁴¹ (340–8)

In the second, Pilate speaks first, then the Jewish leaders:

Pilatus zu den Juden:
    We, nu enweiz ih wc ih tu!
    Ir herren, ratent, es ist cit,
    want unser ere dar an lit,
    vnd uernement die liute dc,
    so gelobent si an Ihesum baz
    danne an alle unser gotte.
    Da von wereden wir ce spotte,
    vnde swechet vns vil sere.
Primus Judaeus:
    Ih rate vf min ere,
    vb ivh geuallet dc
    (olde ir ratent danne bc)
    daz wir dien gesellen
    zwencic phunde cellen.⁴² (435–47)

Unlike many of the other plays of this type, however, it identifies the followers of Jesus as Jews themselves. When asked by a gardener "wen suochent ir," one of Jesus's followers replies:

Jhesum von Nasaret,
den unser uursten viengen
und an daz cruce hiengen.
Des ist der dritte tac,
daz er in des todes banden lac,
want er den tot vershulte nie:
den suochen wir gemeine hie,
als ih dir gecellet han.⁴³ (189–96)

Though this is a brief dialogue, it is important in light of the treatment that the same material would receive in plays composed in the fourteenth and fifteenth centuries. As shall be seen below, the Easter plays from later centuries routinely, and anachronistically, depicted a conflict between first-century Jews and first-century Christians that completely ignored the fact that the latter belonged to the former, both religiously and culturally. Here, however, the spokesman for Jesus's followers refers to the Jewish authorities as "our" princes, not "their" princes. This is done in spite of the strong tendency to introduce anachronistic distinctions in drama, a tendency also reflected in the visual arts, in paintings and manuscript illustrations that introduce physical distinctions – either in dress or in physiognomy – between first-century Jews and followers of Jesus.[44] So strong is the tendency toward anachronism, that the occasional exception to it can be perceived not only as an attempt at historical accuracy, but also as a statement in defense of Jews.[45] Similarly inaccurate – and subtly defamatory – is the conflation of pagan Roman polytheism and Judaism apparent when Pilate says "alle unser gotte," and is not contradicted by the Jewish speaker. The picture of Jews that emerges in this play is, in spite of the identification of Jesus's followers as Jews, predominantly that of enemies of Christ and therefore enemies of Christendom.

The *Trierer Osterspiel* dates from the late fourteenth or early fifteenth century[46] and makes little mention of the role of Jews in the Crucifixion. The one line of dialogue that does treat the matter ascribes sole guilt for the death of Jesus to the Jews:

> Prima maria dicit rickmum "Owe, Owe,":
>> Owe, owe, der vyll grymmygen hant,
>> dye aller werde heylant
>> an das cruycze hayt gehangen!
>> Her hayt dorch den menczschen dye martyge entphangen.
>> Owe, ir judden, wylch eyn groeß mort,
>> wye mychel unde ungehort!
>> Vorsteynt uwer herczen synt:
>> ir hayt gecruzyget dye muetter als dat kynt![47] (19–26)

The reference is a brief one, but the message is clear: the Jews killed Jesus, and the guilt for the "groeß mort" ("great murder") is theirs alone. As meager as this evidence is, it is still safe to say that the play clearly, and anachronistically, distinguishes between the followers of Jesus – one of whom is one of the three Marys – and the Jews as groups.

Even more meager is the evidence of the late fourteenth-century *Füssener Osterspiel*, which only mentions the Jews once in connection with the Crucifixion, identifying them as those to whom Judas betrayed Jesus and who were responsible for Jesus's hanging. The relevant passage is spoken by the third Mary:

> Sy fvrte(n) in als eine(n) diep,
> die iuden, den Judas v(er)reit,
> dez us sine(m) lip geng wasser vn(d) plut.
> Owe, wie ve daz mine(m) h(er)zen tut!
> Sy heten in gefangen,
> zwischnu(n)t zwen schager gehangen.[48] (108–14)

This, the only direct mention of the Jews in the *Füssner Osterspiel*, attributes to them the sole responsibility for the Crucifixion.

Looking to the fourteenth-century *Innsbrucker Osterspiel*,[49] we see no such identification of the first Christians as Jews as seen in the *Osterspiel von Muri*. Instead, we have not only a clear identification of the Jews (not just the Jewish leaders) as the parties solely responsible for the Crucifixion, as in the *Füssener Osterspiel*, but also a definite line between the Jews and the Christians. The distinction between the groups is made clear in the opening speech by the dialogue of the *expositor ludi*:

> Ir seligen cristenlute:
> ic wil uch kunt thon
> (ir mueget gerne hueren czu)
> wy dy Juden dar varen
> vnd daz grab wullen bewaren
> mit rittern mechteg und gruz,
> dy da sint der Juden gnoz;
> sy schullen hute durch gut
> Ihesum halden in irer hut.[50] (30–6)

In their exchanges with Pilate, the Jewish speakers, who are named only "Primus Iudaeus," "Secundus Iudaeus," and so forth, repeatedly identify themselves as Jesus's killers:

> Ihesus der sich nante got
> vnd vns vorstorte vnser gebot
> der is nu tot vnd hindert vns nicht me.[51] (75–7)

And further:

> Tertius judaeus dicit:
> Pylate, edeler konig fry,
> daz dir salde wane by!
> Ich furchte, wir kamen yn gruße not:
> Ihesus den wir schlogen tot,
> der mochte wedir vff ste
> vnd wedir uz dem grabe ge.[52] (103–08)

Their guilt is affirmed also in the dialogue of the three Marys:

> Tertia persona cantat:
> Heu nobis internas mentes
> quanti pulsat gemitus
> pro nostro consolatore,
> quo privamur miserae,
> quem crudelis Iudaeorum
> morti dedit populus.
> et dicit
> Awe, [an] vns armen frawen
> mag man nu wol schawen
> gruz iammer vnd not:
> min lyber herre ist nu tot,
> den dy Juden haben emort,
> an schulde, alz ir dicke habet gehort.[53] (838–49)

Here, again, the Jewish context of Jesus's Messianic claims and the identity of the first Christians as Jews are both fully ignored, making a clear distinction between the moral character of Jews and Christians possible.

Additionally, the *Innsbrucker Osterspiel* includes a brief parody of Jewish religious song, thrice repeated, which adds a tone of outright mockery to its depiction of Jews:

> Tunc Judaei cantant Judaicum:
> Chodus chados adonay
> sebados sissim sossim
> chochun yochun or nor
> yochun or nor gun
> ymbrahel et ysmahel
> ly ly lancze lare

vczerando ate lahu dilando
sicut vir melior yesse
ceuca ceuca ceu
capiasse, amel![54] (57–66; repeated at 89–98 and 157–66)

A similar mockery of Hebrew religious song appears in the *Rheinisches Osterspiel* of Berlin manuscript Ms. Germ. Fol 1219, from 1460.[55] Near the beginning of the *Rheinisches Osterspiel*, a character named "Natan" is asked three times by his fellow Jews to teach them a "juddeschen sang." His response reads:

> Natan respondet:
> Wil uch nu ist also jach,
> so solt ir mir alle singen noch.
> Ich wil uch leren noch juddeschen seden
> den gesang den ich han hie geschreben.
> sic incipit Natan cantum:
> Alba lamazan Messias der sal kommen,
> argel ares sabaoth zu unserem grossen
> frommen, atha berith hie heliodorus
> daz sagen ich uch verware, her amati
> husi mag nit geliegen czware etc.[56] (85–93)

This particular type of mockery seems to have become a common part of the convention of anti-Jewish motifs included in Easter plays in German speaking Europe during the fifteenth century, appearing also in the 1472 *Wiener Osterspiel*, where the stage directions for the scene in which the Jewish authorities go to meet Pilate read "Dy Jodin tanczin tzu Pylato v(nd) singen Jodisch" ("the Jews dance toward Pilate and sing in Jewish").[57]

Two developments, shifting of blame for the Crucifixion to the Jews – all Jews – and creating an anachronistic division between Jews and the first followers of Jesus, have been completed clearly in this and other fifteenth-century texts: the *Rheinisches Osterspiel*, as also in the *Wiener* and *Erlauer* Easter plays, provides the clearest examples of these developments. In the *Wiener Osterspiel*, the three Marys are given this to say:

Awe des jemmerlichen smerczen,
den wir umbe unseren herren tragen,
den uns di juden haben irslagen![58] (719–21)

Another development that is initiated in the fourteenth-century
texts and continued in those of the fifteenth century is the emphasis on
the cruelty and guilt of the Jews in Jesus's death. This development is
perhaps best exemplified by passages from the *Erlauer Osterspiel*.
The play opens with the lamentations of the three Marys. The
character identified as *Secunda Maria* says:

O we, den scheppher heb ich verlorn
den ich derwelt het und derchorn,
Ihesum Cristum, Mariae chind!
Di Juden worn all plint,
da si in punten und viengen
und an das chäycz hiengen.
Des muoß ich an meinem herzen
leiden grossen smerzen,
seid ich mit mein augen sach
daz in ein plinter Jud in sein herz stach.[59] (36–45)

It should be noted here that the blindness referred to here is a spiritual
blindness, one constituted by a theologically based rejection of Jesus
as Messiah. References to this spiritual blindness are common in
Christian polemic, and occur in literary forms that are either wholly or
partially derived from this polemical tradition. These forms include
but are not limited to the Easter and Passion plays and the *Fastnachtspiele*.[60]

Later on in the *Erlauer Osterspiel*, the second Mary, speaking
alone, sings the following:

Owe, du falsche judischait
geschrirn sei über dich waffen!
Das eukch got hat dar zu beschaffen
das ir unser liecht und unser sunne
Ihesum, unsers herzen wunne,
so mardichlichen habt erslagen,
das muss wir heut und immer chlagen![61] (1055–61)

100

Of note in this text is exactly what it is that the second Mary deems worthy of perpetual lamentation: that God made the "falsche judischait," for the purpose of killing Jesus. Though her lament emphasizes the cruelty of the death Jesus suffered, that she describes the Jews as agents who carried out a divinely ordained act demonstrates a tendency of thought that militates against that seen in the Easter plays discussed above. Here, at least implicitly, is an acknowledgment of the theological necessity of Jesus's death in the Christian faith and a statement limiting if not eliminating the guilt of the Jews in the Crucifixion.

In contrast, the cruelty and culpability of the Jews is given even greater weight in the *Erlauer Osterspiel* by the explicit comparison of Jews to vicious animals:

> Wo der herrte nicht enist
> da sint die schaff gar ungewis
> vor den wolfen auf der waide.
> Juden und haiden sind uns immer wolf genuog,
> seid man uns Ihesum ersluog.[62] (149–54)

This explicit comparison of Jews (and heathens) with wolves, animals that had been symbols of gluttony, tyranny, and heartlessness since Greco-Roman antiquity, is a topos that we will encounter again when dealing with the depiction of Jews in the Aesopic fable tradition. It is also a figure that we see in the prophetic literature of the Old Testament – in Jeremiah 8:6–7, Amos 6:12, and Zephaniah 3:3, just to name a few instances – as Mary Callaway has pointed out.[63] However, as Callaway has also noted, the use of this imagery by a non-Jew has altogether different connotations: It becomes a blanket condemnation of an entire group rather than a call for repentance.[64]

In the *Rheinisches Osterspiel*, a similar comparison of Jews to vicious animals is made:

> Maria dicit
> > Daz ist jemerliche
> > <daz <weiz> got der riche,>
> > daz man den guden mit arge lont
> > und die boßen dorch ir boßheit cront.
> > Owe, ir unselgen judden,
> > ir glicht uch woil den dobenden rudden![65] (1158–63)

In these Easter plays, the comparison of Jews to ravening wolves ("Juden sind uns immer wolf genuog") and mad dogs ("ir glicht uch woil den dobenden rudden") is only part of a complex of dramatic and rhetorical developments used in fifteenth-century Germany to place the Jews beyond the pale of normal human morality.[66]

An exception to the general trend in fifteenth-century Easter plays is the *Redentiner Osterspiel*, which is preserved in a manuscript dated 1464.[67] The play begins with two angels addressing the audience and reminding them of the atoning nature of Jesus's death and quickly moves to a scene in which Jewish leaders confer with Pilate:

Primus Judeus:
> Caypha unde gy heren aver al,
> Ene rede ik ju saghen schal:
> desse Jhesus wolde godes zone wesen,
> he sede, he wolde van deme dode wol wezen.
> He sprak sere gruwelike wort,
> de er van manne sint je gehort:
> he wolde up stan an deme drudden daghe.
> Dar umme ik ju dat saghe:
> gy moten dat graf laten bewaren,
> dat he uns nycht kone utvaren.
> Bringet ene sine jungere hemelken van dan,
> So spreken se, he sy van dode up ghestan.[68] (19–30)

This brief passage sets the tone for the characterization of the Jews throughout the *Redentiner Osterspiel* and is, in fact, recapitulated almost verbatim later in the same scene.[69] These two passages dramatize the Jewish rejection of the Resurrection, but they do not contain any of the elements of mockery or derision seen in the *Rheinisches* or the *Erlauer Osterspiel*, both discussed above. An element of condemnation that the *Redentiner* Easter play does share with these others is the attribution of sole guilt for the Crucifixion to the Jews. This attribution is placed in the mouth of Pilate, who declares himself free of any guilt in Jesus's death.[70] Again, it is an attribution of guilt that contradicts the theological necessity of the Crucifixion, a necessity that is affirmed by the dialogue of the angels at the beginning of this very play.

It seems in view of the content of both the Passion and the Easter plays that the adherence to Christian scripture as a model for the plays had some ameliorative influence on the depiction of Jews. Following the New Testament closely forced the compilers of the Passion plays, even the Alsfeld Passion play, to depict Jews as both allies and opponents of Christ. It was when the plays departed from addressing the key theological conflict between Christ, his followers, and the Jewish religious authorities that the plays, most especially the Alsfeld play, degraded the Jewish characters to the greatest degree.[71] This was true of the earliest Passion play, the St. Gall Passion, as of the latest, the Alsfeld Passion play. That all Easter plays and all Passion plays had to depict a conflict between Jewish religious authorities and the first followers of Christ was unavoidable. There was, however, nothing inherent in the Gospel sources that mandated the inclusion of stereotypes, such as that of the greedy Jew, or outright mockery of the Jewish religion.

Because of their reliance on the Gospels, the Passion plays come closest to presenting modern readers with a literary mirror of ongoing theological developments in the Christian attempts to deal with the ongoing rejection by Jews of Jesus as Messiah. One central question, that of the Jews' culpability in their rejection of Jesus, is addressed in all of these plays, and the answers in these plays are as varied as those of the theologians. The diabolically induced hatred of Jesus seen in the Alsfeld Passion, for example, closely resembles the ideas expressed by Gregory the Great, who attributed the Jews' rejection of Jesus to error sewn by "the Enemy" who "ravished the Jewish people [...] extinguishing the faith among them with darts of fraudulent advice."[72] Gregory along with Anselm, Abelard, and Bernard of Clairvaux argued that, their error being unintentional, it could not, therefore, be culpable.[73] Conflicting with this strand of thought was one expressed by Isidore of Seville, Alan of Lille, and Raymond Martin, according to all of whom the Jewish leaders killed Jesus knowing that he was the Messiah and hating him for it.[74]

Bridging these two conflicting positions in his attempt to understand Jewish unbelief, Thomas Aquinas, perhaps the most influential Christian theologian since Paul the Apostle, differentiated between those Jews who were stubborn and malicious, those who were still being taught by the Law of Moses and yet unable to grasp its true meaning, and those who, given the opportunity, could recognize Jesus as the Christ foretold in the Tanakh (the Torah and the prophets).[75] Only the first group could be, in Aquinas's judgment, truly culpable of sin in their unbelief. Aquinas's division of Jews into three groups is closely paralleled by the depiction of Jews in the best-preserved Passion plays here examined. The St. Gall Passion play has its Rufus and its Malchus, the Tiroler Passion play not only a Nicodemus and a Caiaphas, but also a thoroughly Jewish group of Apostles, while the Alsfeld Passion play has figures embodying the acceptance and the rejection of Jesus by Jews. The Passion plays present us not one "hermeneutic" Jew, but a variety of figures, each constructed to dramatize different possible theological explanations for Jewish responses to Jesus.

It seems ironic that the Easter plays, with their focus on the Resurrection rather than the Crucifixion, should provide an image of the Jews that is more unified and in that respect more sinister than that found in the Passion plays. Though the subject matter of the Passion plays afforded their creators the opportunity to dramatize the physical cruelty of Jesus's Jewish opponents, the subject matter – the career, trial, and execution of Jesus of Nazareth – also mandated that they present Jewish characters who were sympathetic toward Jesus. The inclusion of significant roles for Nicodemus and Joseph of Arimathea, both of whom are clearly identified as Jews in the *Alsfelder* as well as in the *Frankfurter Passionsspiel*, undercuts the argument that the Jews were seen by the authors or audiences of these plays as wholly diabolical, unredeemable creatures. No such counterweight to the image of the scheming, deceptive enemies of Christ can be found in the surviving Easter plays, however. Indeed, the Easter plays contain, in their treatment of the Gospel narratives, the sharpest and most anachronistic divisions between Christian and Jew. In the Passion plays, the line between the two groups is hazy and can be crossed. In the Easter plays, we have, with one exception, a body of works that presents a clear and inviolable division between the two groups. This salient difference between the two groups of plays leads to another consideration of the influence of subject matter on the depiction of Jews. We have in the Frankfurt and Alsfeld Passion plays lengthy scenes that dramatize theological disputes between Christians and Jews, covering the key points of theological conflict between them. These scenes treat the fulfillment of Messianic prophecies of Jewish scriptures in the person of Jesus. This being the case, they convey the message that the line between Jew and Christian is neither clear nor inviolable. The existence of converts – in both directions – was a fact of life for Jews and Christians in the Middle Ages and evoked concern from religious authorities in both communities. That being the case, the dramatization of such theological disputations would not have been something abstract and unfamiliar to a Christian (or Jewish) person observing one of these plays, but would have had an immediate referent in their daily life. As we shall see in the following pages, the literary treatment of the Jewish–Christian debate, with its reference to ongoing theological disputes between living persons, also played a role in one of the most widely disseminated of medieval Saints' legends.

Chapter Five: The Legend of Saint Silvester in Medieval German-speaking Europe

Mit einer zunächst vielfach recht problemlosen Symbiose hängt wohl auch zusammen, daß neben der Masse haßerfüllter Stimmen, die so zahlreich im erhaltenen Schrifttum bezeugt sind, auch Vertreter einer menschlichen Gesinnung nie verschwanden – auch für sie muß Zeugnis abgelegt werden. Die Kirche bekämpfte öfter diese Sympathie, sprach von Judaizantes und verfolgte sie zuweilen als Ketzer. Aber selbst im hochkirchlichen Schrifttum fehlen positive Stimmen nicht ganz: Noch die frühmittelalterliche Hagiographie hatte ein recht eigenartiges, neutralistisches Verhältnis zu den Juden, die Ringparabel war schon im Mittelalter bekannt, Päpste schritten zuweilen zum Schutze der Juden ein, und immer wieder fanden sich Menschen, die Verständnis für die Juden aufbrachten....[1]

This quotation, taken from the essay that gave the title to a collection of proceedings from a conference on the Jews in medieval Europe, points to one area of late medieval literature where we might reasonably expect to find a counter-image to the admittedly prevailing negative image of the Jew. If the hagiographic literature of the early Middle Ages had a neutral, "idiosyncratic" relationship to the Jews, one would expect that traces of this relationship would continue to manifest themselves in the hagiographic literature that continued to be produced throughout the Middle Ages. In the above examination of the Passion and Easter plays, we have already, in a manner of speaking, become familiar with the central thematic element of the most influential work of medieval hagiography that treats the Jews as subjects. The work in question is the legend of Saint Silvester and the thematic element in question is the theological disputation between learned representatives of Church and Synagogue. In the concluding remarks to her essay addressing the role of the disputation in the Silvester legend, though, Lydia Miklautsch remarked that the legend used the disputation to define the Jews as "Gottesmörder," as "jene, die den Teufel zum Vater haben," and as "Staatsfeinde."[2] She also calls the legend "exemplarisch" for the depiction of Jews in medieval hagiography.[3] Considering Graus's and Miklautsch's largely contradictory descriptions of medieval hagiography together, we must examine medieval saints's lives anew in order to discern which description comes closest to the mark. Such a reexamination must focus largely on the vast body of medieval German legendaries, but must also concern itself with the integration of saint's legends into popular drama if it is to provide a thorough accounting of the depiction of Jews in medieval hagiographic literature.

We have already become acquainted with the core element of the Saint Silvester legend: the theological debate. In her discussion of the Passion plays, Wenzel characterizes the dramatic representation of abstract theological debate, specifically the open, scholarly disputation between representatives of the two religions, as an alien element introduced into the Passion plays in order to enhance their value as religiously didactic works. In her estimation, the inclusion of this element in the Passion plays only amplifies and focuses the central conflict of the Passion narrative by affirming the truth of the Christian message.[4]

The dramatization of public theological disputations between Christian and Jewish religious leaders unites the Frankfurt and Alsfeld Passion plays with the works that Wenzel treats in the concluding half of her book, namely the *Fastnachtspiele* and *Reimpaarsprüche* of Hans Folz.[5] Folz, a Nuremberg printer, barber, and author, who was most active from the 1470s to the 1490s, will figure prominently in the discussion of the Silvester legend's reception outside of the hagiographic tradition proper. Like the Passion plays, the *Fastnachtspiele* (carnival plays) had their part in public celebrations of a religious nature. The carnival plays as a genre, however, lack the generally sober tone and religiously didactic purpose of the Passion plays, and these factors affect their content. Of particular interest among the *Reimpaarsprüche*, the rhymed dialogues, is that entitled "Christ und Jude." Their concentration on the theological disagreement between Christianity and Judaism connects all of these works to a larger body of Christian apologetic literature, which, as we shall see in this chapter, also includes the most popular, most widely disseminated body of texts from the Middle Ages – anthologies of saints' lives.

Where the Passion plays, particularly the Frankfurt plays, apparently drew much of their material for the disputation scenes from the pseudo-Augustinian tract *Altercatio Ecclesiae et Synogogae*,[6] Folz's plays drew from a wider variety of source material. Specifically, while Folz's works are undoubtedly also indirectly indebted to the pseudo-Ausgustinian *Altercatio*, several also draw heavily from a late fifteenth-century polemic against Judaism: the *Pharetra contra iudaeos*.[7] Those works, namely the rhymed dialogue "Christ und Jude," his plays *Die alt und neu ee* and *Kaiser Constantinus*, reveal a keen interest in the Jewish–Christian theological debate. The central theological dispute between Judaism and Christianity became in these works the matter for direct confrontations between representatives of the two faiths. All of these texts – Passion plays, carnival plays, and rhymed dialogues – can therefore be seen as works animated by Christian thinking about the Jews, particularly about their relationship to God, and the proper Christian response to Jews in Christian society. In each of these literary forms, we see representatives of the two faiths debate theological propositions. In the Passion plays, these representatives were the allegorical figures *Ecclesia* and *Synogoga*. The representatives in "Christ und Jude" and *Die alt und neu ee* remain unnamed, while *Kaiser Constantinus* presents the legendary debate between Saint Silvester, who is referred to throughout the text as "der christen doctor," and an opponent who is only identified as "der rabi" or "der jüd".[8]

The connection of Folz's *Kaiser Constantinus* to the Silvester legend is particularly important for a number of reasons, the foremost of these being that the Silvester legend, which focuses on the conversion of Jews, was one of the most widely attested saint's legends of the Middle Ages. As we shall see in detail below, it appears in numerous versions beginning in the fifth century and is attested in vernacular sources such as the *Kaiserchronik, Der Heiligen Leben*, the *Elsässische Legenda Aurea*, the *Verspassional*, and in a verse treatment by Konrad von Würzburg. As the discussion of Hans Folz's works has indicated, the core of the Silvester legend provided the basis for some of his best-known carnival plays and a well-known rhymed dialogue. The Silvester legend's wide attestation and influence in the Middle Ages has led to its being seen by many modern scholars of medieval literature and culture as one of the most significant works of medieval literature representing then-contemporary thinking about Jews.[9]

The Silvester legend, however, was not the sole medieval saint's legend that contained Christian thinking about the Jews' relationship to God. Certain other legends, frequently found in the same legendaries as the Silvester legend, also focus on the relationships between Jewish figures and the Christian conception of the Jew in medieval Europe. In particular the Marian legend of Bishop Theophilus, that of Saint Basil, as well as the Marian legend known commonly as *Der Judenknabe*, are widely attested throughout the Middle Ages and focus on the character and metaphysical condition of Jews, as conceived of in a medieval Christian context. Because of their wide attestation in a variety of literary forms and their singular focus on the role and place of Jews in Christian society, the legends of Saint Silvester, Bishop Theophilus, the Marian legend of the *Judenknabe,* and the legend of Saint Basil will be examined in these chapters.

As a preface to the discussion of the individual saints' lives, some attention must, necessarily, be given first to the complex of legends that contain the motif of the blood libel, as these legends undeniably speak to one side of the Christian conception of the Jew in medieval German-speaking Europe. As argued with respect to the figures of Rufus and Caiaphas in the preceding discussion of Passion plays, it will be argued here that it is a mistake to think of the Jewish figures in the blood libel legends as representative for all Christian thinking about the Jews throughout the European Middle Ages. The blood libel itself has a history that predates the medieval period and originated in Alexandria, Egypt, not in central or Western Europe. Originally, the blood libel was applied to Jews not by Christians, but by the pagan Roman historian Posidonius. The legend appears to have gained some measure of wider dissemination in the Roman world, as it was repeated by the historian Apion and refuted by Flavius Josephus.[10]

The first medieval attestation of the blood libel and its first use to defame Jews comes from mid-twelfth century England. In 1148, several Jews of Norwich were accused of murdering a boy named William in order to use his blood in an act of ritual magic.[11] Significantly, the accusation met at first with ridicule and mockery, not belief, and only came to be believed after its proponents mounted a lengthy and thorough campaign of propaganda, culminating in Thomas of Monmouth's "Life and Passion of Saint William of Norwich."[12] In the thirteenth century, another ritual murder accusation was made against Jews in England, this time in Lincoln. The second English blood libel became more celebrated than the first: The "martyred" boy Hugh was soon elevated to the status of saint and his Jewish "murderers" were hanged *en masse* in London in 1255.[13] These two famous cases along with a handful of lesser-known ones from the continent established the motif of the blood libel firmly in the canon of European hagiography and folklore by the mid-thirteenth century.

Its acceptance in hagiography and folklore, however, did not guarantee its acceptance by legal authorities. Recall that it was in 1272 that Pope Gregory X issued his most strident condemnation of the blood libel, stating emphatically that "no Christian bringing such a preposterous charge was to be believed" and ordering the immediate release of any Jews held on such charges.[14] Two years later, he would reissue a bull that his predecessor Innocent IV had authored in 1247, ordering all archbishops and bishops in German-speaking lands to defend the Jews from such accusations which, the Pope noted, were only made at times when local men of power wished to enrich themselves at the expense of the Jews.[15] During this same decade, the 1270's, Konrad von Würzburg composed his *Silvester*. He wrote in a time and place when the blood libel was in its ascendance, and, as we shall see, his *Silvester* takes issue with the blood libel, however subtly. Though the first medieval cases of the blood libel originated in England, it was on the continent, in German-speaking Europe, that the legend would reach its height of popularity in the fifteenth and sixteenth centuries.[16]

That blood libel legends became widespread and had a direct, observable influence on the behavior of Christians toward Jews does not mean that they met with uncritical acceptance or that they were not resisted. In recent years research on the surviving legal documents, city chronicles, imperial decrees, and papal documents has revealed that blood libel accusations were the subject of intense partisan conflict in which municipal authorities were often at odds with the papal see, the imperial court, or both.[17] The ritual murder accusation that formed the basis of the legend of Saint Simon of Trent met with particularly strong papal opposition in the fifteenth and sixteenth centuries, and was condemned outright by the Holy See.[18] Nevertheless, the legend of the "saint" Simon, a boy who was allegedly murdered by Jews in 1474, became well known enough to find inclusion in some late fifteenth and early sixteenth-century printed editions of *Der Heiligen Leben*.[19] The 1476 ritual murder accusation levelled against several Jews of Regensburg also met with fierce imperial and papal opposition, and ended with the release of the accused Jews.[20] Similar ritual murder accusations in Endingen and Freiburg, however, ended with the trials and executions of some or all of the accused Jews.[21]

The fact that there were trials, as grossly unjust as they were, and that the Jews found defenders among the co-religionists of those who slandered them indicates that there was no such thing as a uniform conception of Jews in the minds of medieval Christians. By the late fifteenth century, the time of the best-known ritual murder accusations from German-speaking Europe, the blood libel had been propagated for over three hundred years, yet still met with resistance. The cannibalistic, diabolical Jews of the blood libel, the very ideological figures that were created in order to remove or undermine Christian moral restraints on violence against Jews sometimes failed to serve their intended purpose, no doubt in part due to the continued influence of the Augustinian doctrine of limited tolerance. Another possible source of this resistance to the blood libel is the presence of countervailing images of Jews in other widely disseminated and influential religious texts. Legends of Jews who cruelly martyred boy saints were part of a hagiographic tradition, as was the legend of Bishop Theophilus, which, in many versions depicted a Jew as the devil's agent. However, the legend of Saint Silvester, the Marian legend of the *Judenknabe*, and the legend of Saint Basil, all presented different, more optimistic, accounts of Jewish character and Jewish fate in Christian Salvation History. It is to these legends that our attention will now turn, in order to evaluate their consonance or dissonance with the image of Jews in the blood libel legends.

The individual legends will be discussed in the following order: Saint Silvester, Bishop Theophilus, *Der Judenknabe*, and Saint Basil. However, since these legends share, to a large degree, a common attestation history in the medieval collections of hagiographic literature, and since these collected volumes are themselves attested in a variety of different manuscripts, incunables, and later editions, it seems prudent to describe these texts and their attestation history, including their chronological and geographic distribution.

The three hagiographic anthologies known as *Legenda Aurea, Das Verspassional, Der Heiligen Leben* represent between them the most widely disseminated body of literature in medieval German-speaking Europe. The first of the three, the *Legenda Aurea*, was composed in Latin by the Dominican friar Jacob of Voragine in 1267 or perhaps shortly thereafter, and became well-known in German-speaking Europe by 1282 at the latest, and it is to the German translation, the so-called *Elsässische Legenda Aurea* of the mid-fourteenth century, that we will refer here most often.[22] By the end of the thirteenth century, large portions of the Latin *Legenda* had been translated and set into verse to form the basis of *Das Verspassional*, while the earliest complete German prose translations of the *Legenda Aurea* itself date from the middle of the fourteenth century.[23] *Das Verspassional* has an attestation history complicated in part by the fact that the hagiographic narratives collectively known under this title were divided into three books. There exists no medieval manuscript containing all three books of *Das Verspassional* with most manuscripts containing only one book or fragmentary, abbreviated legends drawn from the entire corpus.[24] *Der Heiligen Leben* is a prose redaction of the materials from *Das Verspassional*, the *Legenda Aurea*, and other sources, some of which remain yet undetermined.[25] In recent scholarship, the Bamberg Legendary has been identified as the single most important precursor to *Der Heiligen Leben*.[26] Concerning the medieval dissemination of *Der Heiligen Leben*, editors of the authoritative modern edition remarked:

> "Der Heiligen Leben" (HL) war das mit Abstand verbreitetste und wirkungsmächtigste volkssprachliche Legendar des europäischen Mittelalters. Knapp 200 Handschriften sind erhalten, 33 obd. und 8. nd. Druckauflagen bis 1521 – einige

mit sehr hohem Ausstattungsniveau – bezeugen einen im mittelalterlichen deutschen Erzählschrifttum beispiellosen Erfolg. Die Überlieferungsdaten der Handschriften belegen eine weiträumige und standesübergreifende Rezeption im gesamten ostfränkischen, bairischen und schwäbischen Sprachraum mit Ausläufern ins Alemannische. Die meist hohen Auflagenzahlen der Inkunabeln und Frühdrucke (500–1000 und mehr) lassen annehmen, daß das Legendar in handschriftlicher und gedruckter Form in ca. 30 000 bis 40 000 Exemplaren im gesamten deutschen Sprachraum sowie in Skandinavien und den Niederlanden verbreitet gewesen sein muß.[27]

An earlier study of the corpus gives the exact number of authentically medieval manuscripts of *Der Heiligen Leben* as 197.[28] Abbreviated redactions of the legendary are attested in ten complete and two fragmentary manuscripts.[29] *Der Heiligen Leben* served also as a source for several late medieval legendaries.[30]

The Silvester legend also occurs in *Die Kaiserchronik*, a text that we will not treat in depth here, but which bears mention for the sake of thoroughness. The earliest manuscripts of this rhymed chronicle describing the lives and exploits of emperors from the Roman Empire to the Holy Roman Empire date from the second half of the twelfth century, and the manuscript attestations continue into the late fourteenth century. The *Kaiserchronik* is of interest for the study at hand because its version of the Silvester legend shares a common source history and a common text, for the most part, with the version of the legend found in the *Elsässische Legenda Aurea* and *Das Verspassional*. In addition, it should be noted that the four manuscripts of another chronicle, the *Sächsische Weltchronik*, and one manuscript of the *Schwabenspiegel*, a compilation of laws and legendary history, contain abbreviated versions of texts drawn directly from the *Kaiserchronik*.[31] The intended public of this latter work included members of the ministerial and clerical professions, the upper feudal nobility, and nuns.[32]

From this discussion of manuscript attestation, we must now turn our attention to the place of the Silvester legend in medieval Christian apologetic literature, in particular that of German-speaking Europe. One of the earliest extant theological documents written in Old High German was a translation of Isidore of Seville's seventh-century *De fide catholica contra Iudaeos*. This text provides us with an appropriate bridge into the discussion of the use of theology in medieval German literature. In their own lifetimes, Jesus of Nazareth and his followers found themselves continually pressed to explain his Messianic claims in terms of fulfillment of Jewish prophecy. In the centuries that followed, explaining and defending the Messiahship of Jesus against the objections raised by rabbinic Judaism became and remained a central element of Christian apologetics. The theological works produced in this branch of apologetics appear in such great quantity in Latin, Greek, and every vernacular in Europe from the early Middle Ages onward that providing a detailed overview here would be completely impossible. Heinz Schreckenberg was able to provide only an overview of the principal texts in his three-volume work, *Die Christlichen Adversus-Judaeos Texte*. For this reason, what follows is necessarily limited to texts that were widely known and makes no pretense of exhaustiveness.

Isidore's *Contra Iudaeos* follows in the apologetic tradition of Augustine's *Tractatus adversus Iudaeos* in that it relies primarily on the writings that Jews and Christians shared in order to make its defense of Jesus's Messiahship. Augustine's *Tractatus adversus Iudaeos*, along with another work falsely attributed to him, the previously-mentioned *Alteratio Ecclesiae et Synogogae* formed, together with the New Testament writings, the basis of all Christian apologetics directed toward Jewish audiences in the European Middle Ages.[33] Since the primary points of dispute between Christians and Jews remained unchanged, it is unsurprising that Isidore's text differs little from Augustine's in content and organization. It addresses interpretations of passages from the Hebrew Bible – in Christian terms, the Old Testament – that support the Christian Gospel as well as common philosophical objections to the logic of these interpretations.

Here it becomes necessary to clarify a point made in the first chapter. When Sapir-Abulafia argues that the twelfth-century Renaissance saw an increased emphasis on the role of reason and logic in matters of religious faith, she does not argue that they played an insignificant or even merely supporting role prior to the twelfth century. What she does say is that, with the writings of Anselm of Canterbury, in his *Cur Deus Homo*, (1098) and Abelard, in his *Dialogus inter Philosophum, Iudaeum et Christianum* (1141–42), we see attempts to prove the essential elements of Christian faith on logic alone, with little or no reference to Scriptural revelation.[34] The goal in shifting the emphasis was to prove that the central truths of the Christian faith were not only sound with respect to the history of divine revelation, but that they could be demonstrated by the logically necessary traits of the Supreme Being. What had been the tool and organizing principle behind the arguments of Christian apologists became the argument itself. Augustine, Isidore, and those who wrote apologetics directed at Jews in the centuries before based their arguments on logical inferences from biblical passages revered by both Christians and Jews. The new development that Sapir-Abulafia observes in twelfth-century theology never completely supersedes the argument based on biblical exegesis alone. Judaism and Christianity by their nature preclude any such development, as the principal matter in dispute, whether Jesus of Nazareth was or was not the prophesied Messiah, has no meaning apart from reference to the Hebrew Bible (the Tanakh, specifically) and the New Testament.

Parallel to the developments in Christian apologetics in the Middle Ages was the development of Jewish apologetics, or, more accurately, Jewish responses to Christian apologetics. Rabbis in all of the nations of Europe produced and circulated such documents, and in the late Middle Ages, an anonymous compiler assembled from disparate sources the *Sefer Nizzahon Vetus*, a book of religious argumentation directed against the chief doctrines of Christianity.[35] The overriding concern of the author is the refutation of Christological interpretations of passages of the Hebrew Bible, though he does include attacks on uniquely Christian doctrines, such as the Trinity and the virginity of Mary. Both this book and the earlier *Toledoth Jeschu* were known to Christian religious authorities, as was the Talmud, and the last of these had become the focus both of anti-Judaic religious polemic and legal action in the thirteenth century.[36] Important for our consideration of literary depictions of Jewish–Christian disputations is the degree to which the arguments used by the Jewish figures in dramas, legends, and other literary treatments accurately reflect the arguments used in Jewish religious writings. If there is a large degree of correspondence between theological writings and literary texts, we cannot accurately say that a medieval Christian author necessarily sought to vilify or deride Jews as a group when he put a Jewish figure who argued against the tenets of the Christian faith on the page. The question of the symbolic valence of a given Jewish figure must be settled by reference to other criteria, as depicting a Jew's rejection of the Christian faith on the basis of theological argumentation certainly reflects an author's concern for accuracy and believability rather than hostility. When medieval Christian apologists did turn vitriolic, the preferred mode was open derogation of the character of the Jewish religion or its adherents, which goes beyond merely rehearsing authentic rabbinical teachings.

In sum, one should keep in mind that the documents in question were produced in the intersection of two dynamic, developing religious communities, each of which made mutually exclusive theological truth claims. Medieval Jews, as the very existence of these books of anti-Christian polemic demonstrate, were not passive objects of Christian missionizing activity, but agents in their own right. However, another important aspect of the Christian–Jewish dynamic in medieval German-speaking Europe that also becomes clear in the Jewish polemics is that the central point of friction between the two communities remained completely immutable. The immutability of the central question dividing the two groups, namely whether Jesus is or is not the Messiah, accounts for any apparent stasis in the literary treatments of theological disputations.

It was in the context of these two vital, related religions that the oldest literary depiction of the Jewish–Christian theological disputation, the legend of Saint Silvester, arose. The historical Silvester on whom the legends accreted during the Middle Ages was the Bishop of Rome at the time of the conversion of Constantine the Great in the fourth century, and though very little is known about him factually, he became the subject of hagiography throughout medieval Christendom.[37] Chief among the feats attributed to him are proselytizing and baptizing Constantine, thereby setting in motion the eventual Christianization of the Empire, and bringing about the conversion of large numbers of the Empire's Jews through his victory over twelve rabbis in a public theological disputation. The legend is extant in several versions, some of which do not contain his debate with the rabbis in any developed form. By way of contrast, the disputation forms the crucial and most extensively developed dramatic instance in several well-known versions of the legend, most notably in *Der Heiligen Leben*, where the disputation makes up the overwhelming majority of the text.[38] Similarly, the Latin version of the Silvester legend in the *Legenda Aurea* develops the disputation in great detail.[39] Three widely attested German versions from the Middle Ages are of particular relevance here. The first is Konrad von Würzburg's *Silvester*, which is the only medieval work in which the legend is presented as an independent text and not in a legendary. The second is that of *Der Heiligen Leben*, and the third that found in *Die Elsässische Legenda Aurea*, both provided here as representative examples of late medieval prose treatments of the legend.[40] The subjects of examination shall be the depiction of Jews contained in these three texts, their relationship to images of Jews in the Passion plays, and the relationship of the Silvester legend to the writings of Hans Folz.

Konrad von Würzburg's *Silvester*, composed in the early 1270s, is preserved for us in a single thirteenth-century manuscript.[41] The theological disputation between Silvester and the twelve Jewish masters encompasses in Konrad's version vv. 2415 to 5145, if one includes the first mention of the impending arrival of the Jewish disputants at Constantine's court and the denouement including their conversion. It is the dramatic and structural core of the verse legend.

Konrad begins his treatment of the disputation by introducing the Jewish participants. He describes them in the following manner:

> Si wâren ûzer mâze
> gar wol gelêret alle,
> und sprâchen nâch gevalle
> kriechisch unde latîn wol.
> Swaz man tiefer rede sol
> trîben von der alten ê
> der kunden si vil unde mê
> danne ich alhie betiute;
> kein ungetouften liute
> wurden nie gelêret baz.[42] (2708–17)

118

The Middle High German prose version of the legend from the *Elsässische Legenda Aurea* is significantly less effusive in its description of the mental capabilities of the Jewish disputants, but nevertheless mentions their innate wisdom:

> Constantinus enbot sinre muoter hin wider das sú mit ir brehte die iúdeschen meister, so wolte er kristen lerer do wider setzen, das men vs irre beder lere vnd worten schetzete welre glôbe gewerer si. Do von so fuorte Helena mit ir ein vnd vierzig vnd hundert meister des iúdeschen glôben, vnder den worent sunderliche zwelfe durch lúhtet mit aller wisheit.[43]

The description of the Jewish disputants in *Der Heiligen Leben* also praises their wisdom, though in less extravagant terms than employed by Konrad:

> Noch dem das dy fraw den prieff gelaß, do sampt sy hundert weiß maister vnd sehs vnd sechczig, dy waren dy pesten auß allen landen. Vnder den waren zwelff gar weiß maister. Dy selben procht dy fraw all mit ir zu Rom zu dem kayser.[44]

It is these twelve, the very wisest of the wisest Jewish scholars "auß allen landen" who debate Silvester in all of these versions of the legend.

Of the twelve rabbis who directly engage Silvester, Konrad goes on to say that "die wielten hôher wîsheit / und wâren tiefer sinne vol" ("they possessed great wisdom / and were full of deep understanding" 2744–5). Here he builds up the audience's expectations for the coming disputation by emphasizing the intellectual capabilities of the Jewish teachers whose arguments Silvester must refute. The twelve rabbis are introduced by name, and the conditions of the debate are established, both details common to other versions of the legend.[45] The conditions are that a question-and-answer format will be followed, in which the rabbis will pose Silvester questions related to the central doctrines of Christianity. In both the questions and the answers, the disputants are to confine themselves to the religious texts that they share, namely the Torah, Psalms, and Prophets, in their discussion of the central teachings of Christianity. The emperor articulates the logic of placing this constraint on the debate, saying that the most persuasive argument is to convince a man using only his own learning and tradition ("ûz sîn selbes buochen"). He further asserts that one unable to defend his faith with recourse to its own holy books deserves to lose both the argument and public esteem (2857–65).

Of particular relevance to the question at hand, how medieval writers in Christian Germany depicted and thought about Jews, are two aspects of the dispute. One has already been alluded to, namely Konrad's praise of the intellectual capabilities of the Jewish disputants. While this aspect of his portrayal does serve the purpose of making Silvester's task the more important and more impressive, it also portrays the Jewish disputants as intellectual rivals to be respected, not scorned or ignored. The rabbis are depicted, with one possible exception that will be addressed below, as rational, moral beings. Indeed, what is perhaps most remarkable in Konrad's text is the lack of vitriol directed at the Jews. The discussion of the Messianic prophecies pertaining to one of the most controversial elements of the Christian faith, the Virgin Birth, is instructive in this regard. In describing the exchange between Dôech, the fifth rabbi, Chûsi, the sixth rabbi, Bônôym, the seventh rabbi, and Silvester, Konrad maintains a tone of respectful exchange (3378–3635). Konrad depicts the Jewish characters in this debate not as "blind" or "arg," but as people who seek truth sincerely. This point is made especially clear in the exchange between Silvester and Zêlêôn that precedes the dramatic climax of the poem. Zêlêôn explains that he wants to know why Silvester believes what he believes so that he, Zêlêôn, might determine exactly what is true about Jesus of Nazareth:

Lâ mich bewîset werden
der lasterlichen smâcheit
undes spottes, den er leit
in sîner manicvalten nôt.
Sînen marterlichen tôt
entsliuz ouch nû von grunde mir,
durch daz wir alle noch mit dir
an in geloubic werden
und iemer ûf der erden
den namen sîn hie prîsen.
Mahtû mich underwîsen
von im der wârheit
sô mêre ich unde breite

sîn lop in allen orten
mit werken und mit worten.[46] (4328–41)

Implicit in Zêlêôn's request is the understanding that, should Silvester fail to provide adequate evidence, he will not join the Christian faith. Konrad depicts most of Silvester's debate partners not as debased creatures mired in superstitions, but as intellectually and morally sound beings. In doing so, he develops a conception of the Jews that treats them as both morally and rationally persuadable, echoing the theological concern that Jews be "taught" into the kingdom of Christ found in Anselm, Abelard, and Crispin, among others.[47]

The obvious exception to Konrad's generally favorable image of Jews is the character Zambrî, the last of the rabbis who speaks against Silvester:

Zambrî der zwelfete meister dô
sprach vil zornlîche alsô,
Mir ist leit, waz sol des mê?
Daz unser veterlichen ê
zerstoeren wil Silvester.
Und daz mit sînen worten er
der sinne (uns) wil berouben.[48] (4545–51)

In his remarks, Zambrî departs from the format of theological disputation that had governed the exchanges between Silvester and the first eleven rabbis. Rather than debate Christological interpretations of biblical prophecy, Zambrî affirms the verdict passed on Jesus's person by his ancestors. He repeats a characterization of Jesus that comes directly out of both the Talmud and the *Toledoth Jeschu*: Jesus was a sorcerer and as such was rightly condemned ("verdamnet … mit rehte") by the Jewish religious authorities of his day (4552–57). As previously asserted, Konrad's placing this accusation, as inflammatory as it would sound to a Christian audience, cannot be construed as a use of literature to defame Jews or their religion. In fact, this statement accurately represents what rabbis were teaching about Jesus in the Middle Ages. If anything, it is considerably milder than many of the accusations made against Jesus in the *Sefer Nizzahon Vetus*. By leveling the accusation of sorcery against Jesus, Zambrî transforms the confrontation before the emperor from one of scriptural exegesis and rational argument into a contest of supernatural power. The parallel with the biblical account of Elijah's confrontation with the prophets of Baal may be intended, but this would be difficult to demonstrate with the extant evidence. The consequence is much the same regardless of whether or not the parallel was intended: the stage is set for a contest of supernatural power, not words.

What Konrad then proceeds to do, in the confrontation between Zambrî and Silvester, is to turn Zambrî's accusation back on the accuser. That is to say, he turns the accusation back on the medieval Jewish teachings about Jesus that Zambrî embodies. Zambrî claims that he can, by pronouncing one of the secret names of God aloud, kill a wild bull (4610–15). When asked to explain how he was able to learn the name and its proper pronunciation without being killed by it himself, Zambrî explains that the name was taught him by his master, who wrote the letters of the name using water on the surface of a silver goblet (4710–40). Zambrî has the bull, restrained in strong ropes by strong men, brought to him, whispers the name in its ear, and enjoys his triumph as the bull falls dead immediately on hearing the name (4815–51). Silvester responds to this by asserting that one who truly knows the secret name of God should be able to restore the bull to life, as the true God both gives and takes life; therefore, he demands that Zambrî restore the bull to life. When Zambrî refuses, Silvester challenges the emperor to let him (Silvester) attempt to restore the bull to life by pronouncing the name of Jesus over it. Zambrî refuses the challenge, prompting Silvester to accuse him of having used the name of a devil to slay the bull. Constantine agrees with Silvester's logic, saying:

> Und swie diz wunder hie geschiht,
> das man den pharren lebende siht,
> so wirt erzeiget hie vür wâr
> daz im der tiufel offenbar
> hât den grimmen tôt gegeben,
> sît er im ein gesundez leben
> niht wider mac gemachen.[49] (5023–29)

The emperor then commands that Silvester be allowed to restore the bull to life, if he can. When Silvester commands the bull to rise in the name of Jesus, and it does rise, the crowd is astounded. Adding to their astonishment is the transformed nature of the bull. Not only does it return to life, but it also loses all traces of its previous ferocity. Both the changed nature of the revived bull and the revelation of Zambrî's power as diabolical sorcery are details common to the versions of the legend in every major medieval text that contains it, as is another detail: that the assembled pagans and Jews, Zambrî included, convert to Christianity on seeing the miracle.[50]

Above, Zambrî was referred to as the possible exception to Konrad's generally neutral and in some ways complimentary treatment of Jews in the Silvester legend. Zambrî is certainly depicted as a sorcerer and even named "Zambrî der zouberaere" (4764). Silvester exposes him as wielding power over a name of a devil and not, as he claims, over a secret name of God. Zambrî embodies a stereotype of the Jew that the Silvester Legend shares with some versions of the Theophilus legend: Jew as practitioner of black magic. The legend of Bishop Theophilus will be discussed at greater length below, the focus here remaining on the Silvester legend. Zambrî stands alone in representing the image of the Jew as sorcerer in the medieval treatments of the Silvester legend. Of the twelve rabbis that Konrad depicts, Zambrî alone is described with terms such as "der gar verwohrte jüde" ("the completely cursed Jew" 4810–11) and "der jüde freissam" ("the ferocious Jew" 5040). He seems to embody the worst of the distortions of Rabbinic Judaism: that of the "diabolical cult of secrets" described by Norman Cohn.[51] Nevertheless, he is also depicted, along with his co-religionists, as a man who is capable of perceiving truth and acknowledging it when confronted with the irrefutable evidence of the miracle. This being the case, neither he nor his fellow rabbis are depicted as utterly unreasonable or irredeemably corrupt. The dominant image of Jewish religious authorities in Konrad's *Silvester* is that of a community sincerely concerned with theological truth.

It is important to note that it is only when the debate shifts away from scriptural exegesis and logical argumentation to a contest of supernatural power that the characterization of the Jewish disputant becomes hostile to the point of associating him with the diabolical. This reinforces the thesis that the treatment of serious theological questions in the literary mode forced medieval authors to engage their own faith and Judaism in ways that kept them from freely slandering or vilifying Jews and their religion. The possible influence of theological considerations on the literary representation of religious disputation is common to Konrad's *Silvester* and the numerous later medieval treatments of the legend. In the *Legenda Aurea*, the *Elsässische Legenda Aurea, Der Heiligen Leben,* and *Das Verspassional*, all later than Konrad's work, the presentation of theological argument predominates so completely that the Jewish disputants hardly appear as more than foils for presenting standard arguments against Christian doctrines, most notably that of the Trinity. In all later medieval versions of the Silvester legend, the Jewish disputants more resemble the "theological" Jews of Abelard, Crispin, or Odo of Chambrai – Jewish characters who are not much more than embodiments of theological argumentation – than the lively figures of Konrad.

In presenting the Jews as reasonable beings subject to logical persuasion, Konrad's *Silvester* harmonizes with the work of other medieval writers treating the Silvester legend. The version of the confrontation between Silvester and the rabbis found in a widely attested German translation of the *Legenda Aurea* differs from that of Konrad von Würzburg only in a handful of minor details. Konrad provides agreement between the disputants on the terms of the debate, while the *Elsässische Legenda Aurea* does not.[52] He also has Zambrî provide a detailed account of how he came to possess his occult knowledge of the hidden name of God, unlike the *Elsässische Legenda Aurea*.[53] Similarly, Konrad gives more precise details in describing the gestures and emotional tone of the speakers. Such stylistic elaboration is characteristic of Konrad's works. This brief list of details is not exhaustive, but it does give the reader a clear indication of both the consonance and the variation between Konrad von Würzburg's version of the Silvester legend and that recorded in the German translation of the *Legenda Aurea*. Despite the years that separate them, the two texts agree in their essential content and differ in their presentation of the legend's dramatic highlights.

124

The degree of consonance between the two texts extends also to the generally favorable treatment of the Jewish disputants presented in them. Nowhere in Konrad's version of the Silvester legend or in the *Elsässische Legenda Aurea* are the Jews vilified or characterized as something less than human. The one possible exception, as in Konrad's version, is the character of Zambrî, who, again, is clearly depicted as a sorcerer. The link between "Jew" and "sorcerer" is broken when Zambrî fulfils his promise to convert on seeing the efficaciousness of Silvester's prayer and hearing the invocation of Jesus's name. Here, the image of the Jew as sorcerer is eclipsed by the Jew as honest man who keeps his word and who joins himself to Christ, thereby robbing the Devil of his joy (5142–5).

Similar observations apply to the Silvester legend as it appears in *Der Heiligen Leben*. Here, the confrontation between "Zara," as the twelfth rabbi is called in this version, and Silvester ends with this exchange of words before Silvester restores the steer to life:

> "Ich vnd Siluester mugen den stier nicht wider lebendig gemachen. Macht jn aber sant Siluester lebendig, so wil ich gern gelawben, das sein got ain worer got ist." Das sprachen dy andern juden all.[54]

An important difference between Zara of *Der Heiligen Leben* and Zambrî in Konrad's *Silvester*, though, is that the former is never identified as a sorcerer, nor described with any epithets emphasizing his hostility. While it is true that Zara kills the steer by invoking the name "des posen gaists" ("of the evil spirit"),[55] he is never himself clearly named as a trafficker in black magic. The connection of even one Jewish figure with the Devil is therefore significantly less clear in the later development of the legend that appears in *Der Heiligen Leben*.

The influence of the Silvester legend is reflected in several of the best-known works of the late-fifteenth century author, barber, and printer Hans Folz of Nuremberg. However, the contrast between the Jewish figures in Konrad's *Silvester*, in legendaries such as the *Elsässische Legenda Aurea* or *Der Heiligen Leben*, and the Jewish figures of Hans Folz's *Fastnachtspiel, Ein Spil von dem Herzogen von Burgund*,[56] which also reaches its climax with a confrontation between miracle-workers, could not be starker. Folz's play presents a variation and recapitulation of the key themes of the Silvester legend: representatives of Judaism and Christianity plead their respective cases in front of a nobleman. In place of an emperor, the play presents the Duke of Burgundy, while a prophetess and a "Messias" serve as the representatives of Christianity and Judaism. The "Messias" arrives, together with a group of rabbis, heralding the advent of the "true Messiah," who has come to take the place of Jesus, the "false Messiah" of the Christians.[57] The rabbis then demand that the Christians embrace the "true Messiah," who is, after all, the one they thought they had been serving all along. The prophetess ("Sibilla") denounces the "Messias" as the Anti-Christ, and challenges him to prove himself. The "Messias" faces and fails the test of the wheel of fortune, but demands a second test. The "Sibilla" and her handmaids challenge him to drink poisoned wine and survive, in order to prove that he has power over life and death. He drinks the poison at her challenge and dies immediately. The prophetess then raises him to life and commands him to tell the truth about himself and the rabbis' fraudulent scheme, which he does, exposing the Jews to public ignominy.

Where both Konrad von Würzburg's and *Die Elsässische Legenda Aurea*'s account of the Silvester legend depict Jews as human beings engaged in an earnest search for truth, Hans Folz's *Ein Spil von dem Herzogen von Burgund* depicts them as objects of deserved scorn and contempt. At no point in the play does Folz depict any attempt to engage in earnest theological debate. We see only a mutual exchange of insults and derision, ultimately leading to a contest of supernatural power between the Christian "Sibilla" and the Jewish "Messias." Typifying the tone of the play is the following exchange:

Der ander Rabi
Merck eben, was ich darzu thu:
Ich kund euch hie Messiam, wist,
Der vns lange zeit verkundt ist
Und wird die judischeit erheben.

126

Der Narr

    Ich torst dir wol eins auff das maul geben.
    Du schwartzer hund, was meinst du damit?
    Ge dannen, das dich schut der rit.

Der dritt Rabi

    Was durft ir des narren spil?
    Hie ist Messias schlecht und wil,
    Das ir im all gelobt und schwert.

Der Narr

    Ach das man dir dein maul nit pert
    Mit einem tzellen auß einenm prifet
    Vnd dich nit druß und pewlen anget.[58] (109–27)

Not content to present a dramatization of theological conflict between *Ecclesia* and *Synagoga* or their representatives, Folz exposes the rabbis to the basest of scorn from the time they appear in the play.

Additionally, Folz takes pains to assure his audience that this scorn is deserved. He does not hesitate to integrate the blood libel into his play in a particularly insidious way: he places an admission of factual guilt into the mouth of the Jewish "Endechrist":

Endechrist dicit

    Ja, wann sie [Christians] dennoch dabei wisten,
    Was grosser fluch, was haß und neit
    Wir in stet han getragen seit,
    Wie vil groß guts in abgeraubt,
    Wie vil an irem leben getaubt,
    Der ertzet wir gewesen sein,
    Wie vil der jungen kindelein
    In abgestolen und getot
    Vnd mit irem keuschem plut gerot
    Vnd die euch cristen abgefurt
    Zu smach der jerlichen gepurt
    Jhesu, die ir ewig beget....[59] (352–63)

In her discussion of Folz's plays, Wenzel asserted in her monograph (1992) that the source for the inclusion of the blood libel in a contest of miracles between a Christian and Jewish disputant is the Silvester legend. She points to its inclusion in Folz's *Kaiser Constantinus* and Konrad von Würzburg's *Silvester* as evidence, arguing that the two derive from the same Latin redaction of the Silvester legend.[60] It is true that in *Kaiser Constantinus* the blood sacrifice of 3,000 children is suggested as a cure for leprosy by a Jewish figure, as recounted by the emperor in this passage:

> Verunreint was mein leib und leben
> Und mit dem aussatz ganz umgehen,
> Das jüdisch erzt, heiden und abtgött
> Nichts anders ritten, dann das man tött
> Dreu tausent kindlein keüsch und rein;
> In irem plut allen gemein
> So solt mein leib gepadet werden.[61]

However, this is not the blood libel as properly understood, as it has no specific connection to Jewish mockery of the Crucifixion, nor, given the inclusion of "Heiden" and "abgött" among the emperor's advisors, any specific, exclusive connection to Jews. Furthermore, the Jews' suggestion that children's blood be used to cure the emperor is not a part of the Silvester legend as it appears in the Latin text of the *Legenda Aurea*,[62] nor as it appears in various Middle High German and Middle Low German texts of the *Legenda Aurea, Der Heiligen Leben*, or *Das Verspassional*. In all of these texts, the suggestion of blood sacrifice comes from a priest (or priests) of the pagan Roman gods, and not from the mouth of a rabbi.[63] The inclusion of the blood libel here is therefore a Folz innovation, both a departure from the source material and a rhetorical move that intensifies the dehumanization of the Jews. Recalling the use of the blood libel to "license" violence against Jews, Folz's decision to include it here marks this play as his most inflammatory and most dangerous to the coexistence of Jews and Christians in Nuremberg.

Subjected to the mockery of the fool and his female counterpart throughout the play, the Jews are reduced, upon the defeat of their "Messias" in the play's closing scene, to a state of abject degradation, forced to wallow in the filth of swine. How this revolting spectacle was actually staged is a matter best left unexplored. Relevant to the discussion here is the fact that the degradation of the Jews through this use of scatological humor is entirely typical of the genre of *Fastnachtspiele*.[64] The degree to which these genre conventions that demand scatological and obscene humor determined the treatment of the Jews in this and other of Folz's *Fastnachtspiele* may have been significant.

The dehumanizing treatment that the stage Jews receive in *Ein Spil von dem Herzogen von Burgund* is exactly what Wenzel and others have in mind when they speak of the image of the Jews in medieval German literature. Wenzel and others have argued that the degradation and dehumanization of Jews in *Ein Spil von dem Herzogen von Burgund* was not merely typical or common, but that it was the image of Jews in medieval German literature, with no significant exceptions. The depiction of Jews in *Herzog von Burgund*, revolting as it is, was not the sole image of Jews in Folz's works, though it certainly is the vilest. The core subject matter of the play, though, remains the theological disputation in the mold of the Silvester legend. In other works developing the same theme, Folz, the master of low taste and exploiter of anti-Jewish sentiments in fifteenth-century Nuremberg, presented to his audience Jewish characters with a modicum of dignity.

Jews are afforded this modicum of dignity in those works by Folz that directly engage the theological dispute between Jews and Christians, namely the plays *Die alt und neu Ee* and *Kaiser Constantinus* as well as his rhymed dialogue "Christ und Jude." The close connection between the latter two works, even to the point of identical wording in some passages, was commented on at length by Helmut Lomnitzer.[65] All three works are literary treatments of theological disputations, with *Kaiser Constantinus* treating the same legendary material as Konrad's *Silvester* and the Silvester legend in the Latin and German versions of the *Legenda Aurea* and *Der Heiligen Leben*. Complicating any attempt to read the Jewish figures in *Die alt und neu Ee* and *Kaiser Constantinus*, however, is the fact that both works are carnival plays and as such are required by genre conventions to employ a degree of low humor which undermines the more serious theological elements.[66]

The dissonance between the genre conventions of the *Fastnachtspiel* and the theological material in these two plays has led to speculation that they constitute an attempt by Folz to rehabilitate the genre.[67] That is to say, *Kaiser Constantinus* sinks to degrading Jews through scatological associations because it was written to fulfill genre conventions and audience expectations. The genre convention of bodily humor dictates the use of scatological humor, and so affects the treatment that the Jews receive in the play. Folz's adherence to the genre conventions of the *Fastnachtspiel*, however, varied from one play to the next. There is significantly less of this kind of humor in *Kaiser Constantinus* than in *Ein Spil von dem Herzogen von Burgund*, and less still in the next play here examined, *Die alt und neu Ee*.

Like *Kaiser Constantinus*, Folz's *Die alt und neu Ee* deals with the theme of Jewish–Christian religious dispute. The setting is no longer the court of a fourth-century Emperor, but the modern day, that is, the fifteenth century. After an initial address by the allegorical figures "Die Sinagog" and "Die Kirch," the two actual disputants are introduced to the audience. These disputants are no longer a legendary Christian saint and an even more legendary – in the sense of "fabricated" – group of learned rabbis, but two figures named "der Doctor" and "der Rabi," who carry on the debate. At the prompting of "Die Sinagog," the debate is to focus on the images of God in the Talmud, a move that automatically puts the Jewish disputant on the defensive.[68] We are not to see a defense of Christian doctrines against Jewish objections, but a defense of Judaism by means of the most significant religious text that Jews do not share with Christians. The debate unfolds as a series of challenges and rebuttals, with "der Doctor" and "der Rabi" each, at different turns, playing the part of interlocutor or respondent.

Folz has the Jewish speaker, "der Rabi," begin his defense with a recitation of the Hebrew prayer "Adon olam."[69] Significantly, Folz renders this prayer with a high degree of accuracy, a fact that Edith Wenzel was unaware of at the time of her 1982 study of the text, but which she discussed at length in her later monograph.[70] This, again, contrasts with the treatment of the Jews in *Kaiser Constantinus*. In *Kaiser Constantinus*, the "Judengesang" that Folz employs is a mixture of Latin, Hebrew, and nonsense words that are, taken together, content free, and therefore serve no purpose other than to alienate the audience from the Jewish figures.[71] In *Die alt und neu Ee*, Folz does not aim to produce an alienating effect and thereby prepare his audience to reduce the Jews to objects of derision and scorn, exposing them to the contemptuous laughter of the crowd. Instead, his aim is to deal with theological conflict in a dramatic and serious manner.

What follows consists primarily of a rehearsal of Christian objections to the many anthropomorphic descriptions of God in the Talmud. Occasional references to the Messianic prophecies of the Bible are also present, but they do not make up a significant portion of the argument. Folz's goal in this play is, as Wenzel points out, to demonstrate the errors of the Talmud and other extra-biblical religious texts. To accomplish this goal, he attempts to show, using selected passages from the Talmud and other extra-biblical Judaic religious texts, that there are logical errors inherent in rabbinic Judaism.[72] The concentration on texts that the two faiths do not share enables Folz, through the figure of the Christian disputant, to emphasize the difference of the Jews in using a rhetorical strategy that he was unable to employ in *Kaiser Constantinus*. There, in keeping with the core of the Silvester legend, Folz limits the argument to the sacred texts that Jews and Christians share, thereby emphasizing the commonalities of the two religions:

> Als das, darinn du wider mich pist,
> Das will ich grüntlich dir ercleren
> Und allein auß dein profeten beweren,
> Auß euer eigen schrift und lere.[73]

In *Die alt und neu Ee*, Folz expresses through "der Doctor" the idea that Jews and Christians share not only a common religious heritage, but also a common lineage. "Der Doctor" then accuses the rabbi of slandering their common ancestors with salacious stories about Adam and Eve's sexual behavior in Eden.[74] The accusation against the Jews is not that they misunderstand the Torah and the Prophets, but that they do not afford them sufficient respect. The idea conveyed is that the teachings of the extra-biblical holy writings force Jews to believe things about themselves that are both shameful and harmful to them. The focus on the Talmud and other extra-biblical writings emphasizes the religious difference between Jews and Christians unlike the focus on the Torah and Prophets in *Kaiser Constantinus*. That the Talmud was regarded as harmful to Jews is the

131

core of much thirteenth-century apologetic literature directed against it, and is also a charge appearing in papal condemnations.[75] Ironically – or perhaps logically – the charges made against the Talmud are at their core, reminiscent of the charges made against Christianity in the Jewish religious polemic: That the people of the "other" group (here Jews) believe things about God that are unworthy of Him.

The impact of this difference in emphasis is significant. We do not have in *Die alt und neu Ee* a play that frequently slanders Jews with scatological and bestial associations, as in *Ein Spil von dem Herzogen von Burgund*, but one that asserts that, if Jews truly accept certain of their own teachings, namely those of the Talmud, they are, in effect, slandering themselves. Given this different approach to anti-Judaic religious polemic, it is not surprising that Folz does not resort to the same kind of rhetorical degradation of Jews in this play that he freely employs in *Herzog von Burgund*. He uses, as Wenzel rightly pointed out, a much more refined and subtle strategy in this play than in any of his other writings treating this subject matter.[76] It is also not surprising that the exchange in the play where the rabbi's interlocutor makes his most deliberately slanderous accusation, namely that of bastardry, is the one exchange where the two disputants depart from the argument about religious texts.[77] It is also in this exchange that Folz refers to Judaism, through the figure of "der fallend Jud," as "unsern huntischen gelauben" ("our despicable faith").[78] When the disputation leaves that accusation and returns to the discussion of religious truth, the Jewish and Christian disputants resume a more respectful tone toward one another.

The civility afforded to a partner in a learned dispute is more evident in Folz's "Christ und Jude," presumably because the Jewish–Christian debate is not subjected to the genre conventions of the carnival play. Here Folz presents the confrontation between two equals, each determined to persuade the other of the truth of his beliefs. At no point does he describe the Jewish participant with degrading or derisive language. Indeed, the most striking thing to the modern reader, especially the modern reader who is familiar with *Ein Spil von den Herzogen von Burgund* or his *Reimpaarspruch* "Der Juden Messias," may be the neutrality that Folz portrays between the two disputants. The terms they use to address one another in opening their argument are instructive:

> Des hub ich an und sprach zum Iuden
> wan sich sunst niemant wolt bekrüden
> hie unser red dan wir alleyn
> so heet ich lust das wir uns reyn
> gegen ein ander sollten üben
> do wurden sie uns all gelüben
> und dar zu pey irn eyden swern
> das keiner sein maul mit uns wolt pern
> pis wir gleich wol mit ein gekosten.
> hie mit wir unser seck auff losten
> und schütten raws was drinnen was.
> Doch fragt ich vor den Iuden pas
> wer unter uns solt heben an.
> Do gab der Iud mir zu verstan
> und sprach, "Das zymet mir du, Crist,
> wan ewer glaub ein new ding ist.
> Mein glaub was vor. Das weystu wol."[79] (45–61)

Absent from "Christ und Jude" are any of the direct expressions of hostility and derogation, such as "blind jud" or "schwarzer hund," familiar to us from *Ein Spil von dem Herzogen von Burgund*. This absence alone is significant, as it indicates that Folz is using a subtler rhetorical strategy in "Christ und Jude" than he uses in any of these other works. In his defense of the Christian faith, the "Christ" figure draws chiefly on texts drawn from the Hebrew Bible, particularly the Torah and the Prophets, rather than on a logical refutation of the Talmud or on a defense of Christianity based on the logically necessary traits of God.[80] Herein he follows the pre-twelfth-century line of argumentation that Konrad von Würzburg also followed, turning away from post-thirteenth-century argumentation focusing on the Talmud or other post-biblical writings. Folz also adopts another line of traditional anti-Jewish thought, in that he entertains a grim fantasy about the consequences, should the extant power relations between Jews and Christians be inverted. In painting his lurid persecution scenario, he uses a rhetorical figure that is familiar to us from the *Erlauer Osterspiel* and the *Rheinisches Osterspiel*, as this passage makes clear:

> Ich sprach, "Mein jud, nun hör mit fleis
> Du weyst, das got in peyspils weis
> Gar vil durch die profeten ret.
> Merckt neur, ob die glos verstet;
> Die wilden und die heimischen thir
> Das sint ir juden und auch wir.
> Wan als die schaff sint ane meyl
> Also piten wir umb ewr heyl
> So hapt ir gen uns wolfes mut
> Wiewol ir würcklich uns nicht dut.
> Desgleich mag man auch exponirn
> Die kind pey den gifftigen thirn.
> Die kinder gottes sint nun wir
> Und die vergifften würm seyt ir:
> Wan het ir uns in ewrm gewallt
> Als ir in unserem seyt gezallt
> Kein christ erlebet jares frist." [81] (277–93)

In the comparison of Jews to wolves and poisonous snakes, Christians to sheep and children, it is clear that Folz deliberately and knowingly inverts the real state of power relations in medieval German-speaking Europe. What differentiates Folz's rhetorical treatment of Jews from that seen in the Passion and Easter plays is that Folz presents Jewish hostility toward Christians as an abstract, psychological phenomenon, and not a credible, extant danger to the lives and property of Christians.[82] Where the authors of some of the Passion and Easter plays did project New Testament-era conditions onto their contemporary, medieval European environment through the use of contemporary names and economically based anti-Jewish stereotypes, Folz presents a subtler picture. Jews are not a real danger ("wiewol ir würcklich uns nicht dut"), but only a potential one, against which Christians would be helpless, if European Jews held real political power ("het ir uns in ewrm gewallt"). Folz certainly depicts the Jewish hostility toward and hatred of Christians as a real psychological phenomenon. Any persecution of Christians by Jews is seen, in this text, however, as only potential and not real.

The fact that the *Reimpaarspruch* concludes without any conversion on the part of the Jewish participant is also significant:

"Iud, hie mit ich beschlissen thu
das der der uns erlöset hot
must sein wor mensch und worer Got
den all figur hant figurirt
und all profeten profetirt
die er vor im her hat gesent
und nomen nach im pald ein ent.
Das aber ir noch hört auf in
das ist an euch ein plöder sin
der euch vil iar verfüret hot."
Der Iud sprach, "Nun erleücht uns got
durch seinen aller heylgsten namen."
Do antwurt ich begirlich "Amen."[83] (596–608)

This closing exchange has a tone that is at odds with the tone of most of Folz's other depictions of Jews. The same Hans Folz who depicted Jews in the most degrading terms in *Ein Spil von dem Herzogen von Burgund*, as objects of deserved contempt in "Der Juden Messias," and objects of deserved hostility in "Jüdischer Wucher," depicts in this exchange a Jewish figure who is the intellectual and moral equal of his Christian counterpart. The Jew's last words in the exchange express the wish that God enlighten both parties in the theological dispute, a wish that the Christian affirms, indicating that Folz attributed to Jews both hostility toward Christians and a desire to know God. Ending the dialogue on this note, however, emphasizes the latter, leaving the ostensibly Christian medieval reader (or hearer) with a favorable image of the Jew.

The fact that Folz dealt with his Jewish characters differently in his various dramatic and non-dramatic works is significant to the thesis of this work. We have from the mind of the same author treatments of Jews that range from the vile and degrading to the respectful and thoughtful. Folz's underlying wish in the plays and poetic texts which have the question of Jesus's Messiahship at their heart seems to be to deal accurately and thoroughly with Jewish objections to Christian tenets of faith in a persuasive manner. In the works that deal with theological questions, most clearly in *Die alt und neu Ee* and "Christ und Jude," Folz expresses the wish to see Jews become part of Christian society, not the wish to see them degraded and driven out. The latter wish he expresses clearly and unequivocally in "Jüdischer Wucher."[84] There he refers to the expulsion of Jews from Nuremberg as a "holy work" that should be carried out as soon as possible. If this one fifteenth-century author was capable of depicting Jews in different ways in different texts, it follows logically that the scholarly treatment of the medieval German image of Jews that sees this image as uniformly and unchangingly hostile is untenable.

The Silvester legend received a wide variety of literary treatments in medieval German-speaking Europe. The most sublime of them were those appearing in texts meant for religious instruction, such as *Legenda Aurea, Der Heiligen Leben,* and *Das Verspassional,* while the coarsest were those in the *Fastnachtspiele* of Hans Folz. A necessary consequence of the formal variation among all these treatments of the Silvester legend is the variation in their presentation of the Jews. The central theme of the legend remained unchanged in its various expressions, with the exception of Folz's plays: if presented with satisfactory evidence of the theological claims of Christianity, the Jews would convert. Jews in the corpus of the Silvester legend proper were regarded not as enemies to be destroyed, but as unbelievers to be convinced. Three other influential legends, those of Theophilus, "Der Judenknabe," and Saint Basil, also present modern readers with valuable insights in to the medieval imagination's varied understandings of the role of Jews in the world. To these legends we shall turn our attention in the next chapter.

Chapter Six:
Theophilus, "Der Judenknabe," and Saint Basil

Standing alongside the Silvester legend among influential works of medieval German hagiography in which Jewish figures play an important role is the legend of Theophilus. Moshe Lazar described the legend and its history trenchantly in an article from 1972:

> The legend of Theophilus, the unhappy and despairing cleric who sold his soul to the Devil but later repented and gained salvation through the intercession of Nostre Dame, was probably the most important literary text in Christian civilization on the theme of despair and revolt prior to the elaboration of Faust's legend. The story of Theophilus, first encountered in a VIth century Greek narrative written by Eutychianus (who claimed to have been a member of Theophilus' household), via the IXth century Latin version of Paul the Deacon of Naples, was the forerunner of a series of poetic and dramatic works during five centuries.[1]

Particularly germane to this study is the fact that the motif of the Jew as intermediary between the fallen cleric and the Devil was already fully developed in the account of Paul the Deacon, the first such account of the legend to become known in Western Europe.[2] The earliest known indigenous version of the Theophilus legend in medieval German-speaking Europe was not produced in German, but rather in Latin by the Benedictine abbess Hroswitha of Gandersheim in the tenth century.[3] Like the Silvester legend, the Theophilus legend was widely known in medieval Europe,[4] the first vernacular attestation in German-speaking Europe being a passage from "der arme" Hartmann's narrative poem, "von deme glouben." Hartmann's version of the legend omits the role of the Jew entirely. In another deviation from Paul the Deacon's legend, Hartmann downplays the role of the Virgin Mary. In his version of the legend, God himself confronts the Devil in order to save Theophilus's soul:

Dô begonde sich got irbarmen
des sundigen armen

mit sîner gotelicher kraft,
dâ er alliu dinc mite getuon mach.
den ubelen tûvel er bedwanc,
daz er âne sînen danc
wider gab den selben brief:
daz ne was deme tûvel niwit lieb.[5] (49–56)

The omission of the Jew and the relegation of Mary to a mediating role, as the pre-eminent of many saints interceding with Christ and God on Theophilus's behalf and prompting God to act (37–48), make Hartmann's treatment of the legend unusual in the legend's history.[6] Hartmann's version is unusual precisely because the roles of Mary and of the Jew are central in the legend's subsequent medieval transmission. In the late Middle Ages, the Theophilus legend was the subject not only of entries in collections of saints' lives, such as *Das Verspassional*, or *The South English Legendary*, but also of dramatic treatments. The legend of Theophilus's fall and his deliverance through the intercession of the Virgin Mary is attested in a number of late medieval collections of Marian legends, most significantly in fourteenth-century manuscripts of *Das Verspassional*.[7] The particular collection of Marian legends common to these manuscripts, as has been conclusively demonstrated, was produced in the late thirteenth-century, possibly drawing on twelfth-century Latin sources.[8] A morally and religiously didactic tale, the plot of the legend revolves around sin, repentance, and the need for mediation between God and man. In the legend Mary functions as the intermediary between the sinner Theophilus and God, while the Jew functions as the intermediary between Theophilus and the Devil. The sin that is the focus of the legend is pride: Theophilus, his pride wounded by a loss of prestige and power, seeks to avenge himself on his clerical superiors by selling his soul to the Devil in return for money and power. It is only after he has made his decision to apostasize that he turns to the Jew:

im ranc nâch hêrschaft der sin
als nâch dem âse tut der rude.
Nu was ouch in der stat ein jude,

138

der in den swarzen buchen
die liste kunde ersuchen
daz er mit tûveln umme gie.
Theophilus dô gar verlie
sîn herze ûf disse juden rât.
in der hôsten unvlât
grub er nâch erzedîen,
die in solden vrîen
von der benanten leide.[9] (62–73)

The Jew is identified as a man versed in the black arts, a sorcerer
who willingly seeks out the power of the Devil to achieve desired
ends on earth. As such he has much in common with the Jews of the
blood libel legends, being wholly threatening and thoroughly evil. The
intermediary role of the Jew and his association with the Devil
becomes more apparent in the actual selling of Theophilus's soul, in
which the Jew demands that he blaspheme and abandon his Christian
faith:

als des der jude wart gewar,
dô sprach er "sô wil ich dir sagen
die wârheit und der nicht verdagen,
wie du kumst in die werdikeit.
gotes und der kristenheit
solt du dich verzîen
und dar zu Marien.
tu niewan daz eine
(dêswâr, es ist doch klcine
und lît nicht grôze macht dar an),
sô wirt dir genzlîch undertân
dîn volle hêrschaft als ê.
dir wirt gewaltes dar zu mê,
des dir der tûvel helfen sol."[10] (82–95)

After summoning the Devil, the Jew repeats his demand that Theophilus abandon his Christian faith and repudiate God and Mary as a
precondition to signing the contract that gives the Devil his soul (108–
16). In this version of the legend, the Jew not only assists the fallen
priest in joining himself to the Devil, but he also ridicules the
Christian faith, referring to "Kristenheit" and "Maria" as possessing
little power. With these words the redactor of this version of the

legend identifies the Jew as the human, mortal enemy of both Christianity and its most revered female saint. Once the contract is signed and Theophilus is fully committed to serving the Devil, the Jew's work is done, and he promptly vanishes from the legend.

As Lazar pointed out in his article,[11] the connection of Jews to black magic varied in the treatments of the Theophilus legend. In this variation we see that, as was the case with the blood libel, the legend meant to demonize the Jews by associating them with the Devil did not always meet with an eager reception from medieval Christian audiences. The connection between the Devil and the Jews, to borrow Trachtenberg's influential phrase, was emphasized in the Middle English version found in the *South English Legendary*, but was, as we shall see below, wholly absent in two of the three late medieval Low German Theophilus plays.[12] In the Middle Low German Theophilus play of the Trier manuscript, his encounter with the Jews begins with his expressing the wish to convert to Judaism, having been so disgraced by fellow Christians (430–35). His initial exchange with the Jews does not begin amicably:

Theophilus:
    Gy, joden, got geve ju goden dach!
De Joden:
    De katte byt ju dat hovet af!
Theophilus:
    Gy joden, wêr ju icht darumme,
    Dat ik my mit juwer ê beklumme
    Unde myner kristenheit versoke?
    My sint wol kundlich der kristen boke:
    Mochte my wat geldes van ju wêrn,
    Wy wolden dei kristen unmaten sêrn.
Musin:
    Twâr, her pape, dat wil ik ju seggen,
    Dâr en willen wy nein gelt an leggen.
    Wy wilt ju gêrn mit uns lyden,
    An wy wilt ju na unser ê besnyden.
Theophilus:
    My were liever, dat al gy joden
    In einer heiten pannen soden![13] (436–48)

The tone of the exchange does not improve, as Theophilus attempts to sell himself as a slave to the Jews, who refuse his offer (456–75). When he resolves to sell his soul and body to the Devil, "nu my dei joden nicht en welt," ("since the Jews don't want me"), the response of the Jews is to chide him for it:

Samuel:
    Wo ludy so vêl, leive here?
    Dat weren vyentlike mere.
    My gruwelt, dat ik se hore nomen.
    Woldy wol lyf und sele verdomen
    Um dit arm unselige gôt?
    Lieve here, des nicht en dôt!
    Gy sint ein kristen und ik ein jode.
    Ik wolde nochtant harde node
    Um alle dat gôt up êrden
    Des duvels eigen wêrden.
    Ik meinde, gy weren ein wysen man!
    Begevet der dedingen unde kômt dârvan![14] (480–91)

Here, the Jew tries to dissuade the fallen cleric from pursuing his evil intentions. Especially significant for our understanding of Samuel, one of the Jewish spokesmen, is that this figure is clearly a Jew who has not converted to Christianity, and yet he appears here as the righteous figure who would turn Theophilus away from the damning sin of apostasy. Further, Samuel is horrified that Theophilus would trade his soul for money. As a Jewish figure on the stage, Samuel of the Trier *Theophilus* play contrasts sharply with the figure of the Jew in the Frankfurt Passion play, who considers loaning money at interest a more worthwhile activitiy than praising the Creator (see Ch. 3). When a medieval audience saw and heard Samuel in a performance of this play, they saw and heard a refutation of the *Theophilus* legend's more common and ancient depiction of Jews, as well as a refutation of such economically based stereotypes.

Theophilus responds to the Jew's admonitions by saying that he knows his soul will suffer in Hell if he gives himself to the Devil, but he does not care (492–501). When it becomes clear to the Jew that he cannot dissuade Theophilus from his foolhardy course of action, the

Jew tells him where he believes that he can find the Devil (502–19). Theophilus responds:

> Du jode, du rest my als ein broder,
> Dat mote dy gelden godes moder!
> Kôm ik weder, so wil ik al wisse
> Dy jo brengen eine kermisse.[15] (520–4)

Significant for the discussion at hand is the Jew's reaction to Theophilus's unholy wish: He is horrified that Theophilus would even speak it aloud, more so that he would pursue his wish so determinedly. Unlike the Jew of Paul the Deacon, the originator of the Theophilus legend in the West,[16] the Jew as written by the anonymous Middle Low German dramatist wants nothing to do with the fallen cleric and is, at first, unwilling to help him in his search for the Devil. When Theophilus presses him for information, the Jew tells him where he might find the Devil, but he does not himself accompany Theophilus on his journey, much less summon the Devil or act as a sort of nigromantic business agent.

In contrast to the legend as known from Eutychianus, Paul, Hroswitha, and *Das Verspassional*, the late medieval Low German Theophilus drama of the Trier manuscript depicts the Jews as neither sorcerers nor willing accomplices of the Devil. In the other Middle Low German Theophilus dramas, those of the Stockholm and Helmstadt manuscripts, the role of the Jew disappears entirely. The Stockholm manuscript refers to a "magister in nigromantia" as the intermediary between Theophilus and the Devil, while the Helmstadt manuscript actually begins with Theophilus's meeting with the Devil.[17] In the Trier text of the drama, the Jews act, initially, as comic relief, exposing the foolishness of Theophilus's pride and self-pity. At the same time, the Jewish figures, in their refusal to accept Theophilus's offer to do "great harm" to Christendom, dramatically refute the common medieval conception of Jewish hostility toward Christians. The Jews in this play have no interest in harming Christians or in cooperating with Theophilus in his apostasy. Their attempt to dissuade him identifies them more with Mary and God than with the Devil, whose whereabouts they only know by reputation, not by direct experience, as Samuel's description makes clear: "Dâr gy den duvel vindet wisse, / ist anders recht also ik *gisse*" (504–5, my italics).[18] Indeed, the depiction of the Jews in this text seems to satirize the depiction of Jews as sorcerers common to other versions of the Theophilus legend. The Middle Low German Theophilus drama of the Trier manuscript contains many passages that hint at the satirical, such as Theophilus's asking "God's Mother" to repay the Jew for his advice and his promising to bring the Jew a present after he has concluded his pact with the devil.

Noteworthy also is the fact that this is the latest of the dramatic treatments of the legend from the Middle Ages, having been written down in the fifteenth century. As such, it is contemporary with some of the Passion and Easter plays discussed in the previous chapter, and demonstrates that there was variation in the depiction of Jews in the medieval treatment of the Theophilus legend, just as there was in the medieval treatment of the Passion narrative. The Trier Theophilus drama presented its audience with Jews who would keep Theophilus from the Devil, if he would let them, while the Theophilus legend common to the cycle of Marian legends in *Das Verspassional* depicts the Jew as the Devil's agent.

Another Marian legend common to that same group as the Theophilus legend, however, depicted Jews in a variety of ways, not all of them negative. The legend is known variously as "Der Judenknabe" or "Das Jüdel." At its heart, "Der Judenknabe" is a legend about mercy and conversion. Latin versions of "Der Judenknabe" circulated already in the sixth century in the *De Gloria Martyrum* of Gregory of Tours and in the writing of Evagrius Scholasticus.[19] The earliest attested German version of the legend, dated to approximately 1200, is preserved only in a much later manuscript, while the best-known version is that of *Das Verspassional*.[20] The version of the legend in *Das Verspassional* tells the story of the conversion of a Jewish boy by means of Marian and Eucharistic visions. His conversion prompts his former co-religionists to condemn him to death as an apostate, throwing him into an oven. He is then delivered from death by the miraculous intervention of Mary. The miracles in the tale are associated with both the Eucharist and with Mary, here in the role of protectress more than that of intercessor. Similarly, the depiction of

Jews in common versions of this tale varies far more than does the depiction of Jews in the Theophilus story as it appears in legendaries. A brief summary and discussion of *Das Verspassional*'s version of the legend, including important deviations from its Latin sources and non-German vernacular parallels, follows.

We are introduced first to the father of the central figure, who is described in the following terms:

Ez was ein jude an rîcher habe
gesezzen bî den kristen,
der nâch juden listen
mit wucher gutes vil gewan.[21] (6–9)

The first mention of a Jew in the poem associates him immediately with wealth and usury, and further describes the Jewish father as "ungeloubig," emphasizing his religious alterity. When the son reaches eight years of age, the father decides that it would be beneficial for him to attend a Christian school and learn about their religious beliefs and rituals, and makes the necessary arrangements for him to do so (12–49). Once he has been among the Christians, though, the Jewish boy not only begins to learn about Christian beliefs, but to adopt them as his own, that is, to convert. His conversion occurs gradually, beginning when he joins the other boys in genuflecting before a statue of Mary (50–113). The boy subsequently becomes devoted to Mary, cleaning her image with his own coat and learning all that he can about her (114–69). At Easter, the boy accompanies his schoolmates to Mass, where he receives the Eucharist after experiencing a vision in which the Communion bread is transformed into the Christ child (170–217). The child's relating this event to his father then becomes the dramatic turning point for the legend as a whole, while the father's reaction becomes the key to understanding the depiction of Jews in this version of the tale.

When the father learns that the boy has attended Easter Mass, his reaction is one of consternation and condemnation of Christian observances, as he assumes that his son did not partake of Communion:

"Ey," sprach der vater, "liebez kint,
du hast der grôzen hôchzît,
die nu der kristenheit an lît
den valschen, den unholden,
harte sere entgolden,
wan du noch bist ungezzen.
du soldest sîn gesezzen
zu hûse billîch hûte,
wan die kristenlûte
mit ir feste unledic sint."[22] (218–27)

When the son tells him that he has, in fact, eaten and that what he ate
was the bread of the Eucharist, the father is so horrified that he falls
unconscious, while the entire family becomes saddened with the news
(244–51). Once word of the boy's partaking of the Christian sacrament has reached the Synagogue and become public knowledge, the
father regains consciousness and gives dramatic expression of his pain
at his son's apparent betrayal of their faith, tearing out his hair and
beard and blaming himself for his son's misdeed (251–76). Immediately the boy is confronted by his relatives and neighbors who ask him
to renounce Christ and curse Mary, to turn away from his "ubeltête,"
which the boy refuses to do (277–89). When it becomes clear that the
boy will not renounce Christ and curse Mary, his Jewish relatives and
friends metamorphose into a bloodthirsty mob, demanding that he be
killed for his apostasy and that, in accordance with the Torah, the
father should be the one to carry out the sentence (290–315, cf. Deut.
13:7–19).[23] The father, however, refuses to do so, saying:

"wâfen immer uber mich!
waz bin ich worden, waz sol ich
und waz furbaz sol mîn leben?
ir habt ein urteil ûz gegeben,
daz ich nicht gevolgen mac.
ûwer urteil, ûwer slac
ân aller hande hinderswich
gê uberz kint und uber mich.
tut mir allez daz ir wolt:
ich bin dem kinde alsô holt
daz ichz nicht mac ertôten."[24] (317–27)

In the depiction of the father's unwillingness to kill his son, the German *Verspassional*'s version of this legend departs completely from its Latin sources: In the earlier Latin versions of "Der Juden-knabe," there is no such self-sacrificing and loving Jewish father, but instead a Jewish father who is willing to kill his son immediately and mercilessly.[25] The *Liber de Miraculis Sanctae Mariae* describes the father's reaction to his son's conversion as follows:

> Haec audiens pater ejus graviter iratus eum cum furore arripuit, et videns non longe fornacem ignis ardentem, illuc rapido cursu perveniens eum in ignem jacavit.[26]

The Middle English version in the *South English Legendary*, derived from the same Latin sources, describes the father as being "nei for wrathe wod" and casting his son in an "al bernynge fur" without hesitation.[27] Similarly, the widely disseminated Middle French version of Gautier de Coinci emphasizes the cruelty of the Jewish father and the innocence of his son, the Christian convert.[28] As such, these widely disseminated Latin, English, and French versions of the legend are closely related to the blood libel legends discussed at the beginning of this chapter, in that they depict the Jew as the murderer of the innocent Christian boy. The Middle High German version of the legend, widely circulated in manuscripts of *Das Verspassional*, is exceptional in characterizing the Jewish father as self-sacrificing and merciful toward his apostate son. Other Middle High German versions, such as that of the *Elsässische Legenda Aurea*, follow the Latin tradition and end with the Jewish father's death at the hands of a Christian mob.[29]

The same sympathetic treatment of the Jewish father figure found in the *Verspassional* appears in another German manuscript version of the legend, edited by Heike Burmeister.[30] Known as "Das Jüdel," the text, which is not the same as in the *Verspassional*, describes the father's reaction to the condemnation of his son as follows:

> nu gesah man nie dehæinen man
> als ummæzichlich chlagen:
> er het sich selben nah erslagen.

sein vlæisch er ab den wangen brach,
zu im selben er jæmerlichen sprach:
"owe, ich vil arme!
wie lutzel ich erbarme
den almechtigen got.
sol ich behalten ditz gebot,
daz muz ich nimmer geleben."
er bat, im ein waffen geben,
ein swert oder ein mezzer.
er sprach: "mir ist bezzer,
daz ich mir selben tu den tot,
denne ich dise ungewônlich not
an meinem chinde bege.
ê ich daz tun, ich wil ê
mich selbe ze tode stechen.
so muze denne ein ander rechen
an meinem chinde diese geschiht.
wæiz got, ich entûn sein nicht."[31] (232–52)

Consistent in both German versions and contrasting with the Latin source material is the depiction of the Jewish father as merciful and loving, willing to die rather than harm his own son. Indeed, "Das Jüdel" extends a degree of sympathy to the Jewish religious authorities, emphasizing their "herzenlæit," and "mit læid gemischter zorn" at the news of the boy's conversion.[32] In the *Liber de miraculis Sanctae Mariae* as well as the Middle English *South English Legendary*, all of the Jews with the exception of the boy and his mother are depicted as completely merciless and, in the case of the father, deserving of a fiery death. With its depiction of a soft-hearted Jewish father and conscience-stricken Jewish religious leaders, "Das Jüdel" goes further than *Das Verspassional* in its humanization of the Jews, deviating even further from their common Latin sources.

The deviations from the Latin sources in *Das Verspassional*'s treatment of Jews in this legend do not end with the father's response to the judgment passed on the "Judenknabe." Common to all versions of the legend is that the boy's punishment for his conversion is being thrown into a fire – either by his father, as in the *Liber de Miraculis* and the *South English Legendary*, or by the elders of the Jewish community, as in *Das Verspassional*. What they do not have in common is the consequence of the attempted execution for the Jewish community.

Once thrown into the fire, the boy is delivered from harm by the miraculous intervention of Mary, recalling the deliverance of Shadrach, Meschak, and Abednego from the furnace in the book of Daniel.[33] The version of "Der Judenknabe" from *Das Verspassional* does not differ from others in this detail (330–97). Where it differs is in depicting the effect of the miracle on the Jews. Though delivered from the flames and assured by his father that no harm will come to him if he leaves the oven, the boy refuses to emerge from the blazing oven until he can be received by fellow Christians. He remains fearful of the wrath of his former co-religionists, who have condemned him to death for apostasy (398–469). Where the Latin source depicts a group of Jews in which some remain unmoved by the miracle and would still kill the boy, if possible,[34] the German version in *Das Verspassional* depicts a conversion of many Jews as a consequence of the miracle. The first to be so moved is the father:

> des alden juden sinne
> ein teil begonde erweichen
> diz wunder zeichen
> daz er an sîme kinde sach.
> hie mite ouch in sîn herze brach
> ein licht von deme glouben,
> daz im begonde rouben
> von deme valschen knoten.
> er sante bald sîne boten
> sô hin ûf der pfaffen hof.[35] (470–9)

Once the boy has actually emerged from the oven and been received by the Bishop, he is baptized along with many other Jews (480–555). Presenting the conversion of the Jews, the legend, in this Middle High German version, also presents the universal and inclusive nature of the Christian message, highlighting again a desire to see Jews included in the Kingdom of God, and not destroyed. In the Latin versions, either the boy's father or all of the Jews are put to death, with only the boy and his mother being spared.[36] In accord with the emphasis on mercy and grace in the corpus of Marian legends, the

148

medieval Christian audience saw the Jews in this German version of "Der Judenknabe" depicted as people who receive that grace and mercy when given appropriate signs, and who are welcomed into the Christian community, rather than as heartless monsters who have no place in a Christian society and are rightly destroyed. The contrast between the hostility toward Jews in the Latin sources and the depiction of Jews as human beings capable of self-sacrificial love and eligible to receive divine grace is sharp, and will be seen again in the discussion of Latin and vernacular fable literature in the next chapter.

Of the legends in the *Legenda Aurea*, *Das Verspassional*, and *Der Heiligen Leben*, the legend of Saint Basil, at least in the latter two versions, depicts perhaps the deepest interpersonal relationship between a Jew and a Christian and, not coincidentally, the most unambiguously positive image of a Jew. The friendship between Saint Basil and the Jewish physician, Joseph, is depicted in the narrative of the end of Basil's life. The saint himself grows ill after a long career as a healer and comforter of the sick ("dem kranken ein trost"). This text from *Das Verspassional* describes the physician's visit to the dying saint:

> do quam gegan ein iude ob in,
> den der bischof gerne sach,
> wand er im grozer liebe iach
> durch die hoffenunge,
> daz noch ein wandelung
> wurde in sime lebene
> und er vurwart ebene
> trete uf die rechte straze
> nach des gelouben saze.
> der iude ein gut arzt was,
> wand er die meisterschaft wol las
> an den wisen buchen.[37]

It is in their respective treatments of this particular scene that the deviation of the German *Verspassional* from one of its primary sources, the *Legenda Aurea*, becomes apparent.[38] In the Latin *Legenda Aurea*, Joseph is able to diagnose Basil's condition by feeling his pulse.[39] In *Das Verspassional,* Joseph diagnoses Basil's condition as terminal and untreatable only after bleeding him. A more significant variation, however, occurs in the representations of the character of the two men. Where the German verse legend dwells on the emotional motivation of the saint and the intellectual skill of the physician, the German prose version of the *Elsässische Legenda Aurea* presents a comparatively dry narrative:

> Do sant Basilius an dem totbette lag in grosser krangheit, do hies er zuo im rueffen einen juden der waz Joseph genant, und waz gar ein meister arzot. Der jude greif sant Basilius an sinen puls vnd sprach zuo dem gesinde daz sú bereitetent waz not durftig were zuo der begrebden, wenne der tot were an der túr. Dis horte sant Basilius vnd sprach: "Josep, waz sprichest du? Ich wil noch morne leben." Do sprach der iude: "Herre daz ist vnmúgelich, wenne die nature ist fúrzert daz su nút me sich enthalten enmag."[40]

Relevant to the topic at hand is the fact that the anonymous compiler of *Das Verspassional*, writing in German for a German-reading audience, mentions that the motivating factor in the saint's love for Joseph was his desire for Joseph's conversion ("wann in großer lieb iach"). The detail does not appear in the Latin *Legenda Aurea*, which, as mentioned above, was the source for much of *Das Verspassional*, nor does it appear in the version of the legend in *Der Heiligen Leben*, though a detail about Joseph's own motivation is included in *Der Heiligen Leben* that does not appear in either the *Legenda* or the *Verspassional*:

> Do ging ain jud vber jnn, der hieß Joseph. Den sahe der pischof gern, wann er hoft, er würd gelawbig. Do was der jud ein guter arczt vnd het sand Basilius gern geholffen.[41]

Where the compiler of the *Verspassional* emphasizes the saint's love for Joseph and Joseph's medical knowledge, the compiler of *Der Heiligen Leben* states only that Basil wished that Joseph would become a Christian, with any idea of Christian love or kindness being only implicit ("den sahe der pischof gern"). However, *Der Heiligen Leben* emphasizes Joseph's desire to help his patient as the characteristic that makes him "ein guter arczt." Joseph's defining quality is not his skill, but his desire to heal. The inclusion of these varying personal details may speak to authorial intent, perhaps revealing a concern for psychological depth in creating a credible narrative.

150

In all versions of the legend, Joseph diagnoses Basil's condition as imminently fatal.[42] Saint Basil then questions the accuracy of the diagnosis only to be reassured by the doctor that the illness is not only fatal, but will take his life that very evening. Saint Basil then asks Joseph what he [Joseph] would do if he [Basil] were to live a full day longer than medical science predicts. Joseph replies that this is totally impossible, but Basil presses him on the question again. In *Das Verspassional* Joseph replies:

> do sprach Ioseph, "Ist daz an dir
> unz dar nicht kumt des todes not,
> so wizze, daz ich lige tot.
> da ist dikein zwivel an."
> "got geruches mich gewern,
> wand ichs von herzen wil begern,
> daz du den sunden sterbest
> unde also erwerbest
> ein recht cristenliches leben,
> darinne dir ouch wirt gegeben
> von gote ein vernumftec sin."[43]

Saint Basil turns his own fatal illness into a demonstration of the healing power God manifests in the Christian faith, asking the physician if he would recognize the prolongation of his life as proof of the truth of Christianity and therefore convert. The physician readily accepts the proposition, since, according to his medical knowledge, it would be impossible for Saint Basil to survive even one more day. Were Basil to survive any longer than Joseph's diagnosis stated, Joseph would be compelled to accept it as a miracle and convert:

> do sprach der iude wider in
> "ich verstê wol daz du sagest
> und wahin du mit worten jagest
> als dich leret din gut site.
> ich wil dir werlich volgen mite
> und des min truwe borgen,
> daz ich mich toufe morgen,
> ob du lebest unz da hin.

ist daz mich truget hie min sin,
   so kan ich arzedie nicht,
   wand alle min kunst mir vergicht,
   daz du nicht lebest disen tac."[44]

As was the case with the earlier exchange, the passage of *Das Vers-passional* is considerably more detailed in its dialogue than the corresponding passage from the *Elsässische Legenda Aurea*:

> Do sprach sant Basilie: "Josep, waz wiltu tuon, lebe ich noch denne morne?" Antwurt der iude: "Herre so wil ich morne sterben, lebest du morne zuo sexten zit." Do sprach sant Basilie: "Du solt den súnden sterben, vnd solt Cristo leben." Do sprach der iude: "Herre ich weis wol waz du meinest. Ist es, daz du morne zuo sexten lebest, so wil ich tuon daz du begerest." Do bat sant Basilie got daz er ime sin leben lengerte, wie daz wider die nature were: also bleip er lebende bicz an den anderen dag zuo nonen. Do dis sach Iosep der iude do erschrag er vnd glôbete an Christum.[45]

The text of the legend from *Der Heiligen Leben* is, with dialect differences accounted for, almost identical to that of the *Elsässische Legenda Aurea* in this portion of the the legend.[46] In both versions of the legend, Basil does survive and Joseph does convert, allowing Basil to perform his baptism. The baptism of his friend complete, Basil says a final prayer of thanks to God and dies in peace.

There are strong parallels between this legend and that of Saint Silvester, discussed above. Both legends emphasize the limitations of abstract reason in matters of faith, insofar as Silvester and Basil unsuccessfully attempt to persuade the learned Jews of the truth of Christianity through logical argumentation alone. However, both legends ultimately place the decision of faith beyond the realm of the immediately rationally provable into the realm of supernatural revelation. Saint Basil may, as Joseph says, pursue his goal with words ("ich verstê … wahin du mit worten iagest…"), but the ultimate demonstration of the truth of Christian revelation lies beyond his power and must be provided by an empirically observable miraculous event. Far more than in the Silvester legend, reason, learning, and intellect are depicted as limited in their capacity to encompass ultimate reality. The Silvester legend depicts a certain kind of learning, Jewish theology, as hindering knowledge of the truth of

152

Christ, while the legend of Saint Basil clearly affirms that science and learning by themselves do not provide a full account of the divine mystery.

It is also clear that the legend of Saint Basil and Joseph, his Jewish physician, affirms the necessity of conversion to Christianity for salvation, implicitly rejecting the possibility that Judaism itself would be soterifically efficacious. The same affirmation of the universality of the Christian message runs through all of these legends, informing and undergirding their narratives. It is with this fact in mind that one has to consider the undeniable breadth of variation in the depiction of Jews in the medieval Christian hagiographic narratives. In all versions of the Basil legend, Joseph is depicted as being a morally good man while he yet adheres to the Jewish religion. It is, in fact, Joseph's virtues that evoke in Basil the wish to see him convert and thereby receive eternal life.

The gulf between Joseph and the Jews of the blood libel legends discussed at the beginning of this chapter is so vast as to be unbridgable, and yet both Joseph and those figures are products of medieval Christian attempts to understand what the Jewish rejection of Jesus and persistence in their own religion meant. A similar gulf exists between the Jewish father as depicted in some versions of the *Judenknabe* legend and the same figure as depicted in other versions of that legend. The Jewish man appears as a cruel, filicidal maniac in Latin, French, and English versions of the *Judenknabe* legend, while the same figure appears as a self-sacrificing, loving father in another (German) version of the same legend. Theophilus finds the devil through the direct agency of a Jewish sorcerer in one version of his legend, while in another the Jews are horrified by his diabolical plans, and only tell him a rumor of the devil's whereabouts. The Silvester legend contains within itself a spectrum of Jewish figures, ranging from the theologically interested disputant to the deceptive sorcerer. Seen together these varied images of Jews demonstrate again the validity of Langmuir's observation about Christianity: demonization of Jews is not a logically necessary outcome of belief in the Messiahship of Jesus of Nazareth (see Ch. 1). From this body of evidence, it is clear that Graus's observations about early medieval hagiography apply to late medieval hagiography as well.

Chapter Seven: Representations of Jews in Fables and Related Moral-Didactic Narratives in Late Medieval German-speaking Europe

Late medieval and early modern redactors, scribes, and authors saw no clear borders between the types of literature that we recognize today as fable, exemplum, and allegory.[1] The broad categories of *historia, fabula,* and *argumentum* inherited from classical antiquity and the early Christian aestheticians left much room for redefinition and disagreement among medieval and modern scholars alike.[2] In the Middle Ages, the term *fabula* was used to refer to any kind of fictional story, and while the terms *historia* and *argumentum* were used to classify narratives, the boundaries between them were not strictly observed.[3] Indeed, in his fifteenth-century collection of fables, *Esopus*, Heinrich Steinhöwel was compelled to refine the accepted medieval definition of fable that had been taken from Isidore of Seville's *Etymologies*. Where Isidore had defined fables as fictional stories without further qualification,[4] Steinhöwel defines the fable as follows:

> So ich aber von den fabeln Esopi sagen wil, so ist vor ze merken, waz ain fabel genemmet sye. Darumb wisse, daz die poeten den namen fabel von dem latinischen wort fando habent genommen, daz ist ze tütsch reden, wann fabel synt nit geschehene ding, sondern allain mit worten erdichte ding, und sind darumb erdacht worden, daz man durch erdichte wort der unvernünftigen tier under in selber ain ynbildung des wesens und sitten der menschlichen würde erkennet.[5]

Though certainly more specific than that of Isidor, Steinhöwel's definition still leaves room for confusion between "fabel," "bispel," and "exemplum" or "allegorese." As Klaus Grubmüller pointed out:

> *Bispel* übersetzt im Mittelalter *apologus*, das Wort für die äsopische Fabel, *gleichnis* übersetzt *exemplum* und beides kann dasselbe bedeuten. Rhetoriken, Poetiken, theoretisierende Vorreden (wie z.B. Phaedrus, der sog. "Romulus," aber auch Quintillian) ordnen die Fabel dem Exemplum zu. Die Sammlungen des

Mittelalters zeigen wie schon die der Antike, wie Exempel zu Bestandteilen von Fabelcorpora werden und Fabeln in Exempelsammlungen überliefert sind. So enthält etwa – um nur ein Beispiel zu nennen – das Aviancorpus von altersher das Exempel vom "kahlen Ritter" (s.u.), das auch in der Babrios-Umgebung überliefert ist. Wo Avian als Sammlung rezipiert wird, z.B. im Deutschen bei Boner und im Leipziger Äsop, wird auch dieses Exempel mit übertragen.[6]

Grubmüller goes on to argue that, if there is to be a clear definition of medieval fable – as opposed to *bispel* or *exemplum* – for modern literary scholars, it cannot be based on either the moral-didactic impulse of the story or on its irreality, since these are traits shared by all of these types of literature.[7] Our modern definition of the fable as a moralizing story in which the actors are animals or other personified non-human entities, only appears in the sixteenth century.[8] This modern definition provided the basis for inclusion in Dicke and Grubmüller's extensive catalog of medieval and early modern Latin and German fable literature,[9] and it is this definition which will be used throughout this chapter to differentiate fables from related genres. Here "related genres" will refer to morally didactic narratives and their commentaries, allegorical *exempla*, and brief moralizing stories that include stereotyped human actors (the knight, the farmer, the Jew, the housewife, the king, etc.). With this definition in mind, we can proceed to examine texts of these two related groups. We will begin with the fable "von der äffin," from the early fifteenth-century *Nürnberger Prosa Äsop*:

Zu einen zeiten gepot Jupiter daz allew lebentigew creatur, ez warn leut, vögel, tïr, visch oder gewürm daz daz alles für in chäm. Vnnder den wolt er besechen welchs das aller edlist wär und die schonisten chinden hiet. Vnd do sew chomen vnd prachten mit in irew jungew welff, vnnder den chom dew äffin vnd pracht mit ir irew chind vnd trat für Jouem und sprach: "Nimm war daz under aller creatur, die hie vör dein stet, nicht schöners ist dann mein chind." Vnd do daz Jupiter hört, der lacht und spott ir daz si sich und ïr chind also lobt, wand si wolt von im gelobt werden. Do ward si von aller creatur vmb ïr torhait gescmächt vnd hin gelegt.

Gaistlich: Pey der äffin ist dew Judenschül zu uersten, pey den andern tiern sind ander geslächt zu merken als christen und haiden, und daz die Juden sprechen ïr gelaub sey gerechter wann der vnser. Vnd daran werden sew ze spot, wand si der schrifft vnd spruch der weizzagen nich betrachten noch versten wellen. Vnd da wider redt Paulus vnd spricht: "Si sind hörer der wart und nicht nachvolger."[10]

156

This passage from the early fifteenth-century *Nürnberger Prosa Äsop* presents readers with Jews as foolish hypocrites who have access to the truth but refuse to heed it, "hörer der wart und nicht nachvolger." Elsewhere in the same collection, the fable "von dem ritter dem daz har enphiel in dem turnay,"[11] we are confronted with another popular medieval conception of the Jews: as the bloodthirsty mockers of the innocent Christ. These tales have been placed here, at the beginning of a chapter dealing with didactic literature in order to illustrate one end of the spectrum of "didactic Jews." The spectrum as metaphor implies the existence of other, differently charged figures, while the use of the phrase "didactic Jews" is a reminder that the literature in this chapter belonged to the most widely disseminated body of educational literature in the Middle Ages. The core of the argument is that the images of Jews here, as in other areas of medieval German literature, were more diverse and complex than scholars have hitherto asserted, that they reflect an almost completely unacknow-ledged complexity and diversity of attitudes toward Jews in medieval German culture. Fables and related morally didactic literature afford a particularly rich stock of material in evidence.

The first question to address is whether the image of the Jews in this fable from the *Nürnberger Prosa Äsop* is typical for medieval and early modern fable literature. If so, is the treatment of Jews in this text only typical of vernacular fable compilations or also of the Latin compilations that were their sources? The text itself is obscure, having been preserved in only one manuscript and never widely imitated, and therefore opens this first question for discussion.[12] A second question is whether the depiction of Jews by nominally Christian authors was as one-sided as one might readily believe on the basis of the above sample, or was the depiction of Jews as varied as that seen in other widely disseminated text traditions, such as those discussed in the previous chapters. The third is whether we see in such fables a body of didactic literature that instructed its recipients in how Jews were to be regarded or a descriptive literature that did no more than record attitudes that already existed. That is, did these fables influence popular thought or were they influenced by it? In connection with this question, it is necessary to examine factors that promoted the growth of anti-Jewish attitudes in the late medieval and early modern period and their expression in fables, exempla, and related short literary forms.

The *Nürnberger Prosa Äsop* is an ideal starting point, as the fables with pointedly anti-Jewish epimyths are, as we shall see, common to the prose commentaries in a large body of extensive Latin fable collections of the medieval and early modern periods. The Latin collections referred to here are those belonging both to the *Avianus* and to the *Anonymous Neveleti* fable tradition. The latter, known in the English-speaking world more commonly as the "Fables of Walter of England,"[13] is one of the best-attested works of the European Middle Ages. Nearly two hundred manuscripts of this late twelfth-century Latin re-working of the fables of Romulus exist.[14] The text is of particular import for the study of medieval German fable literature for the reason that, of all the medieval fable collections, the *Anonymous Neveleti* found its strongest reception in German-speaking Europe. It became part of the standard corpus of fable literature in the later Middle Ages, eventually competing with and to some degree replacing the earlier texts that had been derived from the Avianus.[15] As A. E. Wright observes, when he compares the fate of the *Anonymous* and *Avianus* in the modern period to their influence in late medieval civilization:

> In the late Middle Ages, in contrast, the Aesopic fable was not only conspicuously represented among the Latin works every *litteratus* could be expected to know, but was assigned priority of place in that canon, adduced chronologically (if not aesthetically) well before Virgil, Horace, and Ovid; indeed, it was precisely in the marginal notes to the fable books that the medieval schoolboy first encountered these august names. And it must always be recalled that to the late medieval West, still unacquainted with Phaedrus and entirely unaware of his Greek contemporary Babrius, the collections of Avianus and the Anonymous were not thought, as they are today, the curious side branches of a philological tree badly in need of pruning; they quite simply *were* the Äsopic fable.[16]

The *Anonymous* was, together with the *Avianus* fable corpus, a text that every medieval student and teacher of rhetoric was expected to study and master.[17] The images of Jews in the fables of the *Anonymous Neveleti* and Avianus, were the images received by later

158

fabulists, such as the compiler of the *Nürnberger Prosa Äsop*, and are therefore of highest relevance to the topic at hand.

In the Latin prose commentaries on the *Anonymous*, the fables that have attached prose interpretations condemning the Jews are "de lupo et agno,"[18] "de ranis regem petentibus,"[19] and "de musca et formica."[20] These epimyths are reproduced here, as they appear in Wolfenbüttel Codex Guelferbytanus 185 Helmstadensis, a text typical of the medieval commentaries on these particular fables:

> De lupo et agno (Anonymous Neveleti 2)
> Moraliter per agnum intellige Christum in lege per prophetas promissum, qui in humanitate tanquam agnus humilis et manswetus fuit usque ad mortem. Iuxta illud Petri in canonica sua: "Tanquam ouis ad occisionem ductus est." Per lupum vero intellege Iudaeorum congregacionem qui tanquam lupi contra Christum coram Pilato false clamabant in hec verba, "Hic distruit templum Dei" etc. Item, "Si non esset hic malefactor" etc. Quibus Christus mite respondet: "Non veni soluere legem sed adimplere." Iudei vero velut lupi furiosi agnum.[21]
>
> De ranis regem pententibus (Anonymous Neveleti 22)
> Moraliter per Iouem intellige Deum omnipotentem, per ranas Iudeos qui clamaverunt ad Deum pro rege. Qui cum eis daretur ipsum spreuerunt et ei subici noluerunt. Propterea venundati sunt et deuorati gladio sicut legitur de destruxione Iherusalem et captiuitate Iudeorum et interfectionem eorundem tempore Thiti et Vepsianii.[22]
>
> De musca et formica (Anonymous Neveleti 37)
> Moraliter per muscam intellige Iudeos, qui credunt legem eorum esse beatam et illa que faciunt. Sed per formicam spirituales homines designantur, qui sepius ab illis deridentur. Per estatem intelligenda est vita huius seculi, in qua Iudei et multi conuersi Christiani deliciose viuunt. Sed yems, id est diabolus uel dies iudicii, opprimit eos morte et viuunt in iehenna.[23]

From the Avianus come the Latin prose commentaries on the fables "de calvo equite" (Avianus 10) and "de simia" (Avianus 14):

> De Calvo Equite (Avianus 10)
> Allegorice per istum militum Christum intelligere possumus, per comes vero annexos humanitatem eius, que mortua et elapsa fuit et a Iudeis derisa sic dicentibus: "Alios saluos fecit, se ipsum saluere non potest." Et per resurrexionem eius risum Iudeorum deleuit. Vel aliter per turbam deridencium intelligentur Iudei qui euellendo barbam militis, id est Christi, eum deriserunt, quod gratanter accepit quia omnes euntes per viam caput mouerunt in signum derisionis, sed ipse verbis suauibus coram eis se defendit.[24]

De Simia (Avianus 14)
Item allegorice per symeam debemus intelligere synagogam et per alias feras quaslibet alios gentes. Modo synagoga dicet fidem suam esse meliorem, cum tamen ita non sit, et sicut symea clamat ad Iouem, eta Iudei et heretici nituntur destruere fidem nostram christianam, dicentes fidem ipsorum esse optimam, cum tamen sit pessima.[25]

The Nuremberg collection, which drew on the older fable collections of the *Anonymous Neveleti* (Walter of England) and the *Avianus* – and their respective prose commentary traditions – contains five fables with allegorical epimyths that are unequivocally anti-Jewish. In addition to the above-cited "von der äffin," they are "von dem wolff und lamp," "von dem ritter dem daz har enphiel in dem turnay," "von den vier ochsen die der leeb betrog vnd vmb den hals pracht,"[26] and "von den froschen die den got Jouem umb einen chunig paten." The anti-Jewish epimyths of four of these five – "von der äffin," "von dem wolff und lamp," "von dem ritter," and "von den froschen" – derive from the Latin prose commentary tradition and were, in fact, common to the Latin commentaries in their respective fable corpora.[27] The epimyths of three of these fables, "von dem ritter," "von der äffin," and "von den froschen," depict Jews as objects of deserved scorn, as foolish or morally deficient people who are, by their very nature, worthy of contempt. The bad ends that they meet are seen as the deserved consequences of their innate flaws.

In the *Nürnberger Prosa Äsop*'s epimyth to "von dem ritter," the contempt that the Jews earn is seen as just recompense for the contempt that they heaped on Christ at the Crucifixion:

Gaistlich: Pey dem ritter jst vnser herre Jesus christus zu versten. Pey dem har ist zu uersten sein menschaitt. Der ward von den Juden gespott, do si sprachen [Mt. 27, 41] "Er hat ander leut gesunt gemacht, awer sich selben chan er nicht gesunt machen." Vnd do das vnser herre verstuend, der cherret in ir gelächter und gespött in wainen und inn chlagen an dem tag seiner auffart, do sew vernamen daz er mit aignem gewalt erstanden waz.[28]

Of the remaining two fables, "von dem wolff und lamp" affirms the guilt of the Jews in bringing about Jesus's death, just as the older Latin version of the fable in the *Anonymous*:

Gaistlich: Pey dem lamp ist vnser herre Jesus Christus zu uersten, pey dem wolff dew judenschül vnd die juden, die vnsern herrenn valschleich czigen er zerstörat in ïr ee, vnd wie wol daz vnser herre widerrett vnd sprach [Mt. 5,17]: "Ich pin nicht chömen die ee zu störn, sunder zu erfüllen," yedoch halff in sein tugentleich widerred nicht vnd töttn in vnschuldichleich, als dez pilatus selb bechant, do er sprach [Lk 23,14]: "Ich vind an im chain schuld, darumb er zu töten sey."[29]

The fable "von den vier ochsen die der leeb betrog," on the other hand, depicts Jews and heretics as a credible danger to the lives and salvation of contemporary Christians:

Gaistlich: Pey den vïr ochsen sind die gerechten frumen christen beczaichnet die da alleczeicz lëben vnd wonen nach dem gepot vnsers herren. Pey dem leeben sind Juden und checzer beczaichnet, wand die mit allem fleizz dar nach stellen wie sew die gerechten mit iren valschen lügleichen wörter betrïgen vnd ab dem gerechten weg laiten auf den weg dez todes. Vnd daz wïr stät vnd vest pey einander beleiben, daz rätt vns Jsaias vnd spricht, "Stee wïr zu samm vnd nicht aus dem weg, so werd wïr trew geschätz vnd erfunden."[30]

The view of Jews that we find in the epimyths of the fables in both some Latin fables of the *Anonymous* and in all fables mentioning Jews in the *Nürnberger Prosa Äsop* is thoroughly, unrelentingly negative.

Furthermore, it is important to note that the association of Jews with animals that were frequently viewed with fear, contempt, or disgust – such as wolves, frogs, or apes – was common in medieval allegorical literature beyond the Aesopic tradition. Here, we see the animal types common in the Aesopic fable corpus – wolves, lions, apes – through the interpretive lens that is designed to present Jews as hostile and threatening elements in Christian society. In terms of Cohen's "hermeneutic Jew" model, the figures from the *Nürnberger Prosa Äsop* most closely resemble the Jews as conceived of by Isidore of Seville and Guibert of Nogent, neither of whom saw any place for Jews at all in a properly ordered Christian polity.[31] Commenting on the general tendency in medieval allegorical literature to associate Jews with unpleasant or even monstrous beasts, Moshe Lazar writes:

The mythicization and diabolization of the Jews led consequently to their dehumanization. They now become [author's italics] serpents, vipers, aspics, basiliscs, goats, pigs, ravens, vultures, bats, scorpions, dogs, cormorants, hyenas, jackals, vermine, to name only a few among the most frequent zoological qualifiers, to which are added the mytho-zoological ones according to the talent and fertile imagination of the individual theologians and artists.[32]

Canine imagery seems to have been particularly common, as it appears in the Latin allegorical interpretation of "de lupo et agno" seen above, its vernacular counterpart in the *Nürnberger Prosa Äsop*, in Easter plays, and in Hans Folz's *Spil von den herzogen von Burgund*, as noted in previous chapters. As we shall see below, this particular anti-Jewish motif, however ubiquitous, evoked sceptical rejection from one popular medieval moralist.

It is also worth noting that the Latin prose commentaries that gave us these anti-Jewish epimyths were themselves high- and late-medieval innovations, and are not represented in the earlier tradition of Latin fable transmission.[33] The Latin text of the *Avianus* fable "de simia" common to Ellis's manuscripts and the Leyden Avianus manuscript concludes as follows:

> Tunc brevis informem traheret cum simia natum,
> Ipsum etiam in risum copulit ire Iouem.
> Hanc tamen ante alios rupit turpissima uocem,
> Dum generis crimen sic abolere cupit.[34]

The six manuscripts used by McKenzie and Oldfather in their edition of the *Ysopet-Avionnet*, by way of contrast, do contain brief verse commentaries in their Latin texts. Just as the Leyden Avianus manuscript and the texts used in Ellis's edition, though, the Latin verse texts lack the anti-Jewish interpretation of this fable:

> De Iove et Simia
> Moralitas
> Nolo uelis rerum quicquam laudare tuarum,
> Ni sint alterius ore probata prius.
> Sic mos est hominum quicquam sibi fecerit ipse,
> Vile licet maneat, approbat ipse tamen.
> Addicio
> Laus falerat nimis proprio sordescit in ore;
> Incitat in risum laus falerata sibi.[35]

162

Similarly, the version of Avian #10, "de calvo equite," common to the manuscripts used by Ellis and the Leyden manuscript concludes:

Ille sagax, tantis quod risus milibus esset,
Distulit ammota callidate iocum,
"Quid mirum," referens, "positos fugisse capillos,
Quem prius aequaeuae deseruere comae?"[36]

The manuscripts represented in the McKenzie/Oldfather edition contain the following verse interpretation:

De Milite Calvo Paupere
Moralitas
    Ridiculo cuiquam cum sis absoluere temet
    Opposita ueri cum ratione stude.
Addicio
    Fuscata ceruice stude ne preuitearis;
    Crine capillata calue secunda patent.[37]

We have here two texts of the same two fables: an uncommented one in prose and one in verse with a brief verse commentary. Each of these two versions was transmitted in manuscripts that existed alongside those of the fable texts that contained the anti-Jewish prose commentaries cited above.

From the examination of these texts, the group used in the Ellis edition, the Leyden manuscript, and the texts used in the McKenzie/ Oldfather edition, it is clear that the medieval fabulist working in Latin was not compelled to include interpretive commentaries of any kind, much less the specifically anti-Jewish commentaries seen above. Though the practice of including prose commentaries as both translation aids and hermeneutic guides to the fables did become commonplace for both the *Avianus* and the *Anonymous Neveleti* fable collections, there was no compulsion to include any specific commentary at all, and therefore, no attempt to turn the fable collections into systematic treatises on dogma.[38] Commenting on the treatment of Jews in the *Anonymous* in particular, A. E. Wright remarks:

In the commentaries on the fables listed above, the merest narrative parallel, the slightest verbal suggestions are enough to call forth a diatribe *contra Iudeos*; surely, had it been the commentators' principal intention to inculcate such ideas on their schoolboy readers, they would have had no difficulty in finding similar parallels and suggestions in other places as well, making every treacherous wolf, every silly toad, every boastful mosquito a Jew. No such effort can be observed in any of the fable commentaries preserved from the late Middle Ages; the anti-Semitism of the commentaries is, as so much medieval anti-Semitism, breathtakingly matter-of-fact, a convenient material for exposition, and not its purpose.[39]

As noted in the first chapter, the application of the term "anti-Semitism" to medieval culture is problematic. Nevertheless, Wright's conclusions about the depiction of Jews in fabular epimyths are sound. When convenient, fables were adapted to support conceptions of the Jew that were formulated in interpretive frameworks that surrounded the fable tradition, existing independently of it. It cannot be said that fable literature developed its own theologically determined conceptions of the Jew, in the way that hagiographic literature or religious dramas did. Christian theology's ambivalent and conflicted attempts to explain Jewish unbelief were superimposed on the originally pagan fables in a way that was wholly unnecessary in these other literary forms. The Greco-Roman fable, itself a tool used to teach interpretation, became the object of interpretation and integration into a larger, Christian symbol system.

The question that arises when we turn our attention to the vernacular fable tradition is this: How common was it for vernacular fabulists to recapitulate the anti-Jewish material of the Latin models? That is to say, if there was no systematic effort to use fables as vehicles for anti-Jewish thought, was there any systematic attempt to preserve the anti-Jewish thought present in the Latin sources when fables were rendered in the vernacular? As the five texts treated above make abundantly clear, the fabulist who compiled the *Nürnberger Prosa Äsop* recapitulated the anti-Jewish material from the Latin prose commentary tradition, reproducing verbatim the anti-Judaic commentaries found in Latin fable texts, specifically those of the widely disseminated *Anonymous Neveleti*. The fables of the first independent vernacular fable collection, Ulrich Boner's *Edelstein* from 1350,

provide an illuminating contrast to the Anonymous, which they predate by more than sixty years. It is to the *Edelstein* that we will now
turn our attention.

Literary scholars have long established with certainty that Boner's
sources in compiling the *Edelstein* included the *Anonymous Neveleti*,
the *Avianus*, as well as other collections of didactic stories.[40] How
Boner differed from his sources in presenting the epimyths of these
same fables indicates that the inclusion of anti-Jewish epimyths began
to fall out of favor as soon as fables began to be translated into the
vernacular. Boner's version of "de simia" concludes only with a
general moralizing point and no reference to Jews:

> wer rüemt daz nicht ze rüemen ist,
> daz mag wol sîn der affen list.
> wer rüemt, daz er nicht rüemen sol,
> der mag wol spottes werden vol.
> ein ieklîch muoter dunkt ir kint
> schœn, diu doch nicht schœn sint.[41]

The epimyth continues for several lines, ruminating on the im-
propriety of self-aggrandizement and assuring the reader that virtuous
and meritorious conduct will elicit praise from men and esteem from
God. The epimyth of "de calvo equite" or "von einem kalwen ritter,"
similarly emphasizes only the general moral point, interpreting the
loss of hair as a change in fortune and the knight's clever reply to his
mockers as the ability to cope with life's vicissitudes:

> an dirr welt ist kein stætigkeit:
> waz hiut ist liep, dast morne leit.
> er ist hiute siech, der gester waz
> gesunt. dâ von sô spricht man daz,
> daz er nicht wîse müge sîn,
> der sich lât ûf der welte schîn.
> der hêrre verlôr der hûben kleit,
> daz ist der welt unstætigkeit.[42]

From these two examples, both typical for the *Edelstein*'s treatment of
the traditional fables it includes, it is clear that Boner's only interest
in the fable was as a vehicle to convey general moral points and

conventional wisdom. The anti-Judaic commentaries do not appear anywhere in the *Edelstein*. One fable of Boner's collection does treat a Jewish figure, though, as we shall see below.

Comparing the epimyths of the *Nürnberger Prosa Äsop* with those of another vernacular fable collection, the above-mentioned late-fifteenth century *Esopus* of Heinrich Steinhöwel, provides further evidence of the existence of an interpretive fable commentary tradition in the vernacular that was free of the anti-Jewish element. The text contains Latin prose versions of the fables followed by German prose translations of the Latin, followed in turn by Latin verse retellings of the fable (that is, a German prose version sandwiched between Latin prose and Latin verse). As the following example demonstrates, the commentary in the Steinhöwel version is brief and illustrates only general moral instruction, without any moral condemnation of Jews:

> Die ander fabel von dem wolff und dem lamp
> Mit diser fabel will Esopus bezaigen, daz by bösen und untrüwen anklegern vernunft und warhait kain statt finden mag; söliche wolf fint man in allen stetten.[43]

Similarly brief and completely lacking in any reference to the Jews are the conclusions of the texts of "die erst fable von den froschen" (de ranis regem pententibus), "von der fliegen und amais" (de musca et formica), "von dem affen und synem kind" (de symea et nato), and "von vier ochsen" (de quatuor bobus):

> Die erst fabel von den fröschen
> Do gab er (Jupiter) inen (the frogs) den storken, der ward sie töten ainen nach dem andern. Do wurden sie wainend iere stimm uncz in die himel uff erheben und schreyen: O got Jupiter, kom uns ze hilf oder wir sterben all! Do sprach er zuo in: Do ir ains künigs begerten, do wolt ich nit. Do ir wider zuo mir ruofften, gab ich üch ainen senfftmütigen künig. der ward von üch verachtet und under die füß getrett, do gab ich üch umb üwer ungestümes bitten disen künig, den ir iecz habt, den müßen ir behalten, wann ir wollten den guoten nit verdulden.[44]
> Die xvii fabel von der fliegen und amais
> Die amais sprach her wider zuo der fliegen also: Wie gar bist du ain schnöder schantvogel, do du dyn ungestümikait und lästerliche getauten lobest. Sag mir, wer begert dyner zuokunft, wie würdest du von den künigen und rainen frowen, die du meldest, enpfangen, die du trüczlich wider ieren willen anflügest und sprichst, es stand dir alles ze gewalt, und sagst nit, wie ain unwerder gast du bist;

166

wa hin du komest, da vertrybt man dich, man verjagt dich ungestümlich an allen enden als ainen raiczenden fynd. Und bist allain in dem summer etwas. Ze winter zyt vergaust du on kraft, so bin ich allweg wol gemuot. Ze winter zyt bin ich sicher in myner wonung, alle zyt bin ich gesund, ich leb in fröden. Wa du dann bist, so vertrybt man dich mit gaiseln und wedeln, die mit flyß allain wider dich gemacht synt. Dise fabel ist wider die ungestümen zanner, haderer und unnücz güder von den dingen, die schentlich synt.[45]

Die xi fabel von dem affen und synem kind

Do ward der künig innerlich lachen und mit im alle mengy der mütern, und sprach zuo im: Du solt dyner ding kains loben, es sey dann vor andern berümbt und gelobet worden! Wann aigens lob is ze schelten; darum würst du iecz von menglichem verspottet und verachtet.[46]

Die xiv fabel von fier ochsen

Do aber der leo merket, daz sie gezwaiet waren und jeder allain gienge, was er jedem besonder stark und mächtig gnuog, und fraß sie alle nach einander, die er in ainikait nit getörst berüren. Als er aber an den letsten ochsen kam, der sprach ze lere aller tieren: Welher gern ain rüwigs leben füren welle, der mag lernne by unserm sterben, daz er trügenhafften worten synen auren nit licht dar sol bieten, und alte früntschafft nit ringfertiglichen vergaun laße; wann were wir in ainikait beliben, der leo hett uns nit angesigen.[47]

The allegorical interpretations embedded in each of these fables concern universal moral concepts, such as humility, concord, and fidelity as well as their opposites, arrogance, strife, and treachery. In these vernacular versions of the traditional fable material, Steinhöwel does not attempt to associate the vices with Jews, as the Latin tradition and the redactor of the *Nürnberger Prosa Äsop* had done.

Several facts of the transmission and production of these variations on the same fables are important for our consideration of the place of the fable in constructing the image of Jews in late medieval German literature. The first is that there existed parallel, divergent traditions of Latin commentary on the fables over a long period. The Latin texts listed above are drawn from manuscripts of eleventh-, twelfth-, thirteenth-, and late fourteenth-century provenance and exhibit a wide variety in their fable commentary. The Paris manuscripts of the Ellis edition contain no commentary at all, while the fable texts from Wolfenbüttel Codex Guelferbytanus 185 Helmstadensis (the fables of Walter of England) all contain extensive interpretive commentaries. The commentaries of the *Nürnberger Prosa Äsop* are nearly identical to those of the Wolfenbüttel codex in wording and therefore in their anti-Jewish content. This is unsurprising, since, as Wright has pointed out, these interpretations were, in the High and Late Middle Ages, common ones for the five fables discussed above.[48] Nevertheless, the transmission of the anti-Jewish commentary, or any extensive commentary at all, did not become an obligatory part of the transmission of either the *Avianus* or the *Anonymous Neveleti* fable corpus.

In the body of vernacular fable literature, every one of the manuscripts or manuscript groups treated so far has drawn from the same body of source material: the Latin fables of Avianus and Walther of England. In spite of their common source material, the three vernacular fable collections differ in their appended interpretations. Neither Boner's *Edelstein* nor Steinhöwel's *Esopus* contains the anti-Jewish epimyths that appear in the source text, Walter's fables, while the *Prosa Äsop* contains them. Furthermore, though the Nürnberg text was innovative in its treatment of its Latin model, it was in nearly every respect a failure and is transmitted to us in a single manuscript from 1412. A. E. Wright has noted, that though "the Viennese translator's efforts are to assign new functions to the elements retained from the Latin academic tradition" are impressive, "the Nuremberg Aesop was by no measure a success…" and, in spite of its innovative nature as "the first prose fable collection in German," it clearly "appears to have had no influence on the further development of the genre…."[49]

The *Nürnberger Prosa Äsop* failed, at least in part, because it merely recapitulated extant Latin interpretations of its fables and in no way adapted them to a new audience, either as grammatically or morally didactic works. This being the case, it was just as well for the medieval schoolmaster or pupil to refer to the Latin texts of the fables, which were abundantly available. In contrast, Steinhöwel's collection of fables offered only limited and general didactic epimyths, departing substantially from its Latin source material. It soon became one of the most successful printed books in the early modern period, enjoying seven Latin and 31 German printings between the late fifteenth and early sixteenth centuries.[50] If the frequency of a text's reproduction is any index of its popularity, then it is clear that in late medieval Germany, the preferred vernacular fable translation of the Aesopic fables was one that omitted the anti-Jewish elements.

An earlier, specifically late fourteenth-century, version of the fable of the wolf and the lamb from a Middle Low German fable collection also provides a strong contrast with both the Latin version above and that in the Nürnberg text. In place of the anti-Jewish interpretation of the *Nürnberger Prosa Äsop*, the Middle Low German version of the fable has an epimyth that uses the wolves to represent the wealthy and powerful members of society who inflict injustice on those socially inferior to them. The Middle Low German version of "Wolf und Lamm" (Wolfenbüttel Hs. 997 Nov), which dates from around 1370, is attributed to Gerhard von Minden:

> De unschuldige nicht neten enmach
> siner unschult, men nacht und dach
> de weldige boslik darna ringet
> wo dat he en tom dode bringet.[51]

A similar epimyth appears in Martin Luther's sixteenth-century version, with the moral of the fable relating to the suffering of the just in an unjust world, writing, "Der welt lauff ist, wer Frum sein wil, der mus leiden … Denn Gewalt gehet fur Recht … Wenn der Wolf wil so ist das Lamb unrecht."[52]

In their respective interpretations of this fable, both von Minden and Luther, writing almost 300 years apart, emphatically criticize the abuse of power in social hierarchies, following a traditional use of the fable dating back to Antiquity.[53] In the same Middle Low German collection mentioned above (Gerhard von Minden's fables), the fable of the ape and her child is also free of an anti-Jewish epimyth, as is the fable of the four oxen. Gerhard's version of the fable of the frogs and their king also comments on the relationship of the powerful to the powerless, though its epimyth is of an admonitory rather than a cynical character, and is directed at the powerful:

> Sachmödich unde vredesam
> sal sin en here lovesam:
> sin volk sal dem billik hören,
> so endarf se gin tiranne schören.[54]

Of the fables heretofore mentioned, only this one, "Die Fröschen bitten um einen König," or "Von dem Storch und den Froschen," contains, in vernacular versions either indirectly dependent on or wholly independent of the *Anonymous*, an epimyth relating to Jews. The sixteenth-century version by Hans Sachs, derived from the *Anonymous*, contains references to the Bible's account of Israel being punished by God through an unjust king as a response to their having rejected the rulership of God. However, the *Nürnberger Prosa Äsop*, derived from the *Anonymous*, emphasizes the ingratitude of Israel and the resulting inevitable punishment in a way in which the later version does not.[55] Further, Sachs's version of the fable makes it clear that the impulse at work is a general one and that there is no moral difference between the Jews of ancient Israel (the frogs in the fable) and the Christians of contemporary Europe:

> Wan wie ain volck lebt diese zeit,
> so schickt in got auch obrigkeit.
> Wo es mit sünden is behaft,
> so wird es den von got bestraft
> mit tiranischer obrigkeit,
> wie Ysrahel des zeugnis geit,
> die almal pos obrigkait hetten
> wen sie sich von got wenden thetten.[56]

From the above examination of the Latin and vernacular fable collections a number of things have become clear: The first is that there existed parallel, independent traditions of interpretation within the body of fable literature in a period spanning more than 200 years; the second that there was not a compulsory, anti-Jewish orthodoxy at work. In the Latin verse fable tradition, interpretive epimyths are not extensive and do not contain anti-Jewish elements. The Latin tradition of prose fable commentary that derives from Walter of England's compilation transmits five fables having pointedly anti-Jewish epimyths. However, three widely disseminated vernacular collections that derive from this same Latin fable compilation omit these anti-Jewish epimyths. Neither Gerhard von Minden's, nor Boner's, nor Steinhöwel's fable collection relates these anti-Jewish epimyths. The *Nürnberger Prosa Äsop*'s epimyths, nearly identical to those of the

170

Anonymous, are, for the vernacular fable, an anomaly. This anomaly will seem more striking when we consider it in light of the inclusion of another fable from the Latin tradition in Boner's *Edelstein* and its exclusion from the *Nürnberger Prosa Äsop*, a fable that depicts a Jew in a positive, even sympathetic light. The fable in question is known in Latin as *de Iudeo et pincerna*.

De Iudaeo et pincerna is attested in a variety of fable collections, including both the French and Latin verse fables of the *Ysopet Avionnet* and the internationally disseminated fables attributed to Walter of England. The plot of the tale is this: a Jew requests from a king safe conduct through a forest known to be dangerous. The king gives the Jew his own royal cupbearer to serve as a bodyguard on the journey through the forest. Once he is alone on the road with the Jew, the treacherous cupbearer decides to murder the Jew and take his money. The Jew warns the cupbearer that the crime will be found out, saying that a bird flying by at the time of the murder will bring it to light. The cupbearer murders the Jew anyway, only to betray himself by laughing in the presence of the king when he later sees the same bird fly past a window in the palace. The version of the fable common to the London, Paris, and Brussels manuscripts – all of them fourteenth-century and edited by McKenzie and Oldfather – contains the following exchange between the Jew and the cupbearer prior to the murder:

Silua patet, subeunt, Iudeus in ore sequentis
Cor notat, "Ipse sequor," inquit, "obito."
Ille refert: "Scelus hoc ista loquetur auis."
Prosilit a dumo perdix, hanc indice signat;
Alter ait: "Scelus hoc ista loquetur auis?"[57]

Appended to the fable is a brief commentary that lacks any interpretive reference to Jews:

Moralitas
    Vt perimas quemquam, nullum tibi suadeat aurum,
    Nam decus et uitam mesta rapina rapit.
Addicio
    Percipet funus letale uorax gladiator;
    Qui ferit ense minus prouidus, ense perit.

Sanguinus effusor humani sanguine pallet;
Interfectori sanguinis unda fluit.[58]

The moral point illustrated here is, as the expression goes, "murder will out." The innocence of the Jew and the moral perfidy of the cupbearer are evident in the tale, but are given no amplification or generalized allegorical significance.

The simple commentary attached to the Latin verse version of the fable text as it appears in the *Avionnet* manuscripts contrasts to that found in the fables of Walter (fable LIX) and with Ulrich Boner's reworking of Walter's text (*Edelstein*, LXI). In the Latin prose commentary on the version of the fable in Codex Guelferbytanus 185 Helmstadiensis, we read:

> Moraliter: Per Iudeum intellige fidelem animam, que timens accusationem huius seculi, vadit ad regem, id est Deum, petens ab eo conductorem. Deus autem dat ei pincernam, id est corpus inclinatum ad delectaciones, quod interfecit animam auferendo sibi diuicias magnas. Tandem autem in cena, id est in die iudicii, perdices, id est peccata, accusabunt corpus, et tunc rex dampnat corpus cruci, id est eterno supplicio.[59]

In contrast to the anti-Jewish sentiments expressed in other fables of the same collection, the emphasis in this tale is on the innocence and trustworthiness of the Jew, who is an allegorical figure of the faithful soul. The treachery and greed of his Christian companion, however, marks him as an allegorical figure of the sinful flesh.

Similarly, the emphasis in the version of the tale in Boner's *Edelstein* is on the guilt of the Christian and the innocence of the Jew, as the following passages make clear. The first is Boner's depiction of the murder itself:

> der jude troug unmaze
> vil goldes uf der selben vart.
> der schenke des wol inne wart
> in sinem muot er sere vacht
> (wan stunt und stat vil dieben macht),
> wier dem juden taet den tot.
> er gedacht: "du kunst uz aller not,
> wirt dir daz golt. wer wil ez sagen
> oder wer mag uf dich denne klagen?

172

du bist allein: hab guoten muot!
umb disez mort dir nieman tuot."
do der jude daz ersach,
vil tief er siufzet unde sprach:
"ich zwivel nicht, und weiz ez wol,
daz disez mort got offnen sol.
e daz ez würd verswigen gar,
die vogel machentz offenbar,
die hier vliegent, samer got!"[60]

The second passage comes from the conclusion of the tale:

"Sag an schenk, was meinestu
daz du hast gelachet nu
do du an saehe das rephuon?"
Er sprach, "Herre, daz wil ich tuon,"
und seit im, wie er hat getan
dem Juden, mit dem er solte gan
und geleit'n durch den walt,
da sin untriuw was manigvalt.
Also ward offenbar das mort
dem kunge. Daz tet sin selbes wort
der das mort ouch hat getan.
Des muost er an den galgen gan.
Haet er daz rephuon nicht gesehen
des mordes haet er nicht verjehen.
Er wart erhangen, daz was wol!
Der guote man nieman morden sol.[61]

The emphasis on the Jew's piety – his calling out the divine name twice, once in an oath, and thereby making a posthumously successful appeal to divine justice – also contributes to the tale's sympathetic portrayal of the Jew.[62] Here the Jew is not a threat to the Christian faith or the social order, but an honest man unjustly murdered. The revelation of his murder at the hands of the cupbearer is to be understood, in the context of the tale, as an act of divine retribution: God himself avenges the murdered Jew by sending a pheasant past the king's window at precisely the right moment to trigger the cupbearer's confession. The guilt for the moral and social transgressions lies solely with the Christian cupbearer. His execution is lauded as a good thing, his action, the murder of a Jew, condemned as one that no good man would perform. Boner's *Edelstein*, it should be noted, became the standard vernacular collection of the Aesopic corpus for the fourteenth and fifteenth centuries, until it was replaced by Steinhöwel's *Esopus* in the late 1470's.[63]

The presence of anti-Jewish hostility in the body of late medieval German-language fable literature seems to have been limited, in spite of the prevalence of such hostility in the prose commentaries of the Latin fable collections from which the vernacular collections derived. So far, however, we have been dealing with fable literature in a strictly defined sense and have not been considering related genres of morally didactic short narrative and the prevalence of anti-Jewish attitudes there. Above, the comparison of different Latin and vernacular versions of Aesopic fables showed that there was no single interpretation of a given fable common to all collections, but rather a variety of interpretations in the Latin and vernacular fable commentaries.

Similarly, a comparison of versions of the "Ringparabel"[64] found in a Latin version of the *Gesta Romanorum*, an Early New High German version of the *Gesta Romanorum,* and the Early New High German translation of the *Decameron* that was once attributed to Heinrich Steinhöwel shows profound differences. Common to all three versions is the conundrum of a nobleman: he has three sons whom he loves equally, but only one ring that he can give, signifying both his love and the son's legitimacy as heir. In all versions, the nobleman solves the conundrum by having two additional rings fashioned, each modeled so exactly after the original that the copies cannot be identified. The nobleman then gives each of the sons a ring without telling any of them which is the original, though each of the sons believes himself to possess the original, and therefore the legitimate claim to the father's authority. The epimyths of the three versions follow. First, that of the Latin *Gesta Romanorum*:

Carissimi, miles est dominus noster Ihesus Christus, qui tres filios habebat, scilicet Iudaeos, Saracenos, et Christianos. Iudeis dedit terram promissionis, Saracenis dedit thesaurum hujus mundi quantum ad potencias et divicias, Christianis dedit annulum preciosum, scilicet fidem, quia per fidem Christiani possunt varias infirmitates ac languores anime curare, sicut scriptum est: Omnia possibilia est sunt credenti. Item: Si habueritis fidem, sicut granus sinapus, etc. Item: Impossibile est sine fide placere deo.[65]

Second, that of the German *Gesta Romanourm:*

> Nu peid drein suenen verste wir dreue volkh die gotez sun sint mit der geschöpfd. Daz sint Juden, Sarraten und Christen. Ez ist aber offenbar, welhen sun er lieber hat gehabt. Dem selben gab er daz pesser vingerl, daz die plinten erlaeucht, siechtum hailt, und die toten erchukcht. Aber pei den ungelaubhaftigen sind nicht Soeliche zaichen noch tugent.[66]

Finally, the interpretation of the "Ringparabel" from the Early New High German translation of Boccaccio's *Decameron* that was once attributed to Steinhöwel:

> Der dryer gezecz halben die den dreyen geschlechten von got gegeben wurden, dez iglich geschlechte das sein für das peste und gerechtest helt und gelaubt. Aber welches unter den dreyen das gerechtest sey beleybt hangen als der ring beleybt. Dann alleine das got wissent ist.[67]

In the first version of the "Ringparabel," it is the presence of signs and of "tugent" which is interpreted as the sure proof of the true faith, with the implication being that those false faiths are lacking in both signs and power. In the first and second version of the parable, both Jews and Moslems are depicted as less favored creations of God, either "filios" of Jesus or "gotez sun ... mit der geschöpfd." In the third version, the question of relative worth in God's sight and even the question of redemptive power of the three religions is left unresolved. It is noteworthy that even the older of the two does not demonize or vilify the adherents of the other religions, and the latter version by Boccaccio places the three religions and their adherents on the same moral and metaphysical level. The image of Jews (and Moslems) in both versions of this parable is at worst, neutral, and at best positive – seeing them as moral equals of Christians.

Tales that depict Jews in a positive light at the expense of Christians are not unheard of in the collections of fables and related moralizing stories. Returning for a moment to pseudo-Steinhöwel's translation of the *Decameron,* we see in one of the earliest stories – "Wie Abraham der Iude durch freunttschafft und rate Gianotto

kaufman von Parisy, wie wol er der Cristen herren pöse werck vnd
übel gesehen het zuo einem guoten Kristen ward" ("How Abraham
the Jew through the friendship and advice of Gianotto the merchant of
Paris, how indeed he saw the evil deeds and wicked works of the
Christian lords and became a good Christian") – a Jewish figure, the
merchant Abraham, described only in positive terms. He is referred to
as "ein gerecht guot kaufman in seinem iudischen gelauben," "des
güte und gerechtigkeit von Gianotto erkant was," and as "der guot
Iude."[68]

The plot of the story is relatively simple: Abraham's Christian
friend, Gianotto, tries to convince him to convert to Christianity. After
much discussion, Abraham proposes that he undertake a trip to Rome,
the heart of the Church, in order to see what Christianity is really
about. Gianotto tries to convince him not to make the trip, telling
Abraham that what he would see in Rome would be corruption and
licentiousness, not the true Christian faith, and that this would most
certainly convince him not to convert. Abaham makes the trip
anyway, leaving Gianotto to despair of his friend's ever converting.
When Abraham returns, he has converted, and explains to Gianotto
that if true Christianity cannot be destroyed by the corruption and
depravity that he saw in Rome, he is convinced that it must be true
and of God, as he replies to Gianotto:

> Dem der Iude palde antwürt vnd sprach: Lieber Gianotto mich bedünket nichtz
> guotz weder irer wort noch werke got geb in iren lone als vil ir ist, vnd sage dir in
> der warheit do ist weder andacht noch heiligkeit noch keinn guot werck noch
> züchtig leben wol vnkeusch, geitikeit, fraßheit do pey ale vnmessige füllerey,
> neyde haß vnd hoffart … und nach allem meinem bedunken mir nicht anders
> erscheint dann wie sie mit ganczem vleisse suchen den christlichen gelauben zuo
> der erden zewerffen; wo sie des beschirmer und merer sein sölten. Doch wol
> erkenne das sie suchen gen nicht geschehen sol Sunder mer dann ye kristenlicher
> gelaube sich meren vnd stercken sol; Darum für war gelaube got der vater sun vnd
> heiliger geiste kristenlichen gelauben ein gruntfeste vnd auffhalter sein, vmb des
> willen wo ich biß in meinem gelauben herte gestandenn pin vnd mich zuo kristen-
> lichem gelauben han keren wöllen, Nun ich dir gancz zuo sag ein Kriste vnd nicht
> mer ein Iude ze sein....[69]

The object of ridicule and scorn is not the Jew but the entire hierarchy
of the Christian Church. The religious outsider is held up, as in "de

176

iudeo et pincerna," as the righteous figure, the Christian establishment as corrupt and hypocritical. As was the case with Joseph in the Saint Basil legend (see Ch. 6), an emphasis on Abraham's righteousness precedes his conversion, revealing both a willingness to see Jews as morally good persons in their own faith and yet also a commitment to the soterific necessity of Christian belief.

The morally didactic anti-clerical satire of Boccaccio's stories was part of a tradition of anti-clerical satire and was anticipated by the major work of the German schoolmaster, moralist, and satirist, Hugo von Trimberg, who lived and wrote from the late thirteenth to the early fourteenth century. His year of birth is uncertain, appearing on the basis of textual clues and a few official records to have been in the 1230s or 1240s. The year of his death was, by coincidence, the year of Boccaccio's birth, 1313, or soon thereafter.[70] His major work, *Der Renner*, is a collection of fables, short moral admonitions, anti-clerical satires, and lengthier meditations on moral topics. It is also one of the best-attested German texts of the Middle Ages, with 64 complete or partial manuscripts, along with anthologized excerpts and whole or partial print versions extant from the late medieval and early modern period.[71]

Boccaccio and Hugo von Trimberg are best understood as compilers and redactors, more than authors in the modern sense, as they both drew the bulk of their works from earlier sources. The fables of *Der Renner*, for example, derive largely from the *Avianus* and *Anonymous Neveleti* corpora, though none of the fables discussed above are among those that Hugo includes in his collection.[72] Unlike Boccaccio, though, Hugo records his own thoughts and reflections concerning both his sources and the general moral topics they deal with, often directly addressing the reader. Of particular relevance for the study at hand is the fact that the best-known works of both men, Boccaccio's *Decameron* and Hugo's *Der Renner*, contain complex images of Jews and depict Jews not as Christ-and-Christian-hating, but as persons who are in their Jewish faith morally superior to hypocritical Christians. This we see in a brief passage from *Der Renner:*

Tuch, des vadem nie ward gespunnen
des varwe nie quam an sunnen

wirt nu verkauft von boesen kristen
die mit verfluchten boesen listen
gut gewinnet wirs, denn die iuden
die wir doch heizzen des teufels ruden....[73] (4921–6)

Here it is the dishonesty of Christians, who hypocritically deride the Jews as "the devil's dogs," that is held up for moral condemnation. In addressing this hypocrisy, Hugo turns two common anti-Jewish motifs, the association of Jews with dogs – here understood as symbols for moral corruption – and with ill-gotten financial gain, on their heads. By so inverting these anti-Jewish characterizations, he openly challenges their validity. In a later passage, he places Jews, heathens, and Christians on the same level of moral worth when he paraphrases Freidank:

Got hat dreirlaye kint,
die Juden, cristen, heiden sint,
das vierd geschuft des teufels list
daz drit dreir maister ist,
daz ist wucher genant,
und raubet leut un auch die lant.[74] (5231–6)

As in the *Gesta Romanorum* and the *Decameron*, the triad Jews, heathens, and Christians is identified as "gotez kint," each of which is exploited by its "maister," the vice of usury. Hugo flatly contradicts the stereotype that the Jews are uniquely prey to this vice, instead labeling the vice itself as an oppressive progeny of the Devil that preys on all mankind.

Hugo also sees the teachings of both Jews and heathens as potential sources of wisdom:

Juden lere und weiser heiden
hant uns dinge vil bescheiden,
die gar nuetze unde gut uns sint,
an mangen stat sint sie doch plint,
die sie gar tief hant gesuchet
und die nu wenik iemant geruchet.
Plato und Aristotiles,
Seneca und Socrates,

Demostines und Dyogenes,
Tullis, Empedocles,
vnd ander alten meister vil,
Der ich hie niht nennen wil.[75] (8507–18)

Though he acknowledges the usefulness and the wisdom of ancient Greco-Roman philosophers, he goes on to warn against preferring their study to that of Holy Scripture, referring to an episode from the life of Saint Jerome, in which he was castigated by God for just such an error.[76] He also refers to them as being "an mangen stat ... plint," that is, spiritually blind to the truth revealed in Christ. Herein Hugo follows the branch of Christian thought represented by Augustine, Eugippus, Hrabanus Maurus, and Hugh of St. Victor, among others, who see wisdom also in the writings of pre-and-non-Christians and commend their study and use by Christians, within certain hermeneutical bounds.[77] Commenting on this, Erich Seemann wrote:

> Hugos Ansicht ist demnach, dass auch die heidnischen Schriftsteller uns mancherlei Nützliches bringen, das wir ungescheut verwenden sollen, und dieser Nutzen bietet ihm den Massstab für die Beurteilung ihrer Brauchbarkeit. Hugos Urteil deckt sich somit auch in diesem Punkt mit den oben angeführten Kirchenvätern, seine Stellung zur heidnischen Literatur dürfte also ebenfalls von geistlicher Seite beeinflusst sein ... damit entfernt er sich von einer einseitigen und fanatischen Verurteilung der nichtchristlichen Autoren....[78]

Hugo's treatment of Jews and heathens in these three brief passages, then, expresses his own, accepting attitude toward non-Christian thought, seen also in the high esteem in which he holds authors such as Plato, Aristotle, Demosthenes, and Diogenes. Hugo was above all a moralist, who esteemed highly works he deemed of morally didactic value, regardless of the religious convictions of the author. Contrast the words concerning "juden lere und wîser heiden" with his judgment of certain works of the medieval German epic and courtly romance traditions. Hugo gives high praise to the works of Heinrich von Morungen, Walter von der Vogelweide, and Konrad von Würzburg, but derides *Iwein, Tristan, König Rother, Parzifal*, and *Wigalois*, saying of them that "lützzel nützes darinne swebe" ("little that is useful floats therein") and "swer der gelaubt, der ist unwîs" ("whoever believes in them, he is unwise").[79]

In its ambivalence and breadth of variation, the depiction of Jews in the fable and related genres can be said to parallel in large degree the conflicting sentiments in society as a whole. A large body of fable literature with a long attestation history contained pointedly anti-Jewish epimyths. Those epimyths appear in the Latin fables of the *Anonymous Neveleti* and the vernacular fables of the *Nürnberger Prosa Äsop*. There existed throughout the High and Late Middle Ages a widely distributed body of fable literature that was free of appended anti-Jewish epimyths, represented by a wide group of texts: the fables of the *Ysopet Avionnet*, those attributed to Gerhard von Minden, the popular and widely disseminated collection of Boner in the fourteenth century, and Steinhöwel's hugely successful fifteenth-century *Esopus*. If the fable were a repository for public sentiments, one would expect that any steady increase of intolerance toward Jews would be mirrored in the fable corpus. On the other side of the equation, it is well established that fables were meant to shape the opinions and attitudes of the grammar students who used them. The medieval schoolmasters were, judging by the content of text compilations used in medieval schools up to and including the universities, particularly concerned with the morally didactic content of the works they presented to their students:

These compilations show a remarkable similarity in the choice and treatment of material; equally remarkable is the freedom with which they were later modified to meet the tastes of successive generations. Proverb and fable were the universal favorites for inclusion, the former in the abstract and the latter in more concrete story form, satisfying the medieval demand for the ethical and didactic in elementary instruction. Cato and Avianus and similar works had the practical advantage also of being brief, composed of units short enough to be copied on the wax tablets of two lessons and easily memorized, besides serving as satisfactory models of the two types of versification always most popular among those who wrote Latin at all, the hexameter (Cato) and the elegiac distich (Avianus). Also characteristically pagan theology, mythology, and religious usage almost never appear in these particular works, and the moral tone is for the most part quite unexceptionable, at least in comparison with most works of the ancients.[80]

One would expect that if there were any programmatic attempt to increase anti-Jewish feeling using morally didactic texts such as fables, that it would manifest itself in the texts here studied. The fact of the matter is that no such attempt is discernible, with the deliberate omission of the common anti-Jewish epimyths in late medieval vernacular fable collections suggesting a trend in the opposite direction.

The characterizations of Jews in the body of fable literature and related morally didactic literature cover an entire spectrum of attitudes, from rejection and scorn to admiration. Furthermore, the wide variation in the characterization of Jews is present in morally didactic literature throughout the High and Late Middle Ages. Walter's epimyths for "de lupo et agno" and "de iudeo et pincerna" appeared within pages of each other in scores of manuscripts for over three hundred years. In the former, the Jew is a ravening wolf; in the latter, he is a symbol of piety and innocence. If anything, the evidence speaks for a decrease in the frequency with which anti-Jewish sentiments appear in fable collections as the Middle Ages wear on and vernacular fable collections become more common, with Boner and Steinhöwel omitting in their respective German fable collections the anti-Jewish epimyths that had been common to the very texts that served as their sources.

Likewise, the ambivalent, often positive representations of Jews found in many of the fable collections apparently had no ameliorative effect on the attitudes of the public, as the increased intensity and frequency of anti-Jewish violence in the late medieval and early modern period makes plain. As Hsia pointed out in his discussion of the blood libel (see Ch. 1), it is the fifteenth and sixteenth centuries, not the Early or High Middle Ages, that see the highest incidence of ritual murder trials.[81] The fable seems neither to have been influenced by any change in widespread beliefs about Jews nor to have exerted any influence of its own in promoting or hindering the growth of either positive or negative attitudes toward Jews through moral teaching. Fables were commonly put to pedagogical use throughout the Middle Ages, used in teaching the arts of grammar, interpretation, and proper mores.[82] Here we must again note that "proper mores" did not always completely correspond to "dogmatic orthodoxy."[83] The available evidence suggests that the vernacular fable exerted not a strongly prescriptive but a strongly descriptive function with regard to popular Christian European attitudes toward Jews, accurately reflecting public attitudes but not even attempting to shape them to fit a moral or theological ideal. The views held by the overwhelmingly Christian populace toward their Jewish neighbors seem to have been every bit as ambivalent as those that are attested in the fable corpus. If this is an accurate assessment of the situation, then the outbreaks of anti-Jewish violence in the late Middle Ages and early modern period must be attributed to the actions of small but influential political groups rather than to an over-arching anti-Jewish ideology.

Chapter Eight: Conclusion

In a passage titled "The beautiful Gloss," Robert Lerner observes the following about thirteenth-century Franciscan reception of the philo-Judaic prophetic writings of Joachim de Fiore:

> Around 1283, a century after Joachim had come to his central prophetic insights, the Franciscan chronicler Salimbene of Parma observed that an exposition by the Abbot on the conversion of the Jews was "most beautiful and full of truth." Salimbene was referring to Joachim's exposition of a passage in Luke: "And it came to pass that after three days they found him in the temple" (Luke 2:46). Turning to the source we find that Joachim read the incident of the twelve-year-old Christ among the doctors as a sustained prediction of the mercy to be granted to the Jews in the future.... And the family's ultimate return to Nazareth stood for the Jews' future flourishing in the era of the Holy Spirit.
>
> How was it that a Franciscan, late in the thirteenth century, a time of mounting intolerance of Jews throughout Western Europe, could view such a confidently irenic portrayal of imminent union between Jews and Christians as "most beautiful and full of truth"?[1]

The answer to Lerner's question is supplied by his own choice of subject matter. His monograph deals with one strand of Christian thought that was current thoughout the Middle Ages, a strand in which Jews were recognized as God-seeking people wholly loved by God rather than enemies of God and truth. It is certainly true that the predominant movement from the thirteenth century onward is toward less toleration of Jews; it is also true that the movement is neither smooth nor free from opposition. Arguments derived from Christian theology drove the growth of intolerance in many instances, but they drove also the opposition to intolerance in others. Evidence of this can be seen in Bernard of Clairvaux successfully stopping pogroms during the second Crusade, the long flourishing of the Jews in Christian Vienna prior to the horrors of the early fifteenth century, and the suppression of the Rintfleisch and Armleder pogroms. Though the irenic strand of Christian thought did not predominate in the Middle Ages, it did not vanish or remain completely ineffectual, either. Any account of Christian medieval thinking concerning the Jews is therefore incomplete if it neglects the thought of Joachim, his Franciscan successors, and Christians who shared their more irenic vision for the future of the Jews.

In examining the depictions of Jews in religious drama, hagiographic literature, and morally didactic literature from late medieval German-speaking Europe, it has become clear that generalizations about "the image of Jews in medieval German literature" are, at best, ill-founded. Though it is true that literary treatment of Jewish figures tended to be unfavorable, it is not accurate to assert, as some scholars have, that the unfavorable treatments of Jewish figures were the only ones present in the culture. In the particular case of morally didactic literature, we find in the fable and related genres from the late thirteenth to early sixteenth centuries anything but a one-sidedly hostile treatment of Jews. Instead, we find in both the Latin fable tradition and in the vernacular tradition from which it derives, coexisting and competing visions of the moral character of Jews and their place in Christian Europe. The third of the questions posed at the beginning of the previous chapter – whether the thoughts of those who read or repeated these fables shaped the fables or were shaped by them – is complicated by this lack of a uniform view. In the same fable collection, mere leaves apart in a manuscript, Jews were denigrated as arrogant and foolish ("de simia" / "von der Äffin") and held up as figures allegorically representing the soul faithful to God ("de Iudeo et pincerna" / "von einem Juden und einem Schenken"). The absence of a consistency in the literary treatment of Jews in fables may, as A. E. Wright's comments on the use of fables indicate, owe much to the purposes served by these texts: their primary use was in the teaching of interpretation and moral living in the world, not in the systematic explication of abstract theological propositions. The fact is that the most popular and influential vernacular translations of the fable corpus – those of Gerhard von Minden, Ulrich Boner, and Heinrich Steinhöwel – did not contain the anti-Jewish epimyths. Such epimyths were common to the Latin fable tradition and the vernacular prose of the *Nürnberger Prosa Äsop*, a text that remained uninfluential, perhaps even unread, in the Middle Ages. These two conditions

184

suggest that expressions of anti-Jewish hostility were nothing like a *sine qua non* for the didactic fable and fable commentary.

In the broader world of morally didactic texts, the image of Jews was significantly less ambivalent: it tended to be positive, within limits. Hugo von Trimberg could see the Jews as sources of wisdom and as victims, not perpetrators, of the sin of usury. He could not, however, ascribe soterific efficacy to Rabbinic Judaism without raising irreconcilable theological conflicts concerning the Messiahship of Jesus, hence his reference to their being "an mangen stat … plint." The same is true of the unknown composer of the "Ringparabel". Though its medieval attestations vary somewhat in their depiction of Jews, the differing versions of the "Ringparabel" are consistent in presenting Jews as "filios dei," with the question of their eternal destinies left open in Boccaccio's version. In his "Abraham and Gianotto," Boccaccio presents the Jewish businessman as a righteous figure, over and against a corrupt Christian ecclesiastical hierarchy. The morally didactic effect of the *Decameron*'s social commentary may be debatable, but the content of the tale and its (theo)logical implications are not. Also beyond debate is the fact that these texts and with them their ideas found ready reception in late medieval German-speaking Europe.

The situation in fables and related literature contrasts with the developments seen in the Passion and Easter plays in the same period. While the Passion and Easter plays do not follow a gradual telos of "worsening" depictions of Jews, as has been argued in the past, it is clear that the plays that depart most markedly from their New Testament sources are also – and not coincidentally – the most vehemently hostile and crude in their treatment of Jews. It is the degree of reliance on the biblical text, and not the date of a given Passion or Easter play along a given timeline, that proves the strongest index of the play's tendency to vilify or denigrate Jews, the former demonstrating an inverse correlation with the latter. Furthermore, it is a fallacy to assert that all dramatizations of Jewish rejections of the Christian message were, by their very nature, constructed to incite anti-Jewish hostility. Some such dramatizations were, in point of fact, accurate and even restrained in their representation of medieval Jewish theology vis-à-vis Chrisitanity. Others, of course, were not, and instead indulged in mockery of the Jewish religion and the Jews themselves.

That theological emphasis and gravity were themselves, however, no complete proof against the inclination to denigrate Jews, is clear from the various medieval versions of the Silvester legend. The core of the Silvester legend, the learned disputation between Jew and Christian, receives varied treatments even from the same author. The contrast between the vile mockery characteristic of Hans Folz's treatment of Jews in *Ein Spil von dem Herzogen von Burgund* and the generally more elevated tone in *Die alt und die neu ee* illustrates the degree of variation possible. A comparison between the thirteenth-century treatment of the legend by Konrad von Würzburg and all of Folz's various re-workings of the legend is still more illustrative of the breadth of variation in the literary depiction of the Jewish–Christian theological controversy in the Middle Ages. Konrad expends considerable effort in his *Silvester* to emphasize the rationality of the Jewish figures and their desire to know truth. Theological considerations clearly played a determinative role in the subject matter, but little role in the way that the subject matter was developed.

Likewise, the medieval versions of the Theophilus legend reveal varied ways of thinking about Jews. The account of Paul the Deacon, the Theophilus drama by Hroswitha von Gandersheim, and numerous other medieval attestations of the legend depict the Jew as the willing intermediary between the apostate priest, Theophilus, and the Devil. Other medieval attestations, notably that of "Der arme" Hartmann, and those of two Middle Low German dramas, give the Jew no role at all in Theophilus's foray into diabolism. A third Middle Low German drama, that of the Trier manuscript, depicts the Jews *in bonam partem*, as concerned parties who attempt to dissuade the errant priest from his evil intentions. The Trier manuscript, a product of the same fifteenth century that gave us the Shrovetide plays of Hans Folz, reads much as an anti-clerical satire that also takes aim at medieval anti-Jewish hostility. Given that the role of the Jew as diabolist and sorcerer was present in the very earliest attestations of the Theophilus legend, the omission or alteration of the Jew's role in the fall of the priest is significant. The omission indicates a rejection of the "Jew as black magician" calumny by a medieval Christian writer in a text intended for a medieval Christian audience. The complete reversal of the Jew's role that we find in the Trier manuscript reveals not merely rejection of the "diabolical Jew" calumny, but condemnation of it through ridicule. The author or authors of the Trier manuscript found the very idea of the "Jew as nigromantic business agent" ludicrous.

Conflicted and contradictory images of Jews are demonstrably present in a wide variety of literary works from throughout the Middle Ages. The enduring presence of such images suggests that, regardless of the direction in which the influence was exerted – whether literary forms influenced readers' attitudes or readers' attitudes influenced the content of late medieval literary production – we should expect to see similarly heterogeneous Christian–Jewish relations in the historical developments of these three centuries. What develops is not a steady, unrelenting growth in intolerance toward Jews. In the centuries between the fall of the Roman Empire and the First Crusade, relations between Jews and Christians in Middle Europe, albeit strained by ethnic and cultural differences, remained congenial enough to allow the two groups to coexist in peace.[2] If the available sources provide us with remotely accurate documentation of Jewish–Christian social relations in Christian medieval Europe, it is with the First Crusade in 1096 that significant outbreaks of violence against Jews begin.[3] Even that violent turn of events, however, was not sufficient to end all amicable Jewish–Christian social contact in medieval Europe.[4]

According to Michael Toch's research, such incidents of violent persecution, both in terms of their overall number and geographic distribution, remain quite sporadic through the High Middle Ages and beyond.[5] This conclusion is supported by the research of Jeremy Cohen, Frantisek Graus, Robert Chazan, and Anna Sapir-Abulafia, all of whom identify various crises in Jewish–Christian relations in late medieval Europe. Common to the research of these scholars is the conclusion that there were periodic crises, whether political, theological, or material in nature, which provoked sudden, violent outbreaks of anti-Jewish hostility. Cohen, Chazan, Sapir-Abulafia identify crises occurring in the late twelfth and early thirteenth centuries, while Graus deals with the crisis resulting from the outbreak of plague during the late 1340s. In each case, the authors identify some event or constellation of events that triggers a disruption in

187

otherwise peaceful relations between Jews and Christians. One thing which none of these authors seems to emphasize sufficiently, though, is that years and decades elapsed between pogroms throughout the Middle Ages. The greatest growth in anti-Jewish violence does not come until the close of the Middle Ages and the beginning of the early modern era. Anti-Jewish violence reaches a peak of geographic distribution with the plague pogroms of the 1340s, tapers off until reaching a low point in the 1370s, increases again in that decade, and finally reaches a point where there is no year between 1379 and 1559 in which central Europe is completely free of anti-Jewish violence.[6]

Returning to the academic controversy that spurred this work, one thing is clear. Seen together, the heterogeneity of the images of Jews in medieval Christian German-speaking Europe and of the treatment Jews received from their Christian neighbors in the German-speaking lands in the late Middle Ages and early modern period are complex and defy any simplistic analysis. If persons living in the Middle Ages could oppose the blood libel even to the point of defending Jews in the face of it, as the research of historians clearly shows, then attributions of sole causality linking the medieval expressions of anti-Jewish hostility to National Socialist and Soviet Communist pogroms or other modern manifestations of violent Jew-hatred, such as those that are common in the scholarship on "Jews in medieval Christian Europe," cannot be regarded as accurate. Indeed, all attempts to attribute modern or contemporary manifestations of anti-Jewish hostility to the survival of "medieval" thinking about Jews must be regarded as suspect, since it is clear that there was no homogenous "medieval" conception of the Jews to begin with.

Instead of a "medieval conception" of the Jew, or even a "hermeneutic Jew" adapted to various dogmatic needs, what we find in medieval German literature is a variety of Jews, each constructed as an answer to questions that troubled medieval Christians about Jews: why don't they believe Jesus is the Messiah and what is their place in Christian society? When local politicians found social or material advantage in promoting negative answers to these questions, figures such as the Jewish sorcerer, as in the Theophilus legend, or filicidal Jew, as in some versions of "Der Judenknabe," were created in order to convince Christians that any action against the Jews, from con-

188

fiscation of property to murder, was justified and licit. Alongside them, however, were figures such as the righteous Jew who converts to Christianity (Joseph), the righteous Jew who does not convert *(De Iudeo)*, and the Jew as critic of Christian moral failings (Samuel of the Middle Low German *Theophilus* play, the Jews described in *Der Renner*, Abraham in the *Decameron*). The Jewish disputant, a figure appearing in numerous literary forms in the Middle Ages, took on a variety of forms himself, ranging from the learned seekers of truth in Konrad's *Silvester*, to the dismissive and haughty figures of the disputation scenes in the Frankfurt Passion play and *Dirigierrolle*, to the surprisingly respectful figure in "Christ und Jude." All of these figures consitute positive evaluations of both Jews and their place in Christian society, reflecting not only a philo-Judaic strand of Christian thought but also the everyday reality of continued amicable relations that Katz and others spoke of.

Notes

Chapter One

1   *Juden in der christlichen Umwelt während des späten Mittelalters,*
    Zeitschrift für historische Forschung: Beiheft 13 (Berlin: Duncker und
    Humbolt, 1992) 26.

2   Friedrich Battenberg, *Das europäische Zeitalter der Juden: Zur Ent-*
    wicklung einer Minderheit in der nichtjüdischen Umwelt Europas.
    Band 1. Von den Anfängen bis 1650 (Darmstadt: Wissenschaftliche
    Buchgesellschaft, 1990) 101–3. For an overview of the Papal edicts and
    imperial legal documents of the early Middle Ages, see Amnon Linder,
    The Jews in the Legal Sources of the Early Middle Ages (Detroit:
    Wayne State UP; Jerusalem: The Israel Academy of Sciences and
    Humanities, 1997), and Solomon Grayzel, *The Church and the Jews in*
    the XIIIth Century Vol. I (Philadelphia: Dropsie College, 1933), and
    Grayzel, *The Church and the Jews in the XIIIth Century* Vol. II, ed.
    Kenneth R. Stow (Detroit: Wayne State UP, 1980). See also the
    relevant entries in Heinz Schreckenberg's three-volume work, *Die*
    christlichen Adversus-Judaeos-Texte (Frankfurt am Main: Lang, 1982,
    1988, and 1994).

3   Schlomo Spitzer, *Bne Chet: Die österreichischen Juden im Mittelalter.*
    Eine Sozial- und Kulturgeschichte (Vienna: Böhlau, 1997) 14–32. The
    texts of the Sicut Judaeus and other papal bulls concerning the Jews are
    reproduced in *The Church and the Jews in the XIIIth Century*, Vol. I,
    85–356; Vol. 2, 47–232.

4   Max Grunwald, *The History of the Jews of Vienna*, Jewish Community
    Series (Philadelphia: Jewish Publications Society, 1936) 1–30.

5   *Bne Chet* 38–42.

6   *The History of the Jews of Vienna* 32–73.

7   See Jeremy Cohen, "A 1096 Complex? Constructing the First Crusade
    in Jewish Historical Memory, Medieval and Modern," and Robert
    Chazan, "From the First Crusade to the Second: Evolving Perspectives
    on Jewish–Christian Conflict," both in *Jews and Christians in Twelfth-*

Century Europe, ed. Michael A. Singer and John Van Engen (Notre Dame: Notre Dame UP, 2001) 9–26 and 46–62 respectively.

8   Solomon Grayzel, *A History of the Jews* (Philadelphia: Jewish Publications Society of America, 1947. Rpt. 1967) 337–74.

9   Miri Rubin, *Gentile Tales: The Narrative Assault on Late Medieval Jews* (New Haven: Yale UP, 1999) 48–52.

10   *Das europäische Zeitalter* 120.

11   *Gentile Tales* 56.

12   *Das europäische Zeitalter* 120.

13   Michael Toch, *Die Juden im mittelalterlichen Reich*, Enzyklopädie deutscher Geschichte 44 (Munich: Oldenbourg, 1998) 55–65.

14   For a look at the interpersonal side of the equation in the conflict surrounding the status of Jews in late medieval German-speaking Europe, see R. Po-Chia Hsia, *Trent 1475: Stories of a Ritual Murder Trial* (New Haven: Yale UP, 1992). See also Frantisek Graus, *Pest, Geissler, Judenmorde: Das 14. Jahrhundert als Krisenzeit*, Veröffentlichungen des Max-Planck-Instituts für Geschichte 86 (Göttingen: Vandenhoeck and Ruprecht, 1987). See also *Das europäische Zeitalter* 136–71. These three historians agree that both Christian citizens and authorities attempted to halt ritual murder trials and pogroms, though their efforts were often unsuccessful. That the imperial "Judenschutz" and "Judenprivilegien" continued to be enforced while the revenues from Jewish sources declined steadily indicates that the motives involved were more than financial and that these laws constituted something more than an imperial "protection racket." The contention that the Emperors had only, in every single case, protected Jews in order to secure economic gain was the core of Markus Wenninger's argument in *Man bedarf keiner Juden mehr: Ursachen und Hintergründe ihrer Vertreibung aus den Reichsstädten im 15. Jahrhundert*, Beihefte zum Archiv für Kulturgeschichte 14 (Graz: Böhlau, 1981).

15   See *Die Juden im mittelalterlichen Reich* 54–55. Toch's picture of Jewish–Christian relations in the fifteenth and sixteenth centuries is bleak, but the data force him to concede this point. As for the efficacy of the Emperor's intervention on behalf of the Jews, it is no coincidence that the city of Regensburg, which had struggled against the Imperial Crown over the right to expel its Jewish inhabitants, only succeeded in driving them out after Maximilian's death in 1519. See Wilhelm Grau, *Antisemitismus im späten Mittelalter: Das Ende der Regensburger Judengemeinde: 1450–1519* (Munich: Duncker and Humbolt, 1934) 158–64.

16 *Exclusiveness and Tolerance: Studies in Jewish–Gentile Relations in Medieval and Modern Times*, Scripta Judaica 3 (Oxford: UP, 1961) 4–11.

17 (Oxford: Blackwell, 1987).

18 (London: Routledge, 1995).

19 (Ithaca: Cornell UP, 1982).

20 *Daggers of Faith: Thirteenth-Century Christian Missionizing and the Jewish Response* (Berkeley: University of California Press, 1989).

21 *Man bedarf keiner Juden mehr* 20–4, 38–40, 218–36.

22 In *Christians and Jews* 4–10 and 78–82, Sapir-Abulafia attacks the arguments of historians, including Gavin Langmuir, who assert that the hostility toward Jews expressed by many in medieval Germany was a product of irrational or non-rational thought processes.

23 The article is cited here as reprinted in Funkenstein's compilation, *Perceptions of Jewish History* (Berkeley: University of California Press, 1993) 172–201.

24 John M. McCulloh, "Jewish Ritual Murder: William of Norwich, Thomas of Monmouth, and the Early Dissemination of the Myth," *Speculum* 72 (1997): 698–740.

25 (Cambridge: Cambridge UP, 1991).

26 *Corpus Christi* 122–30, 216, 360

27 *Gentile Tales* 53–7.

28 (New Haven: Yale UP, 1988).

29 16–41.

30 50–7.

31 On the unintended "educational" function of ideas, see Slavoj Zizek, *The Sublime Object of Ideology* (London: Verso, 1990) 55–84. See also *Corpus Christi* 57–68.

32 *The Sublime Object* 47–9.

33 *Perceptions of Jewish History* 175.

34 This tension is elucidated most clearly in Romans chapters 9–11. For a brief overview of the ongoing controversy over the role of anti-Judaism in Christian theology, see Nicholas de Lange's "The Origins of Anti-Semitism" in *Anti-Semitism in Times of Crisis*, ed. Sander Gilman and Stephen Katz (New Haven: Yale UP, 1996).

35 For a detailed account of the anti-Jewish violence of 1096 and the varied responses of Christian authorities to it, see Moritz Stern, *Hebräische Berichte über die Judenverfolgung während der Kreuzzüge* (Breslau: 1892. Rpt. Hildesheim: Olms, 1997). This compilation of medieval Hebrew sources is particularly valuable because it transmits

contemporary accounts of the massacres in Speyer and other cities. For a summary of the principal events, see Robert Chazan's article in *The Yale Companion to Jewish Writing and Thought in German Culture 1096–1996* (New Haven: Yale UP, 1997).

36 *The Church and the Jews*, Vol. II. 116–20, 123–6. These two bulls are of particular interest for this study, as they are addressed to church authorities in German-speaking lands. The latter bull, dated to 1274, uses some language from an earlier bull that Innocent IV issued in 1247.

37 The frequency with which the blood libel specifically was invoked to justify personal political vendettas or deflect suspicion from parties guilty of real crimes may never be known. Hsia documents several cases of this kind in *The Myth of Ritual Murder* 62–5, 70–85, and 90–3.

38 *Perceptions of Jewish History* 319.

39 "A 1096 Complex?" 13–20. The use of the adjective "lachrymose" to describe the dominant view in much of modern historiography on Jewish life in medieval Europe originated with the historian Salo Baron. See Ivan Marcus's "The Dynamics of Jewish Renaissance and Renewal in the Twelfth Century," *Jews and Christians in Twelfth-Century Europe*, 27–45 for a discussion of its career and waning influence.

40 *The Devil and the Jews: The Medieval Conception of the Jew and its Relation to Modern Antisemitism* (New Haven: Yale UP).

41 *The Devil and the Jews* 219.

42 *The Devil and the Jews* 36–7.

43 Munich: Dunker and Humboldt.

44 *Perceptions of Jewish History* 320.

45 Moshe Lazar, "The Lamb and the Scapegoat: The Dehumanization of the Jews in Medieval Propaganda Imagery," *Anti-Semitism in Times of Crisis* 37–66.

46 See Cecil Roth's *A History of the Jews* 213–45. See also the one-sided and brief discussion of Martin Luther's influence on the Third Reich in William Shirer's *The Rise and Fall of the Third Reich* (New York: Simon and Schuster, 1960) 236–7.

47 ed. Helmut Birkhan and Klaus Zatloukal (Vienna: Böhlau, 1991).

48 *Ideology of Death: Why the Holocaust Happened in Germany* (Chicago: Ivan R. Dee, 1996) 1–26.

49 *Hitler's Willing Executioners: Ordinary Germans and the Holocaust* (New York: Alfred A. Knopf, 1996) 38–77.

50 *Willing Executioners* 37–9, 52–3.

51 *Warrant for Genocide* (London: Eyre & Spottiswoode, 1967, Rpt. London: Serif, 1996) 26.

52 See Gavin Langmuir, "Thomas of Monmouth: Detector of Ritual Murder," here cited as reprinted in *The Blood Libel Legend: A Casebook in Anti-Semitic Folklore* (Madison: University of Wisconsin Press, 1991) 3–40. In this article, he identifies the case of William of Norwich (1150) as the earliest medieval exponent of the blood libel. For an account of the thirteenth-century origin of the host desecration accusation, see Rubin's, *Gentile Tales*. On the fourteenth-century origin of the well-poisoning accusation, see Graus, *Pest, Geissler, Judenmorde*, 299–334.

53 See *The Origins of Totalitarianism* (New York: Harcourt, Brace, and Co., 1951) 165–84.

54 *The History of Anti-Semitism. Volume One: From the Time of Christ to the Court Jews*, Trans. Richard Howard (New York: Vanguard Press, 1965) v–ix, 3–5.

55 See "Historische Traditionen über Juden im Spätmittlelalter (Mitteleuropa)," *Zur Geschichte der Juden im Deutschland des späten Mittelalters und der frühen Neuzeit*, ed. Alfred Haverkamp, Monographien zur Geschichte des Mittelalters 24 (Stuttgart: Hiersemann, 1981) 1–26.

56 *The Jews in Legal Sources of the Middle Ages* 200–680 for texts relevant to the Latin West.

57 Sander Gilman, "The Madness of the Jews," *Difference and Pathology* (New York: Cornell UP, 1985) 150–62.

58 "'Antijudaismus' und 'Antisemitismus.' Begriffe als Bedeutungsträger," *Jahrbuch für Antisemitismusforschung* 6, ed. Wolfgang Benz (Frankfurt / New York: Campus Verlag, 1997) 92–114 here 109–10.

59 See *Anti-Semitism in Times of Crisis* 21–37.

60 *Toward a Definition* 4–5.

61 *Toward a Definition* 17.

62 "Faith of Christians and Hostility toward Jews," *Christianity and Judaism*, Diane Wood, ed., Studies in Church History 29 (Oxford: Blackwell, 1992) 77–92.

63 (Berkeley: California UP, 1999).

64 *Living Letters* 2–5.

65 *Living Letters* 13

66 *Living Letters* 36–7.

67 *Living Letters* 104–22.

68 *Living Letters* 222–3.

69 (Philadelphia: University of Pennsylvania Press), 2001.

70   *Feast of Saint Abraham* 1–23.
71   *Feast of Saint Abraham* 89–90, 95–7.
72   *Feast of Saint Abraham* 89–94.
73   *Feast of Saint Abraham* 96–8.
74   *Rise and Fall of the Third Reich* 97–113.
75   See Scott McKnight, "A Loyal Critic: Matthew's Polemic with Judaism in Theological Perspective," *Anti-Semitism and Early Christianity: Issues of Polemic and Faith*, ed. Craig Evans and Donald A. Hagner (Minneapolis: Fortress Press, 1993) 55–80.
76   *Communities of Violence: Persecution of Minorities in the Middle Ages* (Princeton: Princeton UP, 1996) 6–7.
77   Jeff Jacoby, "Lady Arafat's Real Mistake," *The Boston Globe*, November 22, 1999. Specifically she accused Israelis of poisoning Palestinian wells. In doing so, she repeated the accusation that prompted the plague pogroms in the mid-fourteenth century. It is doubtful, however, that anyone would be so unreflective as to see her comments as part of any "unbroken line" of anti-Semitic slander originating in the European Middle Ages.
78   A. H. Touber, "Das Donaueschinger Passionsspiel und die bildende Kunst," *Deutsche Vierteljahresschrift* 52 (1978) 26–42. Helmut Lomnitzer, "Das Verhältnis des Fastnachtspiels vom 'Kaiser Constantinus' zum Reimpaarspruch 'Christ und Jude' von Hans Folz," *Zeitschrift für deutsches Altertum und deutsche Literatur* 92 (1964) 277–91.
79   Alfred Ebenbauer and Klaus Zatlaoukal, ed, *Die Juden in ihrer mittelalterlichen Umwelt* (Vienna: Böhlau, 1991) 35–51. Frey admits that the Middle Ages also saw writings sympathetic to Jews, but discounts their possible influence on public thought.
80   This is the volume edited by Ebenbauer and Zatloukal from 1991. The individual contributors referred to are Winfried Frey, Frantisek Graus, and Lydia Miklautsch, all of whom differentiate between "Antisemitismus" and "Antijudäismus."
81   (Frankfurt am Main: Lang, 1986).
82   *Forschungen zur Geschichte der älteren deutschen Literatur* 14 (Munich: Fink, 1992).
83   *Studies in Medieval and Reformation Thought* 55 (Leiden: E.J. Brill, 1995).
84   *Das Bild der Juden* 1–36.
85   *Das Bild der Juden* 49–73

86 Specifically, she adduces the use of contemporary names as evidence for this phenomenon, beginning with the *Frankfurter Dirigierrolle*; see 112.

87 The Benediktbeu, Vienna, and St. Gall Passion Plays.

88 The Frankfurt Dirigierrolle and the Frankfurt and Alsfeld Passion Plays.

89 *Das Bild der Juden* 53.

90 *Das Bild der Juden* 213.

91 *Der Antichrist: Der staufische Ludus de Antichristo*, ed. Gerhard Günther (Hamburg: Friedrich Wittig, 1970).

92 *Das Bild der Juden* 123–5, 179.

93 *Das Bild der Juden* 211–12.

94 See the apparatus to Karl von Amira's edition of *Das Endinger Judenspiel* (Halle, 1883).

95 For a summary of the recent research on the dating of the *Frankfurter Dirigierrolle*, see Wenzel, *"Do worden die Judden"* 31–3. For a discussion of the problems surrounding the dating of the *St.Galler Passionsspiel*, contained in Codex Sangallensis 919, see Larry E. West, ed. and trans., *The Saint Gall Passion Play* (Leyden: Brill, 1976) 27–8; Rudolf Schützeichel, ed., *Das Mittelrheinische Passionsspiel der St. Galler Handschrift 919* (Tübingen: Niemeyer, 1978) 55–60; Hermann Manfred Pflanz, *Die lateinischen Textgrundlagen des St. Galler Passionsspieles in der mittealterlichen Liturgie* (Frankfurt am Main: Lang, 1977) 5–6 and 161. These three authors all agree in dating the text of the play, which we have in a fifteenth-century collected manuscript, to the fourteenth century. They are also unanimous in agreeing that it could date to any decade between 1320 and 1380. Schützeichel alone rules out any date after 1370 on paleographic grounds.

96 She identifies the medieval German Christian society of the ninth through fourteenth centuries as being more tolerant of Jews, and that of the fourteenth through sixteenth centuries as being less tolerant (209).

97 Here it is necessary to note that in her treatment of visual arts, Bremer discusses works dating from the late ninth century through the beginning of the sixteenth.

98 *"Do worden"* 216.

99 *"Do worden"* 38.

100 The editions referred to here are those of Ursula Henning, ed., *Das Wiener Passionsspiel: Cod. 12887 (Suppl. 561) der österreichischen Staatsbibliothek zu Wien,* Litterae: Göppinger Beiträge zur Textgeschichte Nr. 92, and Richard Froning, ed., *Das Drama des Mittelalters* (Stuttgart. 1891, Rpt. Darmstadt: Wissenschaftliche Buchgesell-

schaft, 1964). The Vienna Passion contains an encounter between Jesus and the Pharisee named Simon, but is devoid of any figures even resembling those of the Jewish leadership seen in the other Passion plays here examined.

101 *"Do worden"* 57.
102 *"Do worden"* 154–6.
103 *"Do worden"* 65–72 and 104.
104 *"Do worden"* 87 and 111.
105 *"Do worden"* 134–7.
106 *"Do worden"* 22–30, 98–116, 256–65.
107 *"Do worden"* 116.
108 The summary of his ideas is taken from pp. 2–3 of *The Red Jews*.
109 *The Red Jews* 34.
110 *The Red Jews* 181–2.
111 See specifically Graus's *Pest, Geissler, Judenmorde*, 168–281 and Hsia's *The Myth of Ritual Murder*, 1–57, for accounts of the role that local politics played in pogroms in the fourteenth and fifteenth centuries.
112 See *Pest, Geissler, Judenmorde*, 155–67 for details about the chronology of the plague pogroms.
113 *Trent: 1475* and *The Myth of Ritual Murder*, 1–15.
114 See Heinz Schreckenberg, *Die christlichen Adversus-Judaeos-Texte und ihr literarisches und historisches Umfeld (13.–20. Jh.)* 1994. Throughout the Middle Ages, Popes and emperors afforded Jews legal protection that was generally superior to that afforded peasants and tradesmen, and the fourteenth and fifteenth centuries were no exceptions. Though there was considerable variation in the degree of protection and restriction that various Popes afforded Jews in late medieval Christian society, the balance of Papal decrees in these two centuries was favorable.
115 *Exclusiveness and Tolerance* 7–10.
116 This is his *Juden und Judentum in der mittelalterlichen Kunst.* See above for full citation.
117 *Juden und Judentum* 46–50.
118 *Juden und Judentum* 63–80.
119 *Living Letters* 75–94.
120 *Living Letters* 151–201.
121 The debate concerning the depiction of Jews in Wolfram's *Willehalm* has been particularly fruitful. Those interested in this ongoing scholarly discussion should consult the following:

Wolfram von Eschenbach, *Willehalm*, Nach der Handschrift 857 der Stiftsbibliothek St. Gallen. Mittelhochdeutscher Text, Übersetzung und Kommentar, ed. Joachim Heinzle (Bibliothek des Mittelalters), Frankfurt a. M. 1991; Fritz-Peter Knapp, "Die Heiden und ihr Vater in den Versen 307,27f. des 'Willehalm'", *Zeitschrift für deutsches Altertum und deutsche Literatur* 122 (1993): 202–207; Ralf-Henning Steinmetz, "Die Ungetauften Christenkinder in den 'Willhalm'-Versen 307, 26–30", *Zeitschrift für deutsches Altertum und deutsche Literatur* 124 (1995): 151–162; Joachim Heinzle, "Die Heiden als Kinder Gottes. Notiz zum 'Willehalm'", *Zeitschrift für deutsches Altertum und deutsche Literatur* 123 (1994): 301–308; Christoph Fasbender, "'Willehalm' als Programmschrift gegen die 'Kreuzzugsideologie' und 'Dokument der Menschlichkeit'", *Zeitschrift für deutsche Philologie* 116 (1997): 16–31; Walter Johannes Schröder, "Der Toleranzgedanke und der Begriff der 'Gotteskindschaft' in Wolframs 'Willehalm'", in: *FS K. Bischoff zum 70. Geburtstag*, Köln/Wien 1975, 400–415; Karl Lofmark, "Das Problem des Unglaubens in 'Willehalm'", in: *Wolfram von Eschenbach (FS W. Schröder)* (Tübingen: Niemeyer 1989) 399–413; Joachim Heinzle, "Noch Einmal: Die Heiden als Kinder Gottes in Wolframs 'Willehalm'", *Zeitschrift für deutsche Philologie* 117 (1998): 75–80; Fritz-Peter Knapp, "Und noch Einmal: Die Heiden als Kinder Gottes," *Zeitschrift für deutsches Altertum und deutsche Literatur* 129 (2000), 296–302; Timothy McFarland, "Giburc's Dilemma: Parents and Children, Baptism and Salavtion," in: *Wolfram's 'Willehalm'. Fifteen Essays*, (Suffolk: Camden House, 2002) 121–142.

Chapter Two

1   James Shapiro, "Updating (and Retouching) an Old Passion Play," *The New York Times*, 14 May, 2000, 7, continued on 32.

2   Helmut de Boor and Richard Newald, *Die deutsche Literatur vom späten Mittelalter zum Barock*, Geschichte der deutschen Literatur, IV/I (Munich: Beck, 1962, 2nd ed. 1970) 238.

3   *Studien zur Entstehung und Geschichte der deutschen Passionsspiele des 13. und 14. Jahrhunderts.* Münster Mittelalterschiften 14 (Munich: Fink, 1972) 31.

4   *Das deutsche Drama des Mittelalters*, Grundriss der germanischen Philologie 20 (Berlin: deGruyter, 1971) 64.

5   de Boor/Newald IV.i. 247.

6   de Boor/Newald IV.i. 238.

7   de Boor/Newald IV.i. 239.

8   *Das deutsche Drama des Mittelalters* 33–4; 64–8; de Boor/Newald IV.i. 239–47.

9   (Tübingen: Niemeyer, 1972) 55–60.

10 *Das Mittelrheinische Passionsspiel* 3–4.

11 Author's note: these are the Benediktbeu, St. Gall, and Vienna Passion plays.

12 *Das Bild der Juden* 53.

13 *"Do worden"* 31–3.

14 *Exclusiveness* 3–5; 8–11; 18–21; 134–5.

15 *"Do worden"* 58–62; 67–9; 115–6; 120–2; 174.

16 Bremer mentions the Tirol Passion plays on pages 55–7 of her monograph. She does not treat them in any significant depth, however. Likewise, Wenzel refers to Wackernell's edition of the Tirol Passion plays on pages 78, 79, 123,125, 130, 148, and 153 of her monograph, but does not discuss the plays themselves.

17 Author's note: The texts referred to in this study will all be cited as they appear in modern scholarly editions, following the orthographic conventions of those editions. Here, the St. Gall play is cited from Schützeichel. The text reads: "Hear, o holy Christendom, to you will be shown today how the creator of all the world with public signs, and also with holy teaching and in great suffering, walked on the earth and was martyred for your sake."

18 Then the Jews approach John saying: "You two go over there now and ask that man that he make known to us who he is, right away." Then the two going to John: "Very good man, we implore you, that you tell us truthfully, whether you are Elijah. Dear friend, tell us that now."

19 Then the emissaries: "Since we can surely draw near to the kingdom of God with baptism, come here, and baptize us all in accord with this wish."

20 Specifically, John 1:19–27, which reads: "And this is the testimony of John, when the Jews sent priests and Levites from Jerusalem to ask him, 'Who are you?' He confessed, he did not deny, but confessed, 'I am not the Christ.' And they asked him, 'What then? Are you Elijah?' He said, 'I am not.' 'Are you the prophet?' And he answered, 'No.' They said to him then, 'Who are you? Let us have an answer for those

who sent us. What do you say about yourself?' He said, 'I am the voice of one crying in the wilderness, "Make straight the way of the Lord," as the prophet Isaiah said.' Now they had been sent from the Pharisees. They asked him, 'Then why are you baptizing, if you are neither the Christ, nor Elijah, nor the prophet?' John answered them, 'I baptize with water; but among you stands one whom you do not know, even he who comes after me, the one whose sandals I am not worthy to untie.'" The text is taken from the Revised Standard Version of the New Testament.

21   When the Jews are leading in the woman Rufus alone speaks, saying 'Magister': "Give us your counsel. This woman has committed adultery. The law of Moses, by which we live, gave us such a command, that we must stone harlots, of which she is one." Then Jesus, inclining to the ground, writes and sings, 'Si quis sine peccato,' etc. and says: "Whoever is without sin and without malice, let him throw a stone at this woman."

22   *Das Bild der Juden* 78.

23   Responding, the blind man sings 'ille homo' as above and says 'Der Mensch' as before. Then Cayphas says: "That man is not from God, who, according to your own testimony, helped you on a Sabbath, against God's command." The old Jewish man responds: "Yet I doubt very much that a sinner could perform such wonders." Then Annas says to the blind man: "What do you say about the man who made you sighted?" The blind man responds: "He is a prophet, truly. I believe him to be that, obviously." Then Annas to his servant: "I do not believe the testimony that this man gives of himself. Call his father here immediately. He will tell us the truth."

24   John 18:10: Then Simon Peter, having a sword, drew it and struck the high priest's slave and cut off his ear. The slave's name was Malchus.

25   Then Malchus says: "Consider, all you Jews, whether my thought pleases you. The one who made a blind man sighted, how could such a painful thing happen to him, that he should suffer his friend to die, and in dying endure such great pain?"

26   Then Malchus hastens to the Jews saying: "Hear, you men, a great wonder. Lazarus was our neighbor. I certainly saw him dead. The same man, when Jesus bade him, rose up on the fourth day. I say this truly. This will bring the world to the conviction that they should all believe in him. Consider this report quickly. They shall all believe that he is the Christ."

27   Cayphas responds, singing 'Expedit nobis' [and] says: "You men, hear my advice, which is both pragmatic and truthful. It is better that one man die, than that the whole world go to ruin." Malchus reponds: "Lord Bishop, you have a wise mind. This counsel seems very good to me."

28   Then the Jew to Jesus: "Jesus is a very good man. He can well restore ears. So long as I live, I am grateful for this, I will never do him any harm."

29   Then Rufus deals him a blow, saying: "May you never be happy again! Is this how you answer a prince?" Annas says to the Jews: "Don't any of you know of a misdeed that this man has committed? He ought to tell us about it here, where we are decrying them." Rufus responds: "I want to testify here truly that he has spoken publicly:" And sings 'Solvite templum hoc' and says: "I wish to testify here truly that he publicly called for the tempel to be torn down. And he claimed he could build it up again in three days just as it was before. And in addition to this, he spoke other words; he said that he was God's son. Now listen up, what do you want to do about this?"

30   Then Rufus says to Pilate: "Pilate, we bring to you a man who is well capable of sorcery. Therefore, if you wish to do justice, then sentence him to death." Then Pilate says: "What evil thing has he done, that he should stand here for retribution?" Responding Rufus says: "His evil work, his evil thoughts, have compelled us to bring him here. Otherwise we would not have done it." Pilate responds: "You should best let me determine what he has done wrong." Rufus responds: "He has forbidden everywhere, that anyone should give the emperor his taxes anymore. For this reason he has forfeited his life. He presumes kingly authority for himself and thereby derides the emperor."

31   Rufus: "Know that, by my Jewishness, I will repay you well for your work. You shall have twenty marks if you do not restrain your zeal."

32   Then Pilate says: "Now look at your king. I find him to have no guilt. Yet he has been very badly beaten. For this reason you might well be silent." The Jews respond 'Regem non habemus' And Rufus says: "We give honor to the emperor. We acknowledge no other king." Again Pilate: "What do we do, then, with this man who has never committed any sin?" The Jews respond, 'Crucifige, crucifige eum' And Rufus says: "You should crucify him immediately, for he has led astray this great land, from Galilee to here. Certainly, he deserves it."

33   Herod says: "Welcome, all of you gentlemen. Tell me, what would please you?" Rufus responding: "Sir, we now bring you a man who can deceive the whole world. He is from this country. Pilate thought it a

shameful thing to pass judgment on him at this time, for you are in authority here."

34 Rufus responds: "Sir, to this old woman's dream one should not give much attention. You should mark it as true that if you let Jesus escape you, the emperor will hold it against you, because he claims the kingdom. Whoever presumes for himself the office of king, he must receive the enmity of the emperor." Pilate responds: "If you do not want to waver from that course, that I should hang your king, for that reason you shall have shame all the more, whatever may be said in the land." The Jews sing 'Regem non habemus' And Caiaphas says: "We have no other king here, as our speech affirms, than the emperor, have no doubt. You should let this one be hanged, if you wish to have the favor of the emperor."

35 "Get up, one will hang you. You cannot escape that. You have done much harm to us, for which we now repay you. You spread your teaching very often to our dishonor. That I say to you to hurt you."

36 *"Do worden"* 182–8; *Das Bild der Juden* 179, 212–13.

37 *Das Drama des Mittelalters* 326. See also *"Do worden"* 32, footnote 5 for a complete list of scholars who have accepted the later date. Natascha Bremer is among them.

38 *Das Bild der Juden* 99.

39 *"Do worden"* 32–3; *Das deutsche Drama des Mittelalters* 144–52; de Boor/Newald IV.i. 248.

40 *"Do worden"* 36–45.

41 Bernhard Blumenkranz, *Die Judenpredigt Augustins: Ein Beitrag zur Geschichte der jüdisch–christlichen Beziehungen in den ersten Jahrhunderten* (Basel: Helbing and Lichtenhahn, 1946) 198–209. Blumenkranz's translation of the text is found on 89–110.

42 The clamor having ended, Augustine propounds his sermon as follows: "You gentlemen, quiet your noise!" King David responds to him: "I am called David, God's servant." Isac the Jew responds to him: "Shut up, David!" Augustine to Solomon. Solomon speaks. Bandir the Jew responds. Again Augustine speaks to Daniel: "Hear this all you children of God!" Daniel stands up and says: "According to the Septuagint" And says: "Now hear what I would say to you." Joseph the Jew responds: "Shut up over there! What are you blathering about?"

43 *"Do worden"* 35–9.

44 Kalman the Jew responds: "Now tell me, you foolish man!" Jesus says: "Listen, the holy Abraham – ". Again Mannes the Jew responds: "How this speech is constructed!" Again Jesus: "I tell you truthfully – ".

Again Mannes: "What is this talk good for?" Here the Jews look for rocks, as if they wish to stone Jesus, and Jesus says, "I have done good works – ".

45   *"Do worden"* 41–2.

46   See lines 100–22.

47   The Jewish boys and Simon the Pharisee appear in the scene of Jesus's triumphant entry into Jerusalem 127b–32. Nicodemus and Joseph only appear and approach Pilate after Jesus's death in order to retrieve his body, 243–46a.

48   *Das Bild der Juden* 171–7; *"Do worden"* 42–4. In addition to being depicted as blindfolded, *Synagoga* is frequently depicted with a broken spear or scepter and a tablet or scroll of the Torah falling from her hands, symbolizing a loss of authority.

49   See lines 359–67.

50   *Das Drama des Mittelalters* 279; *Das Bild der Juden* 62–3. Bremer considers it probable that the text originated in the thirteenth century.

51   *Das Drama des Mittelalters* 278–80.

52   Luke 19:1–10.

53   "That today salvation has happened in this house, because you, too, are a son of Abraham."

54   Luke 7:36–50.

55   Again. "Simon, I have something to say to you." Simon Peter: "Master, speak!" Jesus says: "A certain creditor had two debtors each of whom owed him a different sum of denarii: One of them owed him five hundred, the other fifty; but each of them became utterly poor and destitute; since they were not able to repay, he forgave the whole of the debt: Which of the two will therefore love him more?" Simon responds: "I surmise it would be the one who owed more, because he gave him more." Jesus says: "Your discernment has rightly judged this statement."

56   The MS is from the decade 1320–1340, though the text itself is likely of thirteenth-century provenance according to Froning (302).

57   *Das Drama des Mittelalters* 324–5.

58   "This woman has washed my feet with her tears, and sweetly kissed them a thousand times, and anointed my head with good oil: These and other good works I have been deprived of by you, I say this to you now and say that she shall be rewarded with this: Her sins shall be forgiven her and the crown of heaven given her."

Chapter Three

1   J. E. Wackernell, *Altdeutsche Passionsspiele aus Tirol* (Graz: Styria, 1897) I–LXXIX. All citations from the Tirol Passion Play are from this edition, which represents the six manuscripts belonging to the Tirol group together as one edited text. The seventh text, the Halle play, is edited separately. Each of the plays is named after the place where it was discovered, the American Passion Play having been discovered in a collection of early modern German documents in the Cornell University library.

2   *Altdeutsch Passionsspiele* LXXX–CXI, CXIV–CCII.

3   J. E. Wackernell, *Die ältesten Passionsspiele in Tirol* (Wien: Braunmüller, 1887) 22–74, 150–67.

4   *Altdeutsche Passionsspiel* 3–177. All six Manuscripts contain these elements of the Passion in nearly identical texts.

5   Lines 1–73.

6   Annas responds: "Truly it is a lapse in duty not to see to this matter! Therefore, you lords, I tell you, as you hear all of the people here clamoring about Jesus, who calls himself the Messiah, but who is certainly a perverter both of the people and the true law; he harms us all equally with his new teaching."

7   Annas says to Nicodemus: "Nicodemus, what do you advise us to do concerning this matter?" Nicodemus says: "What do you want me to do? I cannot consent to that, for the teaching that he has and the works that he does have come to him from God, one sees that in every way. His miracles make it clear quickly, in a short time, that they have come from God; therefore carry on without concern. I do not advise that he be killed: His teaching and his life are plain and in all things righteous." Annas to Nicodemus: "Fie on you, you evil deceiver! Your heart is empty of all honor! Flee from our assembly immediately and with haste!" Nicodemus leaves the stage

8   Annas inquires of Zedonius: "Zedonius, what do you advise us to do concerning this matter?" Zedonius responds: "Should I plot the death of the man who offered me seeing eyes, I, who was born blind, and had been deprived of sight? Know this in all earnest: He is my Lord and my God! I will say this openly, and whoever says otherwise, he doesn't tell the truth." Annas says to Zedonius: "Get out of here at once! May

misfortune overtake you! If you don't want to give him up, we shall have to teach you otherwise!"

9   The entire exchange between Nicodemus and the other Pharisees takes a mere seven verses in John's Gospel, 7:45–52.

10   Caiaphas says to the Savior: "Don't you hear what they who are here have testified concerning you just now? Great and distressing matters! Why don't you give an account of yourself?" The Savior remains silent. Caiaphas shouts in a loud voice, "I adjure you by the living God, that you tell us, if you are the Christ, the son of God!" And he says: "I adjure you in all seriousness, by the living God, let us know immediately, whether or not you are the Christ, God's son." The Savior says to Caiaphas, "If I told you, you would not believe me; if, however, I asked you, you would not answer, nor would you dismiss me. But truly I say to you all, you all shall see the Son of Man seated at the right hand and coming in the clouds of heaven." The Savior says: "If I tell you the truth now, you will not ever believe me; if I ventured to ask you, you would not give me an answer: And truly you would not let me go. But you shall see with the host of angels the Son of Man appear to you at the right hand of his Father, where a cloud shall set him apart, above all the world's people."

11   Then Joseph with his servant goes to Nicodemus and says: "I ask you Nicodemus, noble man, that you assist me today, that we might bury Jesus, the most esteemed." Nicodemus to Joseph: "Joseph, my dear friend, I will gladly be of help to you. Whatever suffering comes to me because of it, I will pay no mind to it at all: For we should be unfailing to him in all his sufferings. Even if someone should kill us for it; for the Lord Jesus Christ is our God and Savior."

12   Annas says: "Joseph, I now well hear that Jewry should consider you as one who is his disciple. For this reason, soon, your body and your life shall be grimly given over to death." Joseph says: "I will not deny my God, no matter what you do to me!" Caiaphas says to Joseph:

13   The first devil says to Lucifer: "Lord Lucifer, be of good cheer! This matter will yet prove trivial, just wait a short while: We will shoot sharp arrows that are bound to pierce the Jews: Then they will have to sing our little ditty and kill this man for us. Therefore do not doubt: The matter will soon be resolved. Farewell all, we must go! The Jews want to have a council that concerns him specifically: That will be a good starting place. Therefore, let us be off, do not hesitate!"

14   The host to the servant: "Servant, come to me quickly, arrange everything (I'll do that with you). See to it that everything is here that is

according to Jewish custom, when one wants to eat the Easter lamb. You are thirteen in number: it isn't too many." The servant to the host: "Sir, greet your guests now, I will truly do the best!"

15   Then the servant carries the plates and the drinking vessels and says: "Sir, here are the utensils and everything, as is the custom of the Jews, when one eats the Easter lamb. The lamb will certainly be good, too." The host to Jesus: "Lord and master, it is time that you prepare yourselves to eat the Easter lamb quickly, as Moses commanded: Roll up your sleeves and get to it, I will serve it up as best I can."

16   The servant, carries in the lamb, saying: "God bless the meal for you and may he never, ever forget us! The lamb is prepared according to the Old Testament, well done but not burned. Hurry now and eat it quickly, as Moses commanded."

17   Then, while they approach the man carrying water, Peter says: "Good man, let it be known to you, that our master sent us, the two of us, to your master. Where is his house? Tell us that." The water-bearer sets down the water and says: "I will show you the right way: Follow me, I will go before you and show you right now where my master's house is." And they go to the host, who says: "Welcome, good sirs! Tell me, what would you like?" John says: "Sir, that we shall tell you: Our master has sent us, the two of us, to you and said that he wishes to eat the customary Easter lamb here with you: That he and his disciples together wish to be at your home for the celebration."

18   Again, the savior to the disciples: "I will now give you the new law, the Easter lamb shall no longer be. Truly I tell you that it was a fore-shadowing of the new law and nothing else. Henceforth one must regard me as the lamb in the appearance of bread: I am the lamb that bears the pain of the sins of all the world on himself...." Similarly taking the cup he blesses it and says to his disciples: "Drink! This drink contains much joy: This is my blood, which will be spilled for you and for all mankind. The old law has passed away: This is the cup of the new law."

Note on the translation: Manuscript M records the word "salden" for "freyden" in line 416 though the "ey" combination consistently stands for the Middle High German "î", (Modern German "ei") in Wacker-nell's edition. The word seems to be Middle High German "vröude" (Modern "Freude"), even though examples of the "ey" for Middle High German "î" abound: "reych" (376) "leyb" (413) "leydlich" (421) "geyt" (476) are but a few. In manuscript Pf, however, the word appears in Simeon's "nunc dimitis" speech (line 427 on p. 206) as a form of the

Middle High German "fride," modern "Frieden." See Wackernell's note on 499.

19　See *"Do worden"* 53–8 for a summary of discussion on this issue that is still up-to-date.

20　Daniel says: "Now hear what I shall say to you! These words you should well heed. The true savior Christ, who is come for our consolation shall yield and surrender his blessed life for us in bitter death. In this manner he will bear our distress." Joseph the Rabbi says: "Quiet, there! What are you babbling? You got up too early today! Who pays careful attention to your words and interprets the dream that you have presented, see, he would perform a service that would be quite useless. But better still, learn this: Loan money at interest, as I do! That can make you rich! That would help you more than if you were to sing all of this long ditty: 'Baruch otta Adonai.' (Blessed are you Creator)"

21　*"Do worden"* 98–9. See also *Das Bild der Juden* 53–5.

22　*Das Bild der Juden* 111.

23　*"Do worden"* 100–08.

24　Malchus says to the Jews: "Hear, you Jews, a new marvel, that the deceiver has done; he has given speech to the dumb! He is a charlatan, by my very life!"

25　The Savior picking up the ear and replacing it on Malchus. Malchus says to the Jews: Malchus then says to the Jews: "Hear, you Jews, what I say to you. One of my ears was sliced off, the sorcerer took it, Jesus the charlatan, and put it back on me as if it had never come off, as you see here! See, where did this ever happen before?"

26　"Oh, Gotschalg, you should abandon this talk! Jesus is a good man! According to his behavior he is completely good! No sorcerer performs such signs!"

27　Nicodemus says to Caiaphas: "You gentlemen, tell me, on what basis do you think and say this, that Jesus is a bastard? There are many pious people here, to all of whom it is known, that the mother of Jesus, whom they call Christ, had a husband in lawful marriage: Therefore this talk wounds me, and the shamefulness of these lies, for such is a malicious insult."

28　The *Talmud*, the *Amoa Ulla*, the *Mishnah*, the *Sefer Nizzahon Vetus*, and the *Toldoth Yeshu* refer to Jesus variously as "bastard son of an adultress" and "a beguiler." B. Sanhedrin 43 and B. Sanhedrin 67a contain specific references to Jesus as a "deceiver," while b. Sanhedrin 106a refers to him as the son of a woman who "played the harlot with carpenters." See Katz, *Exclusiveness and Tolerance*, 4–22 and 131–5

208

for a discussion of the theological necessity of rejecting Jesus's Messianity in rabbinic Judaism. The collection of medieval Jewish polemic against Christianity presented by David Berger in *The Jewish–Christian Debate in the High Middle Ages, A Critical Edition of the Sefer Nizzahon Vetus* (Philadelphia: Jewish Publications Society, 1979) also contains several derisive references to Jesus's parentage: 100–7, 164, 214–5 specifically refer to him as a bastard or the product of "a womb of impurity." References to Jesus as a sorcerer and idolater are also common in the text: 103–05 and 201–04 serve as representative examples. The *Sefer Nizzahon Vetus* unquestionably reflects medieval rabbinical teachings about Jesus, as it was compiled in the High Middle Ages as a manual of polemic against Christian apologetics. See also R. Travers Herford, *Christianity in the Talmud and the Midrash*, Library of Religious and Philosophical Thought (Clifton, New Jersey: Reference Book Publishers, 1965) 35–95.

29 John 7:42–52.

30 Such assertions can be found repeatedly in *"Do worden"* 41–5.

31 Lieberdrut the young Jew says: "Jesus, son of David, to you be said praise and honor unendingly! Hail to you, son of David, here and on the heavenly throne! You are the true savior, sent to us for our consolation, may you be greatly blessed! You shall rescue all peoples with your divine hands from the false fetters of the devil!" The boys sing a second verse: "You are king of the Israel of David" And a third boy says: "You are a king of Israel born of David's line without fault! You shall be welcome by all of us, in the name of God, your father!"

32 Meanwhile Joseph of Arimathea goes to Pilate requesting the body of Jesus and says: "Lord Pilate, I beseech you, that you should grant me this! Jesus the Lord is dead, his suffering has now ended: Therefore let me take him down, so that we can lay him in a grave. If you fulfil my wish today, I will thank you forever!"

33 John 19:38–40.

34 *"Do worden"* 113–4.

35 *"Do worden"* 86–7, 136–7.

36 *"Do worden"* 58–62, 67–9.

37 A late nineteenth-century monograph and a late twentieth-century article treat the influence of the Gospel of Nicodemus on medieval religious drama most thoroughly: Richard Paul Wülker, *Das Evangelium Nicodemii in der abendländischen Literatur* (Paderborn: Schöningh, 1872). Achim Masser, "Das Evangelium Nicodemii und das mittelalterliche Spiel," *Zeitschrift für deutsche Philologie* 107:1 (1988)

48–66. Both the apocryphal Gospel of Nicodemus and the legend of Joseph of Arimathea were widely disseminated and influential through-out Europe in the late Middle Ages. Joseph appears as the key figure in the legend of the Holy Grail in both Latin and vernacular literature. The second-century Gospel of Nicodemus was the source, directly or indirectly, of all medieval literature about the descent of Christ into Hell, including the Anglo-Saxon "Christ and Satan" and all scenes of the descent into Hell in all of the Passion and Easter plays discussed in this chapter.

38   *"Do worden"* 114–6.
39   *Das Bild der Juden* 133–4.

Chapter Four

1   *"Do worden"* 117.
2   *Das deutsche Drama des Mittelalters* 151–6.
3   Wenzel uses the phrase "Verteufelung der Juden" as a section heading in her chapter on the Alsfeld Passion play 117–88 of *"Do worden die Judden."* However, Richard Froning was the first scholar to remark on the dramatist's use of every opportunity to emphasize the connection between the Devil and the Jews in the Alsfeld play. Froning's remarks are on page 538 of *Das Drama des Mittelalters*.
4   *"Do worden"* 122.
5   *"Do worden"* 120–1.
6   "I am called Raffenzahn: I eagerly incite all kinds of evil, my heart is full of skill in deception. I demonstrated this thoroughly on the Jews: Constantly I advised them that they should feel hate and envy toward Jesus, the pious man! My entire mind was bent on this! I also fomented among them the sentiment that they should wish neither to see nor to hear him, but should slander him as an immoral man, and here he has never sinned at all, nor has he harbored any evil thought in his heart! Lord Lucifer, all this I have accomplished!"
7   "I have roamed the whole world far and wide [and] I have effected much evil there, day and night! But now I wish to leave all of that and tell now of my masterstroke! There is a pious man called Jesus who never knew sin; the Jews have taken to hating him: (That happened on account of his righteousness!) I persuaded them all to do that!"

210

8   (Ithaca: Cornell UP, 1984).

9   *The Devil in the Middle Ages* 11–28; 62–104; 160–207. A summary of systematic Christian theology of sin, the will, and the role of the Devil as tempter can be found in Karl Rahner et al. ed., *Das Lexikon für Theologie und Kirche*, (Verlag Herder: Freiburg). See the entries on "Freiheit" vol. 4 (323–36), those on "Teufel," "Wille," and "Willens-schwäche" in vol. 10 (2–5; 1159–61; 1164–6). For a detailed medieval treatment of topic including theological arguments up to the thirteenth century, see also Thomas Aquinas's influential work on the nature of evil, *De Malo*.

10   *The Devil in the Middle Ages* 208–9.

11   Ludwig Wolff ed., *Hartmann von Aue: Gregorius,* Altdeutsche Textbibliothek 2 (Tübingen: Niemeyer, 1973). When the enemy of the world, who, because of pride and envy, lay fettered in hell, espied this joy and comfort, the honor of the two upset him, (for it seemed to him to be too great).

12   The first thing was erotic desire, which confused his mind, the second his sister's beauty, the third the Devil's malice, the fourth his own immaturity, which fought alongside the Devil against him, until he (the Devil) brought him to the point of considering in his thoughts how he might sleep with his sister. Woe, Lord, woe, over the hell-hound's clever deceit, that he is always so dangerous to us!

13   *Living Letters* 253–65; *The Devil in the Middle Ages* 79–85.

14   *Living Letters* 275–89.

15   *Living Letters* 288–9.

16   Meanwhile they take the coin to Jesus while Jesus stays in the same place until the Jews assemble before him. Then, the fourth Jew, namely Bifus, says in his place, namely Jerusalem: "Now hear, good men, what I say to you all! I was present on a day when Jesus worked a great sign in the city of Bethany: He commanded Lazarus, a dead man to rise from the dead and fully recover! That can come from nothing other than from a true man of God! He had lain four days in the ground! Truly I say to you all, I believe in him because I saw that, because my mind confirmed it as true that he is the true Christ, the one we call Messiah!"

17   A fifth Jew, namely Lendenkile, says: "Truly, you men, I tell you: Here is the true Messiah! I attest that this is true: He makes a blind man seeing, a man who was born blind! God has chosen him as a son!"

18   See lines 2564–2649.

19   See lines 2650–2723.

20 *"Do worden"* 136–7. Compare her dismissal of the vacillating attitudes of the Jewish crowd with the accounts of Matthew 21:1–12 and 27:20–6, Mark 11:1–10 and 15:8–14, Luke 19:30–40 and 23:13–23 and John 12:11–15 and 19:1–16.

21 Nicodemus responds: "Good men, tell me why you say and affirm this, that Jesus was born a bastard! Here there are still many pious people, to all of whom it is known that the mother of Jesus, whom we call Christ, is legally married to his father!"

22 And they go to Pilate, Joseph and the centurion. Joseph says to Pilate: "Lord Pilate, I come to you and ask that you do not deny me Jesus, who hangs there dead and has overcome his suffering. Give him to me from the cross and let me bury him in the earth! This I ask you with sorrow: Pilate, grant me this!" Pilate responds: "Noble Lord Joseph of Arimathea, a Jew both pious and freeborn: The request that you have made I will take into consideration, with the soldiers who stand here, who have just returned from him! If he has really lost his life, then I will gladly give him to you!"

23 *"Do worden"* 134–8. Compare the account in John 19:38–42 with Matthew 27:57–61, Mark 15:42–7, and Luke 23:50–6.

24 See the biblical citations above for comparison.

25 *"Do worden"* 137.

26 *"Do worden"* 184.

27 *"Do worden"* 186–7.

28 On Cusanus, *Die christlichen Adversus Judaeos Texte* 1994, 524–9. On Nigri, *Die christlichen Adversus Judaeos Texte* 1994, 544–7.

29 *Das Bild der Juden* 213.

30 *Das Bild der Juden* 76–7.

31 *"Do worden"* 138.

32 *"Do worden"* 115–7, 135–8.

33 "The New Testament and First Century Judaism," in *Anti-Semitism and Early Christianity: Issues of Faith and Polemic* (Minneapolis: Fortress Press, 1993) 1–16.

34 "The New Testament and First Century Judaism" 6.

35 "The New Testament and First Century Judaism" 11.

36 "The New Testament and First Century Judaism" 15–7.

37 *"Do worden"* 137–9; *Das Bild der Juden* 54–70.

38 All dates and references to the Easter plays discussed in this section are taken from Richard Froning, *Das Drama des Mittelalters*.

39 *Das Bild der Juden* 48–53; *Das deutsche Drama des Mittelalters* 14–62.

40 Unless otherwise noted, all citations from the Easter plays are taken from Froning's edition. It is therefore Froning's citation format that will be followed here. Some other editions of the *Osterspiel von Muri*, such as the Reclam volume, follow a different division of the play into scenes and section numbers without continuous line numbers.

41 "You three should lie here and the others on this side, and those lie there, and these on this spot here! Keep watch and do not sleep, and you will get what is due you. If, however, you do not carry that out, we shall have to be angry with you: Watch out very carefully!"

42 Pilate says to the Jews: "Woe, I don't know what to do! Gentlemen, advise me, it is time. Our honor depends on it, and if the people find out about this, then they will believe in Jesus more than in all our gods. That would make us a great laughingstock and harm us greatly!" The first Jew: "On my honor, I advise this: If it pleases you, (if not, devise something better) that we pay these fellows twenty marks."

43 "Jesus of Nazareth, whom our princes seized and hanged on the cross. Today is the third day that he has lain in the bands of death, although he never deserved death: We seek him here together, as I have told you."

44 *Juden und Judentum in der mittelalterlichen Kunst* 49–62.

45 *Juden und Judentum in der mittelalterlichen Kunst* 63–4.

46 *Das Drama des Mittelalters* 46–7.

47 The first Mary speaks the verse 'Woe, Woe,': "Woe, woe to the very evil hand that hanged on the cross the Savior of the whole world! He received torture for the sake of mankind. Woe to all you Jews for that great murder, how awful and monstrous! Your hearts are turned to stone: You crucified the mother along with the child!"

48 Ulrich Müller et al. ed., *Das Füssener Osterspiel und die Füssener Marienklage: Universitätsbibliothek Augsburg (ehemals Harburg), Cod. II, 4°62*, Litterae: Göppinger Beiträge zur Textgeschichte 69 (Göppingen: Kümmerle, 1983). "They led him away like a thief, the Jews, to whom Judas betrayed (him), out of whose body blood and water flowed. O woe, how it pains my heart! They captured him and hanged him between two criminals!"

49 The manuscript itself gives the date September 1391 at the conclusion of the text.

50 "You blessed Christian people: I shall tell you (and you might well want to listen) how the Jews went there and wanted to watch the grave with knights big and strong who were the companions of the Jews there; for the sake of money they are supposed to keep Jesus in their custody."

51   "Jesus, who called himself God and destroyed our law, he is now dead and is no longer an obstacle for us."

52   The third Jew speaks; "Pilate, noble, freeborn king, may good fortune always be yours! I fear, we may come into great difficulty; Jesus, whom we killed, he might rise again and might come out of the grave."

53   The third person (Mary Salome) sings: "Oh, what sighs rise in us for the sake of our comforter, we poor people are robbed of him, whom the cruel populace of the Jews gave over to death." And says: "Woe, one can now well see on us poor women great sorrow and distress: My dear Lord is now dead, whom the Jews murdered, without cause, as you have often heard."

54   No translation is possible for this "song." It contains recognizable or lightly distorted Hebrew words, such as "chodus chados adonay" ("holy, holy is the Creator"), taken from Hebrew liturgy, comprehensible Latin phrases, such as "sicut vir melior yesse" ("Just as the sweet man/son of Jesse"). It also contains nonsense words and syllables, and is in no readily comprehensible structure.

55   *Das Rheinische Osterspiel der Berliner Handschrift MS Germ. 1219*, Abhandlungen der Gesellschaft der Wissenschaften zu Göttingen, philologisch-historische Klasse, neue Folge Vol. XVIII, I, ed. Hans Rueff (Berlin: Weidmannsche, 1925).

56   Natan responds: "Since you are now so eager you should all sing after me. I want to teach you, according to Jewish custom, the song that I have written here." Natan begins the song. The macaronic "song" that follows is a mixture of comprehensible German phrases, such as "Messiah shall come ... to our great advantage," and "that I say truthfully"; Latin or Latin-seeming words such as "alba" and "heliodorus"; and finally, Hebrew or Hebrew-seeming words such as "Sabaoth" (the Lord) and "atha berith" ("you, my covenant"). As with other examples of this kind, the function seems to be to mock Hebrew religious song. My thanks to Dr. Gary Porton for his kind assistance in confirming the authenticity of the Hebrew words.

57   Eduard Hartl ed., *Das Drama des Mittelalters. Osterspiele* (rpt. Darmstadt: Wissenschaftliche Buchgesellschaft, 1969) 77.

58   "O, woe for the lamentable pains that we must bear for the sake of our Lord, whom the Jews have slain!"

59   "O, woe, I have lost the creator, whom I once sought and chose, Jesus Christ, the child of Mary! The Jews were all blind when they seized him and bound him and hanged him on the cross. Therefore I must

suffer great agonies in my heart, since I saw it with my own eyes, that a blind Jew stabbed him in the heart."

60 *"Do worden"* 160–2, 194–7.

61 "Woe, you false Jewry! May 'alas, alack' be wailed over you! That God made you for that purpose, that you have cruelly slain our light and our sun, Jesus, the delight of our heart, this we must lament today and forever!"

62 "Where there is no shepherd, there the sheep are quite unsafe against the wolves in the pasture. Jews and heathens are always wolves enough to us, ever since Jesus was killed."

63 "A Hammer That Breaks Rocks to Pieces: Prophetic Critique in the Hebrew Bible," *Anti-Semitism and Early Christianity* 21–40, here 26.

64 "A Hammer That Breaks Rocks" 36–8.

65 "That is lamentable, God the mighty knows, that the good are repaid with cruelty and the evil are crowned for the sake of their evil. Oh, woe to you accursed Jews! You make yourselves like to mad dogs!"

66 The brief quotes read in translation: "Jews are wolves enough to us," and "You (Jews) make yourselves like to packs of mad dogs." Similar developments involving the depiction of Jews as epitomes of immorality appear in late medieval host desecration and ritual murder narratives, as discussed by Rubin in *Gentile Tales* and Gow in *The Red Jews*.

67 Carl Schröder ed., *Redentiner Osterspiel*, Niederdeutsche Denkmäler Vol. 5 (Norden: Diedr. Soltau, 1893). The date given appears on the manuscript, though Schröder suggests in his discussion of the manuscript that the text itself may have been written a year earlier (8–10).

68 "Cayphas and all you gentlemen, I shall have a word with you now. This Jesus claimed to be God's son, he said that he would recover from death. He spoke such very horrific words, as have ever been heard by anyone: That he would rise up on the third day. For this reason I say to you, you should have the grave watched, so that he cannot escape us. Should one of his disciples secretly take him away from there, they will say that he has risen from the dead."

69 See lines 43–68.

70 See lines 1018–43.

71 *"Do worden"* 138–42.

72 *Living Letters* 79–80 with the quote from Gregory appearing on 80.

73 *Living Letters* on the non-culpability of Jewish unblief in the works of these individuals: for Gregory 79–81, for Anselm 168–179, for Bernard 221–33, for Abelard 285–7.

74 *Living Letters* for Isidore 94–7, for Alan 310–11, for Raymond 348–57.

75 Living Letters 373–89.

Chapter Five

1   Frantisek Graus, "Die Juden in ihrer mittelalterlichen Umwelt," *Die Juden in ihrer mittelalterlichen Umwelt*, ed. Alfred Ebenbauer and Helmut Zatloukal (Wien: Böhlau, 1991) 59.

2   "Der mittelalterliche Antijudäismus am Beispiel von Konrads von Würzburgs *Silvester*," in *Die Juden in ihrer mittelalterlichen Umwelt* 169–190, here 181.

3   This she does in her introduction and conclusion. "Der mittelalterliche Antijudäismus" 169–70, 181.

4   *"Do worden"* 44–5, 172–4.

5   See Adelbert von Keller, ed., *Fastnachtspiele aus dem 15. Jahrhundert*, Bibliothek des litterarischen Vereins Stuttgart 28–30 and 46 (Stuttgart: Litterarischer Verein, 1853 and 1858) and Hanns Fischer, ed., *Hans Folz: Die Reimpaarsprüche*, Münchener Texte und Untersuchungen 1 (Munich: Artemis, 1961). The *Fastnachspiele* referenced here, volumes 28 and 29 of the Bibliothek des Litterarischen Vereins Stuttgart, will be referred to with the notation *Fastnachspiele* Vol. 1 (Bibliothek des Litterarischen Vereins Stuttgart 28) and *Fastnachtspiele* Vol. 2 (BLVS 29), containing, respectively, *Die alt und neu ee* and *Kaiser Constantinus*.

6   Discussing the history of this text, Heinz Schreckenberg writes: "Nicht sicher bekannt ist der Autor einer letzen einschlägigen pseudo-augustinischen Schrift, der *Altercatio Ecclesiae et Synogogae*, auch überliefert und zitiert unter dem Titel *De Altercatione Ecclesiae et Synogogae (dialogus)*, PL 42, 1130–1140. Der sehr wahrscheinlich in den Jahrzenten vor 476 entstandene Dialog, dessen Trägerinnen im Sinne einer Personificatio (Prosopopoiie) allegorisch für Christentum und Judentum stehen – eine Allegorisierung mit schon längerer Tradition – hatte einen suggestiven Einfluss auf Bildkunst und geistliches Schauspiel (Übernahme in der Liturgie der Karwoche) des Mittelalters…. Synagoga – sie ist Witwe – beruft sich darauf, daß zu ihr die Propheten gekommen seien und daß ihre Verfehlungen keinen Verlust ihrer älteren Rechte zur Folge gehabt hätten. Ecclesia hält der Kontrahentin unter anderen ihr schändliches Verhalten gegen die Propheten vor und beweist mit Zeugnissen des Alten Testaments die Messianität Jesu. Ihr Hauptargument ist aber ein Geschichtsbeweis, nämlich die sozial deklassierte Stellung der Juden, die diese bis zum Ende des weströmischen Reiches (anno 476) hatten. Zum Schluß des

Wortgefechts erklärt sich Synagoga für geschlagen, Ecclesia kann aber triumphieren." *Die christlichen Adversos-Judaeos-Texte und ihr literarisches und historisches Umfeld* 1982, 354.

7   *"Do worden"* 193–202.

8   All references to Folz's *Kaiser Constantinus* or *die alt und neu ee* will be to the Keller edition. All references to the *Reimpaarsprüche* will be to the Fischer edition, cited above. The reference here is to *Fastnachtspiele*, Vol. 2 797–9.

9   "Der mittelalterliche Antijudäismus" 173–75.

10   Gavin I. Langmuir, "Thomas of Monmouth: Detector of Ritual Murder," *Speculum* 59 (1984): 820–46, here reprinted in *The Blood Libel Legend: A Casebook in Anti-Semitic Folklore*, ed. Alan Dundes (Madison: Wisconsin UP, 1991) 3–40. This and other slanders against Jews eppear also in the works of Tacitus, Manetho of Egypt, Lysimachus of Alexandria, and Posidonius of Apamea. See *The History of Anti-Semitism* 4–12.

11   *Myth of Ritual Murder* 2–3.

12   "Thomas of Monmouth" 4–36,

13   Gavin I. Langmuir, "The Knight's Tale of Hugh of Lincoln," *Speculum* 47 (1972): 459–82.

14   *The Church and the Jews:* Vol. II 116.

15   *The Church and the Jews:* Vol. II 122–5. See also *The Church and the Jews:* Vol I 268–71.

16   *Myth of Ritual Murder* 3–7.

17   *Myth of Ritual Murder* 14–65.

18   R. Po-Chia Hsia, *Trent 1475: Stories of a Ritual Murder Trial* (New Haven: Yale UP, 1992).

19   Werner Williams-Krapp, *Die deutschen und niederländischen Legendare des Mittelalters. Studien zu ihrer Überlieferungs- Text-, und Wirkungsgeschichte*, Texte und Textgeschichte. Würzburger Forschungen 20 (Tübingen: Niemeyer, 1986) 460. In *"Do worden"* p. 249 Wenzel incorrectly identifies the legendary as the *Legenda Aurea*.

20   *Myth of Ritual Murder* 66–85.

21   *Myth of Ritual Murder* 14–41, 86–110.

22   Ulla Williams and Werner Williams-Krapp, *Die "Elsässische Legenda Aurea," Band I: Das Normalcorpus*, Text und Textgeschichte. Würzburger Forschungen 3 (Tübingen: Niemeyer, 1980) XIII–XIV.

23   *Die Elsässische Legenda Aurea* XIII–XIV.

24   "Der Heiligen Leben," *Verfasserlexikon*, vol. 5, ed. Kurt Ruh (Berlin: de Gruyter, 1985) Col. 288–9.

25 Margit Brand et al. eds., *Der Heiligen Leben: Band I: Der Sommerteil* (Tübingen: Niemeyer, 1996) XVI–XXXVI. See also *Die deutschen und niederländischen Legendare* 269–92.

26 Werner Williams-Krapp, "Das 'Bamberger Legendar': Eine Vorarbeit zu 'Der Heiligen Leben,'" *Zeitschrift für deutsches Altertum und deutsche Philologie* 123:4 (1994): 45–54.

27 *Der Heiligen Leben: Sommerteil* XIII.

28 *Die deutschen und niederländischen Legendare* 188–238.

29 *Die deutschen und niederländischen Legendare* 317–20.

30 *Die deutschen und niederländischen Legendare* 314–7.

31 My discussion of the *Kaiserchronik* and its connections to related texts is based on *Die deutsche Literatur des Mittelalters, Verfasserlexikon*, Vol. 4, ed. Kurt Ruh (Berlin: De Gruyter, 1983) Col. 949–50.

32 *Verfasserlexikon* Vol. 4, Col. 949.

33 Bernhard Blumenkranz, *Die Judenpredigt Augustins. Ein Beitrag zur Geschichte der jüdisch–christlichen Beziehungen in den ersten Jahrhunderten* (Basel: Helbing and Lichtenhahn, 1946).

34 *Christians and Jews in the Twelfth-Century Renaissance* 1–34

35 Berger, *The Jewish–Christian Debate.* See note in chapter two.

36 *Living Letters* 317–63.

37 David Hugh Farmer, *The Oxford Dictionary of Saints* (Oxford: Clarendon, 1978) 366.

38 In Werner Williams-Krapp's as yet unpublished edition of *Der Heiligen Leben: Winterteil*, the disputation occupies six of the legend's ten manuscript pages. References to this work will be noted as *Der Heiligen Leben: Winterteil.* Here I would like to express my gratitude and appreciation to Professor Williams-Krapp for allowing me access to the page proofs.

39 Jacobi a Voragine, *Legenda Aurea vulgo historia lombardica dicta*, ed. Th. Graesse (3rd Ed. 1890: Rpt. Osnabrück: Otto Zeller, 1969) 73–8. Here, as in Konrad's *Silvester*, the disputation makes up the major portion of the legend.

40 The Silvester legend appears in several prose and rhymed legendaries, its medieval attestation not limited to the widely disseminated texts treated here (*Der Heiligen Leben, Die niederdeutsche Legenda Aurea*, and *Das Passional*). See *Die deutschen und niederländischen Legendare* 460.

41 Wilhelm Grimm, ed., *Konrads von Würzburg Silvester* (Göttingen: Dieterichsche Buchhandlung, 1841) 1.

42   They were all learned beyond all measure and spoke, as it pleased them, both Greek and Latin well. Whatever one should wish to discuss in depth concerning the Old Law, they could do this and more than I can relate here: There never were any unbaptized persons more learned.

43   *Die Elsässische Legenda Aurea* 83. Constantinus, in reply, suggested to his mother that she bring with her the Jewish masters of learning, because he wished to put against them Christian teachers, so that one might judge by their teaching and words which faith was more true. From there Helena took with her one hundred and forty-one masters of the Jewish faith, among whom were twelve especially enlightened with all wisdom.

44   *Der Heiligen Leben: Winterteil* 356. After the noblewoman read the letter, she gathered one hundred and sixty-six wise scholars, who were the best in all lands. Among them were twelve supremely wise scholars. These same ones she brought with her to Rome to the emperor.

45   *Der Heiligen Leben: Winterteil* 356–7; *Die Elsässische Legenda Aurea* 83–4; *Legenda Aurea* 73.

46   Let it be explained to me, the degrading mockery and the scorn that he endured in his manifold suffering. His agonizing death, explain it to me from the very beginning, so that we might all with you become believers in him and praise his name forever here on Earth. If you can pursuade me here concerning the truth about him, then I will extol him and proclaim his praise everywhere, with both words and deeds.

47   *Living Letters* 168–85.

48   Zambrî, the twelfth master then spoke very angrily in this fashion, 'I am pained, and what more need be said about the matter? Except that Silvester wants to destroy our paternal traditions. And that he wishes to deprive us of reason by means of his words.'

49   And however this wonder comes to pass, that one sees the bull alive, it is demonstrated here truly that the devil obviously caused him grim death, since he cannot restore to him a healthy life.

50   *Legenda Aurea* 78, Karl Köpke, ed., *Das Passional. Eine Legenden-sammlung des dreizehnten Jahrhunderts* (Leipzig: Basse, 1852) 88–90, *Dat Passionœl* (Lübeck: Stefan Arndes, 1492) cccxvi–a to cccxviii–b, *Die Elsässische Legenda Aurea* 89–90.

51   See Chapter One.

52   *Elsässische Legenda Aurea* 86. Here, the German translation is only following the Latin model. See *Legenda Aurea* 73. In the Latin text, the debate begins without any agreement on the use of biblical texts.

53 *Elsässische Legenda Aurea* 89. Again, the German translation follows the Latin text of the *Legenda Aurea* 77–8.

54 *Der Heiligen Leben: Winterteil* 363. "Neither I nor Silvester can restore the steer to life. If, however, Silvester does restore him to life, then I will gladly believe that his God is a true God." This the Jews all said.

55 *Der Heiligen Leben: Winterteil* 362.

56 This play is also known as *Der Juden Messias*. However, this title is similar to that of one of Folz's *Reimpaarsprüche*. Since the latter will also be discussed in the following pages, the longer title of the *Fastnachtspiel* will be used in order to avoid any confusion.

57 Note that in the text the character is referred to in the stage directions as "endechrist," and identifies himself as such because he is "ein ende der Cristen." Until he is exposed as a fraud, the rabbis address him and refer to him as "Messias."

58 Klaus Ridder and Hans-Hugo Steinhoff, ed., *Frühe Nürnberger Fastnachtspiele*, Schöningh Mediävistische Editionen, Vol. 4 (Paderborn: Schöningh, 1998) 88–9. The second rabbi: "Mark now, what I add: I make known to you now the Messiah, certainly, who was revealed to us long ago, and who will exalt Jewry." The fool: "I would dare give you a punch in the mouth. You black dog, what do you mean by that? Go over there, so the knight can shoot you." The third rabbi: "For what do you need this fool's play? The Messiah is simply here and wishes that you all should praise him and swear oaths." The fool: "Oh, that no one smacks you in the mouth with a stick out of a cesspool and does not beat you full of bruises and lumps."

59 *Frühe Nürnberger Fastnachtspiele* 96–7. Antichrist: "Yes, if only they knew in addition to that how much cursing, how much hatred and envy we have ever borne toward them, how much property we have stolen from them, how much we have annihilated their lives, we who have been their physicians, how many small children we have stolen from them and killed, and reddened with their own innocent blood, and taken away from you Christians, for scorn of the anniversary of Jesus's birth, which you eternally observe...."

60 *"Do worden"* 248. See also "Konrad von Würzburg," *Die deutsche Literatur des Mittelalters Verfasserlexikon*, Vol. 5, ed. Kurt Ruh (Berlin: De Gruyter, 1985) Col. 287.

61 *Fastnachtspiele*, Vol. 2 797. "My body was so polluted and completely covered by leprosy, that jewish doctors, heathens, and idols advised nothing else than that three thousand pure, innocent, little children be killed and my body washed in their mingled blood."

62   In the Latin, Constantinus plans to bathe himself in the blood of 3,000 boys "ad consilium pontificum ydolorum," "according to the counsel of the priests of idols," *Legenda Aurea* 71. The figures are clearly Roman pagans, not rabbis.

63   *Elsässische Legenda Aurea* 81, *Das Passional* 65. *Der Heiligen Leben: Winterteil* 354 identifies the figures as "ewarten" (priests) and is explicit in identifying the emperor himself as "ain haiden."

64   Eckehard Catholy, *Das Fastnachtspiel des Spätmittelalters*, Hermaea Germanistische Forschungen, Vol. 8 (Tübingen: Niemeyer, 1961) 5–8, 41–7.

65   "Das Verhältnis des Fastnachtspiels vom 'Kaiser Constantinus' zum Reimpaarspruch 'Christ und Jude' von Hans Folz," *Zeitschrift für deutsches Altertum und deutsche Literatur* 92 (1964): 277–91.

66   *"Do worden"* 234–46.

67   *"Do worden"* 196–7.

68   *Fastnachtspiele*, Vol. 1 6–7.

69   *Fastnachtspiele*, Vol. 1 7–8.

70   Wenzel, "Zur Judenproblematik bei Hans Folz," *Zeitschrift für deutsche Philologie* 101 (1982): 79–104. *"Do worden"* 206–08. In the 1982 article, she describes the text as a "Kauderwelsch" that Folz uses to achieve "sprachliche Diffamierung der Juden." In her later monograph, she notes that the text is actually a good phonetic rendering of the Hebrew and that the German translation that Folz provides is nearly perfect. This being true, the characterization of the text as "sprachliche Diffamierung" is inaccurate.

71   For the text, see *Fastnachtspiele*, Vol. 2 798.

72   *"Do worden"* 210–16.

73   *Fastnachtspiele*, Vol. 2 799. "Everything in which you contradict me, I will explain thoroughly and demonstrate solely from your prophets, from your own scripture and teaching."

74   *Fastnachtspiele*, Vol. 1 20.

75   *Living Letters* 317–43, *The Church and the Jews: Vol. II* 3–47. Both volumes of *The Church and the Jews* contain texts of the papal condemnations of the Talmud, which begin appearing in the 1240's and are modified, clarified, ameliorated, or made harsher over the course of several decades.

76   *"Do worden"* 216–7.

77   *Fastnachtspiele*, Vol. 1 27–30.

78   *Fastnachtspiele*, Vol. 1 28, line 6.

79 Hans Folz, *Hans Folz. Die Reimpaarsprüche*, Münchener Texte und Untersuchungen zur deutschen Literatur des Mittelalters vol. 1, ed. Hans Fischer (Munich: C.H. Beck, 1961). Here the text of the edition has been compared with that of British Museum IA 7893, "Item, ein Krieg, den der Dichter dieses Spruchs gehapt hat wid' einen Juden, von Hans Folczen" (Nürnberg, 1479), found in *German Books before 1601* (Cambridge, Mass.: General Microfilm Co.) MF #7726, Roll 28, Item 3. "I began and said to the Jew, since nobody else present wanted to season our discourse but we alone, therefore I desired that we two try ourselves against each other alone, and that they should promise and swear their oaths to this: that none would open his mouth against us until we had both tested one another. Herewith we opened our sacks and shook out what was inside them. Yet I asked the Jew further which of us should begin. Then the Jew instructed me and said, 'Christian, it would be fitting for you, since your faith is a new thing. My faith existed first, as you well know.'"

80 *Christians and Jews* 34–47.

81 "I spoke, 'My Jew, now listen carefully. You know that God shows much through metaphor in the words of the prophets. See now, if this gloss is understandable: The wild and the domestic animals, those are you Jews and we [Christians]. Just as the sheep are without malice, so we pray for your salvation. Nevertheless you harbor toward us wolfish thoughts, even though you really do nothing to us. One can likewise interpret the children with the poisonous beasts. We are the children of God. You are the poisonous serpents. For if you had us in your power as you are said to be in ours, then no Christian would live out the year.'"

82 The Frankfurt Passion play uses contemporary names for its Jewish figures and depicts them as usurers, that is, as victimizers of Christians. Likewise, the Brandenburg and Erlau Easter plays depict the Jews as a source of real, not potential harm, to contemporary Christians.

83 "'Jew, herewith I conclude that he who saved us must be true man and true God who was prefigured by all of these metaphors, and foretold by all of the prophets whom he sent hence before him and which came to an end soon after him. That you, however, still wait for him, that is because of a foolishness among you that has led you astray for many years.' The Jew spoke, 'May God now enlighten us, by his most holy name.' Then I answered eagerly, 'Amen.'"

84 *Reimpaarsprüche*, Nr. 37, 215–40.

Chapter Six

1   "Theophilus: Servant of Two Masters. The Pre-Faustian Theme of Despair and Revolt," *Modern Language Notes*, 87.6 (1972): 31–50.

2   "Servant of two Masters" 31–2. See also Hans Heinrich Weber, *Studien zur deutschen Marienlegende des Mittelalters am Beispiel des Theophilus* (Hamburg: Hamburg UP, 1966).

3   On the earliest manuscript, see Meta Harrsen, "The Manuscripts," *Hroswitha von Gandersheim: Her Life, Times, and Works and a Comprehensive Bibliography*, ed. Anne Lyon Haight (New York: The Hroswitha Club, 1965) 42–4. The text is available in a modern German translation: *Hroswitha von Gandersheim: Werke*, ed. and trans. Helene Homener (Paderborn: Schöningh, 1936) 97–109.

4   *Studien zur deutschen Marienlegende des Mittelalters* 7–24.

5   The text of "der arme" Hartmann's poem is quoted here from the introduction to an edition of a late medieval Theophilus drama: *Theophilus, der Faust des Mittelalters. Schauspiel aus dem vierzehnten Jahrhunderte in niederdeutscher Sprache*, ed. Ludwig Etmüller, Bibliothek der gesamten deutschen National-Literatur, Vol. 27 (Leipzig: Gottfr. Basse, 1849) xi–xii. Then God began to take pity on the poor sinner in his Godly might, since he can do all things. He forced the evil Devil to relinquish that very letter without his payment: the Devil didn't like that at all.

6   *Studien zur deutschen Marienlegende des Mittelalters* 24–39.

7   Hans-Georg Richert, *Marienlegenden aus dem Alten Passional*, Altdeutsche Textbibliothek 64 (Tübingen: Niemeyer, 1965) x–xxi. All texts of the Theophilus and "Judenknabe" legends will be taken from this edition of *das Verspassional*.

8   *Die deutsche Literatur des Mittlelalters. Verfasserlexikon*, ed. Kurt Ruh, Vol. 4 (Berlin: de Gruyter, 1983) Col. 331–6. The entry notes that the source history of *Das Verspassional* is still murky and likely to remain so.

9   Within him, his mind struggled for control, just as the dog fights for a piece of meat. Now in the city there was also a Jew who in the black books could locate the art by which one trafficks with devils. Theophilus completely abandoned his heart to the Jew's counsel. In the greatest vileness, he sought the medicines that would free him from the named misfortune.

10 As soon as the Jew was aware of this, he spoke to him. "So, I will tell you the truth and will not conceal how you may come to a position of prestige. God and Christendom you must forsake, and also Mary. If you only do that one thing (and truthfully, it is a little thing, for not much power is associated with it) then all your lordship will be completely subjugated to you, as before. Yours shall also be additional power, to which the Devil shall help you."

11 32–50.

12 Charlotte D'Evelyn and Anna J. Mill, ed., *The South English Legendary*, EETS ES No.235. (London: Oxford UP. 1967). The three German plays are available both in the two-volume edition of Hoffmann von Fallersleben, *Theophilus: Niederdeutsches Schauspiel aus einer Trierer Handschrift des XV. Jahrhunderts* (Hannover: Rümpler. 1853), and *Theophilus: Niederdeutsches Schauspiel in zwei Fortsetzungen aus einer Stockholmer und einer Helmstädter Handschrift*, 1854, and in a more recent single-volume work: R. Pertsch, ed., *Theophilus: Mittelniederdeutsches Drama in drei Fassungen* (Heidelberg: Carl Winter, 1908). Here all citations will be from the von Fallersleben edition.

13 Theophilus: "You Jews, may God grant you good day!" The Jews: "May a cat bite your head off!" Theophilus: "You Jews, would it be worth something to you, if I were to join myself to your faith and forsake my Christianity? I know the Christian books very well: If you would pay me some money, we could harm the Christians immeasurably." Musin: "Truly, mister priest, I will tell you this, we will not pay any money for that. We will gladly have you with us, but we want to circumcise you according to our law." Theophilus: "I'd rather that all you Jews would boil in a hot pan!"

14 Samuel: "Why are you shouting so much, dear sir? That would be a horrible tale. It terrifies me that I even hear it spoken. You would really damn your life and soul for the sake of miserable, unholy wealth? Good sir, please don't do that at all! You are a Christian and I a Jew. Even for all the wealth on earth I would most extremely unwillingly become the Devil's own. I thought that you were a wise man! Abandon this course of action and turn away from it!"

15 "Jew, you advise me as should a brother! May God's mother repay you for it! If I come back, I will certainly bring you a present."

16 "Servant of Two Masters" 31–2

17 Fallersleben 8–9 (Stockholm MS); 51–3 (Helmstadt MS). See also Petsch 11–13; 43–4.

18   "There you can certainly find the Devil, unless it is other than I guess."

19   Beatrice Kälin, *"Maria, muter der barmherzigkeit." Die Sünder und die Frommen in den Marienlegenden des Alten Passionals,* Deutsche Literatur von den Anfängen bis 1700, Vol. 17 (Bern: Peter Lang, 1994) 29, 245; *Gentile Tales* 7–8.

20   Wernfried Hofmeister, "Das Jüdel im Kontext mittelhochdeutscher literarischer Kinderdarstellungen," *Die Juden in ihrer mittelalterlichen Umwelt* 91–103.

21   "There was a Jew rich in property who lived among the Christians and who, with the art of a Jew, gained much wealth through usury." Again, all citations of the Marian legends are from Richert's edition unless otherwise noted.

22   "Oh," said the father, "dear child, you have greatly dishonored the great Holy Day that the Christians now observe, the false ones, the ignoble ones, for you have not eaten. You should have rather stayed home today, for the Christians are most immoral in their celebrations."

23   This detail of the legend originates with Gregory of Tours's *De Gloria Martyrum.* For a full account of its transmission, see *"Maria, muter der barmherzigkeit"* 144–5.

24   "'Woe is me forever! What has become and will become of me, and what, truly, shall happen to my life? You have given out a sentence that I cannot go along with. May your judgment, your blows fall without any delay on the child and on me. Do whatever you want to me, I love my child so much that I cannot kill him."

25   *"Maria muter der barmherzigkeit"* 155–6; *Gentile Tales* 7–26.

26   *Marienlegenden* 274. "On hearing this his father, gravely enraged, seizes him violently, and seeing not far away a furnace with a blazing fire in it, going to it, he throws him into the fire immediately."

27   Middle English: "nearly insane with rage," and a "furiously burning fire." The text of the legend is taken from *The South English Legendary* 229. In the *South English Legendary* this tale is appended to the Theophilus legend.

28   *Gentile Tales* 12–16.

29   534–5.

30   *Der "Judenknabe." Studien und Texte zu einem mittelalterlichen Marienmirakel in deutscher Überlieferung,* Göppinger Arbeiten zur Germanistik Nr. 654 (Kümmerle: Göppingen, 1998) 252. Here the manuscripts referred to are Vienna ÖNB Cod. 2696, Berlin SB Hdschr. 397, and a manuscript without signature known as the "Seitenstetten Fragment" (Seitenstetten SfB).

31 One never saw a man lament so immoderately: he nearly killed himself. He tore the flesh from his cheeks, and spoke to himself piteously: "O, woe, poor me, how little I move almighty God to pity, if I obey this order, I would never be able to live." He asked for a weapon to be given to him, a sword or a knife. He said, "It would be better for me that I killed myself, than inflict this extraordinary suffering on my child. Before I do that, I would rather stab myself to death. Therefore, another must carry out on my child this fate. God knows, I cannot strike him down."

32 *"Der Judenknabe," Studien und Texte* 268.

33 *"Maria, muter der barmherzigkeit"* 148. See chapter three of Daniel.

34 *"Maria, muter der barmherzigkeit"* 155. The resistance of some Jews and their willingness to kill the boy in spite of the miracle is also emphasized in Gautier's Middle French version. See Rubin's discussion in *Gentile Tales* 19–20.

35 The miraculous sign that he saw on his child began to soften the old Jew's spirit a little. At the same time a ray of the faith broke into his heart that began to steal him from the false dilemma. He soon sent his messengers away to the court of the priests.

36 See *"Maria, muter der barmherzigkeit"* 155; *Marienlegenden* 275; *The South English Legendary* 229.

37 *Das Passional* 136. Then there came a Jew to him whom the bishop liked to see, because he felt great love for him, in the hope that a change would yet occur in his life, and that he would truly and straightway set foot on the right path in matters of faith. The Jew was a good doctor, for he well read the scholarship in the learned books.

38 *Die deutschen und niederländischen Legendare* 13, 27. Williams-Krapp identifies the *LA* as the major source for books 2 and 3 of *Das Verspassional*, noting that other sources were also used.

39 *Legenda Aurea* 126. Note that the detail also occurs in the German text that follows.

40 *Elsässische Legenda Aurea* 148. When Saint Basil lay in his deathbed in great illness, he then had summoned to him a Jew who was named Joseph and who was certainly a master physician. The Jew felt Saint Basil's pulse and told the people that they should prepare everything necessary for a burial, for death was at the door. Saint Basil heard this and said, "Joseph, what are you saying? I intend to be alive tomorrow." Then the Jew said, "Sir, that is impossible, for your body is so ravaged that it cannot endure any more."

41 This text is cited from the as-yet unpublished proof of Werner Williams-Krapp's *Der Heiligen Leben. Winterteil* 410. Then a Jew went over to him, he was named Joseph. The bishop liked to see him, for he hoped, that he might become a believer. And the Jew was a good physician and would gladly have helped Saint Basil.

42 *Das Passional* 136, *Legenda Aurea* 126, *Elsässische Legenda Aurea* 148, *Der Heiligen Leben. Winterteil* 410.

43 *Das Passional* 136. Then Joseph said, "If it happens with you, that the tribulation of death does not come by then, then know, that I myself will lie dead. There is no doubt of it." "May God grant me preservation, for I desire from my heart, that you die to your sins and gain therefore a fully Christian life, in which will be given to you by God a rational understanding."

44 *Das Passional* 136–37. Then the Jew replied to him, "I understand well what you are saying and what it is that you are pursuing with your words as your morally good custom teaches you. I will gladly follow you and vouchsafe my fidelity in that I will have myself baptized tomorrow, if you live until then. If it is so that my intellect deceives me, then I have no knowledge of medicine, for all of my learning assures me that you will not survive this day."

45 *Elsässische Legenda Aurea* 148. Then Saint Basil said, "Joseph, what will you do, if I live until tomorrow?" The Jew answers, "Sir, I will die myself, if you live until the sixth hour tomorrow." Then Saint Basil said, "You ought rather die to your sins and live for Christ." Then the Jew said, "Sir, I know well what you mean. If it turns out that you are alive tomorrow at the sixth hour, then I will do what you wish." Then Saint Basil prayed to God, that he should prolong his life, though it be against nature. For this reason he remained alive until the ninth hour the next day. When Joseph the Jew saw this, he was awed and believed in Christ.

46 Der Heiligen Leben. Winterteil 410.

Chapter Seven

1 Klaus Grubmüller, "Fabel, Exemplum, Allegorese – Über Sinn-bildungsverfahren und Verwendungszusammenhänge," *Exempel und Exempelsammlungen*, ed. Burghart Wachinger and Walter Haug (Tübingen: Niemeyer, 1991) 58–74.

2 Klaus Grubmüller, *Meister Esopus. Untersuchungen zu Geschichte und Funktion der Fabel im Mittelalter*. MTU 56 (Munich: Artemis, 1977) 9–11.

3 Edward Wheatley, *Mastering Aesop – Medieval Education, Chaucer, and His Followers* (Gainesville: U of Florida Press, 2000) 1–51.

4 See the discussion in Gerd Dicke, *Heinrich Steinhöwels "Esopus" – Untersuchungen zu einem Bucherfolg der Frühdruckzeit* MTU 103 (Munich: Artemis, 1994) 29–31

5 Hermann Oesterley, *Heinrich Steinhöwel, Äsop*, Bibliothek des Litterarischen Vereins Stuttgart #117 (Stuttgart: Litterarischer Verein, 1873) 5. Since, however, I intend to talk about the fables of Aesop, it should be noted beforehand, what it is we call a fable. Therefore know that the poets have taken the name fable from the Latin word "fando," that is "to say" in German, because the fables are things which have not happened, but rather have been imagined using words, and were imagined so that, through the imagined words spoken by unreasoning animals among themselves, one might gain in understanding of the nature and moral habits of men.

6 "Fabel, Exempel" 60.

7 "Fabel, Exempel" 62–70.

8 Michael Wissemann, "Fabel: Zur Entwicklung der Bezeichnung einer Gattung," *Fabula: Zeitschrift für Erzählforschung*, 33 (1992): 1–13.

9 *Die Fabeln des Mittelalters und der frühen Neuzeit: Ein Katalog der lateinischen Versionen und ihrer deutschen Entsprechungen*, MMS 60 (Munich: Fink, 1987).

10 In the Latin fable, tradition this fable is known as "de simia," Avianus 14. In Dicke and Grubmüller's *Die Fabeln des Mittelalters und der frühen Neuzeit* it is 12. This and all other citations from the Nürnberg fable collection will be drawn from Klaus Grubmüller, *Der Nürnberger Prosa-Äsop*, Altdeutsche Textbibliothek 107 (Tübingen: Niemeyer, 1994). Once upon a time, Jupiter commanded that all living creatures, be they people, birds, animals, fish, or creeping things, should come before him. He wanted to see which among them was the noblest and

had the most beautiful offspring. And when they came and brought with them all of their young offspring, among them came the mother-ape and brought along her child and went before Jupiter and spoke: "See that among all creatures that stand here before you, none is more beautiful than my child." And when Jupiter hears this, he laughs and mocks her because she so boasted of herself and her child, because she wanted to be praised by him. Then she was mocked and derided by all creatures for her foolishness. Allegorical meaning: By the mother-ape the congregation of the Jews is to be understood, by the other animals other peoples are signified, such as Christians and heathens, and that the Jews say that their faith is more righteous than ours. And for this reason they become a laughingstock, for they neither observe nor wish to understand the sayings of the prophets. And Paul speaks against them and says: "They are hearers of the word, but not followers."

11   Perry 375, known in Latin as "de calvo equite," *Avianus* 10.
12   Aaron E. Wright, *Hie lêrt uns der Meister: Latin Commentary and the German Fable*, Medieval and Renaissance Texts and Studies 218 (Tempe: Arizona Center for Medieval and Renaissance Studies, 2001) 328–36.
13   Aaron E. Wright, *The Fables of Walter of England*, Toronto Medieval Latin Texts 25 (Toronto: Pontifical Institute of Medieval Studies, 1997) 2–3; also *Hie lêrt uns der Meister* xi–xviii.
14   *Fables of Walter* 3.
15   *Fables of Walter* 1–2; *Hie lért* xiii–xviii.
16   *Hie lért* xii.
17   *Hie lért* xiii.
18   Dicke-Grubmüller 632
19   Dicke-Grubmüller 162
20   Dicke-Grubmüller 150
21   *Fables of Walter* 28. Moral teaching: In the lamb understand Christ, promised in the law by the prophets, who, in human form, just like a sheep was led humbly and sweetly to death. Just as Peter (says) in his book: "He was led like a sheep to the slaughter." By the Wolves understand truly the congregation of the Jews, who, just like wolves clamored falsely against Christ in front of Pilate in these words, "This one will destroy the temple of God," etc. And also, "If he were not a malefactor," etc. To them Christ gently responds, "I did not come to destroy the law but to fulfill it." The Jews are truly fierce wolves, the sheep....

22 *Fables of Walter* 72. Moral teaching: In Jupiter understand God almighty, in the frogs the Jews who shouted to God for a king. Yet they would not submit to him when one was given to them. For this reason they are put up for sale and devoured by the sword just as is read concerning the destruction of Jerusalem and the capitivity of the Jews and their destruction during the time of Titus and Vespasian.

23 *Fables of Walter* 100. Moral teaching: In the fly understand the Jews, who believe their law and all they do to be good. But spiritual men are designated by the ant, who are mocked by them in writing. By the place is to be understood life in this age, in which Jews and many perverted Christians live in luxury. But then it is the devil or even the day of judgment which surprises them with death and they live in Gehenna.

24 *Hie lêrt* 84. Allegorical meaning: By the knight we can understand Christ, by the hair truly his assumed humanity, which, being mortal and transient, slipped away, and was derided by the Jews so saying, "He did save others, but himself he cannot save." But through his resurrection he annulled the ridicule of the Jews. Or, rather, by the mocking crowd the Jews are to be signified, who, by tearing out the beard of the knight, who is Christ, mock him, who gratefully accepts everything that occurs through the way they shake their heads in the sign of derision, but who defends himself in front of them with trenchant words.

25 *Hie lêrt* 87. Likewise, the allegorical meaning: By the ape we are obliged to understand the Synagogue and by the other wild animals other sorts of people. Only the synagogue says its faith is better, though it is not, and just like the ape who shouts out to Jove, so likewise the Jews and heretics exert themselves to destroy our Christian faith, saying that their faith is the best, when nevertheless it is worst.

26 Dicke-Grubmüller #450

27 *Hie lêrt* 46–8

28 *Nürnberger Prosa Äsop* 24. Moral: by the knight is to be understood our Lord Jesus Christ. By the hair understand his humanity. He became an object of scorn to the Jews, when they said [Mt. 27,41] "He has made other people well, but he cannot make himself well." But when our Lord rose from the dead, he turned their laughter and mockery into crying and lamentation, when they perceived that he rose, by his own power, from the dead.

29 *Nürnberger Prosa Äsop* 69. Moral: by the lamb is to be understood our Lord Jesus Christ, by the wolf the synagogue and the Jews, who falsely accused our Lord of destroying their law, even though he refuted this charge, saying [Mt.5, 17] "I have not come to destroy the law but to

230

fulfill it." Nevertheless, his virtuous refutation availed him nothing and they killed him as an innocent man, just as Pilate himself affirmed, when he said [Lk 23,14] "I find no guilt in him for which he should be killed."

30 *Nürnberger Prosa Äsop* 37. Moral: by the four oxen are signified the righteous, pious Christians, who always live and carry out their affairs according to the commandments of our Lord. By the lion are Jews and heretics signified, who constantly strive with all diligence to deceive the righteous with their mendacious, false words and lead them off the righteous path to the path of death. And that we must always firmly stand by one another, that is what Isaiah advises us who says, "If we stand together and don't leave the path, then we shall be found true and esteemed."

31 *Living Letters* 119–23, 195–201.

32 "The Lamb and the Scapegoat: The Dehumanization of the Jews in Medieval Propaganda Imagery," *Anti-Semitism in Times of Crisis*, 38–80, here 55.

33 *Hie lêrt* x–xxvi. Neither the Latin texts edited by McKenzie and Old-father in their *Ysopet Avionnet* (1919), nor the texts edited by Robinson Ellis in his *Avianus* (1887), nor the Leyden *Avianus* manuscript (MS Voss. L.O. 89) contain any of the anti-Jewish epimyths mentioned in this discussion. Ellis's manuscripts range from the eighth to the fourteenth centuries.

34 Robinson Ellis, *The Fables of Avianus* (Oxford: Clarendon, 1887) 16. Then the small ape drags away her deformed offspring, even as she moves the angry Jupiter himself to laugther. Nevertheless, this shameless one blurted out a word before all others, generating the kind of offense that she would eagerly do away with.

35 Kenneth McKenzie and William A. Oldfather, *Ysopet-Avionnet: The Latin and French Texts*, University of Illinois Studies in Language and Literature, Vol. 4 (Urbana: University of Illinois Press, 1919) 228. "You should not wish to praise those things which are your own, unless others approve with their own speech first. In this manner the man who would make something of himself rightfully remains in a mean estate, although he approves of himself. Additionally: He who is unworthy in his manner of speech greatly cheats himself of praise and by doing so he incites to laughter."

36 The text is quoted from *The Fables of Avianus* 16. The following translation is from *Minor Latin Poets with Introductions and English Translations*, The Loeb Classical Library, ed. J. Wight Duff and Arnold

M. Duff (London: William Heinemann, 1935) 696–99. "Then this sage one, though ridiculed by the thousands, undoes mockery with a skillful rejoinder. 'Is it strange,' he replies, 'that my wig flew away when previously my own hair deserted me in the same manner?'"

37 *Yzopet Avionnet* 225. You ought to dismiss ridicule with ridicule of your own against men by dint of cleverness. Additionally: A darkhaired head will not protect; even with long hair favorable winds make baldness evident.

38 *Hie lêrt* xvii–xix; 170–89.

39 *Hie lêrt* 47.

40 Christian Waas, *Die Quellen der Beispiele Boners* (Dortmund: Fr. Wilh. Ruhfus, 1897) 66–75; "Boner," *Verfasserlexikon* Vol. 1 (Berlin: de Gruyter, 1977) Col. 947–55.

41 *Der Edelstein*, Ed. Franz Pfeiffer, Dichtungen des deutschen Mittelalters, Vol. 4 (Leipzig: Göschen, 1844) 141. He who praises that which ought not be praised, that is really the practice of an ape. Whoever praises what he shouldn't may be covered in contempt. Every mother thinks her children beautiful, though they are not beautiful.

42 *Der Edelstein* 134. In this world there is no permanence. What is good today is bad tomorrow. He is sick today, who was healthy yesterday. For this reason one says that he who relies on the world's appearance must not be wise. This lord lost his wig, which is the world's instability.

43 *Steinhöwels Äsop* 82. With this fable Aesop wants to show that sense and truth find no place among base and false accusers; one finds such wolves in all places.

44 *Steinhöwels Äsop* 111. Then he gave them the stork, who began to kill them one after the other. Then they began to wail and raise their voices to the very heavens, crying, "O god Jupiter, come and help us or we will all die!" Then he said to them, "When you wanted a king, I wouldn't give you one. When you cried out to me again, I gave you a gentle king, but you treated him with contempt and trod him under foot. Then I gave you the king whom you now have on account of your loud yammering, and you shall have to keep him, since you would not endure the good one."

45 *Steinhöwels Äsop* 131. The ant replied then to the fly thus: "What a base and shameful creature you are, that you praise yourself for your rude and nasty behavior! Tell me, who is it that desires your presence? How are you received by the king and by the noble ladies you talk about, whom you stubbornly fly onto against their will, saying all of

232

this is within your power, and yet you don't say what an unwelcome guest you are. Everywhere you go people drive you away. People drive you off everywhere with great commotion as if you were a belligerent enemy. And you are only something in the summer. In winter you perish without strength, while I am lively the whole time. In winter I am safe in my home, I am healthy all the time, and live in joy. Wherever you are, people drive you away with whips and fans that are made especially and with great industry against you. This fable is against all of the noisy quarrelsome folk, the complainers, and useless things of all kinds that are shameful."

46 *Steinhöwels Äsop* 273. Then the king began to laugh heartily and with him the crowd of mothers, and he said to him: "You should never praise something of your own, unless it has already been acclaimed and praised by others. For self-praise is to be criticized; and for this you have now been mocked and derided by many."

47 *Steinhöwels Äsop* 277–8. "However, when the lion notices that they are divided and that each has gone on alone, he was strong and powerful enough against each one individually, and he ate each one in turn, those whom he had not even dared touch when they were together. But when he got to the last ox, that one spoke for the instruction of all the animals: Whoever would like to live a quiet life, he may learn from our deaths, that he should not so easily give an ear to deceitful words, and should not so thoughtlessly let an old friendship fall apart; for if we had remained united, the lion would not have defeated us."

48 *Hie lêrt* 47.

49 *Hie lêrt* 186–7.

50 See *Steinhöwels "Esopus"* 369–72 for a complete list of the 241 extant pre-1600 copies of the German and Latin print editions, 439–49 for descriptions of the seven extant manuscripts.

51 The problems surrounding the dating and attribution of Gerhard von Minden's *Äsop*, found complete only in Wolfenbüttel Hs. 97 Nov, are dealt with by Albert Leitzmann in the introduction to his edition, *Die Fabeln Gerhards von Minden in mittelniederdeutscher Sprache* (Halle: Niemeyer, 1898; Rpt. Hildesheim: Ohms, 1985) XX–XXIV. This fable appears on page four: The innocent man cannot preserve his innocence, but night and day, the worldly maliciously strive for an occasion to put him to death.

52 Quoted in Adalbert Elschenbroich, ed., *Die deutsche und lateinische Fabel in der frühen Neuzeit, Bd. I: Ausgewählte Texte* (Tübingen: Niemeyer, 1990) 79. The way of the world is this: whoever wishes to

be pious must suffer ... for might masquerades as right ... If the wolf so wishes, the lamb is guilty.

53   *Meister Esopus* 4, 53–6.

54   *Die Fabeln Gerhards* 24. Gentle and peace-loving should a praise-worthy lord be: Then his people will obey him willingly, and they will not have to rise up against tyranny.

55   *Nürnberger Prosa Äsop* 94.

56   *Die deutsche und lateinische Fabel* 136–7. As a people lives in this age, so God sends them authorities. If it is laden with sins, then it is punished by God with tyrannical rulers, just as Israel bears witness; they got all kinds of evil rulers every time they turned away from God.

57   *Ysopet Avionnet* 177. He arrives in the forest. They pass by with the Jew following beyond the edge. His heart marks, "I, myself, follow to death." He [the Jew] replies, "A bird will make known this evil deed." A partridge springs forth from a thorn bush, indicating this as a sign. The other says, "Will a bird make known this evil deed?"

58   *Ysopet Avionnet* 177. Moral: Whenever you kill someone, that one does not press gold on you, for the greedy one takes both glory and life. Learn in addition: The insatiable sword wielder gains lethal death; He who plunders with the sword, less providentially, dies by the sword. The spiller of human blood shall grow pale of blood, a wave of blood flows from killers.

59   *Fables of Walter* 154–5. Moral: By the Jew understand the faithful soul, who, fearful of accusation in this world, proceeds to the king, that is, God, requesting of him safe conduct. God, however, gives him the cupbearer, that is, the body with its inclination to pleasures, which kills the spirit, dragging it off to its own great harm. At length, however, at the banquet, that is on the day of judgment, the moral failings, that is the sins, accuse the body, and then the king condemns the body to the cross, that is to eternal punishment.

60   Franz Pfeiffer, *Der Edelstein von Ulrich Boner*, Dichtungen des deutschen Mittelalters (Leipzig: Göschen, 1844) 106. The Jew carried a great amount of gold on this same journey. The cupbearer became very aware of this and in his mind he schemed much (for opportunity makes many thieves) how he might kill the Jew. He thought, "You will be out of all your troubles, if the gold becomes yours. Who will tell it or who, then, can accuse you? You are alone: be of good cheer! No one will do anything to you for this murder!" When the Jew perceived this, he sighed very deeply and said: "I do not doubt, but know well, that God

234

will bring this murder to light. Rather than it remain completely hidden, the birds will make it known, who fly here, so help me God!"

61 *Edelstein* 107. "Tell me, cupbearer, what did you mean when you laughed just now when you beheld the partridge?" He said, "Lord, that I shall do," and told him, how he had acted toward the Jew, with whom he was supposed to go and accompany through the forest, where his treachery was manifold. And so the murder became known to the king. By his own words this was done, by the one who also committed the murder. For this reason he had to go to the gallows. If he had not seen the partridge, he would not have confessed the murder. He was hanged, and that was a good thing! A good man should murder no one.

62 The invocation of the divine name is a detail not found in the Latin versions of the fable in either the Wolfenbüttel *Äsop* or in the *Ysopet Avionnet*.

63 *Meister Esopus* 411. Grubmüller identifies two print runs of the *Edelstein* in the 1460's, both from Bamberg, one from the press of Albrecht Pfister (1464).

64 This is the same "Ringparabel" which was later used by Lessing in his *Nathan der Weise* (III.vii.). The earliest version yet discovered is one from a 12th-century French text. For an account of its origins, see A. C. Lee, *The Decameron: Its Sources and Analogues* (New York: Haskell House, 1909) 7–13.

65 Hermann Österley, ed., *Gesta Romanorum* (Berlin: Weidmannsche, 1872) 417. Dearest ones, the knight is our Lord Jesus Christ, who has three sons, namely Jews, Saracens, and Christians. To the Jews he gave the promised land, to the Saracens, the treasure of this world, both in respect to power and riches, and to the Christians he gave the precious ring, namely faith, for through faith Christians are able to cure diseases and infirmities of the spirit: as it is written, all things are possible to those who believe. Item: "If you have faith just as a mustard seed, etc." Item: "It is impossible to please God without faith."

66 F. Vetter, ed., *Lehrhafte Litteratur des 14. und 15. Jahrhunderts: Erster Teil, Weltliches* (Rpt. Tokyo: Sansyusya, 1974) 450. Now by the three sons we understand the three peoples who are God's sons by creation. Those are Jews, Saracens, and Christians. It is obvious, however, which son he has preferred. To that same one he gave the better ring, that gives sight to the blind, heals sickness, and brings the dead back to life. But among the unbelieving there are neither such signs nor such power.

67 Adelbert von Keller, ed., *Decameron von Heinrich Steinhöwel*, Biblio-thek des Litterarischen Vereins Stuttgart #51 (Stuttgart: Litterarischer

Verein, 1860) 35. By the three kinds of law, which were given to the three kinds of people by God, each one of the peoples considers and believes his to be the best and most righteous. But which among the three is the most righteous remains uncertain, just like the ring. For God alone knows it.

68 See various references to the character throughout the story in *Decameron von Steinhöwel* 29–32.

69 *Decameron von Steinhöwel* 32. The Jew quickly answered him and said: "Dear Gianotto, there seemed to me nothing good in either in their words or their works, and may God repay them as they deserve, and I tell you in truth that there is neither reverence nor holiness nor any good work nor propriety, but depravity, greed, gluttony, immeasurable drunkenness, envy, hatred, and arrogance … and after I thought about this, it seemed to me nothing other than that they sought with all their energy and zeal to hurl the Christian faith to the earth, when they are supposed to be its protectors and increasers. Yet I see also that what they seek is not happening, but that the Christian faith will increase all the more and grow stronger; For this reason I believe in the Father, Son, and Holy Spirit, and the Christian faith to be firmly established and enduring, for which reasons I had long stood firm in my faith until now, but have wanted to convert to the Christian faith. Now I say to you that I wholly want to be a Christian and no longer a Jew."

70 *Verfasserlexikon* Vol. 4, Col. 268–70.

71 *Verfasserlexikon* Vol 4., Col. 271.

72 For a complete discussion of the fables he did include in *Der Renner* and their sources, refer to Erich Seemann, *Hugo von Trimberg und die Fabeln seines Renners. Eine Untersuchung zur Geschichte der Tier-fabel im Mittelalter* (Munich: Verlag Georg D.W. Callwey, 1923) 41–216.

73 *Der Renner: Ein Gedicht aus dem XIII. Jahrhundert. Verfasst von Hugo von Trimberg*, Facsimile-Druck, Drei Hefte, ed. by the "Historischer Verein Bambergs" (Bamberg: Historischer Verein, 1833; Rpt. Berlin: Mayer und Müller, 1904). Cloth, whose thread was never spun, whose color never saw the light of day, is now being sold by base Christians, who, with cursed, base tricks, win a profit in a worse way than the Jews, whom we nevertheless call the devil's dogs.

74 God has three kinds of children, who are Jews, Christians, and heathens, the fourth was created by the devil's cunning deceit, that is the master of all three, and is called "usury," and robs both people and the land.

75 The teachings of Jews and wise heathens have given us many things that are both useful and good for us, they are, however, blind in many places that they have investigated intensively. but which now hardly anyone contemplates. Plato and Aristotle, Seneca and Socrates, Demosthenes and Diogenes, Tullius, Empedocles, and many other old masters, whom I don't want to mention here.

76 8520–8.

77 *Hugo und die Fabeln* 1–7.

78 *Hugo und die Fabeln* 17–8.

79 *Der Renner* 1251–7.

80 Edith Carrington Jones, *Avianus in the Middle Ages*, MS Thesis, (Urbana: University of Illinois, 1933) 18–9.

81 See ch. 3, above.

82 *Avianus in the Middle Ages* 49–52; *Meister Esopus* 86–97; *Hie lêrt* 74–8.

83 *Hie lêrt* 183–7.

Chapter Eight

1 *Feast of Saint Abraham* 38.

2 *Die Juden im mittelalterlichen Reich* 44–55. See also *Persecuting Society* 27–29.

3 *Die Juden im mittelalterlichen Reich* 56–65; *Das europäische Zeitalter der Juden* 62–65; *Persecuting Society* 30–33.

4 "A 1096 Complex?" 16–18.

5 *Die Juden im mittelalterlichen Reich* 55–7.

6 *Die Juden im mittelalterlichen Reich* 55–65.

Bibliography

Primary Texts

Der Antichrist: Der staufische Ludus de Antichristo. Ed. Gerhard Günther. Hamburg: Friedrich Wittig, 1970.

Hartmann von Aue. *Gregorius.* Ed. Ludwig Wolf. Altdeutsche Textbibliothek 2. Tübingen: Niemeyer, 1973.

Avianus, Flavius. *The Fables of Avianus.* Ed. Robinson Ellis. Oxford: Clarendon, 1887.

Berger, David, Ed. *The Jewish–Christian Debate in the High Middle Ages. A Critical Edition of the Sefer Nizzahon Vetus.* Philadelphia: Jewish Publications Society, 1979.

Boccaccio, Giovanni. *Decameron.* German trans. Heinrich Steinhöwel, 1476. *Decameron von Heinrich Steinhöwel.* Ed. Adelbert von Keller. Bibliothek des Litterarischen Vereins in Stuttgart 51. Stuttgart: Litterarischer Verein, 1860.

Boner, Ulrich. *Der Edelstein von Ulrich Boner.* Ed. Franz Pfeiffer. Dichtungen des deutschen Mittelalters. Leipzig: Göschen, 1844.

Die "Elsässische Legenda Aurea." Band I: Das Normalcorpus. Ed. Ulla Williams and Werner Williams-Krapp. Texte und Textgeschichte 3. Tübingen: Niemeyer, 1980.

Elschenbroich, Adalbert, Ed. *Die deutsche und lateinische Fabel in der frühen Neuzeit.* Bd. I: *Ausgewählte Texte.* Tübingen: Niemeyer, 1990.

Das Endinger Judenspiel. Ed. Karl von Amira. Halle, 1883.

Fastnachtspiele aus dem fünfzehnten Jahrhundert. Ed. Adelbert von Keller. Bibliothek des Litterarischen Vereins Stuttgart 28–30. Stuttgart: Litterarischer Verein, 1853; Rpt. Darmstadt: Wissenschaftliche Buchgesellschaft, 1965.

Folz, Hans. "Item, ein Krieg, den der Dichter dieses Spruches gehapt hat wid' einen Juden, von Hans Folczen." Nürnberg, 1479. Rpt. in *German Books before 1601.* Microfilm. Cambridge, Mass.: General Microfilm Co. MF #7726, Roll 28, Item 3.

_____. *Hans Folz. Die Reimpaarsprüche*. Ed. Hans Fischer. Münchener Texte und Untersuchungen zur deutschen Literatur des Mittelalters Vol. 1. Munich: C.H. Beck, 1961.

_____. *Ein Spil von dem Herzogen von Burgund. Frühe Nürnberger Fastnachtspiele*. Ed. Klaus Ridder and Hans-Hugo Steinhoff. Schöningh Mediävistische Editionen. Vol. 4. Paderborn: Schöningh, 1998.

Froning, Richard. *Das Drama des Mittelalters*. Stuttgart. 1891. Rpt. Darmstadt: Wissenschaftliche Buchgesellschaft, 1964.

Das Füssener Osterspiel und die Füssener Marienklage: Universitätsbibliothek Augsburg (ehemals Harburg), Cod. II, 4°62. Ed. Ulrich Müller, Franz Hundsnurscher, and Cornelia Sommer. Litterae: Göppinger Beiträge zur Textgeschichte 69. Göppingen: Kümmerle, 1983.

Gesta Romanorum. Ed. Hermann Österley. Berlin: Weidmannsche Buchhandlung, 1872.

Gerhard von Minden. *Die Fabeln Gerhards von Minden in mittelniederdeutscher Sprache*. Ed. Albert Leitzmann. Halle: Niemeyer, 1898; Rpt. Hildesheim: Olms, 1985.

Hartl, Eduard. *Das Drama des Mittelalters. Osterspiele*. Rpt. Darmstadt: Wissenschaftliche Buchgesellschaft, 1969.

Der Heiligen Leben. Band I: Der Sommerteil. Ed. Margit Brand, Kristina Freienhagen-Baumgardt, Ruth Meyer, and Werner Williams-Krapp. Tübingen: Niemeyer, 1996.

Der Heiligen Leben: Winterteil. Ed.Werner-Williams Krapp. In page proof.

Der Heiligen Leben und Leiden. Das sind die schönsten Legenden aus den deutschen Passionalen des 15. Jahrhunderts. Ed. Severin Rüttgers. Leipzig: Insel, 1922.

Hroswitha von Gandersheim. *Werke*. Ed. and translated by Helene Homener. Paderborn: Schöningh, 1936.

Jacobus de Voragine. *Legenda Aurea vulgo historia lombardica dicta*. Ed. Th. Graesse. 3rd Edition, 1890; Rpt. Osnabrück: Otto Zeller, 1969.

Konrad von Würzburg. *Konrads von Würzburg Silvester*. Ed. Wilhelm Grimm. Göttingen: Dieterichsche Buchhandlung, 1841.

Marienlegenden aus dem Alten Passional. Ed. Hans-Georg Richert. Altdeutsche Textbibliothek. 64. Tübingen: Niemeyer, 1965.

McKenzie, Kenneth, and William A. Oldfather. *Ysopet-Avionnet: The Latin and French Texts*. University of Illinois Studies in Language and Literature, Vol. 4. Urbana: University of Illinois Press, 1919.

240

Das Mittelrheinische Passionsspiel der St. Galler Handschrift 919. Ed. Rudolf Schützeichel. Tübingen: Niemeyer, 1978.

Der Nürnberger Prosa-Äsop. Ed. Klaus Grubmüller. Altdeutsche Textbibliothek 107. Tübingen: Niemeyer, 1994.

Das Passional. Eine Legenden-Sammlung des dreizehnten Jahrhunderts. Ed. Fr. Karl Köpke. Bibliothek der gesammten deutschen National-Literatur. Vol. 23. Leipzig: Basse, 1852.

Redentiner Osterspiel. Ed. Carl Schröder. Niederdeutsche Denkmäler Vol. 5. Norden: Diedr. Soltau, 1893.

Der Renner: Ein Gedicht aus dem XIII. Jahrhundert. Verfasst von Hugo von Trimberg. Historischer Verein Bambergs. Three vols. Bamberg: Historischer Verein, 1833; Rpt. Berlin: Mayer und Müller, 1904.

Das Rheinische Osterspiel der Berliner Handschrift MS Germ. 1219. Ed. Hans Rueff. Abhandlungen der Gesellschaft der Wissenschaften zu Göttingen, philologische historische Klasse, neue Folge Vol. XVIII, I. Berlin: Weidmannsche Buchhandlung, 1925.

The Saint Gall Passion Play. Ed. Larry E. West. Leyden: Brill, 1976.

The South English Legendary. Ed. Charlotte D'Evelyn and Anna S. Mill. Early English Text Society, Extra Series No. 235. London: Oxford UP, 1967.

Steinhöwel, Heinrich. *Äsop*. Ed. Hermann Österley. Bibliothek des litterarischen Vereins Stuttgart 117. Stuttgart: Litterarischer Verein, 1873.

Stern, Moritz. *Hebräische Berichte über die Judenverfolgung während der Kreuzzüge*. Breslau: 1892. Rpt. Hildesheim: Olms, 1997.

Theophilus, der Faust des Mittelalters. Schauspiel aus dem vierzehnten Jahrhunderte in niederdeutscher Sprache. Ed. Ludwig Ettmüller. Bibliothek der gesamten deutschen National-Literatur Vol. 27. Leipzig: Gottfr. Basse, 1849.

Theophilus: Mittelniederdeutsches Drama in drei Fassungen. Ed. R. Pertsch. Heidelberg: Carl Winter, 1908.

Theophilus: Niederdeutsches Schauspiel aus einer Trierer Handschrift des XV. Jahrhunderts. Ed. Hoffmann von Fallersleben. Hannover: Rümpler, 1853.

Theophilus: Niederdeutsches Schauspiel in zwei Fortsetzungen aus einer Stockholmer und einer Helmstädter Handschrift. Ed. Hoffmann von Fallersleben. Hannover: Rümpler, 1854.

Thomas Aquinas. *De Malo*. Trans. Jean T. Oesterle. Notre Dame: Notre Dame UP, 1995.

Vetter, Franz. Lehrhafte Literatur des 14. und 15. Jahrhunderts: Erster Teil, Weltliches. Rpt. Tokyo: Sansyusya, 1974.

Wackernell, J. E. *Die ältesten Passionsspiele in Tirol.* Wien: Braunmüller, 1887.

_____. *Altdeutsche Passionsspiele aus Tirol.* Graz: Styria, 1897.

Das Wiener Passionsspiel: Cod. 12887 (Suppl. 561) der österreichischen Staatsbibliothek zu Wien. Ed. Ursula Henning. Litterae: Göppinger Beiträge zur Textgeschichte Nr. 92. Göppingen: Kümmerle, 1986.

Wright, Aaron E. *The Fables of Walter of England.* Toronto Medieval Latin Texts 25. Toronto: Pontifical Institute of Medieval Studies, 1997.

Secondary Literature

Arendt, Hannah. *The Origins of Totalitarianism.* New York: Harcourt, Brace, and Co., 1951.

Battenberg, Friedrich. *Das europäische Zeitalter der Juden: Zur Entwicklung einer Minderheit in der nichtjüdischen Umwelt Europas.* Band. 1. *Von den Anfängen bis 1650.* Darmstadt: Wissenschaftliche Buchgesellschaft, 1990.

Bergman, Rolf. *Studien zur Entstehung und Geschichte der deutschen Passionsspiele des 13. und 14. Jahrhunderts.* Münster Mittelalterschriften 14. Munich: Fink, 1972.

Blumenkranz, Bernhard. *Die Judenpredigt Augustins: Ein Beitrag zur Geschichte der jüdisch–christlichen Beziehungen in den ersten Jahrhunderten.* Basel: Helbing and Lichtenhahn, 1946.

_____. *Juden und Judentum in der mittelalterlichen Kunst.* Stuttgart: Kohlhammer, 1965.

"Boner." *Die deutsche Literatur des Mittelalters. Verfasserlexikon.* Ed. Kurt Ruh. Vol. 1. Berlin: de Gruyter, 1977. Col. 947–51.

de Boor, Helmut, and Richard Newald. *Die deutsche Literatur vom späten Mittelalter zum Barock.* Geschichte der deutschen Literatur IV/I. Munich: Beck, 2nd ed. 1970.

Bremer, Natascha. *Das Bild der Juden in den Passionsspielen und der bildenden Kunst des deutschen Mittelalters.* Frankfurt am Main: Lang, 1986.

Burmeister, Heike A. *Der "Judenknabe." Studien und Texte zu einem mittelalterlichen Marienmirakel in deutscher Überlieferung.* Göppinger Arbeiten zur Germanistik Nr. 654. Kümmerle: Göppingen, 1998.

Catholy, Eckehard. *Das Fastnachtspiel des Spätmittelalters.* Hermaea. Germanistische Forschungen. Vol. 8. Tübingen: Niemeyer, 1961.

Calloway, Mary. "A Hammer That Breaks Rocks to Pieces: Prophetic Critique in the Hebrew Bible." *Anti-Semitism and Early Christianity: Issues of Polemic and Faith.* Ed. Craig Evans and Donald A. Hagner. Minneapolis: Fortress Press, 1993. 21–40.

Chazan, Robert. *Daggers of Faith: Thirteenth-Century Christian Missionizing and the Jewish Response.* Berkeley: California UP, 1989.

——. "From the First Crusade to the Second: Evolving Peceptions of the Jewish–Christian Conflict." *Jews and Christians in Twelfth-Century Europe.* Ed. Michael A. Signer and John van Engen. Notre Dame: Notre Dame UP, 2001. 46–62.

Cohen, Jeremy. *The Friars and the Jews.* Ithaca: Cornell UP, 1982.

——. *Living Letters of the Law. Ideas of the Jew in Medieval Christianity.* Berkeley: California UP, 1999.

——. "A 1096 Complex? Constructing the First Crusade in Jewish Historical Memory, Medieval and Modern." *Jews and Christians in the Twelfth Century.* Ed. Michael A. Signer and John van Engen. Notre Dame: Notre Dame UP, 2001. 9–26.

Cohn, Norman. *Warrant for Genocide.* London: Eyre & Spottiswoode, 1967; Rpt. London: Serif, 1996.

Dicke, Gerd. *Heinrich Steinhöwels "Esopus." Untersuchungen zu einem Bucherfolg der Frühdruckzeit.* Münchener Texte und Untersuchungen zur deutschen Literatur des Mittelalters 103. Tübingen: Niemeyer, 1994.

Dicke, Gerd and Klaus Grubmüller. *Die Fabeln des Mittelalters und der frühen Neuzeit: Ein Katalog der lateinischen Versionen und ihrer deutschen Entsprechungen.* Münchener Texte und Untersuchungen 60. Munich: Fink, 1987.

Evans, Craig. "The New Testament and First Century Judaism." *Anti-Semitism and Early Christianity: Issues of Faith and Polemic.* Ed. Craig Evans and Donald Hagener. Minneapolis: Fortress Press, 1993. 1–16.

Farmer, David Hugh. *TheOxford Dictionary of Saints.* Oxford: Clarendon, 1978.

Funkenstein, Amos. *Perceptions of Jewish History.* Berkeley: California UP, 1993.

Frey, Winfried. "Gottesmörder und Menschenfeinde: Zum Judenbild der deutschen Literatur des Mittelalters." *Die Juden in ihrer mittel-*

alterlichen Umwelt. Ed. Alfred Ebenbauer and Klaus Zatloukal. Vienna: Böhlau, 1991. 35–51.

Gilman, Sander. "The Madness of the Jews." *Difference and Pathology.* Ed. Sander Gilman. New York: Cornell UP, 1985. 150–62.

Goldhagen, Daniel J. *Hitler's Willing Executioners: Ordinary Germans and the Holocaust.* New York: Alfred A. Knopf, 1996.

Gow, A. C. *The Red Jews: Antisemitism in an Apocalyptic Age, 1200–1600.* Studies in Medieval and Reformation Thought 55. Leiden: E.J. Brill, 1995.

Grau, Willhelm. *Antisemitismus im späten Mittelalter. Das Ende der Regensburger Judengemeinde, 1450–1519.* Munich: Duncker and Humbolt, 1934.

Graus, Frantisek. "Historische Traditionen über Juden im Spätmittlelalter (Mitteleuropa)." *Zur Geschichte der Juden im Deutschland des späten Mittelalters und der frühen Neuzeit.* Ed. Alfred Haverkamp. Monographien zur Geschichte des Mittelalters 24. Stuttgart: Hiersemann, 1981. 1–26.

_____. *Pest, Geißler, Judenmorde: Das 14. Jahrhundert als Krisenzeit.* Veröffentlichungen des Max-Planck-Instituts für Geschichte 86. Göttingen: Vandenhoeck and Ruprecht, 1987.

_____. "Die Juden in ihrer mittelalterlichen Umwelt." *Die Juden in ihrer mittelalterlichen Umwelt.* Ed. Alfred Ebenbauer and Helmut Zatloukal. Wien: Böhlau, 1991. 53–65.

Grayzel, Solomon. *A History of the Jews.* Philadelphia: Jewish Publications Society of America, 1947; Rpt. 1967.

_____. *The Church and the Jews in the XIIIth Century.* Vol. I, 1198–1254. Philadelphia: Dropsie College. 1933.

_____. *The Church and the Jews in the XIIIth Century.* Vol. II, 1254–1314. Ed. Kenneth R. Stow. Detroit: Wayne State UP and the Jewish Theological Seminary of America, 1989.

Grunwald, Max. *The History of the Jews of Vienna.* Jewish Community Series. Philadelphia: Jewish Publications Society, 1936.

Grubmüller, Klaus. "Fabel, Exemplum, Allegorese. Über Sinnbildungsverfahren und Verwendungszusammenhänge." *Exempel und Exempelsammlungen.* Ed. Burghart Wachinger and Walter Haug. Tübingen: Niemeyer, 1991. 58–74.

_____. *Meister Esopus. Untersuchungen zu Geschichte und Funktion der Fabel im Mittelalter.* Münchener Texte und Untersuchungen zur deutschen Literatur des Mittelalters 56. Munich: Artemis, 1977.

244

Harrsen, Meta. "The Manuscripts." *Hroswitha von Gandersheim: Her Life, Times, and Works and a Comprehensive Bibliography.* Ed. Anne Lyon Haight. New York: The Hroswitha Club, 1965. 42–44.

Heil, Johannes. "'Antijudaismus' und 'Antisemitismus.' Begriffe als Bedeutungsträger." *Jahrbuch für Antisemitismusforschung.* Vol 6. Ed. Wolfgang Benz. Frankfurt/New York: Campus Verlag, 1997.

Herford, R. Travers. *Christianity in the Talmud and the Midrash.* Library of Religious and Philosophical Thought. Clifton, New Jersey: Reference Book Publishers, 1965.

Hofmeister, Winfried. "Das Jüdel im Kontext mittelhochdeutscher literarischer Kinderdarstellungen." *Die Juden in ihrer mittelalterlichen Umwelt.* Ed. Ebenbauer and Zatloukal. Vienna: Böhlau, 1991. 91–103.

Hsia, R. Po-Chia. *The Myth of Ritual Murder.* New Haven: Yale UP, 1988.

_____. *Trent 1475: Stories of a Ritual Murder Trial.* New Haven: Yale UP, 1992.

Jacoby, Jeff. "Lady Arafat's Real Mistake." *The Boston Globe.* November 22, 1999.

Jones, Edith Carrington. *Avianus in the Middle Ages.* M.S. Thesis. Library Science. Urbana: U of Illinois Press, 1933.

"Kaiserchronik." *Die deutsche Literatur des Mittelalters. Verfasserlexikon.* Ed. Kurt Ruh. Vol. 4. Berlin: de Gruyter. 1983. Col. 949–50.

Kälin, Beatrice. *"Maria, muter der barmherzigkeit." Die Sünder und die Frommen in den Marienlegenden des Alten Passionals.* Deutsche Literatur von den Anfängen bis 1700. Vol. 17. Bern: Peter Lang, 1994.

Katz, Jacob. *Exclusiveness and Tolerance: Studies in Jewish–Gentile Relations in Medieval and Modern Times.* Scripta Judaica 3. Oxford: UP, 1961.

de Lange, Nicholas. "The Origins of Anti-Semitism." *Anti-Semitism in Times of Crisis.* Ed. Sander Gilman and Stephen Katz. New Haven: Yale UP, 1996. 21–37.

Langmuir, Gavin I. "The Knight's Tale of Hugh of Lincoln." *Speculum* 47 (1972): 459–82.

_____. "Thomas of Monmouth: Detector of Ritual Murder." *Speculum* 59 (1984): 820–846. Rpt. in *The Blood Libel Legend: A Casebook of Anti-Semitic Folklore.* Madison: Wisconsin UP. 1991. 3–40.

_____. *Toward a Definition of Anti-Semitism.* Berkeley: U of California Press, 1990.

_____. "Faith of Christians and Hostility to Jews." *Christianity and Judaism*. Studies in Church History 55. Ed. Diane Wood. Oxford: Blackwell, 1992. 77–92.

Lazar, Moshe. "Theophilus: Servant of Two Masters. The Pre-Faustian Theme of Despair and Revolt." *Modern Language Notes* 87.6 (1972): 31–50.

_____. "The Lamb and the Scapegoat: The Dehumanization of the Jews in Medieval Propaganda Imagery." *Anti-Semitism in Times of Crisis*. Ed. Sander Gilman and Stephen Katz. New Haven: Yale UP, 1996. 37–66.

Lee, A. C. *The Decameron: Its Sources and Analogues*. New York: Haskell House, 1909.

Lerner, Robert. *The Feast of Saint Abraham. Medieval Millennarians and the Jews*. Philadelphia: University of Pennsylvania Press, 2001.

Das Lexikon für Theologie und Kirche. Eds. Karl Rahner and Josef Höfer. 10 Vols. Freiburg: Verlag Herder, 1957–1967.

Linder, Amnon. *The Jews in the Legal Sources of the Early Middle Ages*. Detroit: Wayne State UP; Jerusalem: The Israel Academy of Sciences and Humanities, 1997.

Lomnitzer, Helmut. "Das Verhältnis des Fastnachtspiels vom 'Kaiser Constantinus' zum Reimpaarspruch 'Christ und Jude' von Hans Folz." *Zeitschrift für deutsches Altertum und deutsche Literatur* 92 (1964): 277–91.

Masser, Achim. "Das Evangelium Nicodemii und das mittelalterliche Spiel." *Zeitschrift für deutsche Philologie* 107 (1988): 48–66.

McCulloh, John M. "Jewish Ritual Murder: William of Norwich, Thomas of Monmouth, and the Early Dissemination of the Myth." *Speculum* 72.3 (1997): 698–740.

McKnight, Scott. "A Loyal Critic: Matthew's Polemic with Judaism in Theological Perspective." *Anti-Semitism and Early Christianity*. Ed. Craig Evans and Donald Hagener. Minneapolis: Fortress Press, 1993. 55–80.

Michael, Wolfgang. *Das deutsche Drama des Mittelalters*. Grundriss der germanischen Philologie 20. Berlin: de Gruyter, 1971.

Miklautsch, Lydia. "Der mittelalterliche Antijudaismus am Beispiel von Konrads von Würzburgs *Silvester*." *Die Juden in ihrer mittelalterlichen Umwelt*. Ed. Ebenbauer and Zatloukal. Vienna: Böhlau, 1991. 168–181.

Minor Roman Poets with Introductions and English Translations. Ed. J. Wight Duff and Arnold Duff. Loeb Classical Library. London: William Heinemann, 1935.

Moore, R. I. *The Formation of a Persecuting Society*. Oxford: Blackwell, 1987.

Nirenberg, David. *Communities of Violence: Persecution of Minorities in the Middle Ages*. Princeton: Princeton UP, 1996.

Patschovsky, Alexander. "Der Talmudjude. Vom mittelalterlichen Ursprung eines neuzeitlichen Themas." *Juden in der christlichen Umwelt während des späten Mittelalters. Zeitschrift für historische Forschung*; Beiheft 13. Berlin: Duncker und Humbolt, 1992. 1–27.

Pflanz, Hermann Mannfred. *Die lateinischen Textgrundlagen des St. Galler Passionsspieles in der mittealterlichen Liturgie*. Frankfurt am Main: Lang, 1977.

Poliakov, Léon. *The History of Anti-Semitism. Volume One: From the Time of Christ to the Court Jews*. Trans. Richard Howard. New York: Vanguard Press, 1965.

Roth, Cecil. *A History of the Jews*. New York: Schocken, 1970.

Rubin, Miri. *Corpus Christi: The Eucharist in Late Medieval Culture*. Cambridge: Cambridge UP, 1991.

_____. *Gentile Tales: The Narrative Assault on Late Medieval Jews*. New Haven: Yale UP, 1999.

Russel, Jeffrey Burton. *Lucifer: The Devil in the Middle Ages*. Ithaca: Cornell UP, 1984.

Sapir-Abulafia, Anna. *Jews and Christians in the Twelfth-Century Renaissance*. London: Routledge, 1995.

Schreckenberg, Heinz. *Die christlichen Adversus-Judaeos-Texte und ihr literarisches und historisches Umfeld (13.–20. Jh.)*. 3 Vols. Frankfurt a.M.: Lang, 1988, 1994, 1997.

Seemann, Erich. *Hugo von Trimberg und die Fabeln seines Renners. Eine Untersuchung zur Geschichte der Tierfabel im Mittelalter*. Munich: Verlag George D.W. Callwey, 1923.

Shapiro, James. "Updating (and Retouching) an Old Passion Play." *The New York Times*. 14 May, 2000. 7, continued 32.

Shirer, William. *The Rise and Fall of the Third Reich*. New York: Simon and Schuster, 1960.

Spitzer, Schlomo. *Bne Chet: Die österreichischen Juden im Mittelalter. Eine Sozial- und Kulturgeschichte*. Vienna: Böhlau, 1997.

Toch, Michael. *Die Juden im mittelalterlichen Reich*. Enzyklopädie deutscher Geschichte 44. Munich: Oldenbourg, 1998.

Touber, A. H. "Das Donaueschinger Passionsspiel und die bildende Kunst." *Deutsche Vierteljahresschrift* 52 (1978): 26–42.

Trachtenberg, Joshua. *The Devil and the Jews: The Medieval Conception of the Jew and its Relation to Modern Antisemitism*. New Haven: Yale UP, 1943.

Waas, Christian. *Die Quellen der Beispiele Boners*. Dortmund: Fr. Wilh. Ruhfus, 1897.

Weber, Hans Heinrich. *Studien zur deutschen Marienlegende des Mittelalters am Beispiel des Theophilus*. Dissertation. Hamburg: Hamburg UP, 1966.

Weiss, John. *Ideology of Death: Why the Holocaust Happened in Germany*. Chicago: Ivan R. Dee, 1996.

Wenninger, Markus. *Man bedarf keiner Juden mehr: Ursachen und Hintergründe ihrer Vertreibung aus den Reichsstädten im 15. Jahrhundert*. Beihefte zum Archiv für Kulturgeschichte 14. Graz: Böhlau, 1981.

Wenzel, Edith. "Zur Judenproblematik bei Hans Folz." *Zeitschrift für deutsche Philologie*. 101 (1982): 79–104.

_____. *"Do worden die Judden alle geschant." Rolle und Funktion der Juden in spätmittlalterlichen Spielen*. Forschungen zur Geschichte der älteren deutschen Literatur 14. Munich: Fink, 1992.

Wheatley, Edward. *Mastering Aesop – Medieval Education, Chaucer, and His Followers*. Gainesville: U of Florida Press, 2000.

Williams-Krapp,Werner. *Die deutschen und niederländischen Legendare des Mittelalters. Studien zu ihrer Überlieferungs-,Text- und Wirkungsgeschichte*. Texte und Textgeschichte 20. Tübingen: Niemeyer, 1986.

_____. "Das 'Bamberger Legendar': Eine Vorarbeit zu 'Der Heiligen Leben.'" *Zeitschrift für deutsches Altertum und deutsche Literatur* 123 (1994): 45–54.

Wissemann, Michael. "Fabel: Zur Entwicklung der Bezeichnung einer Gattung." *Fabula: Zeitschrift für Erzählforschung* 33 (1992): 1–13.

Wright, Aaron E. *Hie lêrt uns der Meister: Latin Commentary and the German Fable 1350–1500*. Medieval and Renaissance Texts and Studies 218. Tempe: Arizona Center for Medieval and Renaissance Studies, 2001.

Wülker, Richard Paul. *Das Evangelium Nicodemii in der abendländischen Literatur*. Paderborn: Schöningh, 1872.

"Konrad von Würzburg." *Die deutsche Literatur des Mittelalters Verfasserlexikon*. Ed. Kurt Ruh. Vol. 5. Berlin: De Gruyter, 1985.

The Yale Companion to Jewish Writing and Thought in German Culture 1096–1996. Ed. Sander Gilman. New Haven: Yale UP, 1997.

Zizek, Slavoj. *The Sublime Object of Ideology*. London: Verso, 1990.

Index

Gospel of John 39–47, 49, 53, 63, 75, 77, 78, 91
Gospel of Luke 56, 57
Gospel of Matthew 49
Gow, A.C. 19, 20, 26, 27, 29
Grau, Wilhelm 10
Graus, Frantisek 13, 17, 26, 108, 153, 186
Grayzel, Solomon 20
Gregorius (Hartmann von Aue) 84–5
Gregory the Great (Pope Gregory VII) 31, 103
Gregory X (Pope) 7, 111
Gregory of Tours 143
Grubmüller, Klaus 155, 156
Guibert de Nogent 31, 161

Habsburgs 2
(Der Arme) Hartmann 137–8, 186
Hartmann von Aue 84
Heil, Johannes 14
Der Heiligen Leben 31
Heinrich von Morungen 179
Hilter, Adolf 18
host desecration 2, 6, 12
Hrabanus Maurus 179
Hroswitha von Gandersheim 137, 142, 186
Hsia, R. Po-Chia 6, 10, 181
Hugh of Lincoln (Saint) 111
Hugh of St. Victor 179
Hugo von Trimberg 177–9, 185

Innocent IV (Pope) 111
Isidore of Seville 16, 30, 103, 114, 115, 116, 155, 161
Iwein 179

Jacob of Voragine 113
Jerome 179
Jesus (general) 6, 15, 17, 21
    as Jew 30, 51, 52, 65
    in Passion plays 42–52, 55, 57–62

in saint's lives 107, 108, 109, 115, 116, 117
Jew(s)
    as animals 101–2, 161–2
    as filicide 147
    as loving father 145, 146, 147, 148
    as sorcerer 123, 125, 137–40, 143, 153, 186, 187
    as one who warns against sorcery 141–2, 153, 187
    conversion of Jews 7
    decline in legal status of Jews 2, 4, 7, 13
    "irrationality" of Jews 17
    language 98–9, 130
    legal protections of Jews 2, 4, 28
    medieval definition of Jews 10, 13–18
Joachim de Fiore 16, 17, 183, 184
Josephus, Flavius 110
Judaism 4, 5, 13, 14, 15, 55, 68, 70, 71, 72, 85, 96, 108, 109, 115, 116, 123, 124, 153
"Judenknabe" (Marian legend) 110, 112, 113, 136, 137, 143–9, 153, 188

Kaiserchronik 109, 114
Katz, Jacob 4, 13, 29, 37, 189
Kisch, Guido 20
König Rother 179
Konrad von Würzburg 109, 120–7, 133, 179

de Lange, Nicholas 15
Langmuir, Gavin I. 10, 15, 16, 17
Lazar, Moshe 137, 140, 161, 162
Legenda Aurea 31, 113, 118, 124, 128, 129, 136, 149, 150
Lerner, Robert 16, 17, 183
Leyden Manuscript (Avianus) 162
Liber Miraculis de Sancta Mariae 147
Lomnitzer, Helmut 19, 129
Ludus de Antichristo 22, 23, 31

251

253

Studies in German Jewish History

Peter D. G. Brown
General Editor

Representations of Jews
in Late Medieval and
Early Modern German Literature

Studies in German Jewish History

Peter D. G. Brown
General Editor

Vol. 5

PETER LANG
Oxford · Bern · Berlin · Bruxelles · Frankfurt am Main · New York · Wien

By the same author:

Guaranteed Electronic Markets: the backbone of
a 21st century economy

There is a web site dedicated to *Guaranteed Electronic Markets* where
readers may wish to comment on this book: www.gems.org.uk

net benefit

Guaranteed Electronic Markets: the ultimate potential of online trade

wingham rowan

First published 1999 by
MACMILLAN PRESS LTD
Houndmills, Basingstoke, Hampshire RG21 6XS
and London
Companies and representatives
throughout the world

ISBN 0–333–76009–3 hardcover

A catalogue record for this book is available
from the British Library.

This book is printed on paper suitable for recycling and
made from fully managed and sustained forest sources.

10 9   8   7   6 5   4   3   2 1
08 07 06 05 04 03 02 01 00 99

Editing and origination by
Aardvark Editorial, Mendham, Suffolk

Printed and bound in Great Britain
at The Bath Press, Avon

contents

···

section two

···

A new democratic capitalism: the impact of public
electronic markets   **55**

What trading revolution? Electronic commerce for the perplexed

In 1997 it was still possible to dismiss the Internet as a harmless hobby: now it has become the backbone for what is widely described as a 'new economy'. This is a world in which holiday flights, for instance, can be booked by calling up a travel agent or airline Internet site then selecting a departure, typing in a credit card number and address for delivery of tickets. The information is sent instantly from the shopper's computer down phone lines to the seller's machine which can be on the other side of the world. Flowers, clothes, wine, toys plus countless other goods and services can likewise be browsed, then bought, by visiting suppliers' sites on the Internet's World Wide Web. This shopless shopping offers several advantages over a visit to the high street. It is more convenient and allows access to a wider range of suppliers. More significantly it can be much cheaper: retailers no longer have to fund high-street premises or significant numbers of staff. Increasingly, online customers are expecting to see this reflected in lower prices. British insurance company Eagle Star, for example, offers its premiums at an effective 25 per cent discount to shoppers at its web site.[1]

The new dynamics of Internet trading have caused turmoil in some business sectors. Amazon Books has been mentioned in reverential tones at almost every e-commerce convention of the past two years. This start-up operation in Seattle, which sells only through the Net, offers titles at up to 40 per cent off high-street prices. It now claims with justification to be 'earth's biggest bookstore' and has left comfortably established book retailers scrabbling to build a comparable operation online. Similarly, Auto-by-Tel offers 'pain relief for car buyers' through the Web. Anyone typing in details of their dream vehicle will be contacted soon afterwards by a local dealer who has that model in stock and will confirm an immediate non-negotiable price. Web-based car buying services now account for 15 per cent of auto sales in the US, the figure will be 50 per cent by the year 2000 according to one research firm.[2] Some of the new players emerging on the Net come from industries unrelated to the service they offer. Peapod for example is a home grocery delivery service with order-taking online. It is a software company whose expertise is in automated processes; they have simply found suppliers for the groceries.

Predictably, perhaps, the US leads the world in consumer electronic commerce. But the new marketplace is global in its reach and can undercut national suppliers. A New York delicatessen that set up an order-taking web site was surprised to find an initial customer was in Tokyo. When staff queried his order for $50 of food that would cost him $100 to be delivered they were assured the same ingredients would cost $300 to purchase locally.[3] Alongside this price advantage are unique tools that can attract shoppers from around the world. The Amazon online bookstore, for instance, features software that can advise a browser of new titles he is likely to enjoy: it registers his tastes at each successive purchase and compares what he has already bought with similar lists from other shoppers. This 'relationship technology' that allows automated sales pitches is an area of frenetic development activity at present. More advanced still is the facility, offered by several major parcel companies, whereby a package can be tracked through their delivery chain from departure to delivery by keying in a unique code number at their web site. As their staff scan barcodes on each parcel the information from their vehicles on the road is beamed by satellite to a central computer, which constantly updates the site. Worryingly for many Net sellers, software called 'intelligent agents' is becoming increasingly sophisticated. This can be used by someone seeking perhaps a copy of The Beatles' *Hard Day's Night* CD to call up all the online music stores and compare prices before displaying the cheapest in seconds.

Despite having been the spine of the world's financial markets for decades, electronic trade is in its infancy. The next big step is likely to come from a trend towards 'pervasive computing': computers so intuitive to use and accessible that they become almost inescapable. Already some portable phones can connect to the Internet and shop. NCR Corporation have revealed a serious commitment to developing a microwave oven that allows banking activities, such as account queries, to be carried out from the kitchen.[4] The crucial development, however, is likely to be interactive television. With an estimated 90 million personal computers in the world but 900 million TV sets, it is clearly a technology with which nearly everyone is comfortable. Cheap, enticing, efficient shopping with the remote control is expected to have enormous impact. Around the world, governments are having to grapple with issues of regulation and tax collection in a new marketplace which crosses national borders and allows sellers to migrate to favourable regimes without losing any of their presence for customers.

The significance of this trading revolution is not in what has happened so far but what is to come. Without so far making a cent in profits Amazon Books has been valued by the stock market in billions of dollars. Its potential lies in having established a commanding lead that will reap its full worth when we are all shopping online. Already Wal-Mart, the world's biggest retailer, has ordained that their new stores must be convertible to housing units in anticipation of a time when they no longer need costly bricks and mortar across the country.[5] Even companies who ignore the potential of online trade are unlikely to escape its effects. Car dealerships in the US, for instance, are predicted to shrink from 22 000 today to 10 000 in the near future, as services like Auto-by-Tel mentioned earlier erode margins and allow dealers using the system to reach far more customers. Analysts talk of the Auto-by-Tel effect sweeping across 'industry after industry'.[6] The rapidity of change can be bewildering: no one knows quite where the trading revolution is heading. That is where this book hopes to make a contribution.

Notes

1. Building sites for sales, *Information Week*, 10–23 December 1997, p. 95.
2. JB Power quoted by Kevin Turnbull, Chief Executive of Auto-by-Tel, speaking at Non-Shop Shopping: dealing with the real issues, conference, London, 17 September 1998.
3. The Digital Earthquake, Stop the Technology Madness, *Daily Telegraph/Sun Microsystems*, 1998, p. 15.

4. Surfing for your supper, *Future Shopping*, October 1998, p. 3.
5. *The Grocer*, 6 September 1997. Quoted at Non-Shop Shopping: dealing with the real issues, conference, London, 17 September 1998 by Helen Bridgett, Marketing Manager, Tesco Direct.
6. The quote comes from Matt Eriksen of Boston Consulting Group quoted in Evan I. Schwartz, How Middlemen can Come Out on Top, *Business Week*, 9 February 1998, electronic edition.

Acknowledgements

Many people have contributed to this project, not all of whom would wish to be named.

Particular thanks for help with research are due to:

Adrian Duffield, Mikael Estvall, Peter Jaco, Tracy Muirhead and Peter V. Thomas, Reuters Transactional Products, London; Alan Sayers, British Shops and Stores Association; Brad Trask and Walt Reiker, McDonald's Hamburgers, Chicago; Cheryl Artim, International Liaison, Auto-by-Tel, US; Chris Sundt, security consultant, ICL solutions, UK; Colin Brown, Consumers' Association, UK; Francis Aldhouse, Deputy Registrar, Office of the Data Protection Registrar, UK; Julie Ros, editor, *FX Week*, UK; Keith Collins, London Pride Waste Action Partnership, UK; Michael Linton, Landsman Community Services Ltd, Canada; Professor Adrian Wood, University of Sussex, UK; Ray Eglington and Peter Heath, UK representatives, SABRE; Rupert Hodges, British Retail Consortium; Sam Eaton PRO and Paul Dale, Senior Service Creator, British Interactive Broadcasting; Sigurd Hogsbro, Head of IT, London Financial Futures Exchange; Stuart Norris, Association Cambiste Internationale – The International Financial Markets Association; Tammy Lindsay, Time Warner Cable, US; Tina Kane, Electronic Broking Services, London

The following have contributed valuable encouragement, criticism or advice:

Adam Singer, Chairman, Flextech, UK; Alison Gray, *The Scotsman*, UK; Arjay Choudry, Head of New Media, United News & Media, UK; Ashley Faull, Director of Programmes, Telewest, UK; Bill O'Neil, Editor, *Guardian Online*, UK; Bruno Giussani, *New York Times*; Charles Cohen, Managing Director, Thought Interactive Internet Services, London; Charles Handy, author, UK; Colin Lloyd, Chief Executive, Direct Marketing Association, UK; Cotton Ward, *.net*, UK; Dave Birch, Hyperion Payment Systems, UK; David Gold, PA Consulting, London; David Pringle, *Information Strategy*, London ; David Wilcox, Communities On-line, UK; Deborah Jenkins, Common Purpose, UK; Dee Hock, Founder, President and CEO Emeritus, Visa International; Dianne Nelmes, Granada Television, UK; Don Tapscott, Alliance for Converging Technologies, US, author of *The Digital Economy and Digital Blueprint*; Dr Roger Till, Chairman, Electronic Commerce Association, UK; Dr Jay M. Tenenbaum, founder, CommerceNet, US; Dr Michael Chamberlain, Managing Director, Transactions, Informed Sources, UK; Dr Rafael Guzman Llorente, University of California at Santa Cruz; Duncan Lewis, then CEO Granada Media Group, UK; Ed Mayo, Director, The New Economics Foundation, London; Edward Bonnington, Chairman, Greenland Interactive, UK; Emmett Power, Editor in chief, Electronic Commerce Briefing, UK; Esther Dyson, President, Edventure Holdings,

US; Eva Pascoe, *Independent*, UK; Evan Davis, Economics Correspondent, *Newsnight*, BBC TV; Frances Cairncross, *The Economist*, London; Frank Wainwright, Editor, *DM Business*, UK; Gail Rebuck, Chief Executive, Random House Publishing, UK; Gavin Howe, President and CEO, Reed Elsevier Technology Group, Cambridge, US; Glenda Cooper, *Independent*, UK; Heather Stark, Senior Consultant, Ovum Technology Consultancy, UK; Ian Hughes, Chairman, The Direct Marketing Association New Media Council, UK; Ira Magaziner, electronic commerce advisor to The President, US; Jason Finch, Port 80 Internet Consultancy, UK; Jock Gill, Penfield-Gill consultants, US; John Elkington, Chairman, Sustainability Ltd, author of *Cannibals with Forks;* John Harvey Jones, author, UK; John Seely-Brown, Head of Xerox Palo Alto Research Centre, California, US; Jon Epstein, ResultsRUs Data Services, UK; Keith Ferguson and Shirley Williams, NatWest Electronic Markets, London; Khalil Barsoum, Chairman and Chief Executive, IBM UK; Lester Thurow, Professor, Massachusetts Institute of Technology, US; Lord Hollick, Chairman, United News & Media, UK; Mark Radcliffe, Gray Cary Ware & Freidenrich, Palo Alto, US; Martin Bartle, PRO, The Direct Marketing Association, UK; Mary McAnally, Managing Director, Meridian Television, UK; Melanie Howard, co-founder, The Future Foundation, London; Mike Flood Page, Commissioning Editor, Information Technology programmes, BBC TV, UK; Monika Kosmahl Aring and Rebecca Bischoff, Education Development Centre Inc., Massachusetts, US; Neal Rimay-Mvranyi, The Database Group, UK; Nicholas Booth, Times Interface, *News International*, UK; Nicholas Negroponte, Massachusetts Institute of Technology, US, author of *Being Digital*; Paul O'Reilly, MD, Invaco software, UK; Peter Grimsdale, Channel 4 Television, UK; Professor Tony Davies, Director, British Telecom Electronic Commerce Innovation Centre, University of Wales, UK; Ray Hammond, author of *Digital Business*; Robb Wilmott, Robb Wilmott Associates, Palo Alto, US; Rosabeth Moss Kanter, Professor of Business Administration, Harvard Business School, US; Steve Johnston, Director of Development, Interactive Media in Retailing Group, Europe; Steven Rutt, Isobel Munday and Louise Crawford, Macmillan Press, UK; Sugra Zaman, Watson, Little Literary Agents, London; Thomas Blum, Product Planning & New Product Development, Consumers Union, US; Tim Jackson, founder Quixell, UK; Tony Davison, Head of Futures, IBM UK; Victor Keegan, Economics Correspondent, *Guardian*, UK; Violet Berlin, Presenter and Toby Murcott, Producer, *Soundbyte*, BBC World Service, UK

The potential of Guaranteed Electronic Markets was first recognized by the non-aligned London think-tank Demos. Particular thanks are due to:

Geoff Mulgan, George Lawson, Debbie Porter, Lindsay Nash, Ian Christie, Richard Warner, Perri 6, Tom Bentley, Helen Perry.

Thanks also to Dr Mike Fitchett for resourceful support over the years of this project.

The final frontier for electronic trade

A new technology can be slow to reveal its full potential. Rail, for instance, revolutionised the coal industry many years before their promise of mass public transport and universal postage was fulfilled. The history of broadcasting likewise reveals a pioneering phase when the new invention was perceived primarily for its usefulness to existing organisations: it finally allowed shipping companies to communicate with their fleets at sea. The radical concept of a home entertainment industry took two decades to emerge. More recently, hardware that enabled computers to communicate with each other was seen by its developers as an important contribution to US defence systems. Only when the World Wide Web was launched a quarter of a century later did the full potency of their work become discernible. Now we are witnessing the emergence of new trading technology. This book suggests that electronic commerce, even though it is overturning retailing and business practices around the world, is still only in a relatively insignificant pioneering phase, akin to mine railways or early ship-to-shore radios. There is an, as yet, unanticipated impact that will go much further in reshaping societies, largely for the good. To explore this lurking potential it is necessary to divide online purchasing into two distinct strands. The first is sales channels, in which specific retailers, manufacturers or service companies offer their output. The second is interactive marketplaces, in which anyone can sell.

The first strand of online commerce, sales channels, has its roots in a chance meeting between two Mr Smiths on a 1953 flight from Los Angeles to New York. IBM representative R. Blair Smith found himself seated next to the President of American Airlines C. R. Smith and, making the most of a captive prospect, began persuading the aviation magnate to automate his company's seat booking procedures. A conversation continued between the two companies until in 1959 consumer electronic trade, on any significant scale, was born with the launch of American's SABRE reservations system. At first travel agents seeking a reservation used their telephone to speak to a clerk in the computer room, who would confirm availability and fares. Then terminals were moved out to retail premises so agents could interrogate the database and make bookings online. As other suppliers saw the advantages of such a facility SABRE allowed additional airlines, hotel chains and car hire companies on to their computer. By the 1990s it was so profitable that American's CEO reputedly let it be known that if he had to choose between selling SABRE or selling the airline he would 'let the planes go'. Based on core computers in a vast high-security cavern deep beneath Oklahoma's Tulsa airport, SABRE is now the world's largest online order-taking system, processing thousands of messages from around the globe every second. Along with competing systems set up by other big airlines in the 1970s, the Tulsa goldmine defined electronic trade as a gateway to inventory, set up to offer customers increasing convenience and sophistication of choice. Online consumerism in the 1980s and 90s has been overwhelmingly driven by the same model. The French Minitel, Time Warner's Full Service Network and virtual malls were in turn overhauled by more focused operators including stellar performers of Internet trade such as Amazon Books, Cisco components and Dell Computer. All are channels to market operated by or on behalf of specific sellers. It is for the benefit of companies like this that a new generation of software for 'relationship marketing' to individual online customers is being developed. Interactive television, which simplifies remote shopping with on-screen versions of well-known high-street stores, will further advance this form of electronic trade.

Open markets: a second tier of electronic trade

It is online sales channels that have attracted most of the coverage of electronic commerce, but the true potency of the new trading technology rests in its secondary strand: open online marketplaces. One undercutting sales channel, like Amazon Books, can re-orientate a retail sector but a computerised marketplace available to any seller can rewrite the rules of trade. Developments in global money markets over the last decade demonstrate the difference. World-wide currency deregulation in the 1980s created trading opportunities for finance houses which their floors full of brokers using telephones and e-mail-based 'conversational' online purchasing facilities were ill equipped to exploit: continued moves towards online trading were inevitable. These could have taken the form of each bank setting up an interactive selling site enabling purchasing dealers to shop around among vendors they trusted in search of the best deal for their needs of the moment. Instead, in 1988, financial information supplier Reuters took a hotel room at the annual gathering of currency dealers in Hawaii to demonstrate a prototype for something they called the 2000–2 matching service. At its heart would be a computer on Long Island accessible by any dealer whose employers subscribed and on which they could list ever-changing requirements for funds they wished to buy or offers of currency they needed to sell. The central computer would instantly match a buyer with the best value supplier for their needs of the time, underpin each trade by checking the credit status of the two parties and issue a confirming contract.

Launched four years later, the new trading forum was received with some disdain. 'At first it was junior traders who were assigned to the electronic services, their colleagues called them the Gameboys', recalls the editor of a foreign exchange newsletter.[1] This distancing eventually gave way to enthusiastic embrace, particularly among smaller banks who were now able to trade directly in the market instead of having to constantly use a larger, more trusted institution as a costly intermediary. Market entry costs dropped to near zero: any company with the required funds can trade on 2000–2 without need of existing business relationships, awareness raising or means of order taking. This, coupled with gossamer-thin transaction costs, has kept the electronic currency markets ever widening. As new players join, prices increase in competitiveness, so trading became more attractive, swelling market turnover, which creates new opportunities and a wider spectrum of deal sizes that entice further resources into the system: a classic virtuous circle for the participants. It is this creation of a coordinated market for the benefit of financial institutions that underlies the billions of dollars of 'hot money' now ricocheting around the world.

There are Internet sites that appear to operate open marketplaces for the public: Auto-by-Tel[2] for pre-owned cars is one example, e-bay[3] for general goods and OnSale.com[4] majoring in computer supplies are others. Verification of sellers is a constant problem for their managements. Each has had to make a choice: to restrict providers to those who can be vouchsafed in some way, Auto-by-Tel, for instance, will only sell used cars from their affiliated dealers not ordinary motorists, or to allow all sources of supply and then find some way of enforcing honesty. Anyone buying a second-hand soldier doll at the e-bay site, for example, is not only charged up to 5 per cent commission for being matched with the seller, but also asked to e-mail a final analysis of that person's integrity for display to anyone else contemplating trading with him. It is a time-consuming and fallible mechanism: National Consumers League statistics in 1998 found online public auctions as a sector were home to a variety of enduring scams.[5] Databases that pair buyers and sellers are obviously valued by Net users who have taken the time to understand how their risks can be minimized. Indeed, e-bay, the leading net auction provider, is a a rarity: an Internet-based company that is already profitable. But such services fall far short of the trading environment that currency dealers can take for granted: a truly secure market, fully informed, preserving confidentially, with automatic deal enforcement and minute transaction charges. Reuters' task was made easy because financial institutions are so highly regulated. On the Internet there are no immediate solutions to problems associated with unknown sellers, hence the continuing rise of reassuringly branded online sales channels.

Secure electronic marketplaces open to any seller?

If the mechanisms that underpin electronic currency markets could be adapted from transfer of digital millions to more tangible goods and services, online markets that were completely secure, convenient and available to any seller would be realisable for almost anything. Imagine further that such marketplaces were universally accessible through the Internet or interactive television. That is the breathtaking potential of the new trading technology. Take, as one example, a hypothetical marketplace in car hire, running on one central computer, within which Hertz or Avis were as welcome to offer vehicles as a local garage with only three autos available or even an individual motorist who did not need his car for a weekend. Someone requiring transport for a day would input their location and desired standard of vehicle to be matched with the cheapest, closest option available, regardless of supplier. These as yet unrealised marketplaces have been christened Guaranteed Electronic Markets: their complex underlying procedures, that would make sure each deal was as safe as any presented to a foreign exchange dealer, are outlined in section one of this book. In the case of car hire, for instance, the central computer would need to satisfy itself that any vehicle being hired was provenly roadworthy, that the hirer could easily be made to pay for any damage or late return and it was only displayed to people who met requirements pre-selected by the owner (a long record of safely returned hired vehicles in the past perhaps). This would take a level of programming and support from state agencies (who need a way to assure the central computer that a putative hirer has a valid driving licence, for instance) that would be considerably more sophisticated than anything envisioned for interactive television or public Internet services at present. Demand for car hire simply does not warrant that level of investment. But auto rentals could be only one sector among thousands offered from a core computer which had developed the basic software and liaison required to underpin truly reliable open electronic markets in every area of legal trade. As the money markets have shown, making such a facility available should lead to sharply reduced costs of selling, which widens each market and attracts new resources, and which in turn should increase the 'granularity' of deals on offer. In such a market, for example, it may be possible to hire cars for a period of one hour and, because the vehicles on offer were no longer clustered at company depots but more evenly dispersed, there would be more likelihood of one being available close to any enquirer. This can sound improbably utopian (for everyone except the big car hire corporations of course) but as later chapters will show, money and resources behave very differently in genuinely open electronic markets.

To be truly useful this potential car hire forum would need to be flanked by additional markets running on the same core computer. Delivery would be one, allowing anyone who wished to trade as a car transfer driver to be verified and then price themselves competitively into work, with each assignment contracted and enforced by the computer. Insurance would be another, again not on the basis of a link to a favoured company but an automatic match with whoever offered the lowest price of the moment for the exact requirements of that hire. Once this technology was working it could be extended to marketplaces that scarcely exist at present. Motorbike hire? Child's tricycle hire? It would be up to individuals and companies whether they wished to sell in these virgin sectors but, like currency dealers, they would be able to call up data showing the extent of demand at any time.

Guaranteed Electronic Markets could trade goods with the same protection as services. Books provide a convenient example. An Internet user accessing Amazon's site at present can buy the latest John Grisham novel for 30 per cent less than the price a high-street book-seller with far greater overheads is likely to charge. But in a Guaranteed Electronic Market a purchaser might be matched with someone nearby who had just finished that novel and was willing to sell it second hand for 50 per cent off the published price. Assuming a flourishing market in local deliveries it could be at his door in less time at lower cost than anything despatched from Amazon's warehouse for carriage by the postal service. A local market in door-to-door hire of popular titles might even emerge from enterprising individuals around the country. Like every other deal on the putative system, such transactions would fully protect the property of the seller while ensuring adequate redress against anyone defaulting on a transaction. In time, marketplaces like this might trade contracts for periods of employment, training, groceries, household services, raw materials for industry and so on. Each sector should lower prices and constantly widen the range of suppliers by abolishing market entry costs and providing full informa-tion on levels of demand. As it gained momentum, a system offering these markets should demolish many economic realities currently taken for granted: oligopoly suppliers, market distortions and lack of price information for example. In their place an atomized economy of count-less individual traders and ever-changing suppliers should emerge.

Could electronic commerce ever deliver this theoretical potential?

On current trends the kind of trading just outlined looks set to remain conjectural for some time. In the early days of electronic commerce it was widely assumed that online trade would inevitably graduate to an ultra efficient marketplace and unleash countless suppliers. That is now questioned: certainly new trading software is offering benefits to small outfits but, as section three will show, it offers hyper advantage to large corporations. The trading revolution is not the information revolution. Big players are understandably developing the new infrastructure to increase their corporate profitability; there is no equivalent of the shared incentive to grow a new medium that powered the World Wide Web's growth. Additionally, a simple, wide-open online marketplace would require coordination of software standards well beyond the comparative simplicity of web site construction. Issues to be resolved would include payment systems, authentication of traders, deposit taking, protection of privacy, connections between disparate market-places (making a purchase then selecting delivery from an open pool of carriers for instance), bonding of sellers and dispute resolution. Emergence of common standards in these areas is likely to be protracted, not least because pioneers now have to invest so heavily to create the programming, after which coming second is not an acceptable outcome. Years of 'browser wars' give some taste of the possible road ahead. Since inception the Web needed a consistent software platform for those who wanted to set up sites and those who wished to access them. What emerged was Netscape and Microsoft warring to own crucial technology, incompatible programming deliberately developed and outsider's attempts to promote an emerging standard, Java, obfuscated through proprietary modifications.[6] Yet this winnowing process does not necessarily deliver the best technology: many attribute Internet Explorer's ascendancy in the browser wars to marketing advantage rather than incontrovertible superiority.

Aside from the struggle for standards, a justifiable fear of commoditisation is likely to stop the Internet moving towards a series of truly open marketplaces. Consumer finance companies, for instance, are migrating to the Net and investing in 'relationship management' software. But the real bonus an online economy could bring to their customers would be if it allowed individuals to access one big pool of all the cash currently available for consumer lending in the way foreign exchange dealers trade direct in the market, not with a retailer who has only a small proportion of overall merchandise on offer. Within such a pool a borrower would be likely to find a loan of exactly the size and duration required at a fiercely competitive rate. But, were one massive effectively underpinned consumer loans market to be set up, the financial companies would become redundant. They have to cripple the potential of the new marketplace to retain a place in it.

Entrepreneurial capitalism, it is argued, should ensure that if the finance industry will not pool its resources for the benefit of clients, it is sidelined by a new competitor who, assuming standards issues have been resolved, sets up software in which lenders and borrowers meet each other for secure transactions with charges representing little over the cost of running such a straightforward service. Who might do this? Computing companies certainly have the technological might required, but each of the hundreds of finance company Internet sites at present requires a server computer, probably bought from IBM, Sun or Compaq, then software developed by specialists such as Baan, SAP or Oracle with regular upgrades from the same companies' consultants. None of these companies has any incentive to promote truly open markets akin to the Reuters 2000–2 that runs, very efficiently, on one machine with no need for expensive relationship technology. Unsurprisingly, they unite to promote electronic commerce as a fragmented mass of individual sales channels.[7]

Establishing pure online markets with all the attendant liaison to make them completely trustworthy would be expensive and unpredictable. Might someone like Rupert Murdoch nevertheless scent profitable possibility in making the full capabilities of electronic markets universally available? Were he to decide to do so, his problems would be twofold. First, the very precise laws required to underpin such an operation are not in place and would be difficult to envisage in a globalizing economy. How, for instance, could the putative marketplace operator conclusively avoid being a counterpart in disputed deals? It would need the legal status of say a telephone company, which is deemed not liable for the conversations its customers conduct. That principle could not be extended lightly to a profusion of Internet marketplaces. Second, the neonate Murdoch service would require expensive advertising to rise above the babel of often hyperbolic customer propositions from competing marketplaces. It might then be difficult to maintain momentum towards critical mass because start-up operators could also offer buyer–seller matching with the same features but charging much lower commission. There are, for instance, hundreds of forums which trade second-hand personal computers online, all with their own formulae for 'adding value' and individual charging structures, ranging through various kinds of auction to straight sales or exchanges. No software can compare like with like in this mass of uncoordinated marketplaces. Together they certainly offer a more convenient way of shopping compared to phoning or physically visiting a range of outlets but do not make the major market-widening advantages, currently enjoyed by global money dealers, available to all. In the fast-mutating online world Rupert Murdoch will not make his money from long-term commitment to realizing the deep social benefits of electronic trade. Safer returns are available from setting up a fully featured trading environment using interactive television then selling exclusive use to big retailers. It is the same model adopted by companies like AOL/Netscape which concentrate traffic towards 'portal' sites where prefential retail display can be sold for millions of dollars. Foreign currency dealers could attest to the likely desire among ordinary people for a new pure marketplace. The febrile electronic commerce industry is unlikely to be able to provide it for the foreseeable future.

Government's role as initiator of new technology

History shows a way these hindrances have previously been bypassed and the full promise of an infant technology made real. It is, however, a possibility completely at odds with current thinking in the computing establishment. Study of the last 200 years shows how frequently politicians have transiently involved themselves in emerging technology, not as regulators but as initiators. In a latter-day version of this scenario a government could decide it wanted one simple, fully protected, electronic markets system for its population, perhaps funded by flat rate commission on each deal and built by private enterprise. These Guaranteed Electronic Markets could centralize technologies such as bonding, verification and payment transfer for low-cost use by franchisees running thousands of markets as diverse as household services, transport and accommodation. Certain privileges that only government can bestow could be outlined in legislation that shapes a clear business opportunity for whoever funds the system. These benefits might include: direct legal protection of contracts between buyers and sellers on the system, courts willing to accept disputes forwarded by the software so accusations of unfair trade can be automatically resolved, a right to mesh the system with licensing authorities and other state bodies (without compromising its independence) and a prominent channel on the country's interactive televisions alongside major broadcasters.

There would be commitments to be extracted from the operators of these markets to reflect the scale of opportunity inherent in being sole beneficiaries of these government-awarded rights. They might, for example, have to pay for a network of dedicated terminals in public places so that even those with no connection at home could enter the new markets. Once these terms were decided, competing consortia would bid to build and run the nation's Guaranteed Electronic Markets system using whatever technology standards were practicable at the time. Selection between them need not involve politicians picking winners. It could be as simple as each group specifying, in a sealed bid, the flat rate percentage on each deal they proposed charging if awarded the contract, with the lowest commitment winning.

This would be a nation-by-nation initiative, rather than a global scheme. It would not involve restraining existing electronic commerce in any way: a country's Guaranteed Electronic Markets (GEMs) system would exist alongside the multiplicity of sales channels and Internet buyer–seller matching services. It simply provides an alternative for those who wish to trade in a wide, more convenient, marketplace. The legislative process described is not always popular but it is common and it can work. When Margaret Thatcher wanted a Channel tunnel built, for instance, she pragmatically sidelined her aversion to government-initiated schemes to ensure a successful consortium which, although having to compete with ferry, hovercraft and airline services, was granted an officially enforced monopoly on tunnels between England and France until the end of the year 2020. Anyone else seeking to burrow a competing route, however well funded, will be stopped because protecting one operator was the only realistic way to find the large investment required for a long-term project without taxpayers absorbing any risk.

Parliamentary initiative to enable new technology swiftly to reach its full potential was a conspicuous feature of Britain's economic supremacy during the technological chaos of the Industrial Revolution. The birth of public water supply, in particular, forms a useful analogy with the kind of act that might eventually realise a GEMs service anywhere in the world. Until the 1850s hundreds of water companies were exploiting early pumping and piping technology to supply well-off homes in their locality. Dozens of incompatible pipe networks were spun across the new cities by branded suppliers who delivered marked variations in quality and pricing. A typical company piped water to customers for two hours or less on alternate days with the product then needing to be filtered and boiled before consumption. In 1842 a report looked into appalling public health problems of the time and mooted the notion of a mass water system to run alongside existing companies, growing to offer an affordable 24-hour, immediately drinkable, supply to anyone who wished to plumb in to the new network.[8] Many people found the idea so ambitious as to be inconceivable.

Owners of the water companies at first dismissed, then vehemently opposed, mass supply, which would commoditize their carefully nurtured customer relationships. They ensured a vigorous campaign labelling the idea of an officially instigated water service as unacceptable centralizing of power by politicians.[9] Nevertheless, and despite a parliamentary commitment to *laissez-faire* at the time,[10] the 1848 Public Health Act initiated such a service. It did not banish existing suppliers. Records from 1867 show London having nine water companies alongside the municipal pipes, for instance.[11] But the posited mass system was awarded advantages that would have been of little use to small operators: primarily, access to new large-scale sources of supply.[12] These new resources brought the cost of domestic water down by a claimed 30 to 50 per cent.[13] Coming in the age of Municipal Socialism it was largely local government money that inaugurated the new network but, at a different time, investment could as easily have originated in the private sector. The Act's significance was the focus and momentum it created by outlining and facilitating a bold vision for water that went way beyond industry aspirations or market demand. The masses were not clamouring for 24-hour water: still relying on communal bore holes and delivery carts, they had little conception such a facility could exist. By making the leap of faith as to a new technology's ultimate capability the UK government ensured a low overhead service and created a potentially profitable mass market harnessing the economies of scale.

Would it have eventually happened without parliament? More companies would almost certainly have entered the market for water provision in later decades, lowering costs and extending reach. The Byzantine tangle of piping would eventually, through expensive attrition, have been whittled down to a small handful of dominant providers. This cartel would probably then have set common standards for pipe sizes, junctions and valves and begun discussing intake and outfall siting. But the unique efficiencies of a system planned from the start for mass use would have been missing. Piping expertise soon travelled around the world. It is worth comparing provision in London 60 years after the act with nearby Paris, which had to rely on market forces alone: a 1911 study found 96 per cent of the British capital's households were connected to a water supply against only 17.5 per cent in Paris.[14]

The role of government as initiator can be seen in most of the infrastructure considered essential to modern life. Table 1 shows how governments in just two countries, the US and Britain, have been crucial in supplementing a pioneering phase of genuinely useful technology with a vision for its maximized public usefulness. A notable exception on this chart is the Internet for which there was never an Act to create focused commercial opportunity. There did not need to be: the US government directly paid out cold war tax dollars to build a computer communication backbone. This funding, starting in 1965 with the Advanced Research Projects Agency and eventually through the National Science Foundation, did not end until 1995.

Competition between governments: a coming force in electronic trade?

It is the contention of this book that universal access to reliable electronic markets will become as essential to a healthy society in the networked computer age as was provision of quality water to industrializing cities. Further, the only decisive way to ensure its realization would be for government to craft a combination of opportunity and obligations which amounts to a viable business opportunity for private enterprise. Electronic markets, however, would be a considerably more sensitive public utility than facilities like water supply. A centralized system would forever have the potential for misuse of user data or skewing of markets to favour predetermined outcomes. It would be unacceptable for such a system to be run or even supervised by government; instead control would be in the hands of a web of companies

Table 1   The role of government in the US and UK in turning new technology into public infrastructure

TECHNOLOGY	PIONEERING PHASE	GOVERNMENT ACTION
Public gas supply	Experimental intermittent supply to factories and workshops.	**1817:** (US) Baltimore facilitates first gas lighting in streets. **1820:** (UK) Public Utility Act launched a uniform gas supply in Manchester then the rest of Britain.
Public water supply	Regional water enterprises, differing in standards, reliability and level of service.	**1848:** (UK) Public Health Act made water supply the responsibility of regional government. **1895:** (US) Metropolitan Water District of Massachusetts – the first regional supply system.
Mass postage service	*Ad hoc* stagecoach services.	**1839:** (UK) Penny Postage Act. **1847:** (US) Use of stamps legally recognised.
Public railroad system	Assorted mine and factory railways.	**1840s:** (UK) Various Railway Acts. **1850s:** (US) Federal Land Grants financed construction in return for cheap carriage of government goods.
Telephone	Experimental local systems.	**1880:** (UK) Court ruling bought co-ordinated planning of a telephone system under jurisdiction of the Post Office. **1921:** (US) Graham-Willis Act exempted phone companies from antitrust laws.
Public electricity supply	Sporadic service to factories using differing voltages and AC/DC.	**1882:** (UK) Board of Trade starts licensing companies to provide regional domestic supply. **1920:** (US) Federal Power Commission created. It encouraged building of transmission lines on public domain.
Road system for the motor car era	Countless local track-laying initiatives.	**1909:** (UK) National Road Board. **1916:** (US) First Federal Highways Act.
Radio transmissions	Ham radio, point to point communications, manufacturers' output.	**1927:** (US) Radio Act creates FRC for station licensing. **1927:** (UK) BBC Charter.
Television transmissions	Manufacturer's experiments, unlicensed test stations.	**1936:** (UK) BBC Charter extended to TV. **1941:** (US) FCC authorised first commercial TV station.
The Internet	Experimental computer bulletin boards.	**1960s:** US Defence Dept funding. **1970s/80s/90s:** US Education Dept funding.

making up a winning consortium and more importantly their franchisees operating thousands of individual market sectors. Additionally,
inspection regimes exceeding that of any existing utility and designed to
nullify this damaging potential will be detailed in later chapters. The
most important guarantee such a system should give users is constant
proof that if ever they lost faith in the core computer's security or
integrity they could immediately close their account and in doing so
irrevocably destroy all personal data.

Within the short lifespan of electronic commerce, so far parliaments
have been largely content to act as unimaginative backstays: promising
regulation, or, more often, the absence of regulatory restrictions, to
keep new sales channels competitive. But politicians are of course
themselves subject to competitive pressure and have much to gain from
offering their electorates unique benefits. A Guaranteed Electronic
Markets system would cost the originating country's taxpayers nothing
to build and no citizen would be coerced into using it. If properly
executed and widely taken up, however, it could open up new vistas of
work and consumption opportunities for users. It should bring new
resources into the economy because market entry costs and the chances
of a deal going sour have withered. However, the possibility of public
electronic markets poses enormous threats as well as opportunities for
politicians. Their danger lies in a temptation to launch compromised
markets, aiming to shield existing industries or power bases from the
brutal efficiencies of such a reliable marketplace. Protective forays into
computer trading by the London Stock Exchange (LSE) demonstrate
the perils that could one day be faced by entire countries. As Europe's
overwhelmingly dominant exchange, the LSE moved tardily to electronic trading in 1993 with their TAURUS system. This enshrined
labourious, but politically sensitive, settlement procedures in the new
process, which then collapsed under the resulting complexities. A
second system similarly protected the LSE's legacy of market-making
procedures from the brunt of electronic market forces. Meanwhile,
Frankfurt's less historically encumbered stock market had moved unre-
servedly to a simple open electronic marketplace, attracting an ever
increasing proportion of trade. Eventually out-traded by the German
exchange, London was compelled by its senior customers to merge with
Frankfurt and trade on their software.[15] Any country attempting to
constrain their embryonic public markets would be likely to find them-

selves similarly overtaken by other nations who learned from that mistake. Significantly, it could be Second World countries, where opposition would be less formidable, who would be first to launch Guaranteed Electronic Markets systems. If those public markets were incorruptible they could remove many of the factors that can often make such nations financially unstable. Like the Frankfurt bourse they may then start dramatically catching up with previously implacable international rivals.

Net Benefit aims to introduce all aspects of this emerging potential for electronic trading technology. Section one, overleaf, demonstrates how a Guaranteed Electronic Markets (GEMs) system might enact a variety of transactions. Section two explores the impact such a system might have in the country of operation, including the effects of a possible official online parallel economy to include those with little hard cash in the new way of trading. In section three the steps necessary to launch a GEMs service are discussed, as well as the probable opposition to such a move and its possible tactics. The fourth section asks how businesses might adapt to a world of genuinely open electronic markets for all. Finally, Appendix one outlines the five principles of Guaranteed Electronic Markets that define a system in which every aspect of operation is genuinely guaranteed for the good of all users and Appendix two offers a tentative business model for any consortium looking to build a first GEMs system.

The effects of online consumerism and business-to-business purchasing are now inescapable. If its ultimate potential is ignored by governments, the rewards of this trading revolution are likely to accrue progressively to those with dominant seller sites: firms that are employing decreasing numbers of people. Yet, as following chapters will show, this technology, with a nudge from politicians, offers an answer to many pressing contemporary problems: economic inefficiency, social exclusion, crime and national determination in the global age. The downside, if significant numbers started using public market systems, would be felt by many organizations that form the backbone of today's economy who could lose their previously unquestioned status as economic activity widens. The battle over whether electronic trade should be left to reinforce concentrations of economic power, or moulded to drive a newly inclusive, atomized, economy of widening participants, could be one of the defining political issues of the next decade.

Notes

1. Julie Ros, Executive Editor of *FX Week Newsletter*, published by Waters Information Services. Interview with the author 28 August 1998.
2. www.autobytel.com
3. www.ebay.com
4. www.onsale.com
5. Evan I. Schwartz, At Online Auctions, Good and Raw, Deals, *New York Times*, March 5 1998 – electronic edition.
6. Susan B. Garland, Sun takes the stand, *Business Week*, 26 October 1998, p. 49.
7. Proving the exception to the rule, Microsoft does run matching services including Expedia for travel and Carpoint for cars. They are heavily restricted on the seller side.
8. *Report of the Sanitary Condition of the Labouring Population of Gt Britain*, written by three Poor Law Commissioners assisted by Edwin Chadwick, Secretary of the Commission. Its eventual recommendations were so radical the former had their names taken off the cover and Chadwick alone is credited with recognising water supply as an essential utility (M. W. Flinn, *New Introduction to the Report*, University of Edinburgh Press, 1965, p. 46).
9. S. E. Finer, *The Life and Times of Sir Edwin Chadwick*, London, Methuen, 1952, p. 320.
10. In 1846, for instance, the protectionist Corn Laws had finally been repealed.
11. *Encyclopaedia Britannica*.
12. In 1850, for example, the new system was allowed to develop wells at Farnham and Hindhead to supply London 30 miles away. Smaller water enterprises were still drawing from the River Thames, an inhibitor for the private market because it was then the capital's main sewer. (S.E. Finer, *The Life and Times of Sir Edwin Chadwick*, London, Methuen, 1952, p. 394).
13. Ibid. p. 394.
14. Jean-Pierre Goubert, *The Conquest of Water: the Advent of Health in the Industrial Age*, Princeton University Press, 1986, p. 196.
15. Melanie Bien, Traders Force the Rate of Exchange, *The European*, 13–19 July 1998, pp. 8–10.

The ultimate potential of e-trade: how open public markets might work

In 1993, after nearly three decades of networked computing, the Internet consisted of 800 unrelated networks with a mass of incompatible operating systems and programming languages.[1] A group of particle physicists in Switzerland constructed an additional network based on what they called the http protocol and designed to allow them to easily exchange documents. Unofficially they christened it The Web. It was this creation of one very simple way of reliably accessing data or adding new pages of information in a maelstrom of options that turned the combination of computers and telephone lines from an academic accessory to a social force. Within a few years, users opting for the http protocol far outnumbered those using any of the established networks. This chapter assumes a GEMs system has achieved something similar for the more complex requirements of secure online trading: offering a single convenient entry into an enormously varied marketplace in which anyone can sell anything instantly. There would be no controlling authority acting as gateway to the new markets, only automated procedures to ensure each deal was safe. I have further assumed that dependable public markets were initiated by a government, motivated either by political expediency or egalitarian conviction, who enshrined two crucial principles in the enabling Act. First, the putative system is confined to providing only the services that can be most efficiently delivered by a public markets service. The consortium running GEMs is not allowed to leverage that pole position, through technological domination or contact with customers, into a commanding lead in further areas. Their profits come only from continuing investment in neutral, confidential, relentlessly inspected public markets. Second, that there is no social engineering attached to the project: no attempt to manipulate markets or arrive at a planned outcome. The only aim is finding a best possible match for each buyer's enquiry across every area of trade that is legal in the country of operation. Consequences of such a system, not least as outlined in later pages of this book, can only be speculative.

Any citizen in the country of operation could open an account then buy or sell in the new marketplace, which would be available through the Internet or interactive television sets. They would need to prove identity and banking arrangements, at a Post Office perhaps, where they would receive a PIN generated on the counter clerk's GEMs terminal. On first logging in, the system would ask for a link to their bank account enabling it to add and subtract funds as they trade. Alternatively they could use a smart card. Such a system would start modestly and grow as new sectors were added. The following scenarios, however, demonstrate the operation of a mature, widely used system.

1 Demonstration: booking overnight accommodation in a GEM

It is half past six on a Friday evening. A couple looking for a weekend on the coast have turned to the GEMs system to find somewhere to spend tonight. After the customers have entered their PIN (personal identification number) and navigated to the 'overnight accommodation' marketplace, an initial screen asks 'do you want to rent a room or do you wish to sell accommodation?' One click tells GEMs they are buyers rather than potential providers: they are then asked for detailed requirements. On completion their screen might look like this:

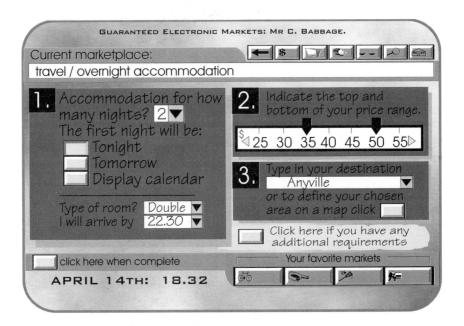

It has taken seven clicks to tell the central computer they seek a room in nearby Anyville for tonight costing $35–50 and they will be arriving by half past ten. Immediately GEMs displays a map of accommodation it has still available that most closely matches their demands.

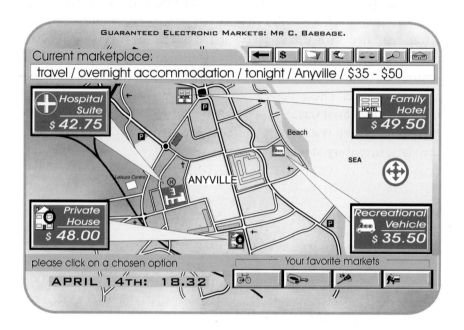

Market entry

Any individual or organization can sell in this market which will offer a room in a branded chain hotel as readily as accommodation with a householder letting out a spare bed. It is up to the purchaser to decide which they favour. Market entry is an automated process with no charges levied by GEMs: anyone with a room to sell simply completes three tasks. First, they must prove their accommodation complies with any relevant legislation. They might, for instance, need to acquire a fire safety certificate for which the Fire Officer would give them a GEMs compatible PIN (Box 1.1). Then they need to transfer a specified sum of money that will be held as a bond from which compensation can be paid if they default on any deal. This would not be as arduous a requirement as it may seem: interest accumulated on the bond is paid into the room owner's account, anyone having problems raising the cash could turn to a GEM for insurance. Their supplier could then have their commission automatically extracted from each transaction. Finally the market entrant will be asked to input a pricing formula. This can be as simple as a flat nightly rate or it can change according to the day of the week, time of year, length of stay, the arrival and departure times of guests, advance notice with which a booking is received, occupancy level at time of sale and so on. The formula can also be set to attract particular customers; those who can prove to GEMs that they are *bona fide* students maybe. These details are used to calculate a price for each individual potential buyer. Hotels letting dozens of rooms may want to link their existing reservations computers to GEMs so both are trading the same inventory at identical prices.

Box 1.1

VERIFICATION OF TRADERS BY STATE AGENCIES

This would probably be achieved through encryption algorithms. In the case of fire certificates National Fire Service Headquarters would be given a PIN which they use to identify Senior Fire Officers to the system. Each of them is then allocated an algorithm by GEMs. When they certify a premises as safe they type the address into a GEMs terminal, it is fed through their algorithm and the 4 letters returned are the owner's proof to be typed into a GEMs market entry page. The key principle is that GEMs does not centrally store assessments of any individual's fitness to trade: the only information it holds on a user is that he has chosen to input, with proof where required. Fire stations could charge for this service just as they currently charge for a paper certificate in most countries.

This instant access to the market should make many new resources available. The offer of accommodation in a hospital, for instance, might be the result of cancelled operations tomorrow and an administrator releasing the patient rooms as bed and breakfast for that one night. He has nothing to lose, if there are no takers at his minimum price the hospital has suffered no costs for market entry, its sum in bond being transferred back in full in the morning. The recreational vehicle option may seem implausible but again the owner who has an expensive asset parked on his drive has nothing to lose by putting it in the market occasionally on the terms of his choice.

It is the private house that appeals to the couple seeking a place to stay. They click for a details page on that option.

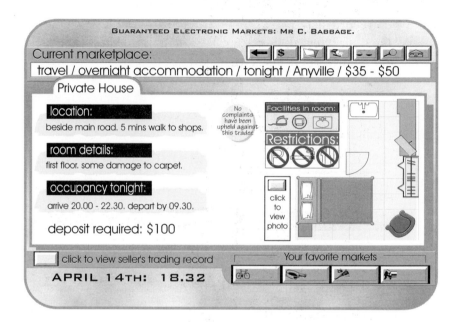

This information was input by the owner. It is no place for hyperbole, the details given become part of a binding contract with any buyer. Some sellers would opt to provide only the most basic information, others could click through GEMs' detailed questions for overnight accommodation market entry, including sections on availability to the disabled, views, historical significance of their building and so on. There may be potential buyers for whom one of these headings is a key selection criterion. Sellers who want to offer still more enticing detail can use a friendly interface to assemble a floorplan of the room or have a photograph of the building scanned and sent to GEMs. The symbols in this details page show the facilities available in the room: a kettle, television and sink, and the restrictions imposed on hirers: no parking on the premises, no smoking and no eating in the room. Again, this becomes part of the contract.

GEMs' ability to compile a trading record for each user is essential to faith in the marketplace. The system can monitor a buyer or seller's number of trades and any complaints upheld against them. No user has to release this personal information to potential trading partners but those that do not might be judged to have something to hide. The owner of the room in Anyville, still anonymous to browsers, has chosen to make her record across multiple categories available to potential buyers. One click reveals a background of unimpeachable reliability throughout a range of GEMs market sectors.

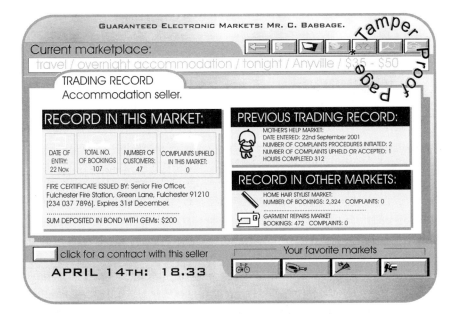

Satisfied that they are dealing with a solid individual, the couple click for a contract with which to book tonight's stay.

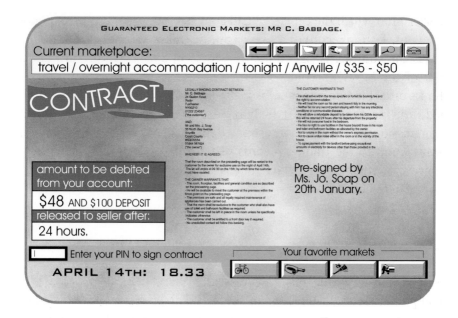

Written by GEMs lawyers, this is the system's standard contract for overnight hire of a room at the $50 or less price point. The core text is immutable, specifying legal minimums for this particular trade but sellers can remove additional clauses, one stipulating towels will be provided perhaps. Or they can add their own: a demand for 'complete silence after 23.00', for instance. Any such changes show up in red. Without these eye-catching amendments a buyer knows they are dealing with the typical agreement, one that does not favour the seller as is the case in owned sales channels but is designed only to facilitate the market. As experienced GEMs users the couple do not bother to read the contract, they know it will be firm but fair on both sides. One standard stipulation is 'no unsolicited approaches', the seller cannot use this transaction as a launchpad for relationship marketing unless a buyer clicks to remove the clause.

The room owner pre-signed this contract when laying out her terms of trade, the couple now sign their side by re-entering his GEMs PIN. The system now reveals the address of their place of residence tonight and offers a map. Simultaneously a booking information page is sent to the room owner, she can use this to confirm details when the couple arrive on her doorstep. A copy of the contract is sent to each side's files and GEMs retains its own version for a month in case of legal comebacks, after which the centrally held copy is wiped. The system does not keep any lasting record of a user's specific transactions.

As the contract is signed the agreed sum, plus a deposit, are taken out of the buyer's account and held in escrow by the system until 24 hours after the booking is over. If the system does not hear from either side during that period it will release the fee, minus GEMs' own commission, to the seller, return the deposit and add another successful transaction to the trading records of both parties. During this period, however, either buyer or seller may freeze the cash by instigating a complaint about the other.

Complaints procedures

Safe electronic trade rests on dependable and prompt resolution of complaints between buyers and sellers with sanctions applied against offenders and compensation for victims. GEMs would address this need with an automated three-stage process once a completed transaction in any one of its markets was disputed. It would be demanding but that commitment to fairness should minimize the times it was called upon by deterring defaulters. The deals complained about could range from the supply of hundreds of thousands of dollars worth of ingredients for industry to lowly domestic breakages. Each transaction in every market would be bonded with funds held by the system for a safety period after completion. Let us assume as an example that the room owner in Anyville finds the couple have broken her kettle during their stay. She would call up her archived copy of the contract and click a box marked 'I wish to complain about the room occupier'. As a first stage, all the money involved in the transaction, the fee, deposit and supplier's bond would be frozen. The room owner is now invited to type in her account of the problem and click on the amount of compensation she believes is her entitlement, under the published scale of fines for this market. As a second stage, that resulting page is sent electronically to her former guests and GEMs asks if they accept culpability for the problem as outlined. If they do so, restitutive payment is deducted from their frozen deposit, transferred to the owner and the matter is closed. If they resist, the software asks for their version of events, the amount of any fine they would accept and seeks agreement from the other side. If agreement is not reached, the complaint is finally forwarded to arbitration.

Every GEMs sector would be backed up by a relevant adjudication authority, either an existing organization or a panel brought into being by system staff when they launch a particular market. In both cases judgements are financed by the bond/deposit mechanism and buying or selling in that marketplace are conditional on accepting the results. The overnight accommodation market might be overseen by tourist development bodies, for instance: any unresolved issues are electronically forwarded to their panel which reads the accounts of both sides. It can also speak to those involved by phone and, more usefully, ask to see their GEMs trading records, if available. Should the couple have a track record of complaints against them by diverse landlords, or if they choose not to release their record to the panel, their credibility would be diminished and they would be more likely to find the cost of the kettle and adjudication coming out of their bond. Particularly serious allegations would be forwarded to the courts.

Persistently misbehaving sellers or buyers would be automatically barred from a given market after a certain proportion of upheld complaints. Likewise, wilful complainants would be purged from GEMs trading after a specified number of groundless grievances. This is the same principle by which bad drivers are banned from the roads: no one has an incontestable right to use GEMs, they do so only as long as they obey the rules that make the market safe for everyone else. No trader would be immune from this relentless drive for a quality marketplace. If a big name hotel in one city was accruing too many upheld complaints and failing to live up to the standards laid out in GEMs' contract for luxury accommodation it would be mechanically ejected from that level of the market for a predetermined period, as would any caravan owner who failed to live up to the less extensive demands at the budget end of the accommodation sector. No member of GEMs staff makes judgements about who is in or out of the markets: it would be an automatic process, based on ground rules available to all.

chapter

2

Growing the new markets

Market overviews

Finding a room in Anyville that most comprehensively matched the buyers' requirements from the widest possible pool, then putting together a deal that could be promptly enforced would have taken seconds. Market entry would be equally effortless and made all the more enticing by GEMs' market overview capability. Available to any user in any sector, these screens could bring data interrogation to an entire population as they constantly collate market information that can be displayed according to a user's individual preferences. A house-holder in Anyville with a spare room, for instance, might call up this screen before deciding whether to start offering bed and breakfast.

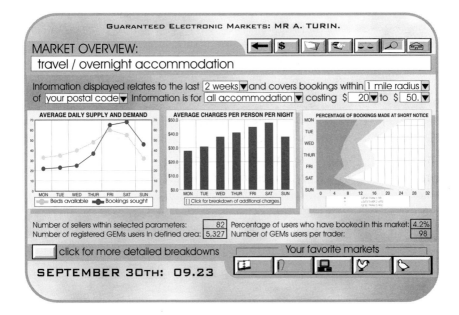

This screen shows there is unmet demand at weekends with predictably high prices being charged. The householder may now want to check levels of supply already available for next weekend and, if they remain low, perhaps take five minutes to go through GEMs' step-by-step market entry process for bed and breakfast. The parameters defining information displayed in a market overview can be changed continuously. However, if an enquiry focuses on too narrow a segment of the market, no data will be shown. A rigid commitment to user privacy prohibits display of information that may be used to deduce the income or sales patterns of any one user, corporate or individual. Only market overviews drawing on multiple anonymous sellers can be compiled.

A market in everything

GEMs would trade goods with as much thoroughness as services. A seller in the men's shirt market, for instance, would answer basic questions about size, style, sleeve length, colour (selected from an on-screen palette) and quantities available, which would then become details pages for each variant on offer. Additionally sellers could have illustrations of the garment being modelled, or a life-size patch of the material scanned for display to putative purchasers. It does not matter if the seller has a warehouse full of clothes to shift or one second-hand calico garment: as long as they set a price and describe the condition truthfully their goods will be offered to interested buyers. A contract between the two ensures that any inconsistency between what is described and the item received will, ultimately, be referred to trading standards officers for judgement. Shirt sellers would also have to specify how promptly and securely they will despatch goods. Will they manufacture the garment specified in 10 minutes and then access the 'rush deliveries' GEM for the best deal on same day transit? Or do they only check their nearest GEMs terminal once a fortnight and then send anything sold by second-class mail? Either way, if a buyer can prove non-arrival within the promised time, compensation from stored bonds awaits them. Cautious customers may want to check and only deal with a supplier, whether an individual clearing his wardrobe or an international designer label whose trading record demonstrated that they have much to lose from any lapse in integrity.

Standardised goods – refrigerators, roof tiles or bulldozers, for instance – would have their details held in GEMs archives. A seller need only input a product number for a picture and full specifications to immediately appear on their details page.

It would take several years of evolutionary development, but a mature GEMs system could eventually provide the levels of service just described across thousands of sectors. This would not take the form of one uniform market structure into which diverse trading requirements are shoehorned: instead each sector is run by a GEMs franchisee, one person handling the market for aircraft components for instance, another motivated to grow trade in a GEM for fresh vegetables. Both would develop the adjudication procedures and levels of bonding required to ensure users had unquestioning faith in the market. Additionally, each franchisee would look continuously at how a centrally provided range of electronic trade tools might make their area of responsibility more attractive to likely buyers or sellers. Anyone shopping for a second-hand car in GEMs, for example, might find a range of sellers had clicked to enable a 'purchased hold' option. This could allow potential purchasers, on payment of a fee determined by each owner, to have the vehicle taken out of the market for, say, a week until they had time for a test drive. In the plumbers' market the supply side could be offered a geographical component in their pricing formula: towards the end of each day they might choose to automatically lower charges for jobs that brought them ever nearer home. A GEMs for carpets might allow prospective purchasers to assemble a floorplan by entering room measurements on a grid. Using details input over similar squares by sellers, the core computer then demonstrates whether a proffered carpet of shape A can be made to fit room B and, if so, exactly how the new owner should proceed with dissection. Because GEMs is an all-sellers-welcome marketplace, it should steadily build the turnover that amortizes the costs of ever-increasing sophistication in its service.

3 The system's relationship with users

A GEMs system would have multiple responsibilities to its users. Crucially, it must prove that it does not abuse its position by compiling information about any company or individual's activities, apart from an optional generalized trading record. Unlike the Balkanized world of uncoordinated electronic commerce channels, users can be sure there is no data capture at any stage in the buying process. Instead, GEMs offers a user questionnaire which asks for ever-changing individual preferences in all sorts of markets. The couple seeking a weekend away, for instance, might have both clicked that they prefer a vegetarian cooked breakfast option in the overnight accommodation section of their questionnaire and GEMs would make that a search priority in ranking their options for any particular location. Persuading users to be completely at ease with GEMs, however, would take more than peerlessly detailed software. Non-binary aspects of system stewardship must be equally reassuring. To this end GEMs should operate by the principles of Guaranteed Electronic Markets (listed in Appendix one). These mandate neutral markets, distance from government or any particular seller and the right of a user to leave the system and have all their details expunged at any time. This would be enforced by transparency of operation (Box 3.1). The likelihood of being found out notwithstanding, a GEMs consortium would have no incentive to invade users' privacy. Restricted by statute to running passive electronic markets, the system has no application for individual information. The greatest business risk faced by operators would be analogous to a run on a bank: users lose faith in the system and exit *en masse*. It should be commercial logic more than regulatory threat that keeps the public markets system acting according to its published aims.

Box 3.1

TRANSPARENCY OF OPERATION

The operating consortium's commercial secrecy would be a secondary consideration to open publication of GEMs' core programming. Anyone technically competent could devise their own ways of checking that this code did not allow sensitive information to be compiled, nor markets skewed. They could then devise endless ways of confirming that the programming as published matched that actually running on the central machine. Testing would be random and never-ending, not at the hands of a potentially corruptible national body which would inevitably have links to politicians. Groups from across the geographical and ideological spectrum would be paid to visit the country of operation and pursue the inspection regime of their choice. Would this openness be a boon to hackers? GEMs' central computer would not allow remote access to restructure the core code by anyone, there is no authorization to fraudulently replicate. Users should be able to read the core programming at home should they wish but otherwise have only very low level access to the system from remote terminals. You cannot hack into a bank's computer from a cashpoint however much you know about its core programming because access is physically not possible. GEMs could follow the same protocol with security at the central control room to rival that in a missile command bunker.

Unlike existing e-trade channels, GEMs would want to go largely unregistered in its users' consciousness. Its combination of unobtrusiveness and universality would probably be a key appeal. The system would do everything possible to avoid imposing its own values on the trading process: government defines which goods and services can be legally traded, multiple sellers determine the breadth of each market and relevant outside organizations operating adjudication panels shape the acceptable behaviour in each sector. GEMs' software should aim to be like the equipment involved in a telephone call, having no character that impinges on the process it facilitates. Other companies have mastered this transparency in similar areas already. De La Rue, for example, print banknotes for over 150 countries but, despite a pivotal role in those economies, impose no values, beyond an objective commitment to quality, on any of them. Even the most persistent monetarist would not think of lobbying De La Rue to print fewer notes for a client economy; it is understood that the company implements decisions made elsewhere. Certainly GEMs' operators would have to make constant editorial decisions about which organizations to involve in markets, how to present options to users and the system's navigation paths. But those decisions, uniquely among online services, would be focused on reducing GEMs and its enforcement procedures to a commoditized service. The system should be no more than a timeless trading platform on which others build a vibrant marketplace of the moment.

chapter

4 Demonstration: connected transactions – hiring a van and driver in GEMs

A key advantage that public markets would have over piecemeal e-commerce networks is the way in which diverse marketplaces could interlock. A deal can be constructed that fits together something bought in market A, from a wide pool of informed sellers, with goods or services purchased in the same conditions from market B. Imagine, as an example, a plastic moulding company in a small town that just before 7.00 p.m. on a weekday has received a rush order for a van-load of their wheeled bins required 250 miles away by 9.00 a.m. the following morning. The company's van and driver are elsewhere, vehicle hire depots that may still be open are far away and the trusted driver hire agencies with local presence have all closed for the night.

For a harassed factory owner the solution might be found in a GEM for *vehicles/hire/vans/immediate*. By clicking through on-screen diagrams and questions he specifies overnight hire of a box van capable of at least 1000 kg payload and 10m^3 capacity. (GEMs could offer illustrations showing vehicle size relative to an adult figure to help illustrate these characteristics.) He is shown a map of his surroundings flagged with suitable vehicles and their prices for his assignment. He browses details pages before selecting a Ford belonging to an electrical goods company 4 miles away. They have chosen to put their vehicle in the market until 10.00 p.m. (when their security guard goes home) on nights when it is not required for their own deliveries. A glance at the relevant GEMs market overview showed high prices being paid for such hires, meriting the increase in cover required for all drivers, input against a PIN issued over the phone by their insurer. Since they already sell their electrical products in GEMs, the firm had no problem topping up their interest-paying bond with the system for this extra liability (Box 4.1). To protect their property, they specified additionally that only someone with at least 100 complaint-free vehicle hirings on their trading record could be eligible as a buyer. GEMs checked that the factory owner cleared this hurdle before allowing him to see the vehicle as an option. This kind of restriction on buyers, available to any seller in any GEM, should be an important factor in coaxing cautious providers to make their resources available. It encourages buyers to act responsibly because a creditable trading record then allows them to shop in a wider market, where they can expect more competitive prices.

Box 4.1

THE GEMS INSURANCE MARKET

GEMs' requirement for insurance to underpin every deal can seem intimidating. If trading on the system requires that much effort might not sellers simply go elsewhere? But insurance itself could be traded in a GEM so the most competitive cover for a very precise liability and period could be constructed instantly. Had the company letting out their van chosen to go down this route they simply would have clicked on 'find my bonding' in the market entry screen and it would have been put in place at once. Sellers of insurance could link their pricing to market overview information so that, when there is clear demand for van hires, for instance, they might opt to offer commission-based cover.

Back at the wheeled bin company the factory manager signs his half of the contract. His account is debited for price and deposit, both to be held by GEMs, this time for 72 hours to allow sufficient time for symptoms of any mechanical damage inflicted during the hire to emerge. A booking confirmation screen is sent to the supplier, it includes an eight-letter codeword, selected by the van owner and revealed to tonight's hirer after the contract has been signed. Without it the security guard would not hand over his set of keys.

Although constructed in seconds this deal would provide full back-up for both sides. If the Ford were not available for collection when promised, for instance, the hirer would tell GEMs. The system then automatically accesses the defaulting owner's bond to rent an equivalent or better vehicle and engage a driver to deliver it to the hirer. Next time the van's owner logs in he would then be asked whether he admitted culpability and reminded that, if so, he must top up his bond before trading again. If the owner denied that his vehicle was unavailable, the system would relay a message to the hirer and ask him to click on a resolution that it can administer if both parties agree: perhaps splitting costs of the replacement vehicle equally if the problem was misunderstanding on both sides. If the hirer maintained that the fault was wholly with the owner and the owner disagreed, GEMs would freeze the required sums to finance adjudication, probably in a small claims court, and then instantly forward the contract plus allegations and responses in the complaints page, to court officers.

A new world of work

After signing his contract for van hire the mouldings company manager is asked 'do you require a driver for this hire?' Clicking on 'yes' would tell the central computer he needs someone immediately for a journey and return that should end by 5.00 a.m. The system would then need to know how much he is willing to pay.

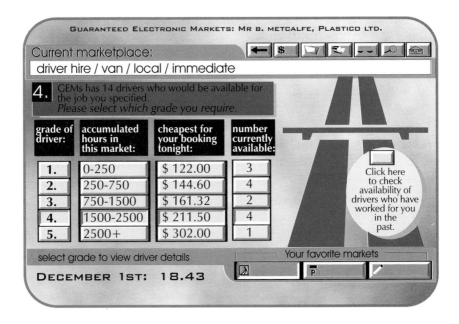

Anyone wanting to sell their services as a van driver in GEMs would have to input proof of a driving licence, renewable with a fresh PIN every

6 months as additional security to show they have not been banned from the roads in that time. Then they pinpoint their home location and specify the hours they will work, while GEMs enforces any legal restrictions on their individual timetable of availability. Finally, the aspiring driver is asked to input a pricing formula. This could be a crude hourly rate or a sophisticated set of percentages by which that basic fee is to be increased or reduced depending on, for example, length of booking, with how much notice of it was given, time of day, destination, even type of vehicle to be driven and whether the driver is allowed to smoke at the wheel. Cancellation fees could also be specified and would be relentlessly enforced. Additionally, workers could drop their prices for employers for whom they have enjoyed working and discretely raise them for less acceptable clients. GEMs computes their price for each incoming assignment from this information, which can be changed daily, perhaps in the light of intelligence from the appropriate market overview page.

GEMs would grade drivers, automatically promoting them through its ranks as the hours they have been booked mount, assuming that the number of complaints upheld against them is low. As they move up the grades, workers can charge more for their services while remaining competitive. For the mouldings company, tonight's delivery is critical enough to merit a grade 4 driver, of whom four are available. One click reveals their details sheets, cheapest first.

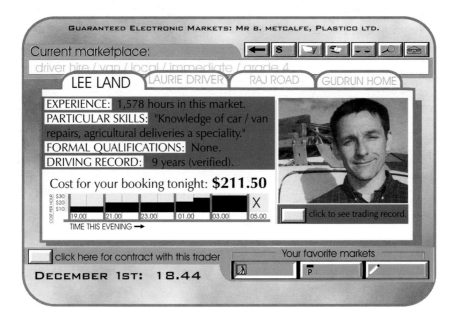

Clicking for the first driver's trading record would reveal what was already obvious: he has many hundreds of hours and dozens of satisfied customers behind him, with a negligible number of upheld complaints. Without this resumé he would not be trading in grade 4. His enviable career is a precious asset, he would be highly unlikely to endanger it with a cavalier attitude towards tonight's assignment. Once more a contract is offered, the mouldings company's transport department PIN is entered and the driver is hired. His first job will be to pick up the van, confirming that it is roadworthy in the process.

Several miles away the driver, who has told GEMs he will be at home and available for short-notice bookings all evening, is automatically paged and told to check his GEMs terminal. Once there he sees details of his night's work, including a suggested timetable calculated by GEMs based on legally permitted maximum driving periods and its ability to time the journey between two postal codes.

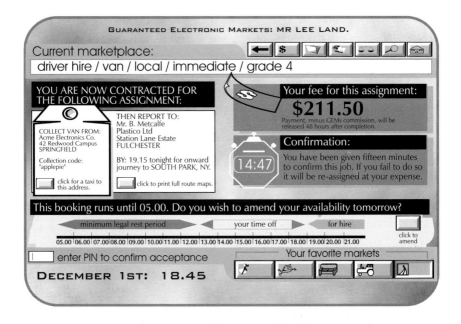

This driver would be charging a premium to be available at such short notice. He is now given only 15 minutes to enter his PIN signifying that he is on his way. Should that not happen, GEMs will re-assign the job and compensate the employer from the driver's bond. Once he has signed, GEMs might ask if he wants to book a taxi to the pick-up point: one click would then bring the nearest available, best value cab to his door with the destination already displayed on the driver's dashboard panel and the fare transferred automatically into escrow. Assuming the journey passes without incident, payment would go across to the taxi man the following evening. Before the van driver leaves home, however, GEMs is looking ahead to his next booking and asking if he wants to adjust tomorrow's availability in the light of tonight's income and hours on the road.

5

Contractual
chains

Although taking less than a minute, the process for hiring a van and engaging someone to drive it just described would be unnecessarily arduous. It would be far quicker to access a GEMs template for 'van and driver hire' which could calculate the combined costs and arrival times of multiple options for van and driver, then allow the chosen package to be bought with one PIN entry, both payments going into escrow separately so any link in the chain can become the subject of a complaint. GEMs could memorize its users regularly used settings. If a company makes regular deliveries from their factory to a customer depot utilizing drivers of the same grade, it should take less than half a dozen clicks to have fully a qualified worker and vehicle ready for a long journey at the factory gate in 20 minutes. Both would have come from a widening, competitive, informed marketplace and be contracted for exactly the company's requirements at that moment.

A firm that had used this facility for occasional out of hours emergencies when their own delivery fleet was overtaxed might begin to see advantages in arranging the ebb and flow of daily transport arrangements through GEMs instead of relying on a dedicated fleet and employees. Staff drivers, too, may decide they could have a better life if self-employed and selling their services in GEMs to a pool of buyers, accumulating a trading record while using market overviews to price themselves into desired opportunities. Further potential of this new way of working will be examined in later chapters.

More complex packages

The van and driver scenario demonstrates a basic, two link, contractual chain: GEMs could construct a far more complex series of commitments. Preparing a funeral could be one example. A 'When Someone Dies' template would examine the availability and pricing of a sequence of provenly competent local traders in the funeral business who were selling their time on the system, then assemble a timetable and overall price for a buyer's particular needs. Once contracted, each individual is then responsible for vouchsafing the work of their immediate predecessor in the chain. So, a qualified mortuary assistant collects the deceased and delivers them to a chapel of rest that has availability for sale in GEMs, later a freelance undertaker lays out the body and confirms to GEMs he has completed his tasks in the period he had originally offered. When the embalmer arrives at the chapel of rest inputting her PIN signature not only attests that her job is done but also that she found the body ready for her ministrations. If not, she would instigate a complaint procedure: if the dispute was not immediately resolved GEMs would use the undertaker's bond to hire a replacement, extend the timetable if necessary and compensate the buyer. Later judgement by a funeral trades body would rule on whether the undertaker or the embalmer was in the wrong and bonds would be rearranged accordingly. It is a complex process with multiple layers of protection built in, but as ever with GEMs, it would be presented to each user in a very simple display of their best options at the time.

Only traders who could prove insurance cover sufficient to reconstruct the whole chain, should they default, would be offered in a template. Insurers are likely to demand a credible track record of bookings before providing such cover, so templates will naturally assemble their components from middle to high grade traders. Families who wish to use less-experienced, cheaper providers would be able to bypass this template and make individual bookings, but they would be responsible for ensuring that each stage was completed satisfactorily. Equally, they could choose to buy all their needs from one full-service funeral company. GEMs has no bias for or against particular kinds of business; it is interested only in the best value for each individual enquiry. However, it is unlikely that a company constructing off-the-peg funeral deals from a small number of employees and facilities, then adding their own overheads and mark-up, could match the prices constructed by GEMs from its pool of informed, infinitely flexible individuals in a personalized chain.

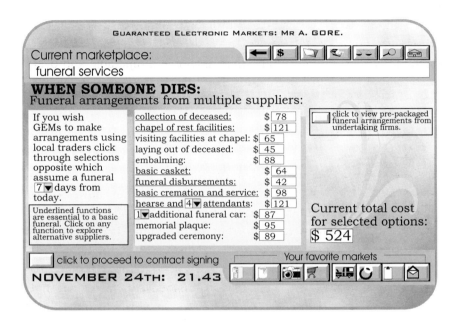

Would grieving relatives be in the frame of mind to want to turn to their interactive television and then point and click to make a loved one's final arrangements? When the telephone first appeared it was widely derided as a device for 'nattering shop-girls'. Now of course it is used unquestioningly for even the most important arrangements. The device's sheer usefulness has made it emotionally and culturally neutral. If GEMs could match that reliability and convenience, it could lead to a population pointing and clicking their way to a far wider range of goods and services than is currently envisaged. Its appeal is, not least, that customers will be hiring providers who are decentralized, working for themselves, and each treasuring a trading record of continuing good faith, even among clients who may not be a ready source of repeat business.

Other GEMs templates might include screens that construct entire journeys, from availability offered by train, long-haul bus and taxi companies, to move a GEMs user from one precise postal code to another at the times of their choice. A separate codeword printed or copied on to a piece of paper would constitute a prepaid ticket for each segment. Should the first leg, say on a train, be delayed beyond the 20 minutes specified in the contract and as a result the traveller misses his coach connection, then the train company's bond is used to finance automatically re-booked legs of bus and taxi travel and, of course, to fund nominal compensation to all passengers. In industry a manufacturer with spare capacity on their bottling line could hire it out in GEMs, specifying which of their staff were required to make it operational. GEMs would then parcel up the line's availability with their staff's individual pricing formulae and raw materials as specified, thus enabling another drinks maker to investigate availability and costs for his excess production requirements. GEMs could enable holidaymakers to construct their own package from flights, rooms, transfers and representatives' services. Like inclusive funeral arrangements, complete package tours could still be offered in this market, of course, and when they fitted a user's requirements they would be put forward as an option, but they would be a blunt way for providers to trade in such a sophisticated marketplace. Instead, tour companies might enter a details sheet and pricing formula for each room in a hotel or each seat and level of service on a flight. No longer need mass market tourists be charged the same for a room overlooking the bins as for a panoramic view just because none of the dozens of tour company sales channels warrants the detailed programming for more precise marketing.

chapter

6

Easy access to capital

A public markets system would allow users to lend and borrow money without incurring the overheads of a financial institution, or the fragmenting of the marketplace for capital under multiple sales channels. The GEM for loans would be an anomaly within the system, the only market in which one user could be in danger of defaulting on another. Elsewhere, contracts cannot be signed unless funds are available to go into escrow. GEMs' commitment to guaranteed trading precludes the uncertainties of debt chains or potentially defaulting creditors. Users without reserve funds of their own would need to turn to the loans market, where lenders decide the level of risk they are willing to assume. Once again the matching between suppliers and purchasers is of fine 'granularity': a typical transaction might involve lending $100 for a week.

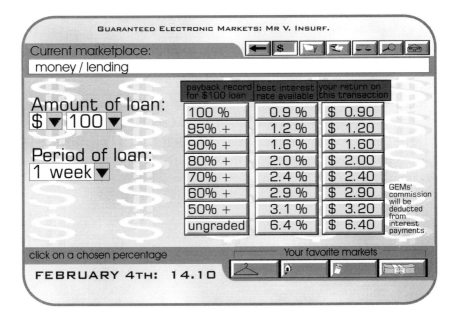

GUARANTEED ELECTRONIC MARKETS: MR V. INSURF.

Current marketplace:

money / lending

Amount of loan:
$ ▼ 100 ▼

Period of loan:
1 week ▼

	payback record for $100 loan	best interest rate available	your return on this transaction
	100 %	0.9 %	$ 0.90
	95% +	1.2 %	$ 1.20
	90% +	1.6 %	$ 1.60
	80% +	2.0 %	$ 2.00
	70% +	2.4 %	$ 2.40
	60% +	2.9 %	$ 2.90
	50% +	3.1 %	$ 3.20
	ungraded	6.4 %	$ 6.40

GEMs' commission will be deducted from interest payments

click on a chosen percentage

Your favorite markets

FEBRUARY 4TH: 14.10

Here, the lender is being asked to select the grade of borrower with whom he is willing to sign a contract for the loan of his $100. GEMs would compile a borrower's payback record on past loans. Someone who regularly needs $100 or more to tide them over the last week of the month, and just as reliably transfers the money plus interest back on time, will start to build a payback record for that sum in the 95 per cent plus range. This enables them to access ever cheaper money, reaching a point where the continued value of their rating outweighs any short-term gains from non-fulfilment of an individual loan. Cash providers with an appetite for risk can opt for higher-return, lower-grade, borrowers who are still climbing this ladder, but are then more likely to find themselves pursuing their claim through the courts at payback time. Details of the borrower would be revealed by GEMs once a contract is signed. It may often be that one user is borrowing large sums and entering into qualified agreements simultaneously with dozens of lenders, or that the $100 is split between five users each needing $20 and backed by the selected credit rating. Matches do not have to be one to one.

Borrowers with a 100 per cent grading qualify for 'automatic resched-uling' and have clicked for that option. If there is not $100 plus interest in their account on the day for payback GEMs will automatically take out an ungraded loan in their name to pay off the debt. They would have longer to pay off the new liability, but at much higher interest, and their credit rating will be scaled down thereafter. Alternatively, one user can be underwritten by another, an indulgent parent perhaps. In that case, the borrower would attain instant 100 per cent status because GEMs has been authorised to deduct any unpaid accounts from the parental bond.

There is no human input to the process of setting interest rates. Instead the computer assesses demand and supply for each grade of borrower from second to second and calculates the ever-changing figure that will generate maximum turnover. Alternatively, a borrower, for example, can specify the rate they will pay and see if they obtain a match but they are likely then to be either beached below the day's trading range or paying over the market rate to a lucky seller. This forum, as accessible to major institutions with millions to lend as to thrifty 6-year-olds with their weekly allowance to invest, would obvi-ously be influenced by the country's official exchange rate and global demand for its currency. But its spread between lending and borrowing rates, representing only GEMs' tiny commission, should undercut anything available in the outside economy. Additionally, users should find significant liquidity, responsiveness and equilibrating market overview information.

A flexible money market

Much of the time GEMs users were harnessing the system's capital markets they might not be aware they are so doing. The couple signing a contract for overnight accommodation earlier in this section, for instance, had to put down a $100 deposit. It may have been that those funds were not available in their account, so GEMs borrowed the sum automatically for 48 hours on an 'automatic rescheduling' basis building the interest into the room cost it constructed for them. The sum would then be returned, without any involvement on the users' part, two days later. Similarly suppliers who cannot wait for money owed to come out of escrow can click to try selling their unpaid debts in the loans market. If they can attach a solid trading record with no previous freezing of payments they should be able to receive immediately 98 per cent or more of the money due. Days later GEMs would transfer the funds leaving escrow to the debt purchaser. 'Autotrade' functions could further feed the cash pool; for instance a user telling GEMs that every time her bank account exceeded $300 credit the surplus was to be instantly invested in $50 blocks for two weeks as long as the interest rate is 2 per cent or more. The less well off might instruct GEMs to assemble an automatic overdraft at the best rate for which they qualified, once their resources dipped below a certain level. Pressure in the market-place should quickly limit any drift towards excessive debt because their trading record would indicate such a degree of risk that only the highest rate money would remain available.

This beguiling process for 'vanilla' loans would be the bedrock of a financial exchange which might cautiously develop a range of instruments for users. In time the system might be able to parcel serial loans together into seamless debt for house purchasing. Authorized lawyers would hold deeds as collateral for non-payment. Templates for futures contracts in which one party constructs the deal of their choice, backed up by a contract, and awaits any takers could be offered. So too could long-term funding agreements, enabling pensions to be accumulated according to an individual's requirements. Financial services companies would, as ever, be welcome to trade in the GEMs money market and, initially at least, could find a niche acting as 100 per cent borrowers then lending back at a higher rate to unproven users lower down the credit rating ladder. However, as swelling numbers of ordinary borrowers attained the proven solidity that ensures eligibility for the 100 per cent 'automatic rescheduling' option, and with confidence in the market building, as bad debtors were mechanically evicted, the financial companies would probably find their overheads, and comparative inefficiency, made them uncompetitive. GEMs should de-brand the flow of money, turning capital into the atomized commodity that a truly inclusive digital economy requires.

chapter

7 **Would populations start to use a GEMs system?**

Public electronic markets would be particularly vulnerable to the law of network externalities: the more who use the system, the more valuable the service to each of them becomes. Starting with only a handful of sectors and growing to the scale of operation outlined in this section, GEMs' need for secure trades in an open market would demand its users follow procedures that are going to be unfamiliar to most and daunting to some. A cultural leap would be needed to take computer issued codewords from their currently rarefied status in, for instance, ticketless business travel to routine use between neighbours hiring each other's lawnmowers. Likewise, we are so used to entering into unstated webs of contractual protection, and shrugging off their periodic failures, that signing a written contract for transactions as small as buying a second-hand music CD then engaging a teenager to cycle round and deliver it could seem frighteningly formal.

New infrastructure always imposes unfamiliar requirements on users: early adopters of the telephone struggled to attach a string of digits to each acquaintance. Cashpoint machines required widespread use of PINs. This unprecedented need for users to hold a number in their memory did nothing to stop take up of cash cards far exceeding original projections. In the case of GEMs, would the inconveniences of registration and adjustment to alien procedures be offset by the benefits from the fledgling system? Anyone shopping in GEMs could escape the cacophony of promotional offers, loyalty schemes, spurious discounts, relationship marketing, loss leaders and bundled merchandise through which we must currently pursue value for our needs. New efficiencies in online technology presage a sharp increase in this blizzard of information which shopping software will be able to penetrate only partially.[2] In contrast, the GEMs buyer compares like with like, gets the best deal available at once and then knows it will be ruthlessly enforced. More appealing still, he escapes the costs inherent in sellers making themselves heard in an uncoordinated marketplace. Gone too is the expense of fraudulent traders, levied on prices generally in the non-GEMs trading environment but paid by a defaulting buyer or seller's bonds or deposits within the system. The sophistication of matching offers with users' enquiries in a growing any-seller-welcome marketplace should better that of any one company's sales channel or squeezed buyer–seller matching service. Facilities such as buyer's clubs (Box 7.1) would bring unique benefits to users. With this elaborate programming, masked behind friendly interfaces focusing in intuitive steps on a user's specific enquiry, buyers would be unlikely to scythe their way through competing sellers' claims in search of the outside marketplace's best deal.

Box 7.1

GEMS' BUYERS' CLUBS

Guaranteed Electronic Markets would work very much on the principle of buyer 'pull' rather than provider 'push'. The infrastructure for purchasing is passive, not set up to favour the seller's objectives as is the case in sales channels. One way this can be exploited is for geographically close purchasers of a particular commodity to be banded together by the system for bulk buys. Everyone on a particular housing estate who regularly bought Marlboro cigarettes, for instance, might be asked if they wished to join with other smokers of that brand. The system might then buy 1000 packs with pooled funds and engage someone locally to act as a point of delivery and disperse the smokes according to a printable list. Every link in the chain would be completely bonded, the deliverer could disappear with the cigarettes but as he would have had to put more than their value into bond there would be little point. More complex buyer's clubs for groceries in neighbourhoods, stationery between businesses or over-the-counter drugs for the long-term ill could be available to anyone willing to sacrifice immediate realization of the order for likely cost savings from combined purchases.

Could distrust of such a large, potentially all-knowing, central computer be an inhibitor? The world aviation industry was founded on a concept once considered unthinkable by many: hundreds of thousands of people hurtling through the air in converging tubes of thin metal, flammable fuel sloshing around on either side of them. Customers have been largely persuaded to set aside fears about the technology because everyone working for an airline is imbued with a commitment to safety procedures that becomes ingrained. The public electronic markets industry likewise would have to grow alongside unending efforts to maintain and assert its probity.

Individual market sectors could be slow to take off and might require experimentation until the right balance was found between over-easy entry and costly verification procedures that deter even the most desirable sellers. Take a highly sensitive marketplace such as childcare, for instance, in which there could be deep scepticism about an automated market. Would even a provider who had attained grade 5 or 6 in GEMs' child-minding be sufficiently trusted? To attain that level they might have had to pass examination by both police and a local government panel every 6 months of, say, a 10-year career. If that was still not sufficient, further vetting requirements would be added by the franchisee. Would personal endorsement by the child's school, at candidate's expense obviously, be sufficient? Or proof of bookings with friends of the family who had been entered as acceptable referees? Proven acceptance by a well-established agency? Or perhaps a system of mutual imprimatur whereby, say, five local baby-sitters agree to be bound by shared responsibility: if one of them is found guilty of unprofessional behaviour they all lose their bonds? Maybe a free visit to meet the parent in advance arranged by the system would tempt the ultra-cautious buyer? GEMs will always allow users to enter the lower rungs of its markets easily, in this case perhaps as mother's helpers who only work with children while a parent stays in the house. Providers can then begin to climb a ladder of increasingly profitable verification that could see top-level customers paying enormous sums because so few suppliers clear the hurdles they have demanded.

Public electronic markets have been seen by some as a potentially useful service for downscale consumers while more valuable deals could be expected to remain in less utilitarian, branded channels. It is a dangerous assumption to make, which mirrors early predictions for the phone system and cash machines. In the first case, Bell's device was seen as something for people who could not afford messenger boys: in the second, banks widely saw ATMs as a facility for the kind of customers who withdrew small amounts and were probably intimidated by a human teller. It is usefulness to users generally, not an emotional hierarchy of business, that drives long-term take up of new technology. A system that can allow van drivers to structure a career on their own terms could easily do the same for management accountants. Attractiveness to those seeking overnight accommodation suggests a similar appeal to buyers of 6-month leases on office blocks. In each case there would be a GEMs franchisee, who understood the needs of that specific market, shaping the service.

Would sellers enter such a competitive marketplace?

Sellers on GEMs would probably be self-selecting. Anyone offering genuine value and able to deliver what they promise has little to fear in this new sales regime. If company strengths are more in marketing than manufacture, with hefty margins reaped from the advantages gained, boardroom strategists need to be sure the brand will continue to merit a premium in a wider marketplace. Once GEMs were established, however, any seller choosing to exclude the system from their channels to market would be vulnerable to an upstart competitor, the GEMs-friendly newcomer having all the facilities of interlocking electronic markets with which to launch a business. Once a GEM for selling portable office buildings was written, for example, if no-one started to sell in it and if the market overview showed customers looking but not finding, an opportunist might decide to begin fabrication. He could use GEMs to find raw materials, production line capacity, workers, haulage and then, if he remains alone in the market, add a substantial mark-up to his costs. An additional danger, assuming selective distribution is not legally protected in the country of operation, is that manufacturers who baulk at the system find unwanted middlemen selling their output in the public markets. A century ago, Edison predicted that one day every going concern would have its own electricity generating division within the organization. That vision soon gave way to the efficiencies of a secure mutual supplier. There may yet come a day when competitive pressure will push companies away from the costs of maintaining and updating their own sales servers, security systems, payment mechanisms and back office functions, in favour of one independent mechanised market.

Cost of transactions has yet to emerge fully as a competitive edge in Internet buyer–seller matching services. The efficiencies of online-pairing are so far ahead of any comparable function in the world of physical commerce that services like the e-bay auction site can easily offer value with up to a 5 per cent take. However, the GEMs model could be planned from the start as a business driven by currently inconceivable volume. That was the rationale behind an equally radical development in Britain in 1839: nationwide flat-rate postage. Before that date, mail was carried using a combination of local and national stage-coach services, with charges paid by the recipient of each letter according to distance travelled and weight of missive. Outside *ad hoc* local cheap postage schemes a typical letter delivered across London cost 4 pence and a one sheet communication between the capital and Scotland around 16 pence. The campaign for a flat rate of just one penny, paid by the sender, for an envelope of less than half an ounce (14 grams) between any two points in the country was considered laughably naïve. The then Secretary of the Post Office described the plan as 'a most preposterous one, utterly unsupported by facts and resting entirely on assumption'.[3] It was an understandable assessment in the market conditions of the time, given that few people could read or write and fewer still knew anyone outside their locality. Once realised, however, penny postage fully justified all the unsupported assumptions underlying its business model. It sparked an explosion of literacy as workers began to move away from home knowing they could now keep in touch. It took only 14 years for the new mass service to become more profitable than all the old postage schemes combined, a short time indeed given the relatively slow pace of Victorian business cycles.[4] It is possible that what could appear an absurdly cheap GEMs commission rate could induce individuals and firms to trade in ways that can scarcely be imagined until e-trade is truly commoditized: an eventual system might deduct as little as 0.25 per cent of each deal.

GEMs would have their limitations, of course. As a dumb utility, restricted by law to core functions and with no exploitable customer knowledge, the central computer could not advise users which new books they might enjoy, or pass them to an online consultant to help shape hazy requirements, nor send e-mail to remind husbands when it is time to buy their partners birthday flowers. (There would of course be nothing to stop GEMs users subscribing to any number of companies that provided these facilities.) Similar objections about low levels of service were made by opponents of penny postage. They pointed out that in the patchwork postage market a sender could in effect tell the deliverer 'if the recipient of my letter is not in, you'll find her at her friend's house with blue curtains further down the street or try the shop next door'. Replacing this customer-friendly flexibility with tightly timetabled operatives who would simply shove mail through a hole in the door, which householders would have to cut for the purpose, appeared retrograde to many.[5] But they had failed to appreciate the extent to which populations were ready to move beyond a confusing, often irritating and cost-heavy process into an environment where sending a letter was an untaxing mundanity. For postage in the 1840s, perhaps, read buying and selling in the 2000s?

Notes to
section one

1. *The Glory of the Geeks*, Channel 4 Television, (UK) 3 October 1998, Programme 3 of 3.
2. Powerful retailers, for example, are learning how to block automated enquiries by coding price displays in ways that software cannot read or bundling goods so true prices cannot be ascertained. (Shopbots – Friend or Foe? *Information Strategy*, July/August 1998, p. 42.)
3. Douglas N. Muir, *Postal Reform and The Penny Black: a New Appreciation*, The National Postal Museum, 1990, p. 50.
4. Ibid. p. 181.
5. Colin G. Hey, *Rowland Hill: Genius and Benefactor*, Quiller Press, 1989, p. 69.

A new democratic capitalism: the impact of public electronic markets

chapter

8 The effect of GEMs on business: a decline in big institutions

It was a surreal morning, even for hardened financial journalists. On Easter Monday 1998, Wall Street opinion formers were invited to the opulent Hilton banquet room at Manhattan's Waldorf-Astoria to be told that Nations Bank was merging with BankAmerica to form the largest bank in the US. 'Bigger is indeed better' a beaming head of Nations Bank told the press conference.[1] Two hours later the financial commentators trooped back to the same building's Empire banquet hall to learn that First Chicago and Banc One had followed suit, creating the continent's fifth largest bank. Both mergers were explained in terms of advantages of size in a globalizing economy and economies of scale: BankAmerica and Nations Bank announced plans to shed between 5000 and 8000 jobs within two years of fusing. The creation of megabanks represents one part of a long historical trend in business: the need to be big. Factories and centralized distribution facilities in the Industrial Revolution spawned big business. Craft-based worker alliances then metamorphosed into big union power as an essential counterweight. When the weaknesses of those antagonistic forces were painfully revealed in the depression years, big government emerged to provide a safety net.

The trend towards 'bigness' is being accelerated in surprising industries as we move to an online economy. An oil company's optimum size is obviously large; it requires hugely expensive installations and worldwide operations, but there are no comparable physical factors in the drive towards big accountancy. The big eight companies did not become the big six, en route to becoming the big four or fewer, to maximize their usage of desks, telephones and chairs. They are melding not least because a crucial currency in the online uncoordinated market is 'mind-share'. By being big you offer the reassurance of a widely recognized

brand name. The possibility of becoming a 'one stop shop' for globalizing clients can then be staked on this, widening the range of services to
include, for instance, consultancy within your all-important brand
values. Under this philosophy, once humble banks are expanding into
big finance offering, for instance, stockbroking and insurance services to
exploit the flexibility that comes with their size. There is an argument
often raised about the Internet asserting that it creates 'a level playing
field' in which small players can easily challenge the big boys. In reality,
establishing an upstart brand to entice customers away from entrenched
and – when they get it right – massively efficient corporations on any
appreciable scale is so costly that few will attempt it. Consumers do not
use the Net to constantly shop around for new suppliers to meet their
every need. They prefer a simple life. Industries based on human
resources, which might have been thrown open to diversified players by
the digital economy, are evolving into the kind of battle between titans
reminiscent of the motor industry, with its need for participants to
possess a gargantuan asset base. It is hard to see how customers benefit,
except in the sense that it helps them navigate an otherwise bewildering
marketplace. There is little evidence it brings lower prices. In 1998, for
example, The Federal Reserve reported US banks' net interest margin
between lending rates and borrowing costs had widened from around
3.5 per cent in the mid 1970s to 4.3 per cent, despite waves of mergers in
that time.[2] 'As these banks get bigger, they'll get more confident that
they can get away with [increased] fees, because they'll have such a large
captive customer base' commented a spokesman for the US Public
Research Group.[3] It was a point not explicitly raised in either presentation at the Waldorf-Astoria.

The pursuit of bigness has had its critics of course. A former
economic adviser to the British National Coal Board, E.F. Schumacher
published *Small is Beautiful: A Study of Economics as if People Mattered*
in 1973. In it he suggested smaller units of work and production could
be both more productive and more rewarding for participants than
large unified organizations. His message was not without its detractors.
During subsequent tours of the USA, Schumacher was provided with
police protection because of threats, deemed serious, from 'pro-busi-
ness' groups.[4] But even those who supported his analysis and sought to
apply it to the developed world came up against an unarguable reality:
in the uncoordinated marketplace capital can usually be more effec-

tively accessed and exploited by a large firm than by small traders. As money continues to acquire a newly aggressive mobility from digital transmission and the imperatives of big finance, human considerations are in many cases receding even further.

A Guaranteed Electronic Markets system would reverse this situation, making small units not only more humane but, crucially, more economically efficient than large corporations. Banking is not a useful example: GEMs could render banks, big or small, largely irrelevant in the core area of straightforward lending. Instead, consider as an illustration the market for long-distance bus travel in the UK. It is a sector dominated by large providers, notably the Stagecoach group. Dominance in routes, numbers of drivers employed and vehicles owned bodes well for their future in the uncoordinated online marketplace. With high brand name recognition and corresponding 'mindshare' their Internet or interactive television page will be a logical first stop for anyone wanting to travel from say Cardiff to Liverpool. As Stagecoach takes in details of individuals' travel requirements and pricing sensitivities it can start to make them personalized offers while building an increasingly sophisticated database of patterns in demand. This likely growth in business will be combined with enhanced efficiencies in driver rostering and vehicle utilisation across the organization. As long as adequate standards of service are maintained, the sheer size of Stagecoach creates an escalating barrier to entry for competitors.

Now consider a typical coach operator that might trade in a public electronic markets system. Three qualified drivers in Cardiff could band together and, given easy access to capital by GEMs' loans market, lease a 52-seater which they take in turns to drive on a self-employed basis. Each buys bus station slots and sells seats in GEMs, perhaps using market overview information to see which routes out of their hometown are likely to offer the best returns. On a typical day one of them might depart from Cardiff at 6.00 a.m. on a run to Liverpool, returning 8 hours later for the second man to operate a late afternoon service to Holyhead, returning in time for driver number three to operate his overnight journey to London. They do not need the resources of a big organization for flexibility. If one of them is ill one day he can hire his replacement in the appropriate GEM. If a problem with the vehicle makes a journey impossible, they can turn to the bus hire marketplace. Were only ten seats to be sold on one of their departures they might hire a minibus that provides the levels of comfort stipulated in that contract and rent out their own vehicle for those eight hours. Because they are trading on a GEMs contract with money in bond as potential compensation, they do not need a brand name to reassure potential customers (Box 8.1).

Box 8.1

CUMULATIVE CONTRACTS

GEMs could aggregate contracts of purchasers in case of supplier default. This would provide a level of customer assurance well beyond anything offered by a brand name. If a self-employed bus driver, for instance, operates a service that is late departing or with a vehicle in unacceptable condition a number of passengers are likely to call up their contracts for that journey and initiate a complaint. If the driver accepts culpability, or is found in fault after arbitration by the panel for long-distance bus travel, all the passengers automatically have an amount in compensation transferred from his bond to their accounts. The underlying principle is that the driver is held personally responsible to each passenger.

In this environment Stagecoach would be disadvantaged. They are obviously free to list their departures and sell seats in the GEMs travel market but their prices will carry marketing, scheduling and central office overheads for which smaller operators have no need. Nor are their centralized decision-making processes likely to rival local busmen who can respond to immediate market conditions with new routes, times and prices, on a weekly basis if they wish. This eclipse of Stagecoach would not be a temporary phenomenon awaiting the emergence of a new big player but a lasting consequence of a diversified marketplace. However successful the three drivers in Cardiff were to be, they would find it hard to build an extended empire of owned vehicles and employed drivers in this new era. There would be no market advantages to being big, just additional costs. Instead of aspiring to size they might look to market diversification for more profitable opportunities: trading up to a more luxurious bus perhaps, or starting to offer week-long tours of North Wales.

Would large scale manufacturers retain the current benefits of their size? The advantages of bulk buying of ingredients or components are likely to be minimized in a truly efficient, more fluid marketplace. Additionally, the market for distribution would now be both decentralized and probably more active, so the benefits of a fleet of vehicles and warehousing agreements disappear. GEMs would be driven largely by consumer pull. A buyer's club on the system seeking, perhaps, 500 1 kg boxes of cornflakes with no brand specified would have delivery costs automatically factored in, when shopping for the best deal. That is inevitably going to favour more dispersed manufacture: the advantages centralized companies enjoyed in the producer push model of grocery distribution would have evaporated. The quality levels required for cornflakes would be contained in a cumulative contract with all purchasers, any maker who cleared those levels would no longer need bigness to create consumer awareness: buyers would find him regardless (Box 8.2).

Box 8.2

SETTING MINIMUM STANDARDS FOR GEMS TRADES

A criticism sometimes made of GEMs is that they would hand control of market standards over to the operating consortium who could then make or break sellers with their stipulations. It is true that GEMs' franchisees would need to establish quality levels in their sectors: someone would have to decide for instance what is the legal definition of a cornflake, otherwise all sorts of cereal by-products could be marketed as cornflakes. Setting those definitions would obviously rest on existing consumer law where available. Where there are no existing statutes and customers have previously relied on brand name trust for a fair deal, GEMs will have to originate a definition. This would be crafted not with an eye to positioning GEMs as an arbiter of food standards but simply to grow that market. What paragraph of legalese will define a cornflake acceptable to shoppers but not so daunting to manufacturers that no seller will want to comply with the definition? Shoppers of course need not spare a thought for this complex contractual small print. They could take it for granted that GEMs will satisfy their basic expectation of a cornflake as much as could Kellogg's or Nabisco. The system could not, however, guarantee the distinctive taste of a known brand. Although there will be shoppers who will trade down in this wider marketplace, it should not signal a death knell for distinctive and well-marketed products that could, of course, also be sold on the system if the makers wished.

This economic model, based on ever-changing, easy-to-enter markets would move a country closer to the vision of thinkers like Adam Smith and Friedrich von Hayek who defined capitalism. By making the buyer truly sovereign it should promote flexibility and bring increasing resources to market. In 1776 Smith himself wrote 'people of the same trade seldom meet together, even for merriment and diversion, but the conversation ends in a conspiracy against the public, or in some contrivance to raise prices'.[5] Public electronic markets would do much to end an era where a key aim of so many enterprises has been to achieve the scale necessary to manipulate their market. As huge opposing forces give way to competition among millions of individual protagonists trading in a near perfect market competitiveness, stability and efficiency should all increase. It is the 'snowballing' effect of this trend, sweeping through sector after sector, that can make the truly atomized, post-GEMs economy so difficult to envisage from our current perspective.

9 GEMs and employment: the rise of portfolio working

A database enigmatically named Monster Board is currently the Internet's most popular means of finding work.[6] Its twin pools of job seekers and job openings are diluted by dozens of rival marketplaces; nevertheless, it is indisputably useful, attracting nearly two million visitors a month. But the service it performs – matching employers and candidates – is becoming an anachronism. The world is drifting inexorably towards fragmented employment, with individuals shouldering the costs and time required to find work and then juggling any competing requirements. An online facility for putting the two sides together in this ever-splintering marketplace would have to be far more exacting than any existing job matching service. PeopleBank, the UK Internet employment matching service offers probably the most sophisticated programming for matching employers and potential workers but, even so, does not foresee a future trading in short-term work contracts as a low-cost automated service.[7] 'I couldn't see us getting into temporary work placements unless it was with the involvement of a major agency', says Bill Shipton, MD of PeopleBank, 'the administration and vetting would be too complex'.[8] Guaranteed Electronic Markets could of course crack this problem and embrace the new reality of work, offering increased stability for an evolving workforce. Fifty years ago it was firms who largely absorbed the risks and cycles of business, shielding employees from the ravages of each downturn. In today's marketplace, profitability frequently survives a slowdown in demand: it is the workforce who immediately suffer the consequences. Individuals seeking a flow of customers for their services, rather than the erstwhile security of life on a single payroll, is the way of the future.

GEMs would trade periods of work like any other commodity, using the mechanisms already illustrated to enforce each deal. A window cleaner could be hired for 15 minutes with only a few more clicks required to engage an experienced management consultant for two weeks. Both individuals would have to prove any qualifications necessary for that market and be able to display their past trading record, with identifying details removed, to prospective hirers. Each could use a pricing formula to prioritize the opportunities they sought. Payment would be through the system, allowing everyone involved to enjoy accurate diary keeping, accounting and issuing of contracts. With end-to-end automation of the drudgery of finding work, the need for one main employer, or even a specialized profession, would disappear for many. British management theorist, Charles Handy, pioneered the concept of 'portfolio working' in which individuals construct a customized range of part-time jobs that together build a discernible career path. With GEMs, that attractive option, already easily available to a $150 000-a-year high flier, would come within reach of a blue-collar worker surviving on a tenth of those earnings. For example: a typical week's diary for a 25-year-old male working sometimes as a window cleaner but also as a car mechanic and general cleaner might look like this.

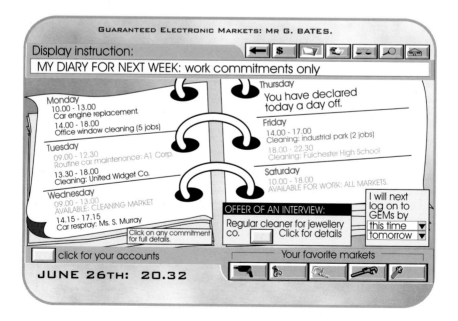

Every GEMs user would be offered a diary from which blocks of time can be sold. A business version, trading assignments for a musical instrument repair company maybe, would be far more complex than the illustration above. The bookings in black on this diary are confirmed, automatically accepted by GEMs because they fall within the user's availability and pricing as currently defined. Periods of work in grey are offers still available for which he qualifies but which require approval because the hours or compensation are outside his formula. The cleaning work on Friday for instance is being offered by an educational establishment that regularly needs three operatives for an evening at the end of each week. Instead of taking on permanent staff, they have a pool of ten local cleaners who understand the building and are regularly given work. GEMs offers contracts from the school in randomized order to all ten: the first three to sign, or automatically accept, are rostered. More hierarchically minded employers could choose to rate their approved workers. GEMs would then offer jobs to the most favoured first, descending down the list if they are not available. The offer of an interview at the bottom of his screen demonstrates how GEMs might replace the hunt through classified adverts for its users seeking new openings. A local jewellers could be looking for someone to join its roster of cleaners and has told GEMs to contact individuals with more than 1000 hours experience in that market, living within a

---

Box 9.1

GETTING PRE-GEMS ACCOMPLISHMENTS RECOGNIZED BY THE SYSTEM

A public markets system could very simply capture a true record of a user's past bookings. However, there would have to be a transition period in the early days of the system, when people who had perhaps been office cleaning for years wanted to sell their time on the system but understandably did not feel comfortable about joining in a starter grade. The solution owes more to the 'old world' of imperfect judgments than the new order on GEMs. It would involve traders paying the adjudication panel for that market to review their resumé, references and maybe tax statements or bank accounts and to assign a grade that would have been achieved had the bookings been through GEMs. These awards, which could never match the concrete standards demanded by the system, might be flagged to potential buyers: GEMs bookings in black, for instance, calculated previous bookings in grey.

mile of their depot. They specified five applicants be interviewed for the post at times compatible to both diaries. If the system does not get five qualified interview acceptances within a mile after two days it has been authorized to extend the range to two miles and so on until the desired number of pre-screened locals are scheduled for a meeting in the manager's office (Box 9.1).

Anyone hiring themselves out in this way would have to bear occasional costs that might previously have been carried by an agency or employer. If the worker above were to fall ill and be unable to fulfil his commitment to visit an individual's garage and change his engine on Monday morning, for example, he would call up that contract and click 'I can no longer complete this obligation'. GEMs would re-assign the task to the next available trader who most closely matched the car owner's original requirements, trading up the grades rather than down for customer peace of mind. Additional costs would be met from the defaulting worker's bond. Corporate employers, too, would have to be compensated with a potentially higher grade operative to replace an ill contractor. It would be an unusual convention for workers to pay for the cost of their replacement in cases where they were not at fault but a reliable automated market can only work if each trader carries total responsibility for every commitment into which they enter. Users who feared illness would of course be able to insure against costs of their replacement. They could certainly console themselves by comparing the flexibility and low overheads of GEMs trading against overhead ridden agency work or staff employment.

Widespread portfolio working would realize a holy grail of international competitiveness: a fully adaptable and responsive workforce. In a world of monolithic employers this has to be achieved largely by weakening employee protection. With momentum in a public markets system the workers would have as much to gain from new-found pliancy as their former masters. Fresh opportunities can be painlessly sought, for instance. The window cleaner/mechanic/school cleaner might actually dream of life as a ski instructor. Equipped with PIN evidence of the required qualification and an increased bond he can start to price himself into occasional work for individuals seeking basic instruction at nearby slopes. He might chose to make his trading record of reliability in current markets available to prospective customers knowing that new on-piste bookings will similarly mount up allowing him to climb an additional set of grades. He would have every reason to diversify like this rather than spend a life majoring in window cleaning. The top grade in a household services market would probably be attained after 5000 hours of bookings. It is hard to envisage a home-owner so punctilious as to pay a further premium for a window cleaner with, say, 10 000 hours of window cleaning behind them. The trader with 5000 hours would have every incentive to parlay them into new and more lucrative markets.

Of course there is no reason why an individual's work diary should not be blocked out to one employer. GEMs would be equally helpful to seekers of long-term posts. An experienced production line controller, for instance, might release her trading record into the GEM for senior factory personnel and set a salary formula that would make her attractive to manufacturers in areas which she wished to live. As soon as a potential match with a prospective employer was found the system would schedule an interview at a time when both had specified availability in their diary. Even if offered a five year contract the production controller may ask that GEMs remain an intermediary in their agreement. By signing the system's contract for factory personnel rather than the company's document she would be assured of an impartial framework that was in use across the country. By utilizing her diary on the system for rostering she would be assured that all conditions in her contract about hours of work, periods of leave, even levels of support staff on duty during her shifts were adhered to. GEMs would not allow managers to roster her beyond the levels allowed in that initial agreement. Payment would be calculated according to the contract, independently of management, then transferred to her account. The employer could not trade in GEMs without a bond, part of which could be frozen awaiting outside adjudication if she had a dispute about conditions or remuneration.

If the manufacturer planned to be a reliable employer they would have much to gain from hiring and then rostering all staff on GEMs. Automatically compiled trading records in a mature system would be more reliable than potential candidates' resumés for instance: a US study has found that a third of job applicants lie about their backgrounds.[9] It is a problem that the uncoordinated market in Internet job matching simply moves online. 'I don't see how we could ever get into verifying [career resumés] and make it financially viable', says People-Bank's Shipton. In return for GEMs' infinitesimal commission on salaries, however, employers would be certain they were hiring the level of experience and previous employer satisfaction claimed. As part of a government's package to enable GEMs, education authorities could provide PINs to accompany individual exam grades, perhaps for an additional fee. Subjective achievements, samples of past work by an advertising copywriter for instance, could be loaded on to an individual's details page to be bound into any contract they sign. Any lack of veracity is then a legal offence with no confusion possible about which work the employee had claimed to have created.

Employers would also be relieved of the need to administer payroll, holiday scheduling or sickness cover. Audit costs should disappear: their tamper-proof accounts on the system would show who had been paid what and when. A factory handling human resources this way, for instance, might decide to replace centrally imposed duty rotas with market-based rostering, in which workers actively trade their daily willingness to work. Approved members of staff could each set a pricing formula and GEMs would buy their time to construct the cheapest possible timetables of cover, based on required grades of staffing. White and blue-collar workers could then increase their rates for unpopular periods while charging less for more convivial shifts. Anyone tempted to form a cartel with their colleagues and push up prices may need to be reminded how easily a GEMs-empowered manager could increase his pool of available employees and how attractive those positions would look if market overview screens are showing generous rates being paid.

Employers already geared towards part-time workers would have every incentive to trade likewise. A teenage burger flipper, once authenticated with a PIN from his local McDonalds or Burger King might input availability to them alongside his willingness to serve in half a dozen other markets. GEMs then follows his pricing formula to construct a diary of commitments that might lead to increasing amounts of time spent, perhaps, in storeroom work for local warehouses, rather than in ketchup application. Why should the burger boss choose to hire his front-line staff this way instead of tying them to rigidly timetabled weeks that suit his average business flows? First, he gains flexibility: by training then approving a larger pool of workers he can change his requirements from day to day without the delay in feeding new workers into his system or the awkwardness of disengaging them during temporary downturns. Wages also become more competitive among a thick market of licensed employees in which any absenteeism is sorted out by the defaulter. No longer need the manager fear epidemics of calling in sick on unexpectedly fine weekends, for example. Each of the sun seekers would automatically finance their own replacement from his pool of employees. Second, he gains a motivated workforce. The individuals who report for duty are there because burger assembly is the best available job for them that day in a wide-open market of multiple opportunities, not because their dreams of stumbling across something better in the uncoordinated marketplace have yet to be fulfilled.

It would be up to government how ruthless this market for work was allowed to become. Can employers in sought-after sectors drop rates to the minimum needed to maintain a required level of workers? Are individuals with qualifications in scarce supply permitted to resign and seek better-paid jobs week after week? Or are minimum wage levels and contract completion enshrined in law to dampen swings in the market? These are political decisions, outside the remit of GEMs which neutrally enforces any legal restrictions. There would, however, be some factors unique to Guaranteed Markets which need to be decided: how punitive the system is on traders who accumulate complaints, for instance. If a carpet layer trading in grade five of that market has a complaint against him upheld after 4000 hours of flawless assignments, does that sit permanently on his trading record, a handicap for years to come, or does it become spent at some point? The answer stems not from ideology but from the GEMs' consortium's overweening need to earn back its huge investment in building the system. In other words: what balance does a franchisee need to strike between unquestioning faith in his market by buyers and the need to remain attractive to sellers if market turnover is to be maximized? It may be that the carpet fitter is automatically given a chance to have the complaint expunged if he will agree to having 500 hours wiped from his record, thereby dropping a grade. Even while cursing the professional panel that found him in the wrong after a publicly accountable adjudication process, he might find solace in the fact that the response of GEMs itself is fully automated. The scale of sanctions for particular offences in any market could be published openly: unlike employers or agencies the system can not be ageist, racist, homophobic, religiously prejudiced or misogynist. It is simply programmed to grow the market. There would, however, be discrimination between professions and grades, recognizing the differing seriousness of unprofessional behavior. An entry level hairdresser who inadvertently applied too much perming fluid to one of her GEMs clients would be treated more leniently on the system's scale of sanctions than a grade five childminder judged to have left her charge alone in the house.

A new market in local services

To be fully useful to its clients GEMs would need to create new categories of employment. Individuals who deliver goods traded on the system around their area are one example. Anyone hiring a child's paddling pool on a sunny afternoon maybe, or a video game console for a rainy weekend or a scientific calculator to finish a college assignment could well find the best possible deal came from a nearby household. They could choose to collect the item but would be more likely to click for 'include delivery in price'. GEMs would not of course employ people to do these deliveries, or decide who provides the service. The consortium simply sees that a 'local deliveries' market is written with all the back-up of any other Guaranteed Electronic Market. Individual traders can then define their area, rates for different journey lengths and particular times of day. The competitiveness of this pricing formula would determine how much they work. For small goods, some of the work might go to teenagers with a carry rack behind their bicycle saddle: higher levels of the market would demand proof of a driving licence and currently insured vehicle. Anyone who was providing this service may choose to sell additionally in other local markets such as taxi journeys. Given the short notice with which most bookings would arrive, they may eventually opt for a simplified GEMs terminal on their vehicle dashboard; using this they could constantly vary their prices, increasing them perhaps on days when market overview showed a paucity of competitors willing to trade. They could also allow GEMs to price them into a logical pattern of trips. If they have won a trip from town A to town B, for example, they could then automatically undercut all other players for a fare or delivery from B back to A. All their obligations would be displayed in a diary broken down minute by minute using GEMs' estimates of their journey times. They could obviously override their automatic diary at any point. Full-time traders in this market may chose to paint their vehicle with the name of their area in a bid to persuade GEMs shoppers to tell their user questionnaire which individual was to be their first choice for all neighbourhood delivery jobs. As these localized traders criss-crossed their patch they could become a vital component in an intangible community spirit, unlike the effect of fleets of vans from UPS, FedEx or TNT delivering from remote depots.

Another market would provide for 'holders': individuals who look after goods for their neighbours. Someone renting out a vacuum cleaner for the 99 per cent of the time it had previously idled in the cupboard under the stairs, for instance, may not want to have to keep track of a GEMs diary of commitments and be constantly answering the door to their new-found customers. They might deposit the machine, together with any other household assets for which market overview screens were showing local demand, with a nearby pensioner who undertook to remain at home and handle the mechanics of letting. GEMs would insert hirings for the cleaner in his diary and construct a contractual chain for each booking that automatically deducted his stipulated percentage. A combination of 'holders' and deliverers could solve the problems that dog home delivery in the uncoordinated online market-place. While someone currently ordering a parcel of clothes from an Internet site usually needs to be in for their arrival, GEMs would effort-lessly route delivery to a nearby holder who signs for acceptance. The purchaser could then click 'deliver now' when she arrived home. Anyone entering the 'holder' market with a capacious freezer could cash in on grocery deliveries, perhaps breaking up loads bought by a neighbourhood buyers' club. Once again, all stages in the contractual chain would be bonded, individually competitive and subject to prompt arbitration in case of dispute.

The rise of sole traders

In the 1940s in the USSR Joseph Stalin turned a blind eye to limited decollectivisation of agriculture, allowing transfer of land from large state enterprises to individual holdings. Painfully, a generation of Soviet planners then had to adjust to the reality that small farms produced more food for less expenditure. Furthermore, not that it mattered to anyone in Moscow, the newly empowered farmers were much happier working for themselves. In an uncoordinated capitalist marketplace the big is beautiful mantra makes sense as much as it did for Kremlin strategists determined to build the USSR into a global competitor. A sprawling 4000 hectare farm in East Anglia or Kansas today merits the biggest, most cost-effective machinery or can allow one hand to tend thousands of animals and permit bulk purchase and delivery of feeds. GEMs could change this rarely questioned principle, not through penalties on the large operators or any Stalinistic switch in government policy, but by opening the marketplace while dramatically reducing the risk and overheads of trading.

A farmer with 50 hectares might own one tractor which he hires out 80 per cent of the time, but only to those with at least 75 complaint-free agricultural equipment rentals on their record. At the same time he could hire in implements for the precise times required. GEMs market overviews will show if local farms are having to hire, say, a muck-spreader from miles away with each hire involving high transport costs. That would represent an opportunity for any local contractor purchasing their own model, possibly in the GEMs market for second-hand agricultural machinery, perhaps with a GEMs facilitated loan. Anyone who wanted to join a GEMs buyers' club for feed or fertiliser could enjoy the benefits of bulk buying with one farmer being paid by the group to break up the load and deliver the required amounts to each member. Staff would be available according to precise demand in the kind of market described for van drivers earlier. Livestock could be sold within precise time periods: a farmer with good quality pasture might, for example, use GEMs to automatically buy cattle between 9 months and 1 year old, inputting a formula that maintained his herd at 30 beasts through automatic buying and selling as they aged. One motivated individual, with full local market information to hand and comprehensive trading ability only a few keystrokes away, is likely to get more out of a patch of land than a remote manager averaging cultivation methods across one monocultured strip. He would also be able to contribute to a more varied market. In Britain for instance the demand for organic produce is not matched by supply, 70 to 80 per cent has to be imported.[10] A nimble small farmer could check the prices being paid in his locality and shift to this kind of output knowing GEMs would ensure customers find him, can trust him and could have delivery speedily arranged without intermediaries, before the expiration of shelf life. As the advantages of large farms were progressively nullified their owners should find the newly realized value of small plots reflected in prices they could charge in the GEM for farmland.

It is hard to think of a service industry on which a public markets system might not have similar shattering impact. Instead of turning to a breakdown organisation's easily recalled phone number or web site when her car will not start, a motorist away from home accessing the GEM for immediate car repairs would be likely to find a local high-grade repairer was cheaper and could guarantee to be at her side faster. A manufacturer seeking round-the-clock security for a new plant could turn to a GEMs template that would ensure all the individuals involved had cleared comprehensive vetting: no company need be involved. High street bookmakers might find themselves losing out to individuals offering their own odds on a race in the GEMs betting market. The system would ensure they had sufficient funds in bond to pay out on any stake accepted: in case of dispute between punter and bet taker all moneys would be frozen until resolution. Even companies with assets that are genuinely most efficient when large could find the fringe 'value added' parts of their operations under threat. The telecom companies, for instance, are unlikely to be challenged by very small providers selling in GEMs. But their legions of installers and repairmen, who currently rely on, say, Australia Telecom or Bell Canada for work, might go free-lance and hire themselves out to a mix of individual householders, companies with telephone problems and their former employers. Would these fragmented traders miss the social aspects of a workplace? If so, they could turn to GEMs to find others who wanted to jointly rent office space. Six self-employed data entry clerks for example might hire convenient accommodation and if they enjoyed each other's company deepen their relationship by accepting joint liability on GEMs, then trading as a group able to tackle large assignments. Like shocked Polit-buro members in 1945, many senior managers could find this loss of centralization inconceivable. The likely extent of opposition to public electronic markets will be examined later in this book.

Starting work in public electronic markets

A youngster wanting to start work through GEMs might be shepherded on to the system by her school. Senior teachers would be able to issue a

PIN that proved their endorsement of a student to enter selected low-level markets as a provider. Pet walking might be one such sector. Once endorsed, a 13-year-old uses her PIN to shop for bonding from an insurer, perhaps on a pay-per-booking basis. Then, with a blank trading record, she must price herself into work. There would be little incentive for teachers to endorse unsuitable pupils. Once a proportion of their protégées became the subject of upheld complaints, that educator's ratification would be downgraded by GEMs' software, hurting the chance of their more meritorious scholars obtaining insurance cover.

Having opened a bank account, proven their identity at a Post Office and obtained an initial GEMs PIN, a teenager would find entering the markets for work as easy as any other user. The following example assumes another 13-year-old, trading with the blessing of his school, perhaps with a nominated teacher offering guidance on his embryonic career, which would be automatically confined to legally allowable hours for his age group. He has no clear idea of what he wants to do, relying instead on GEMs to reveal where there is likely to be demand for his services locally. His first step would be calling up the 'work for under 16s' template and choosing a sector.

He is not being shown available jobs here. It is unlikely there would be any for someone his age. Instead GEMs is telling him in which of the markets he is legally entitled to enter he could earn the highest rates per hour locally at the moment. He could chose any combination of them, or try to price himself into an already saturated sector not on the list. GEMs' helpfulness is not to be mistaken for control of users. Assuming he opts for delivery work he is then asked to construct a pricing formula starting by stipulating which hours he wants to be available for jobs. This is done by sliding a pricing bar up and down within each hour that he is allowed to work next week. GEMs assists by underlaying last week's market overview information about average earnings around his home postal code at those times in this market. He can go above that level for times he will only work under duress, below it perhaps for slots he is keen to be out delivering. The bottom of each rectangle represents the legal minimum he is allowed to charge for his labour.

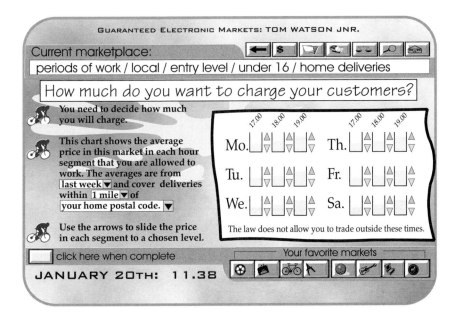

He might chose to maximise his competitiveness early in the week with a pricing level below last week's average. By dragging the pricing bar above the top line for all three periods on Thursday he could tell

GEMs he does not want to be in the market at all that evening, the TV schedule is too good. Because he is a probationer GEMs might only allow him to set out a timetable of availability for two weeks in advance; the software needs to see some proof of reliability before letting him schedule further ahead. If he turns out to be a rogue trader he could damage the system's most valuable asset: users' faith in the markets. Were he to prove unreliable in the first fortnight, by not logging on to check for work when he has said he would, for instance, GEMs would politely evict him from the marketplace. His jobs would be reassigned with costs borne by his bond and he might be told he can try again in 3 months.

Now, a screen asks for details of his bike's carrying capacity and whether he wishes to define local areas in which he will not work. Then it seeks to underline the seriousness of his new commitment.

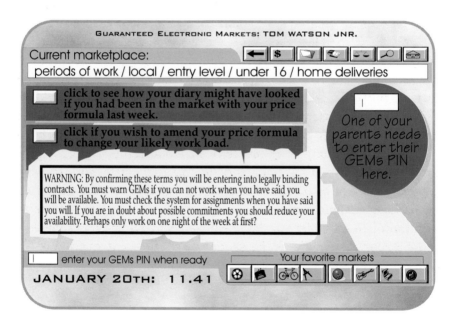

This could be many youngsters' first introduction to obligations in the unforgiving world outside home and school. GEMs should ease them in gently. Any bookings he wins in the following few days would be spelt out clearly. 'Go to 12 Station Road, ask for Mr Jones, collect casserole dish and deliver by 5.30 p.m. to Miss Smith, 17 Avenue Terrace', for instance. Maps could be provided along with estimated journey times. Market mechanisms such as codewords might come with expanded explanations and acceptable levels of service could be reiterated. The software might issue sporadic reminders, for example that standard contracts forbid bikes being chained to a client's property without permission or that deliverers are expected to carry their own padding for fragile items. A wise GEMs franchisee running this marketplace would see that the system allowed extra time for journeys, even above its normal allowance for cyclist speeds, to anyone entering through the under-16s template. Further facilitating the callow suppliers might be a facility allowing purchasers to say they wish to give priority to students of a named school for their household services. Parents could be persuaded to do this by teachers in weeks where they have new entrants making a first step into GEMs trading.

Any teenager choosing to begin working this way should accumulate a trading record that could amount to several hundred hours by the time they are 16. They would then have wide-ranging proof of reliability, independence, competitive trading and people skills to show insurers or college interview panels. Some students would want a more focused portfolio of evening or Saturday work and GEMs could, in time, help by providing templates for those hoping to enter specific careers. If the boy in the example above, for instance, had set his heart on working ultimately as an architect, he could call up a GEMs page that might show him his chances of finding immediate work or work experience doing home improvements or assisting with exterior work on building or landscaping. He would then come to formal training with thorough grounding in the practicalities of his chosen profession. More importantly perhaps, he should be sure that it really was the course for him.

Training: out of the classroom into the community

'There has been sustained demand for chefs in your area, click to see availability of training' is a message that might confront someone in their thirties idly shopping for a new career on GEMs. Having checked the appropriate market overview, to ensure there were not already hundreds of aspiring cooks in the pipeline, the user might cautiously pay for an initial 2 hour trial lesson to be scheduled into his diary. His tutor could be anyone with the required accreditation to teach catering skills, working freelance or for a college. If she was freelance, GEMs might only schedule her appointments when it could simultaneously hire a kitchen for teaching sessions. Commercial kitchen hire would be a new market realised by GEMs. It would be a means for perhaps a school or restaurant to generate income by renting out their facilities after hours: they are likely to do so only to tutors with flawless trading records. Tuition could be one to one or based on a class of stipulated maximum and minimum sizes: GEMs would ensure the availability of all registered participants. After one introductory lesson, the system could help both sides construct further periods of study, allow the pupil to buy a slot with an examining body and, assuming he could then input a 'pass' PIN, enter the market for lower-grade chefs.

Universities would be free to trade course vacancies in a GEM tailor-made for the purpose. They might want to build the flexibility offered by the system into personalized blends of work experience and conventional study. The responsiveness of a public markets system should ensure the end of skill mismatches and make a reality of just-in-time learning. It should ensure that uneven supply, like that in Britain where engineers able to fix washing machines and dishwashers can currently name almost any price they choose, is resolved.[11] It also allows for training in 'soft' skills too often considered uneconomic within the inefficiencies of the uncoordinated market. The girl who spends two hours after school every day walking dogs and feeding cats, for example, might use accumulated proof of that responsibility as a first rung on the ladder into a childcare market. With hundreds of hours of animal supervision on record she should be able to hire herself out as a mother's help, looking after children while under supervision from a parent in the house. Trading record proof of periods of volunteer work in a youth group would also help her career plans. Simultaneously she could be studying child welfare, first aid, cooking for children and maybe a tourist board-led series of evening classes and visits examining facilities for youngsters in her locality. That might put her onto a first step in unsupervised child care from where she would continue to be rewarded for her continuing investment in non-academic but thoroughly practical training. It would be very much in each GEMs franchisee's interest to promote depth and variety in the market for which they were responsible.

What impact would GEMs have on overall levels of work?

'When I was growing up, we used to read that by the year 2000 everyone would have to work only 30 hours a week and the rest would be leisure time. But as we approach 2000 it seems likely that half of us will work 60 hours a week and the rest of us will be unemployed.'[12] The writer, quoted in a study on the future of work, crystallizes the irony of employer-run software packages in the computer age. Such packages rigorously produce efficiency within their tiny segment of the economy. That tends to mean fewer workers, who develop a monopoly on skills, while the costs of rising unemployment are foisted upon other parts of society. GEMs, conversely, should foster equilibrium across the economy as a whole. It spreads the available work around and evens out inequalities, not by redistribution of wealth but by constant distribution of opportunity. It should be radically different from the way workplaces are set to move, as localized efficiency for employers continues to dominate the uncoordinated marketplace for work. A major study into employment environments found most US companies remain 'wedded to a low-trust, low-skill, authoritarian route to competitiveness'.[13] Annualized hours, for example, is an increasingly popular scheme that enables employers to pay for a certain number of hours from their workforce, who are then rostered, often at short notice, as the company requires.[14] GEMs would counterbalance the need for employers to extract increasing value from their workforce with the means for employees to exploit flexibility in industry for themselves. This is likely to include fewer hours of conventional work for many, creating new openings.

As a public markets system evolved, new patterns would emerge. Inevitably, there would be those who would lose their jobs because of efficiencies offered by GEMs. Factory payroll departments, for instance, could have a limited future. But most of those jobs could be judged under threat if the employer invested in a proprietary software package. In that case, however, much of the cost savings would go on licensing fees and computing consultants rather than to the firm. At least those who lose their jobs to GEMs should stand a chance of retraining for a former employer. If not, they should find a newly vibrant work market outside. Labour intensive provision of services could thrive in new areas at the expense of automated manufacture. Were caravan owners, to take one example, to start renting out their trailer homes for the 48 weeks they had previously sat on their drive-ways, there would be demand for delivery and maintenance that scarcely exists in an economy where so many mobile holiday homes are unused for most of their life. Even if all restrictions on employers and hirers were removed, it is hard to envision GEMs leading to full employment in a technological age. However it could end the dismal prospect of structural unemployment, entire households who have no work, barely remember employment and have very little prospect of any member ever coming off benefits. The system may not create employ-ment for all, but it could at least spread realistic hope of work through all tiers of society.

10 GEMs and society: new initiatives made easy

Once a public market system is built there are additional social features that could be added at little cost. As well as creating an additional revenue stream for the consortium funding the system they would do much to promote social stability. These features delivered by a sophisticated but low-cost system offer advantages that a mass of individually targeted Internet sites could never achieve.

A national parallel economy

In 1932 the Mayor of Worgl in Austria, dismayed at 35 per cent unemployment in his jurisdiction, took the unlikely step of authorizing and printing his own currency for the town. As this money, backed by bank deposits of official Austrian schillings, intentionally lost 1 per cent of its value every month the new notes were circulated rapidly. Anyone holding them had every incentive to seek out traders already accepting the secondary currency or persuade newcomers to join the circle of acceptance. With a powerful disincentive for hoarders, the notes achieved a circulation velocity 14 times that of the national currency. Two years later Worgl was the first Austrian town to achieve full employment as citizens used their new scrip to improve houses, replant forest and engage their fellows for activities they could never previously have afforded. Two hundred Austrian communities had appropriated Worgl's idea before their Central Bank deemed such currencies illegal. The point proved in the Tyrolean town – that a well-run but restricted currency can dramatically stimulate economic activity – resurfaced in the 1980s. A therapist in Canada's Comox Valley, Michael Linton, tackled the problem of a falling clientele by issuing his own notes and persuading local traders to accept them in part payment. After 15 years of proselytizing, Linton has inspired hundreds of similar Local Exchange Trading Systems (LETS) around the world. His message is 'Anyone can start a currency and persuade people to use it'.[15] Carpenters can now be hired for LUPP tokens in Uppsala, Sweden; in Rotorua, New Zealand shopping will be done in return for RIBS vouchers; in Mexico City slum dwellers are being offered the chance to trade their labour with each other for Tlalocs. Notes issued by the majority of these regional projects are not backed by any tangible assets, it is the continuing faith of a circle of users that assures their value. This limits the scale of any one scheme. Linton admits 'As you get up in scale you get more fraud, more scam artists'.

GEMs could create its own money for users. Because the deals enacted would be enforced in the same way as any other transaction there should be no problems with defaulters. On joining GEMs each user might be awarded say 500 Parallel Official Economy Tokens (POETs) to sit in an account on the system. They would be digital only, with no validity outside GEMs, and paid over in tranches, perhaps every few weeks to avoid flooding the supply. Any user could then offer goods and services in return for POETs. This would be particularly tempting to anyone who was getting little business when charging 'real' money. The parallel economy points would have to be restricted in their useful-ness or they would simply devalue the main economy. They would certainly only be available to personal, as opposed to company, users and might be limited to transactions within 1000 homes of the user's postal code, confined to low-level markets like local household services and second-hand goods from around the country. A user in a depressed area, for instance, might offer to do neighbours' washing for POETs, which she then uses to purchase counselling sessions or pre-owned VHS movies. She may even use them to purchase surplus food from a neigh-bour. All her deals would be underpinned by GEMs' mechanisms for deal protection and could be scheduled in her GEMs diary while a trading record of demonstrable reliability is being accumulated. She would no longer be excluded from economic activity just because her country's main currency is being deployed elsewhere.

How would the GEMs consortium make its money on this service? Initially POETs would be worthless but as the supply stabilized they could begin to acquire meaningful purchasing ability. At that point the system would offer an exchange, where POETs and the main currency floated freely against each other (Box 10.1). Wealthier users who had spent their initial 500 POETs would be unlikely to hire themselves out to earn more but they might scent a bargain in converting hard cash into the parallel points, then using them to hire someone, perhaps to dig their garden. The second currency should find a value that puts it well below 'real' money while remaining useful for labour-intensive transactions and perhaps second-hand goods. GEMs will take its cut from each of these contracts and automatically convert the POETs it gains back into the primary currency, at the going rate, through the exchange. It would be an uncertain cash flow until the parallel currency hardened but the benefits to the consortium of bringing the underclass into economic activity go beyond any immediate return. Someone who cleans neighbours' cars for POETs through the system and builds up a credible trading record might then enter the GEMs market for truck cleansing, being paid this time in hard currency. High-spending companies that can meet all their needs, including vehicle valeting, from ever-open and competitive markets, are likely to take the system more and more for granted. GEMs' progress to wide acceptance would come about from a constant search of ways to extend each marketplace. For users, POETs would provide stability against movements in the primary currency. The parallel points could not be traded outside the system or abroad, would not be available to companies and, because of their increasing supply, should have little value as a savings medium. They should continue circulating whatever wider economic conditions might prevail and could appreciate dramatically in times of depression in the outside economy.

Box 10.1

GEMS' EXCHANGE BETWEEN THE MAIN AND PARALLEL CURRENCIES

Like every other aspect of GEMs' day-to-day operation, the exchange between primary and secondary currency would be completely mechanical. The computer would be programmed to deal as if holding two pools of money, say $1m and 5 million POETs. As demand fluctuates it sets the price between them at whatever level will facilitate the maximum number of trades while keeping the two pools as close to their original level as possible. This would ensure liquidity, removing the need for an immediate counterpart with whom to swap currencies.

It is not only not-for-profit community schemes that have emulated that of the mayor of Worgl. Large consumer companies are widely expected to start issuing their own currencies to customers for online shopping. Someone holding American Airlines Advantage points after a series of foreign business trips, for instance, might be able to use them to purchase groceries online through a tie-up between the airline and a retailer. As these points are backed by concrete assets, the right to air travel in this case, they are much more desirable than community currencies. The *Wall Street Journal* has already labelled frequent flier miles 'a second national currency'.[16] Going further, individuals can trade loyalty points among themselves, perhaps even asking an employer for payment in points, which can then be sold online. Former *International Herald Tribune* correspondent David Brown has researched the potential impact of these privatized currencies. He concludes: 'The electorate's leverage over its own social and economic policy will then further erode... this will further heighten the dangers of systemic collapse'.[17] It is primarily the well off who benefit from tax-free trading in loyalty points, they are the ones who have both points and Internet connections with which to fully exploit them. But, as Brown points out, any damage done to the main economy by proliferating sidebar currencies will be borne by all.

GEMs would not make decisions about money supply and, following its doctrine of maximum usefulness, must allow users to trade both in community currencies and loyalty points. In South Africa, for instance, a householder looking for a coffee table might want to pay from her alternative currencies account. The country's GEMs system would show her tables most closely matching her requirements, converting each price from rand into say 'Johannesburg Johans' or loyalty points from the Pick'n'Pay supermarket chain at the going rate if asked. However, the system could not set a pool level between these extraneous currencies and the rand because that would involve management, rather than the market, assessing their value. Instead of an automatically calculated rate based on two pre-set pools, the exchanges would have to work on the lumpen principle of bid and offer. Multiple currencies for the electronic age is an idea that has its supporters who point out it would be equivalent to international trade between companies, who simply transact in a mutually convenient and stable denomination regardless of its country of origin. In reality it is possible governments will eventually try to restrict trading in loyalty points because of the destabilizing impact of multiple currencies being used to replace 'real' money by individuals in the top income percentiles. POETs, available to anyone through public access GEMs terminals and automatically restricted to pockets of the economy which hard cash has so often largely vacated, should have an opposite effect. Sealed within a system committed to transparency and widening markets, they could finally make the full promise of secondary currencies for the less well off an undemanding daily reality.

Community organisation

British statesman Edmund Burke called them the 'little platoons', people who find reward in grouping together to serve their community. At present the arduous administration and problems of overcoming a tendency towards social isolation make such projects hard work. It is easier, and often considered safer, for a youngster to play a virtual soccer game online in his bedroom than to organize a real team with his peers in the outside world. A GEMs system could breathe new life into communal activities, not through centrally directing resources and individuals but by extending its technology for running markets into social functions. The system would not initiate, it merely offers to organize. This would allow anyone willing to act as prime mover in setting up a drop-in for local people with mental handicaps, for instance, to call up a GEMs template showing the extent of unmet demand for such a facility locally. The template would then help him find a room and furnishings from the appropriate marketplaces before calculating a cost for the whole package for his proposed period. If grants were available, the system would match him with them; if not, a cost per user would be calculated. Finally GEMs could act as a bridge to potential users, who would sign a contract with the initiator that would be bonded like any other GEMs transaction.

Recent decades have seen considerable imagination applied to community ventures, spurred on by able people who find themselves released from downsized mainstream organizations. GEMs could do much to release this 'third sector' (after private enterprise and government provision) from the momentum-draining requirements of marshalling users and materials in an uncoordinated marketplace. A local minister setting up a weekend away for pensioners, for instance, would be able to do so with all the instant back-up and verification with which a currency trader currently moves millions around the world. So would a family wishing to start an Irish club one night of the week. Or someone instigating a system of 'Civic Guards', as pioneered in Holland, to schedule volunteers who will patrol public places in the locality so the general public feel safe using them. Collectively GEMs' social initiatives could lead to a re-birth of 'civic society'. If individuals start connecting with their neighbours and are able to easily sign up for a range of secure but very low-cost activities there might be less fear of walking the streets, greater pride in the collective environment and improving local facilities.

Grass roots initiatives to replace government provision

On a bleak evening four days before Christmas in 1844, the door opened on a remarkable new store in Rochdale, UK. Initial sales stock was limited to butter, sugar, flour, oatmeal and candles: the bare essentials for families blighted by endemic poverty during the darkest days of 'the hungry forties'. Crucially, the new emporium was committed to honest trading in the days before effective consumer legislation and was run for the benefit of its member shoppers, not to make a profit. It was the success of the Pioneer's Society store in Rochdale that assured a future for the British cooperative movement which went on to encompass affordable insurance, burial services, banking, education and wholesaling. It proved a point often eclipsed today by relentless focus on capital assets: entrepreneurial drive can extend far beyond the profit motive.

GEMs would allow local entrepreneurship to flourish, probably at the expense of centralized provision. Consider, for example, a trio of experienced state sector teachers demoralized by bigger classes and dwindling resources. A GEMs system could, if permitted, reorganize services like education: it might facilitate the three in establishing and then running their own school. Clearly, there would be enormous hurdles to be crossed with standards and commitments to be enforced at every step. GEMs might, however, offer a standard page for seeding a junior school that would follow similar steps to its templates for establishing all sorts of organizations. As setting up an institution for children would be, quite properly, among the most demanding of activities, it is worth describing the scenario in full. The funding mechanism here assumes British-style municipal education provision but it would as easily work in other systems: the key point is that scale of operation would no longer be important.

The group of teachers, perhaps gathered in one member's kitchen, would navigate to the GEMs marketplace for school formation and call up a market overview page. It might show that 50 parents, within a mile radius of the postal code they identified, have tried to move their 5–11-year-olds out of the existing school into something smaller without success so far. The teachers have a market. Before going any further each of them in turn must prove their identity to the system by entering their name and PIN: this also brings up their trading records for group inspection. Now the system asks them to decide on a headteacher, perhaps pointing out a legal requirement that it be someone with at least 10 000 hours complaint-free experience at the chalkface in junior schools. Additionally, they must nominate how much extra that individual is to be paid. After the longest-serving member of the group is nominated, GEMs offers a business contract that binds all three into joint liability for the venture, while their newly appointed boss is held to additional legal responsibilities. A crucial function of this contract, it would be pointed out, is to define the ethos of the new operation. Democratic social initiatives in the past have often failed because they had no means of embedding values to which potential subscribers either acquiesced or moved on to a more like-minded grouping. The British co-op movement nearly foundered on this rock as it became demonstrably successful. 'It appears to me wrong for persons to enter a Society with whose principles they disagree, and then destroy its constitution' wrote William Cooper, one of the Rochdale Pioneers.[18] It is at this point that the principles of the new school are laid down decisively. They will be inserted into any eventual contract with parents, changeable only by a vote involving everyone concerned.

Now the three each need an insurer who will provide the substantial financial bond from which any compensation in case of wrongdoing can be paid. Like all the GEMs insurance markets, the forum for educationalists' bonding matches details of the candidates' experience, previous complaints upheld and potential liabilities with formulae input by insurers pricing themselves into different niches in the market. Each applicant for insurance specifies how they wish to pay for cover and the system will find the best match.

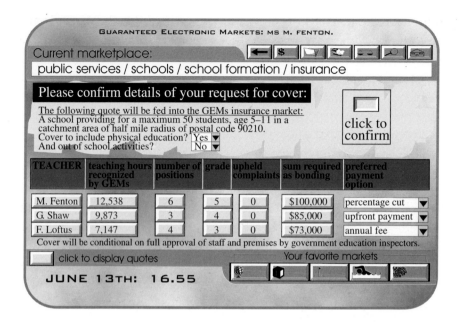

The insurance cover cannot be booked until some further procedures have been completed. GEMs simply needs to know that the three were insurable in current market conditions before continuing. Their next step is to locate a building. The GEMs franchisee running the template for school formation has input current legal requirements for a fledgling establishment and GEMs pulls together options from across its property market. Anyone selling property is offered the chance to answer detailed questions that determine whether their offering could additionally be made available in the schools template. For instance, someone putting a small office suite up for sale might be asked not only for room and outside area dimensions but also about the plumbing: are toilets and handbasins cemented to the building or only bolted? If the latter, then they can be easily replaced by child-sized facilities, for which GEMs can display the best price currently available in its sanitary ware marketplace and factor in the charges for such a job from local plumbers. Likewise, a suitable property that does not have the minimum space required for a playing field will be paired with the nearest sports facilities available for hire in that market. This process can sound prohibitively complex. In reality it would require a fraction of the computing power currently used daily by big banks to construct and trade exotic financial instruments around the world. Buildings, in the area the teachers have defined, that matched the requirements for a small school and were available for at least a two-year period would be displayed on a map.

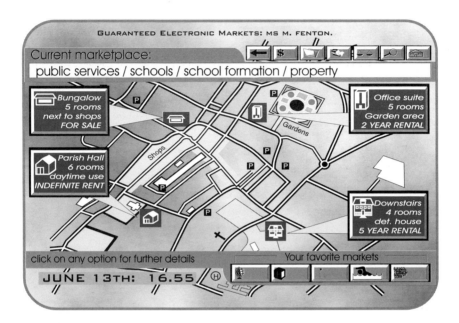

These are not properties that would normally appear in the market for education space. It is because savvy sellers have seen the advantages of answering precise questions that assess the suitability for school use that they appear in this context. Other questions for anyone putting property up for long-term rental or sale might be geared to assessing the building's potential for use as a doctor's surgery or community drop-in centre. No seller has to answer these non-essential questions in their contract but doing so increases the pool of potential buyers. It would also be in the vendor's interest to commission a survey of the property from a surveyor willing to put final gradings into GEMs against his PIN. They could then be browsed by any potential buyer.

Each of the available options is backed up by a details page about the property. After viewing these it might be that the teaching threesome decide that the ground floor rooms in a detached house are their best option. They could now opt for a 'purchased hold', paying the owner through GEMs to take his property out of the market for 24 hours until they have seen it. Simultaneously they tell GEMs to schedule a viewing in the seller's diary at his convenience and the group adjourns until after that appointment.

The following evening they reconvene having visited the suite of rooms and benchmarked it against a list of legal minimum requirements printed out from GEMs. They like the rooms and after haggling with the owner have persuaded him to discount his price to them: he inputs that instruction into GEMs which then constructs a provisional contract between the two sides. A further sum is transferred to the owner to allow for a new 'purchased hold' extending for another month. The teachers do not have capital to buy their potential school outright; they turn to GEMs for the best possible mortgage. As with the insurance, it will be found by matching specifics of price, surveyor's assessment, location and intended use against the pricing formula of providers. As well as offering that figure, the system now asks for precise details of modifications they need, then prices each in the appropriate market. The screen might look like this.

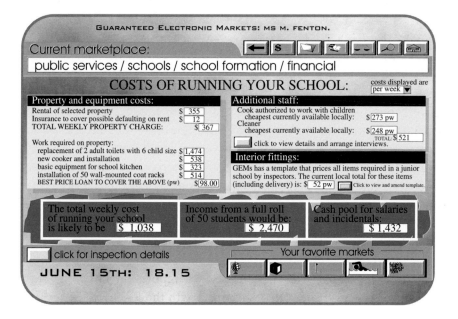

This would probably be as far as a new school could go without approval from the education regulators. Clicking to put their plan forward would schedule them into the local authority's diary for reviewing new school openings and give them a code-word to bring up all the details they had decided so far. Inspectors might, at the teachers' expense, spend a day interviewing them individually, visiting the proposed premises, and studying their conversion plans and costings as assembled by GEMs. If the venture passes this scrutiny it is then awarded an inspection PIN which, when entered into the template, allows the project to move into the next phase: recruiting students. Would education authorities be obstructive to start-up schools, to protect their empire of existing establishments? Central government would have to decide if it wished to encourage small schools: if so, vetting would have to be separate from administration of existing schools and clear, publicly accountable grounds for acceptance and rejection established. Additional grants might be made available through the system, perhaps to pay for inspection of potential enterprises.

A parent who tells GEMs they sought to move their child from an existing school in the area would be given the option of receiving a message from anyone licensed to operate a community alternative. The three teachers would now be able to activate this facility, throwing their combined GEMs diaries open for meetings with parents. As parents came away from their discussions with the entrepreneurial teachers they could call up the GEMs contract that would govern their child's education. This would set out the level of service to be offered covering hours of religious education, sports activities, facilities to be provided and so on. If the state allowed funding to follow a child to the school of choice, parents could then sign up and their youngster would be provisionally booked to spend his next term at the new enterprise. Once the required minimum had signed, all would be sent a message confirming their place, while purchase of the building, structural modifications and hiring of cleaners and caterers was activated. Once the school opened, GEMs would see that it was inspected regularly, the input of an inspector's PIN being necessary before pupils could be enrolled for each further term. Additionally inspectors' reports might be circulated to all parents as a term of their contracts with the teachers. As with any small organization trading in GEMs, there would be full flexibility to engage replacement teachers in case of sickness and to hire extraneous facilities. Innovative schools might use the public markets system to shop for, say, old people's homes in the vicinity that were looking for activities for residents and had clicked on 'would welcome visits to schools'. Children could then study oral history with pensioners, with GEMs scheduling their get togethers and arranging any transport required, perhaps drawing on funds for those specific journeys made available by charities to promote activities for the elderly. Specialist outside help could be bought in, perhaps with a local freelance nurse engaged for six Tuesday mornings to teach first aid or an experienced football coach hired for one day a month to train players for county little league trials. In all cases, GEMs would be attesting to the individual's solidity through a trading record and by status as someone verified by police as approved to work with children.

This changed model for education provision would not need central administration. The efficiencies of a market economy would dictate which institutions succeed and, because the schools are smaller and more evenly distributed, parents would have more choice about moving their offspring out of a failing institution. Inspection would be bought in a dispersed market that could expand and contract with demand. If teachers around the country preferred setting up their own neighbourhood schools to working in centralized education facilities and if parents enthusiastically supported those new ventures, there could be an exodus of students and staff from existing places of education. This is no concern of GEMs which exists only to bring the unbridled benefits of electronic markets to users, not to shape their impact. That task falls to elected governments. However, politicians who wished to encourage a newly realised efficiency for smaller schools might reflect that declining old schools could begin to sell their textbooks while renting out fixed assets, like laboratories and gymnasiums, to surrounding start-up institutions. Given the purity of the marketplace in which these transactions would take place, there should be little loss in the use of resources as the education system evolved. Community-based schooling with only two or three teachers per institution has been tried before: it is how education for the masses started in the UK with schools provided by church and parish in Victorian times. A demand for ever bigger places of learning emerged not from the needs of children but from the efficiencies of scale required to make universal provision, administered from above, cost effective in an industrial-age economy. Governments wanting to give their electorate the choice of returning to provision on that scale would need only to free parents to allocate the funds for their child's education. The market mechanism on GEMs would do the rest.

It is not just existing schools that could be affected by a grass roots revival. Local government services such as street cleaning could be taken over by locals, not in a voluntary capacity but as paid contractors who are answerable for any complaints. Suppose a town hall sectioned off its jurisdiction on a GEMs-provided map and invited contracts to regularly clean each square of the grid. This could mean agreements specifying that a contractor 'keep Station Road, High Crescent and Main Street from numbers 32 to 98 swept twice weekly with public litter bins emptied at least every other day'. The term of engagement might run for a month at a time. Anyone could bid for the part-time contract with the lowest tender automatically winning. Each winner would then have to put a sum in bond and be subject to adjudication at personal expense if their patch was not diligently tended. Any resident can complain through GEMs about the level of service. That might then be treated as a dispute with the cleaner, bypassing local officials. The market mechanism should maintain a high level of service: if a bad job is being done at a high price, someone else can undercut the current contractor next month. Local policy makers might choose that the rate being paid for each sector be made public on GEMs to increase this competition. Anyone who thinks they can do better for the money can then price themselves into next month's contract for that area. In the past, regional governments have shied away from engaging local people to provide local services because in the uncoordinated market it is almost invariably cheaper to contract-out a large area to a company big enough to possess expensive equipment and skilled staff. GEMs-empowered street cleaners would have the advantage of a pure market for trading second-hand bin trolleys, hiring brooms and shovels or engaging a street cleaning truck to pass through their sector for half an hour. A GEMs buyer's club among adjoining sectors could book the truck for a morning, with each contractor automatically paying their share of the cost through an individual agreement for the driver and equipment.

Social networks: using computers to increase human contact

The mechanisms that match buyers and sellers in electronic market-places could be adapted to unite those who want to set up a particular group nationwide and those that want to join it. Someone wanting to launch a mountaineers' ornithology club, for instance, or a recovery network for Christian alcoholics, could call up a contract for club formation. They would input a title for the proposed group, a brief summary of its aims then a longer paragraph of description and perhaps have some photographs scanned for a details page. Details of any charges to be made on those who join, to cover production of a club magazine or Internet site, perhaps, would also be required. The founder's identity would be clear in the contract that any new member signed and he would have to put a sum of his own in bond in case of misbehaviour. Unlike the Internet, groups could not be set up by concealed individuals who then abscond with the funds. Once initiated by a user who was taking responsibility for its management, the club would need to be categorized in a GEMs directory of groups available for joining. Anyone interested could see the details sheet and sign a joining contract. Meetings would then be arranged at times when the maximum number of members had availability in their diaries and all would pay a share of communal costs. GEMs would audit each club on behalf of its members, showing in which markets the founder or his approved signatories had spent funds and whether they had been allo-cated on a rational basis. If the joining contract specified a quarterly magazine, for instance, GEMs would report to members how much had been spent on printing and show that the treasurer had genuinely selected the best value operator in the market that day and not just opted to place the job with a friend's print works. Because many of these clubs could be operating on a no charge basis, the system would deduct a flat fee for this service but, assuming management adopt a 'penny post' pricing model sacrificing short-term margins to long-term development, the sum involved should be small enough not to put a brake on anyone's social life. The social networks facility on GEMs could allow for evolution as flexibly as any of its markets. If two near identical clubs are formed, for example, the initiators of both can propose a vote for members on whether to merge. GEMs would arrange the poll, while highlighting areas of difference in the two contractual constitutions that needed resolution. The social facilities available from a public markets system could be infinitely more reliable than anything offered on the open Internet with its lower grade levels of protection.

A particularly heartwarming social facility GEMs could offer, again for a flat fee, would be a friendship and dating function. Committed to fantastically sophisticated matching functions across thousands of varied markets, management would have little problem adding programming that brings together individuals by interests, locality and multiple additional fields. Likely to far exceed the pool of potential suitors, criteria in selection and cheapness of any agency outside the system, this function could be a killer application to attract many individuals on to GEMs.

Universal legal services

A GEMs system in mass use would be constructing millions of contracts a day for its users, each one underpinned by law. Why not spin off that facility into a feature, allowing users to write their own agreements and have them deposited in the GEMs registry of legally binding contracts? A home owner who agrees to sell half his garden to a next door neighbour, for instance, does not need matching with a buyer through the system. But he might want a contract specifying the extent of the land and the terms of any rights of way signed by them both banked on the system for an insubstantial fee rather than negotiated by the hour in a lawyer's office. (The latter option would of course also be available through GEMs.) Nearby a trio of builders agreeing to work jointly on a row of new garages might want a contract limiting their liability to each other. A comprehensive public markets system could easily include blank contracts which users then complete themselves, before depositing with the time and date of creation certified by the central computer. If this was deemed too casual, government may decide that signatories have to call up their contract and re-sign it a week later and then a month later before it is valid. That way they would have time to reconsider. Some businesses not selling their entire capacity on GEMs might still choose to impose the system's contracts on all deals. A small guesthouse, for instance, might invite a guest, who walked into reception and asked for a room, to sign a public markets contract for overnight accommodation, if he was a user. That would immediately clarify their relationship and facilitate the business's accounting by GEMs. Wills, house share agreements and affidavits about substandard goods or services could be created just as easily.

This facility could force government into new rulings on what constitutes an acceptable agreement between two consenting parties. Obviously a contract drawn up between two individuals committing to a bank raid or other criminal act would not be upheld in court. But what of prenuptial agreements, declarations of marriage by gay couples or a pact to split possessions and child custody between a long-wedded couple who have no wish to involve the divorce courts? At present these social contracts are expensive to instigate and carry little weight because they are dispersed. A GEMs registry would be more accessible and would show up numbers of any given type of social contract. This could lead to a situation where sheer weight of contracts signed led to pressure for a law underwriting their legitimacy being passed.

Electronic voting: 'participative democracy'

GEMs could transform the way citizens in its country vote. It could also allow them to have a genuine say on a far wider range of issues. Voting through the system would be a logical extension of its markets software but not one from which it could legitimately make any money. Even the most enterprise-focused countries would find it unacceptable to charge their populace for access to the ballot box. If voting through the system is to be offered, it must be a cost carried by the consortium, negotiated as part of their deal with parliament when setting up the operation.

How would it work? On election day the system makes a voting page available to every user, computing their constituency from its map of postal codes. Individuals tapping into GEMs at home, work or on a public access terminal then click against a chosen party, or rate a list of candidates in countries with transferable votes. Entering their secret PIN then sends that vote to the central computer where results are tabulated through the day to be released at poll closing time. The fact that an individual had completed his page would be recorded to forestall any attempt at voting a second time, but no record of the candidate he personally selected would be kept. The scores for each contender are compiled by GEMs' central computer without any reference back to who voted for them. A complication to this vision of a low-cost democratic utopia is the overriding principle that no one would ever be compelled to use GEMs: voters who want to walk to a local church hall, enter a booth and place a tick on a piece of paper must be free to do so. Losing sight of this principle would turn GEMs from a freely entered market system to a potential instrument of statist control, unacceptable in a democracy. The system's voting capability has to run in association with returning officers around the country. Each would have a GEMs terminal displaying the local electoral register. It is on this rather than the printed register that they mark who has been given a ballot paper. As individuals vote on GEMs they are removed from the display to local presiding officers, signifying they are not to be given a ballot paper at the polling station. When the polls close, electronic vote tallies are published immediately by the system to all its users; the paper count is then added for each constituency (Box 10.2).

Box 10.2

VOTING AS A BELL-WETHER OF TRUST IN THE SYSTEM

An electorate would only vote through GEMs if they trusted the system completely. A corrupt system might either falsify returns or reveal to officials how individuals had voted. The purity of a country's public markets system would be crucial to its economic and democratic well being and requires new forms of inspection. GEMs would be relentlessly probed both by outside organizations paid through a trust established by the consortium and by its own more technically minded users. Because the millions of lines of programming code driving the central computer are published openly and available to be checked (but not tampered with) by anyone with a GEMs terminal, conspiracy theorists could think up ways that data might be tampered with and confirm that it is not happening. Willing uptake of the voting facility by trusting users could be a useful target for consortium management to set themselves.

GEMs voting would be convenient and cost the state nothing. It need not be confined to election days. In Switzerland the value of national referendums has long been recognized. Collecting signatures from 0.7 per cent of a population of 7 million guarantees a national plebiscite on any proposed law. Anyone attracting 1.4 per cent of his countrymen to sign a petition can initiate legislation. Swiss political culture hands sovereignty directly to the people: when a Zurich newspaper reports 'The Sovereign has decided' it is simply saying the population have voted. GEMs could offer its users in any country the capacity to initiate Swiss-style referendums to which other users can choose to add their PIN signatures in support. However, its sheer convenience could lead to abuse. 'We get a lot of wacko things on the ballot' grumbles the governor of Oregon, one of the US states in which members of the public can initiate a referendum once a threshold of signatures has been crossed.[19] Any GEMs facility for petitions would need automatically to separate out the frivolous polls launched by users from the democratically useful. This could be achieved by grading petitions on offer by the number of votes, for or against, they had so far attracted. Thus anyone launching a petition, calling for the abolition of government rent controls perhaps, would have every incentive to also initiate a profile-raising campaign that should ensure the measure started to move up the list of polls available to users. GEMs would see that an individual only signed each petition once. The system would need a cut-off period after which a petition was removed. When drafting the act that launched GEMs, politicians would have to decide how far they wished to use it as a means of widening democracy. The potential for letting the public, or at least those who had enrolled with GEMs, stage a well-regulated poll could haunt them. How, for instance, would UK parliamentarians react to a definitive poll demanding the return of capital punishment? In the wake of atrocities there is inevitably evidence of an overwhelming desire to bring back hanging which the House of Commons has always resisted. One way to avoid this hysteria-fuelled rush to judgement in an age of effort-free polling would be to establish rolling referendums. The same question could be posed four times with perhaps a month's gap between each polling day. Those with an abiding concern for the issue would be likely to welcome the opportunity for a more measured sampling of public opinion, the uncommitted and media-frenzied might disqualify themselves by not bothering to cast a vote on each of the four days. GEMs' referendums should never be given the weight of Swiss petitions because they would perpetually exclude that segment of the population who choose not to use the system. However, if say 90 per cent of the populace have a GEMs account and 70 per cent of them consistently support a change of law, however abhorrent to parliament, it would take skilful dissembling by politicians to negate the impact.

A GEMs vote need not be national. Unions could ballot members on the system, with only those who had paid their subscription invited to vote. Clubs and democratically minded employers could do likewise. Most empowering of all, perhaps, would be community polls, displayed only to those who live within specified streets. For example two mothers living close to a patch of communal land could instigate a petition calling for pets to be banned from the grass so toddlers could play there in safety. They would word a question, define the street on which it impacted then launch a campaign among their neighbours. If a proportion of them, decided by government, voted and a sufficient number opted for the change of use GEMs might automatically pass the results on to local government. One of their officials would confirm that the question posed was fair and the new status of the contested land had now been enshrined in local legislation. The system would then collect subscriptions from any of the recent voters who wanted to contribute towards legally approved signage, then hire a contractor to install notices warning all comers that dogs were now to be walked elsewhere. Eventually this facility could lead to communities defining themselves. An area of many elderly residents might, if allowed, vote for a low noise ordinance. Zones with a large population of small children might collectively decide that they wanted their street car-free at weekends. Such polls might have to be reaffirmed every year; the decision would rest with local officials. In Glasgow, Scotland, residents of the council-run Langstone Place tower block were recently allowed to interview and rule on new applicants for apartments. Those suspected of drug dealing or antisocial activities are now rejected by a panel of locals.[20] It is a step that does have wider social implications but, if permitted by government, GEMs could allow countless other communities to take control of their destiny for far less effort. It might also allow for cost-effective voting for local officials, even to the level of school governors or hospital administrators.

Where would this world of newly reliable, instant, popular decision-making leave politicians? In Switzerland, few electors know the name of their premier. The culture of *subsidiarität*, whereby decisions are made at the lowest practicable level, makes him or her a far less influential figure than foreign counterparts. The politically active Swiss citizenry, though, has strong cohesion without a high profile leader to unite them: despite having four main languages spoken by its population the country has been stable for centuries. Other nations, where democracy is increasingly defined by adversarial politics driven by personalities, would probably not want to lose that capacity for a clear sense of leadership. But the progressive centralization of power in several first world countries in recent decades could easily be reversed as a public electronic markets system was taken up. It might demonstrate that a politically empowered population led to a more content and stable society.

User boycotts: forcing the supply chain

Any GEMs user could list companies or individuals who were not to be presented to him as trading options. A motorist who was not satisfied with the durability offered by a particular tyre company, for example, might click on 'I do not wish to have this seller's products offered to me again'. If a public markets system were truly committed to offering its users every benefit of which the technology is capable, however, it would empower buyers further. Users could be offered a 'current boycotts' page. Here they could list ingredients they preferred to avoid in their purchases or companies with whom they had no desire to trade, even indirectly. Ecologically minded consumers could tell this page, for example, that they wished to punish agrochemical giant Monsanto for its enthusiastic propagation of genetically modified crops. They would be telling GEMs that when shopping in food-related marketplaces they want priority in matching given to any supplier whose contract attests to no Monsanto involvement in their output. Any seller could call up the boycotts page and transfer an automatically generated clause confirming this commitment to their standard sales contracts. Were one of these sellers found subsequently trading with the boycotted company their new-found customers would all be automatically compensated from funds in bond. GEMs has no input into which companies are listed on the boycotts page of course, but market overview information will show sellers how many potential buyers are giving preference to manufacturers who have purged their supply chain of, say, Monsanto produce.

This facility could put buyers back in control of market regulation rather than abdicating responsibility for industrial processes to negotiations between big business and government. The resources of global corporations, combined with an ability to play governments off against each other, are, many believe, diminishing politicians' ability to act effectively as arbiters of the public interest. 'I am not sure' British Agriculture Minister Jeff Rooker is reported to have told government conservation agencies seeking a moratorium on gene modification 'that we are in the driving seat'.[21] Individual consumers certainly are not: modified food is rarely labelled in supermarkets because it originates so far down the processing chain. With a GEMs boycott gathering momentum, however, individual farmers might see advantages in decisively switching away from the merchants supplying seeds from boycotted companies, inserting the appropriate clause in their contract and making their harvest more valuable to processors who now wished to act likewise. If public distaste for biotechnology was overwhelming, as some surveys suggest, it would be mass market consumers who decided the fate of companies involved, not lone regulators.

11 GEMs' impact on parliament: technologically literate politicians and small government

British Prime Minister Tony Blair has famously joked that he has trouble finding the on switch for his official laptop computer. Bill Clinton came up with a similar quip for reporters at the launch of his government's electronic commerce policy statement. This affected naiveté would probably not be a vote winner in a country where a significant section of economic activity was happening in GEMs. Politicians would need to understand the dynamics of electronic markets, including the dizzying speed with which they can respond to events. In October 1997, for instance, the London stockmarket launched its SETs share dealing service with a speech from Chancellor Gordon Brown who, in the course of his remarks, appeared to suggest diminished enthusiasm for European monetary union. As his talk progressed the enormous SETs screen behind him progressively turned red as dealers used their new-found technology to immediately sell shares in companies reliant on the European market. When the frenzy abated, stock prices had been pushed way below their true value. Consumers given similarly fluid markets may conceivably respond in the same way to a report criticizing perhaps a specific make of car. Parliament, like the ruling bodies of Stock Exchanges, would need to decide whether the more illogical aspects of market forces were to be tempered with trading limits. They might, for example, rule that the price of any tangible asset on GEMs is not allowed to drop more than 15 per cent below its previous average in a 24-hour period, to put a brake on panic selling. Alternately they might opt for 'capitalism red in tooth and claw'. GEMs would not force any ideology on governments, merely give them a new forum in which their convictions can be applied.

A government launching GEMs would need to decide how much responsibility it was willing to abdicate to market mechanisms. Some regulatory issues might be better resolved by individual GEMs franchisees working to cultivate buyer confidence than by edicts from central government. In the UK, for instance, policymakers have repeatedly tussled with the question of whether nannies should be regulated or whether, as one official report put it, an enforced code would create 'a false sense of security' for parents.[22] A guaranteed market for childcare would sideline these quibbles, automatically building in ongoing checks to a depth far beyond that feasible in the uncoordinated marketplace. Parents would still be free to hire an unregulated nanny, through a newspaper classified advertisement perhaps, but they might ask themselves why she had decided not to trade in the very convenient, but heavily vetted, market on GEMs. Regulation currently puts an enormous cost burden on economic activity: supervision of financial services alone in the US costs over $700m a year according to studies by the London Business School.[23] With automated checking of market entrants and enforcement of deals, GEMs would not require anything like this level of policing (Box 11.1). As government regulators started clearing their desks, central administrators could be doing the same. In the USA, 15–20 per cent of the cost of healthcare is estimated to go on administration.[24] But in a GEMs environment, hospitals and health providers could trade their services on a day-to-day basis. A 50-year-old user requiring physiotherapy, for example, could be given a PIN by his family doctor which allowed him to decide on a supplier and have GEMs schedule the appointments as available. No one need predict demand for these services or oversee the premises on which they are given. Once insurers or state health services attach payment to the patient all provision can be left to the market which would have full overview information to ensure demand and supply attain rough equilibrium at the best possible price. It may lead to hospitals shrinking to core functions as staff who do not need operating theatres or centralised equipment shift to self-employed status.

Box 11.1

POLICING THE MARKETS IN GEMS

Each GEM would be self-policing. Sellers' claims are not evaluated by anyone, instead compliance relies on 3 C's: customers, competitors and consumer groups. Suppose, for example, a camping equipment manufacturer releases a new line of rucksacks in the appropriate GEM and types in that the product is '100 per cent waterproof'. A first buyer to discover it was not would instigate a complaint and, if successful, receive recompense according to the publicly known scale for misleading claims in that market, double the cost of his back-pack perhaps. However, if hundreds of the rucksacks have been sold, competitors or consumer groups might initiate tests and, if the bag's repellent qualities are not 100 per cent, launch a complaint of their own. If the case against the bag maker has foundation, and the waterproofing claim has been untrue throughout a long production run, the company will experience the punitive effects of cumulative contracts. GEMs will automatically access its month of stored contracts with buyers of that model and send them all a warning about their purchase plus compensation from the camping suppliers' bond. Would competitors endlessly complain without justification about each other? There would need to be rapid judgement by trading standards officials and perhaps a three-strikes-and-you-are-out rule for wilful complainers. The kind of preventative policing that can so encumber existing routes to market should not be required in this bonded environment.

Politicians around the world are already aware of the potential for online efficiencies in the delivery of government services. This awareness has spawned multiple computer systems at enormous start-up cost for the taxpayer. At time of writing, for instance, the UK government is having to explain embarrassing overruns in a scheme called BA-Pocl that will eventually computerize welfare payments at a price in excess of $1000 million.[25] Nearby, civil servants in the agriculture ministry are setting up CTS, the Cattle Tracing System to record movements as livestock are bought and sold.[26] Elsewhere officials are grappling with a late-running system that should one day simplify tax calculations.[27] All these projects and their related expenditure in the uncoordinated online marketplace would be irrelevant with a fully functioning GEMs system. It could pay benefits, register cattle as they changed ownership and constantly compute individuals' tax liabilities. As provision of official services came to be governed more by the transparent GEMs marketplace, and less by coteries of administrators, problems of accountability should diminish. The Pentagon, for instance, has been criticized for the opacity of its accounting, but if it were purchasing through GEMs, and choosing to release its auditing on the system to Congress, any missing millions could be quickly tracked back to the individuals concerned. Other countries who have a problem, not with official ineptness but with full-scale corruption, could likewise find a solution in public electronic markets. Civil servants might be told they can buy only through the system and be given assigned levels of purchasing responsibility then have their record of transactions made public to all users. GEMs need not release full details of course, simply showing that a certain amount was spent in the market for uniforms by someone in the police procurement division and attesting that the deal for which he opted was the one offering best value for his requirements at the time. His specifications could be made public, to ensure they were not skewed to favour a particular supplier, and the state of the market that day recorded: were there sufficient suppliers to ensure real competition? As the smallest of deals would be open to automatic scrutiny, the favouritism and incompetence that can tarnish an entire government should disappear. While dishonourable politicians would be unlikely to welcome this facility, as online technology spreads it is possible it could be forced on them. The World Bank for instance might one day make the launch of a GEMs-style system, with its facility for transparent government accounting, a condition of any financial bail out.

Government control of a GEMs economy: precision and imagination required

The telephone played a pivotal role in the 1929 Wall Street crash. No one had anticipated its capacity for allowing sell orders to snowball. Governments launching GEMs would need to exercise some foresight about the broad effects it could unleash. They might feel that, instead of a traditional industrial policy, they had a role in promoting sectors that offered new sources of employment, for example. Tourism is one obvious category. Inbound visitors to the country of operation could open a GEMs account and assemble personalised itineraries for travel, accommodation and activities, each component of which would be found in a market moving towards direct payments to individuals and away from corporate coffers. The traditional levers of government control over a democratic economy would remain unchanged by GEMs but they should each become much more responsive to policy decisions.

Tax and social policy

Taxation of transactions across the Internet is currently a fraught issue. At which end of the deal are goods dispatched from one US state to another charged sales tax? How is tax calculated when a Swedish customer orders clothing from an Australian company? Can retailers follow banks in moving their computers to offshore tax havens to escape revenue officials? Unlike the global complexity of controls on uncoordinated electronic trade, a GEMs system would be national and could immediately calculate current tax payable on each transaction. Consortium management would need to ensure this ease of collection did not tempt policymakers into using GEMs as a cash cow for higher taxes, which would price users off the system. A more intelligent use of public electronic markets would be to drop the revenue department's take from very specific transactions. Politicians might do this to achieve social ends: lowering the tax on lorry and driver bookings between midnight and 6.00 a.m. for instance, to ease road congestion or allowing parents of a registered disabled child to buy a quota of clothes, in the appropriate size, every year free of sales tax, to reflect their increased costs of care.

Selective tax rates could also be used to tempt traders out of the grey economy. The untaxed money-in-hand sector has expanded around the world three times as fast as official economies in the last three decades.[28] It now amounts to some 15 per cent of the cash turnover in developed nations. Enticing thousands of hairdressers, plumbers, drivers, builders and catering staff from the fringes of criminality and on to the system would be a rich prize for both government and management. Politicians might drop tax rates in these markets on the pragmatic grounds that a small cut from 15 per cent of gross domestic product is better than no cut and that society, as a whole, has much to gain from cleaning up the grey market so that crime detection can focus on a remaining hard core. As it downsized government, GEMs should reduce public spending. The resulting leeway for policy makers could be applied in many ways through the system. They might, for instance, want to reflate particularly depressed areas by zoning tax payments, allowing anyone living in specified postal codes 25 per cent off their employment tax. This zoning need not be as crude as previous attempts, where residents on one side of a street often find themselves paying local taxes well above those of households they see out of their front windows. If politicians define an epicentre to be given full tax relief, GEMs could graduate the percentage outwards over a variable radius.

GEMs does not demand this kind of sophisticated taxation policy to become workable. But a government choosing to ignore its potential would be opting for very blunt supervision of their economy in a new era. Bold politicians might one day go further in harnessing the system's capacity to collapse the criminal economy. It would be a radical step indeed, but if underground drugs were made legal and their supply (heavily restricted, of course) moved on to the system, an entire infrastructure of sustained crime would cave in. The social ramifications would need thinking through in great detail but for GEMs the operation of a restricted sector would be routine. The system's marketplace for explosives, for instance, might only be accessible to buyers with authenticating PINs to prove their status as licensed quarry blast managers plus verification from an approved employer. Their every purchase would be recorded for public safety officials who could set limits on the amounts that could be bought. Similarly, a heroin addict, once registered with a drugs counsellor, might be given a PIN enabling him to purchase a small personal supply, day by day, as long as he continued submitting to supervision and getting new PINs. Legitimate sellers could sell in this market in transparent competition with each other. It might be that the supply side is restricted to established pharmaceutical companies because they have experience of distributing controlled substances. They would obviously not be allowed to promote their new product range. This market should end the 500 per cent or so street mark ups typically enjoyed by many dealers.[29] Would the implied imprimatur of respectability increase drug use? Its immediate effect could be to destroy any channel for recruiting new users. As existing addicts realised they could find their fix much more cheaply on GEMs, they would be likely to enroll with a counsellor and then purchase controlled amounts from a supplier trading on the system. Not only would long chains of profit-taking intermediaries be broken but the sector would be working on a customer pull model, rather than having thousands of small sellers around the country motivated by high margins to push their product on to new customers. Once a hard drug began trading at commodity prices in a transparent market limited to supervised buyers and suppliers, it should be relatively easy for government to stifle current levels of growth in the sector. Auditing the supply would become precise to the last milligram.

Unlike the uncoordinated Internet marketplace, it would be virtually impossible to commit a crime on GEMs. Markets would only be written for legal sectors of the economy and, as each deal is enacted through a contract provided to both parties, it would be difficult to launder money without leaving an incriminating audit trail. The disposal of stolen goods would be similarly affected. As opening a GEMs account requires high-level proof of identity and every transaction involves a contract that is copied to both parties, only the dimmest racketeer would choose this route for his underhand activities. However, this automated enforcement should be the extent of GEMs' role in the fight against crime. What it must not do is spy on its users. For example, the system could, on request, compile earnings accounts for every user, simultaneously calculating their tax owed on each transaction. At financial year's end one click would send this statement to revenue officers, perhaps accompanied by a signed declaration from the individual testifying he had not earned any money outside the system so they were a complete record. A transfer of the appropriate funds to the tax authorities could be authorised with a few more clicks. However, it would be crucial that GEMs' management do not allow any user to be coerced into deepening his reliance on the system. An individual who wished to file a paper tax return would be free to do so, even if he had traded exclusively in GEMs that year. If tax authorities queried his figures they could not have access to his accounts page on the system, which would be available only to him and which he could choose to destroy irrevocably at any time. It may seem inconsistent that GEMs, a system predicated on enforcement of honest trading, would stand back and allow a user to commit a crime by destroying his true accounts. But it is on a par with another principle implicitly accepted in most advanced democracies: photographers and television crews covering, say, a rowdy demonstration do not hand over unpublished material to police, even though it may identify perpetrators of criminal behaviour. It is preferable that some miscreants go unidentified rather than communications media lose their independence from state bodies. Revenue officials, dubious of a paper return from a GEMs user, could obviously call up market overview archives to show what he would have been likely to be earning at the times stated in his area. Such information would be in the public domain. Tax authorities might choose to offer a discount to anyone filing their system accounts as a tax return and then concentrate their enquiries on those who do not, but they could not snoop on GEMs users' details.

Environmental policy

Thousands of Berliners belong to a scheme called *Stadtauto* (city car). In return for a joining fee, deposit, monthly charge and usage payments calculated by time and mileage, they can use hundreds of cars based at dozens of sites in the city. Members make a phone call to establish the identity of their nearest vehicle, then use a pass key to open a kerbside deposit box for the ignition keys. They abandon their transport at journey's end. 'A lot of people like the idea that there's no hassle, no trouble and no responsibility', according to the manager of one of more than 300 such schemes, born of Germany's green movement.[30] Proponents reckon that each city car removes four privately owned vehicles from the roads. This sort of venture would have much to gain from public electronic markets. First, the pricing and car location process could be made much more convenient; second, the fixed pool of cars could be supplemented by individuals letting their car out, perhaps during their two weeks of holiday, into contractual chains of drivers each with an impeccable trading record. Whoever managed the car pool would have overall responsibility for the vehicle. Finally, city car schemes could be extended to cover much longer journeys. If a family required one way transport from Berlin to Nuremberg, for instance, a German GEMs system could automatically price the vehicle into an immediate return journey then arrange transfer between drivers, or via a local 'holder', with identifying code-words. It may be that this facility would become indistinguishable from the GEMs car hire market if thousands of dispersed owners were to decide to let out their vehicles when not required. Government could do much to encourage this activity. Tax breaks would be one step, so would GEMs terminals and reserved parking places for communal cars around city centres. Kerb-side boxes could be opened with PINs issued seconds earlier by a public access GEMs terminal at the car park. A couple who went to the theatre in one car might drive home in another, then deposit it on the rank near their house. The PIN they use to open the key deposit case on a nearby lamp post might be wired to another terminal that automatically registers the car's new position and the end of their hire. None of this would require particularly advanced technology, just government will.

Other low-cost, eco-friendly transport options that would become much more practicable in a coordinated marketplace include Middle Eastern-style shared taxis, summoned immediately via a GEMs display on the driver's dashboard and particularly valuable for regular journeys such as school runs. For shorter trips involving children, GEMs could, of course, draw up and underpin rotas of parents to walk from a neighbourhood to the school gates. Other environmental schemes particularly suited to public electronic markets might include a marketplace for squatters, allowing responsible inhabitation of temporarily empty buildings, or an urban greening initiative where scraps of land are identified for grants that local people can access to spend on approved plants. Once a small group of neighbours had accessed the money, signing contracts to accept responsibility for planting their purchases, officials from the grant provider would be able to use their copy of such contracts to check that the work had been done.

A sophisticated tax structure could help to consolidate deliveries, reducing road use. If the rate on a local delivery journey was highest for a one drop-off assignment and lowered for each additional job accepted through GEMs, automatic calculation of prices that include tax should ensure that, in a case where all local deliverers were pricing themselves equally, the first one to win an assignment for an hour hence would then collect other jobs in that vicinity, ahead of rivals. It would be up to government whether to distort the market for environmental ends.

Recycling could be driven by the GEMs market mechanism, rather than central administration. If aluminum cans, for instance, were made to carry a deposit repayable at the recycling plant, as is the case in some countries already, a market that moves their supply towards the smelter should develop organically. A family with perhaps 40 cans, accumulated in a bin under their sink, might put them up for sale with a couple of clicks in GEMs. Bought in a competitive market by a local 14-year-old who comes round to pick them up, crush them and add them to his hoard in the garden shed, they are then sold to a consolidator who will only collect once the teenager has 1000 cans, and so on. A chain in which each member subtracts their share of the value of the deposit ebbs and flows with the supply of cans. This is the kind of low-level market, largely infeasible with current overhead-heavy trading, that GEMs could originate.

Officially imposed quotas, too, could evolve from those rigidly imposed restraints on individual traders to market-driven controls across a whole industry. Trawlermen out at sea, for instance, landing their nets to discover an over-catch of plaice could use their GEMs terminal in the wheelroom, linked to land by a mobile phone, to purchase other boats' plaice quotas for that day. If plaice is easy to catch, the rising quota price should tempt a proportion of trawlers to stay in port and make their money on quota sales from a wide open market. Similar transfers between countries given a limit on polluting emissions have already been proposed. GEMs would roll out this kind of facility, like so many others, to individual traders.

People on benefits

Public electronic markets could easily handle social security payments for claimants willing to use the system. In time the system might even automate the process of deciding who is paid what. A GEMs user wishing to claim benefits could release their tamper-proof availability for work and pricing records to social security staff. If it is clear he has found bonding, then offered his services for sustained periods in active markets at minimum wage levels without finding work, he is obviously a temporary victim, rather than a shirker. If his claim is legitimised, state funds can be transferred to his account in successive weeks. In addition they might be earmarked for spending in specific markets on GEMs, food, transport and rent, for instance. This would benefit those claimants currently prone to extortion attempts on the day funds are moved into their account. Should he choose not to open his records to officials, GEMs obviously would not permit any surveillance of his activities on the system and even allow him to wipe his records, if he wished. Would this facility encourage traders to claim while working in the cash-in-hand economy? By releasing their records they would show that they had genuinely been available for work in GEMs and had been checking regularly for assignments, the non-completion of which would have resulted in fines being deducted from their bond and eventual expulsion from the system. More importantly, if the levers of tax and regulation had been adjusted to entice people into legitimate GEMs trading, there should be little incentive for buyers to hire, say, a car mechanic for cash. They would be ignoring the contracting and bonding mechanisms that would ensure a job well done, and any price advantage would be minimal. Once a GEM for car repairers achieved critical mass it should find pricing equilibrium at a level below which only cowboys were willing to trade.

The allocation of funds to the unemployed could be made automatic if politicians set up formulae for calculating allowances according to previous availability for work, circumstances and area of residence. Applicants would then fill in a GEMs template to learn of their entitlement, which would then be paid over as decreed by the formula. A PIN issued by the local doctor might be required if sickness payments were sought. This would be an area of enormous sensitivity. The consortium running public electronic markets would have to see that the system was constantly apart from government. Even a suspicion that they acted as an arm of the state could damage business prospects for GEMs systems in other countries. Despite the loss of the small fee subtracted from every payment, it would be very much in management's interest to see that a robust core of sceptics claimed their benefits the old-fashioned way.

This vision for electronic commerce aims to offer all citizens the right to trade on their own terms within a secure market. That capability could be extended to the lowest tiers of society, who may need extra help achieving the self-sufficiency that should be available from GEMs. Take, as an example, a former decorator who had hit a bad patch in his personal life and who repeatedly failed to turn up for bookings the system had found him, sacrificed his bond and he had been automatically banned from GEMs trading for 6 months. Instead of sitting idle on benefits, or trying to find work in what could be a very restricted market outside the system, he might join a closed GEMs market, overseen by social workers or perhaps a charity. Buying and selling in this forum would be open only to a local circle of people in a similar position. Although barred from selling in the wider market-place, they could engage each other to cut lawns and to do shopping, house cleaning and countless other tasks that would require adherence to a diary of commitments. Payment would be either in points, valueless outside that specific market, or in parallel economy points if a charity could persuade better-off users to donate them. GEMs would not dilute their value by doing so. By demonstrating consistent reliability in this market, the former decorator should find it easier to re-obtain an insurance bond when he is allowed back into the wider marketplace. To further widen the experience of participants, anyone overseeing these closed markets might persuade selected local people to tell GEMs they specifically wanted to hire from the closed market. The system would make it clear the trader they hired was not bonded and the trade could not be guaranteed.

12 A country with GEMs in a global economy: international advantage

Around 500 BC, the Kings of Lydia achieved dominance of their region by inventing money to replace direct barter of goods. In the 1980s, Singapore automated all export/import paperwork on a computer called TradeNet and became the busiest port in the world in terms of shipping tonnage. Countries that use technology in unique ways to develop their economic workings have often done well. A nation with fully functioning public electronic markets should be able to stand aloof from trends that other nations will have to accommodate in the age of linked online economies. New efficiencies and a galvanised domestic economy could create unequalled appeal for investors that transcends short-term considerations, such as interest rates or business cycles. The nation would, for instance, be particularly attractive to inward investors. Take, for example, a Korean company debating where to set up their European manufacturing facility. If, say, Spain had a GEMs system the company could open an account in a Madrid bank, then a GEMs account, based perhaps at their Spanish lawyer's address. Before leaving Seoul, they might access GEMs on the Internet and use their account to book an office suite and hire bi-lingual secretaries willing to work particularly long hours. Long-stay accommodation for a forward team and dependable support for their domestic lives could likewise be arranged in minutes. After putting purchased holds on various production facilities for hire on the system, then selecting a site, they could engage highly flexible staff, in their hundreds if necessary, to start work the following Monday. If there were a shortage of skilled workers, fitters qualified to work on a certain make of machine for instance, the company's demand would show up on market overview screens studied by mechanics around the country, who should then be able to click their way to the training required.

Might the Koreans be deterred by the competitiveness of the market in which they would be selling output from the new factory? If Spain was unique in its development of GEMs and the company planned to distribute across Europe, the advantages of purchasing and manufacturing in an efficient coordinated marketplace while selling in a price-heavy, relatively uninformed, uncoordinated equivalent could be overwhelming. As European integration proceeds, a nation willing to go it alone with public electronic markets alongside its adherence to all EU agreements on Internet trade could emerge as disproportionately attractive to foreign investment. Members of NAFTA, Mercosur or other regional trading pacts could be in a similar position. Individual companies in the country with GEMs would be equally equipped to extend their efficiencies abroad. A Spanish yacht maker, for instance, could send out a diaspora of representatives equipped with laptop access to GEMs over the Internet. Sitting beside a Cayman Islands millionaire, one of them would be able to input requirements for the construction of the desired craft for immediate costing. With not only company facilities but materials, additional labour and a delivery crew available for contracting instantly, the millionaire could have all his requirements competitively costed, timetabled and contracted during one visit to his poolside.

How would a country with GEMs interact with a globalizing economy? The existing online economy is dominated by US firms, who generated 85 per cent of global Internet revenues in 1997 even though only 62 per cent of Net users are thought to be Americans.[31] Because most households in the USA enjoy free local phone calls the country is likely to remain at the forefront of Internet take up for some time. Despite this dominance, there is currently widespread agreement between governments world wide about the need to encourage online transactions. Within four months in 1997, Europe, the USA and Japan issued separate policy documents focusing on the coming digital economy.[32] All three agreed broadly on a key principle for the trading revolution: government's role should be minimal, confined to the bare necessities of enacting unified new laws in cases where industry self-regulation did not work. The corporations driving the new technology are to be left free to decide how it develops. Freed from geographical restraints, companies trading digitally can site their computers anywhere in the world and still reach a global customer base. Countries with strong traditions of social welfare partially paid for by corporate taxation are unlikely to find favour with these nomadic institutions. As many commentators have already pointed out, collectively they are likely to play governments off against each other and base themselves only in the most capital-friendly havens.

Many see this lifting of national restrictions for businesses as a good thing. Both *Business Week*[33] and *Wired*,[34] the monthly bible of digital aficionados, have written approvingly of the 'long boom' anticipated from the descending prices and increased productivity of online business. From the perspective of their readership this is probably a reasonable long-term economic assessment. Elsewhere, however, a down-page news report in August 1998 shows the wider implications of these changes. British wine merchants Victoria Wine and Thresher are to close 300 shops and shed 1500 staff as they merge. The cutbacks come not as a result of traditional merger efficiencies or poor sales but because 'their online shopping profits have never been so good'.[35] Increased unemployment, caused by digital shopping, accompanied by low taxes, to placate the companies involved, form a potentially explosive social cocktail.

A GEMs country could stand back from this race to the floor of social provision. Instead of trying to tempt international money by minimizing negatives, it should be able to offer distinctive positives. Social and economic stability, corruption-free trading, low government expenditure plus a responsive and motivated workforce could be some of the points to be talked up by trade delegates. The social order and lower public spending that should accompany a GEMs system would give politicians room for manoeuvre that might be used to further protect their population from the economic buffeting of 'hot' money flashing around the world. Chile, for example, has experimented with minimum investment periods for outsiders to engender stability, but few Western countries could risk alienating the financial markets by acting likewise. If public electronic markets were to deliver their full potential, their country of operation would have a unique proposition for investors that could add considerable long-term value to its currency. Politicians need not live in fear of upsetting the markets.

Invisible trade, too, could benefit. Unless government decided otherwise, any foreign company could trade in the GEMs country by setting up a subsidiary. A Turkish hotel owner, for instance, might choose to sell his rooms in a Belgian public markets system rather than *en masse* to one of the country's tour operators. As soon as he had found insurance, or provided his own sum to go into bond, he could be in the market. Were other East Mediterranean hoteliers to do likewise, the Turkish tour companies may find it advantageous to open a 'brass plate' subsidiary in Brussels and start buying rooms for domestic tours departing from Ankara or Istanbul in GEMs, rather than over the phone. The longer a country could retain a monopoly on public markets in its region, the greater the advantage to be gained. A problem for politicians might be that foreign manufacturers were able to gain a toehold in the economy, previously denied to them. If they are able to undercut domestic suppliers in a pure market, the government might opt for protective tariffs.

As national cultures homogenize, with the continuing spread of global entertainment and cross-border business, GEMs could offer a tantalizing but intangible asset: national pride. Countries around the world have 're-branded' themselves in recent years. This project would create a sustainable difference beyond shallow perceptions: a sense of governmental purpose, rising above the confusing uncertainty that few doubt will engulf us as the unfettered digital economy really builds momentum. To quote a slogan of Silicon Valley's Palo Alto Research Center in 1970: 'the easiest way to predict the future is to invent it'.[36]

Notes to
section two

1. Hugh L. McColl Jr quoted in David Greising *et al.*, Trillion Dollar Banks: are megabanks – once unimaginable, now inevitable – better for customers, the nation's economy or even for the banks? *Business Week*, 27 April 1998, electronic edition.
2. Doing Business, *Business Week*, 31 August 1998, p. 55.
3. Edmund Mierswinski quoted in March of the Banking Behemoths, *Observer*, 19 April 1998, p. 5.
4. Barbara Wood, *E. F. Schumacher: His Life and Thought*, Harper & Row, 1984, p. 363.
5. *Wealth of Nations* (1776) Bk 1, ch. 10, Pt 2.
6. www.monster.com
7. www.peoplebank.com
8. Interview with the author, 4 August 1998.
9. How the Land Lies During Interviews, *Daily Telegraph*, 18 June 1998, p. A6.
10. *Voyager*, British Midland Airways in-flight magazine, September 1998, p. 43.
11. Analysis: Jobs and Pay, *Guardian*, 16 July 1998, p. 11.
12. Thompson P. and Warhurst C. (eds) *Workplaces of the Future*, Macmillan, 1998, p. 18.
13. Ibid. p. 9.
14. Open All Hours, *Commercial Motor Magazine*, 16–22 April 1998, p. 36.
15. Interview with the author, 3 September 1998.
16. Evan I. Schwartz, *Webonomics: Nine Essential Principals for Growing your Business on the World Wide Web*, Penguin, p. 140.
17. David Brown, *Cybertrends, Chaos Power and Accountability in the Information Age*, Viking, 1997, p. 116.
18. John Pearce, *At the Heart of the Community Economy; Community Enterprise in a Changing World*, Calouste Gulbenkian Foundation, 1993, p. 18.
19. Governor John Kitzhaber, quoted in How Far Can we Trust the People? *The Economist*, 15 August 1998, p. 41.
20. Drug Tower Tenants get Power to Ban Dealers, *Observer*, 26 July 1998.
21. George Monbiot, Gene Prince, *Guardian*, 9 June 1998.
22. Melanie Phillips, They say they reject a register of nannies because Mr Blair doesn't want a nanny state. Is this a joke? *Observer*, 12 July 1998.
23. Missionary Government, *Demos Quarterly*, 7, Demos, 1995, p. 47.
24. Peter Kellner, We can Pay, But What About the Cost? *Observer*, 12 May 1998.
25. Alexander Garrett, Why Everyone's Keen to Take a Swipe at Plans for a DSS Card, *Observer*, 9 August 1998, Business p. 7.

26. Keeping Tags on Cattle, *Daily Telegraph Connected*, 12 August 1998, p. 6.
27. EDS Humbug, *Private Eye*, 4 September 1998, p. 9.
28. *Thriving in the Shadows, The World in 1998*, Economist Publications, 1987, p. 16.
29. England's Green Unpleasant Land, *Observer*, 9 August 1998, p. 8.
30. Joachim Schwarz quoted in Car Sharing Means Less Jam Today, *Guardian*, 6 March 1996.
31. Interactive Media in Retail Group, *Electronic Commerce in Europe – an Action Plan for the Marketplace*, 1998.
32. *A European Initiative in Electronic Commerce*, April 1997; *Towards the Age of the Digital Economy*, MITI (Japan) White Paper, May 1997; *A Framework for Global Electronic Commerce* (US) July 1997.
33. The 21st Century Economy, cover story, *Business Week*, 31 August 1998.
34. The Long Boom, cover story, *Wired* (5.07), July 1997.
35. Check Out Hassle-free Online Shopping, *Guardian Editor*, 29 August 1998, p. 14.
36. Antony Sampson, *Company Man: The Rise and Fall of Corporate Life*, HarperCollins, 1995.

section
three

The battle for public markets: electronic trade becomes politicised

The German philosopher Schopenhauer wrote that truth 'passes through three stages. First it is ridiculed, then violently opposed. Finally it is accepted as being self-evident.' He could as easily have been writing about campaigns aimed at persuading governments to instigate new infrastructure for public use. Because Schopenhauer's stage three has now so obviously been reached with services such as postage, nationwide rail links, water and other everyday services, originally initiated by government, it is easy to lose sight of their earlier phases. The campaign for universal flat-rate postage for instance started in the UK and was widely derided by those in authority. Parliamentary commissioners who finally agreed to consider the idea were told by the British Postmaster General that 'of all the wild and visionary schemes which he had ever heard... it was the most extraordinary'.[1] Toll road and canal companies in the UK, who eventually realized parliament was serious in its consideration of acts to spur railway growth, were appalled that 'whereas all were free to use the roads... the villainous new railway companies would hold a monopoly of the traffic on the iron roads which they proposed to build across England'.[2] Playing on the conservatism of a little-travelled public, they invoked fears that cows would stop giving milk, as fiery machines blazed by killing the grass and stopping farm animals breeding. More ridiculously still they suggested 'ladies would have to travel through tunnels with pins in their mouths to stop anyone kissing them'.[3] Ten years later, when a crusade for centrally provided clean drinking water was underway, its opponents had refined the art of opposition to infrastructure proposals. Having overcome collective incredulity at politicians offering a vision for their industry, the existing supply companies in Britain bought a newspaper, the *Daily News*, in which they relentlessly attacked the individuals advocating a mass water network.[4] The possibility that electronic trade might also be developed for social benefit could follow a similar three-phase progression. Were a clear strand of opinion to emerge that wanted public electronic markets underpinned by government, it could lead to the first campaign for mass infrastructure in a developed country in living memory. The Internet, the most recent example of a centrally initiated infrastructure, was inaugurated without public debate by Pentagon chiefs. Before that, broadcasting was directed towards mass usage by governments on both sides of the Atlantic amid little significant opposition, possibly because the companies who were to be its main victims remained complacently in a Schopenhauerian phase one. As late as 1946, Darryl F. Zanuck, head of Twentieth Century Fox and Hollywood opinion leader, believed '[television] won't be able to hold on to any market it captures after the first six months. People will soon get tired of staring at a plywood box every night.'[5]

This section looks at the possibility that the evolution of electronic commerce might become a dominant political issue. Should development be left to short-term commercial forces, with perhaps a little backstop regulation, or would Guaranteed Markets be made available to all who want them? The first route already has its priorities clear: it is driven very much by a vision of super service for a generation of restless online buyers. 'Right here. Right now. Tailored for my idea of useful or cool. Dished up the way I like it. Stripped to the core, that is what the new consumer's expectations are', writes consultant Regis McKenna, author of *Real Time: Preparing for the Age of the Never Satisfied Customer*.[6] But individuals are multifaceted and often want more from life than instant material gratification. They also seek intangibles, such as a stable society, personal empowerment and richness of experience. These social factors do not necessarily flow from a world in which formidable new technology is developed primarily to woo the most rapacious customers. The first chapter of this section explores the possibility that e-trade with no accompanying vision from government could become its own worst enemy, causing inequalities and market distortions likely eventually to provoke a backlash against the technology. Assuming individuals in their capacity as voters, rather than customers, will eventually become a force in the trading revolution, the next chapter outlines steps politicians might take to instigate electronic markets for mass benefit. Likely opposition to such a move is discussed in the chapter that follows. There are valid concerns to be raised in response to the idea of government-initiated markets, not least the undesirability of one operator being awarded certain advantages by the state and the perilous consequences of any system failure. These are examined. So, too, is the possible reaction of powerful organizations who would have much to lose as an economy atomised. A final chapter in this section asks which countries would have the most to gain from launching a first public electronic markets system.

chapter

13 Could there be a backlash against electronic shopping?

The disproportionate benefits of online trade for large sellers

US phone company AT&T used to run a seductive commercial in which two young women, dismayed at the shortcomings of their hard plastic sunglasses, set up in business making a more pliant alternative. Although the mechanics of manufacture present no problem, their newly founded company, Rubbereyes, cannot find retail distribution. In despair, they turn to AT&T Web Site Services, start selling over the Internet and enjoy swift success. This notion, that Net selling will, by its nature, create one level playing field in which a small newcomer can immediately reach world-wide consumers, has been enthusiastically propagated, not least by companies who would like to see every corner store and lone trader setting up a website. The reality, however, is shaping up very differently. 'People say there are no limits to channels on the Internet. But that's not the limiting factor here. The real limits are how to get through to people and get their attention', explains one commentator.[7] The number of online enthusiasts who will enter, say, 'sunglasses' into Internet search software then laboriously peruse even a few of the 190 000 sites returned at time of writing is diminishing sharply. Instead, interactive shoppers increasingly call up a 'one stop' site that allows them to shop with a manageable number of pre-selected retailers. These Net 'portals' are widely seen as the way forward in Net commerce because they simplify a range of online facilities, including shopping. With millions of users visiting a typical portal every day, the operators can sell their virtual real estate to the highest-bidding retailers. A regular visitor to the Netscape Netcentre, for instance, who clicks for finance information will find the subsequent display favouring the product range of Citibank. The US institution is reported to have agreed to payment of $40 million over three years for this prime cyber-space location.[8] Other portals offer customers the facility to search product databases of several partner retailers in search of their require-ments. Without one of these expensive relationships, restricted to big suppliers who keep the number of virtual storefronts manageable, outfits like the fictional Rubbereyes will probably find benefits of the new marketplace pass them by. To quote *Fortune* magazine: 'launching an e-commerce site without a Portal partner is like opening a retail store in the desert. Sure, it's cheap, but does anybody stop there?'[9]

It is not just issues of visibility that are beginning to conspire against small traders in the uncoordinated marketplace. Another problem arises from the changing role of computers in organizations. In its early days, business computing was seen merely as a way to cut costs by automating administration. Now intricate exploitation of information is at the core of many corporations' activities. The bigger the enterprise, the more intelligence it possesses and the greater sophistication with which this can be applied. In 1985, the airline People Express was an early victim of this potential. Running a strictly no-frills service and undercutting major carriers, the company was for a while the fastest growing in the US. It was SABRE, American Airlines' enormous order-taking system, that largely reversed their growth. Using the system's vast reserves of data on load patterns and pricing sensitivity, American began to offer dozens of fares for any one departure, automatically changing the mix in response to demand until the gate closed. Seats that could only be filled with backpackers willing to accept travel restrictions were priced below People Express rates, while high-revenue generating business travellers were still sold expensive open tickets. Within a year of SABRE being unleashed in this way, People Express, with no market insights on a comparable scale, had lost half their market share. The company was sold off in 1986.[10]

Today, it is not only information about market sensitivities but details of individual customers that offers added leverage to those who possess it in enormous quantities. US retailer JCPenney, for instance, holds records on 98 million customers including particularly detailed records on the transactions of 17 million store card holders.[11] In the early days of vast databases this information could have been processed through online analytical processing (OLAP) software to answer questions such as 'what were our five top selling lines last year?' or 'how many customers closed their account with us in the last six months compared to the first half of the year?' That simplistic interrogation has now been superseded by complex 'data mining' capabilities that predict behaviour. Store chiefs can ask 'which customers are likely to switch their accounts to a competitor in the next six months?' or 'which additional products are most likely to be sold with a purchase of men's shoes?'[12] Desirable individuals whose spending traits suggest they are in the process of switching to a competitor can then be targeted with lower prices or extra services. Any male footwear buyer can be offered the additional purchases that he is most likely to accept. Corporations using these predictive tools keep their findings to themselves but there is little doubt of their efficacy as they continue to mature. A 1998 presentation from Swiss Bank Corporation, 'Using Data Mining to Identifying Behaviour', showed how such systems can teach themselves: drawing together strands that mere humans in the marketing department may have missed.[13] The resulting leanness of operation and understanding of the marketplace extracted from bigger and bigger data pools are crucial drivers towards ever larger corporations.

AT&T's idealized two-women-and-an-idea business would probably suffer additionally for its lack of a recognized brand name. Unlike three dimensional shopping, which at least imbues traders who set up a premises with some measure of solidity, the online buyer cannot see behind a web site. There could be a keen and professional outfit waiting to despatch his sunglasses or a group of fly-by-nights who will take his money and disappear. It is always a temptation to confine credit card details to known names that have been around for some time. Certainly, fledgling brands are emerging on the Net but they increasingly represent a new big name, not a diversity of small traders. Amazon.com, for instance, became a force in book retailing in just a few months but it is one monolithic organization that displaced others slow to understand the winner-takes-all potential of Net trade. Few industry leaders will be so slow in the future.

This landscape, where big players are able to lever their strength in the old economy to near domination of the new, will be set in stone when interactive home shopping graduates from the complications of Internet access to less intimidating two-way television services. You cannot create a web site of your own on a TV set. Nor can companies not approved by the broadcaster offer their wares. *Information Strategy* magazine reports 'broadcasters are prepared to fight tooth and nail rather than use digital television to give their viewers direct Internet access'.[14] The technical requirements of retailing by interactive television form an additional barrier to entry. Because they demand richness of broadcast content that can be manipulated by a user who has no significant processing power in his set, such sites will cost between $800 000 and $1 600 000, according to one software company already geared up for this market.[15] Viewers must then be confined to these sites, not free to seek out bargains from cheaper operators. The intention is to retain viewers and their spending potential within a 'walled garden', explains a senior executive at the ironically named Open TV, a company providing underlying operating software for two-way television.[16]

As a highly convenient and reliable new marketplace on interactive television sets is unrolled for the exclusive benefit of powerful retailers, market diversity will diminish further. In the bricks and mortar world of, say, travel agency anyone could still set up their own high street premises and draw some customers from the existing operators, by virtue either of a niche specialization or catchment area. The first advantage is not sustainable in the digital age; if a niche is worth having, the Thomas Cook store on Open interactive television can enter it immediately. They no longer need additional salespeople or display space. The uniqueness of a catchment area disappears likewise; Thomas Cook's Open front end becomes the nearest, most convenient travel agent to anyone connected to the system. Walter Forbes, an early visionary of online shopping and former chairman of Cendant Corporation, one of its undoubted success stories in terms of consumer take-up, has predicted a shake-out of companies selling online 'which will make the restaurant business look stable'. He believes fewer than 15 companies will end up making 80 per cent of online sales.[17] The worst consequences of this 'closing of capitalism' are suggested by recent actions of supermarket chains in the UK. Having underpriced and out-convenienced a former tapestry of neighbourhood stores, the now unchallengeable chains responded to their new playing field by ruthlessly controlling suppliers, increasing margins to the point where British shoppers pay a third more than those in Germany or the USA, and becoming a significant force in political lobbying in an attempt to maintain their *status quo*.[18]

There will always be specialized suppliers who find a niche and develop a level of customer relationships with which no large player can compete, a site selling art deco lamps to appreciative enthusiasts for instance. But if the new very attractive marketplace is left to develop with no wider vision than immediate commercial considerations it is likely to emerge as a platform on which the bulk of activity flows through large corporations. Unlike the paternalistic firms that signified national achievement in previous decades, tomorrow's big players are likely to be increasingly unpopular. They will certainly be free of the need to employ anything like the numbers they have in the past. The consequence of cheaper goods and hassle-free shopping could be dramatically increased unemployment. In Britain, to take one example, over 10 per cent of jobs are retail related. Interactive shopping needs only offer a small advantage to tip high streets into the beginning of a downward spiral of increasing relative prices and reduced ranges, accompanied by progressive job cuts. But even this scenario does not reveal the full extent of the social and economic damage new trading technology could conceivably cause if left purely to the uncoordinated market.

Market force: the black arts available to online marketeers

The business elite currently driving the trading revolution enjoy a rarefied life. As they relentlessly pursue new frontiers in profitability, dealing with the highest levels of the aggressive companies who fund their activities, they are in danger of developing values that may not play well once they become more widely recognized. 'A battle is imminent' averred a 1998 statement from Britain's well respected Interactive Media in Retailing Group 'to own the consumer and to control these new channels to them'.[19] In other words it is not enough to be a powerful player, the aim is then to distort the electronic marketplace. The phrase 'owning the customer' was much in vogue in e-commerce publications and presentations in late 1997 and early 1998. It translates as controlling the information that a consumer must give about themselves as part of an initial transaction to see that they subsequently have little incentive to shop anywhere else. This should be presented as a

benefit offered by your company. An airline, for instance, to which you
have told your credit card details plus seating and meal preferences for
an initial ticket, then automatically applies them to every future flight
booked on their site. If you are in a hurry you are likely simply to book
with them rather than shopping for a better fare which might entail
repeating the information to a second carrier. Additionally, the
company owning the information can contact the customer with offers
based on past patterns of purchase. More advanced programming is
being developed by other sellers hoping to reap the same benefit. A
marketing newsletter tells the story of North Carolina-based
Textile/Clothing Technology Corp. who have introduced a scanning
device in stores that can pinpoint more than 300 000 points on the body
using an array of cameras. Once measured, a consumer can then order
personalised garments from the company. The newsletter notes 'the
challenge facing [the company] is making sure the customer can't walk
away with measurement data that can be carried to a competitor and
used successfully'.[20] In the GEMs model, by contrast, this kind of
personal data could be input by any user, in this case with a tape
measure or through a device attached to the system by someone
charging for its use, and harnessed by them to shop around at will.

Facilities like body scanners do not come cheaply and for maximum
profitability need to be concentrated on customers who have plenty of
money to spend. This is no longer difficult to achieve. The practice of
charging richer customers lower fees to retain their business has long
been practised, among credit providers for instance: it is becoming both
widespread and more finely honed. An emerging science, Customer
Value Management, enables individuals to be assessed by a company's
computer for their profitability to the firm. Instead of the market as a
whole supporting a certain standard of service for everyone, as has
previously been the case, a firm's resources can then be targeted at the
well off. The leading evangelists of this movement are Don Peppers and
Martha Rogers who run a Stamford, Connecticut, marketing consultancy and published the seminal *Enterprise One to One: Tools for
Competing in the Interactive Age* in 1997.[21] They advise companies to
segment customers by profitability potential, present and future, so
someone identified as a student, for example, might have low value for
a furniture retailer but is worth cultivating for their spending potential
after graduation.

At the bottom of the Peppers and Rogers metric are 'below zeros' or BZs, consumers who 'will probably never earn enough profit to justify the expense involved in serving them. Every business has some of these customers, and our objective should be to get rid of them.'[22] The duo admit 'dealing with BZs is definitely a ticklish problem',[23] not because of any social concerns but for fear of a public relations disaster. Their book documents the story of First Chicago bank whose goal was 'to find a gracious way to help its unprofitable customers become some other bank's unprofitable customers'.[24] The solution: to charge clients with little money in their accounts more for certain transactions.[25] Doing so did eventually contribute significantly to reduced costs of operation but the tactic was spotted and made headlines. As Customer Value Management tools become increasingly sophisticated, there are fewer examples of such a blunt approach to the dumping of undesirable customers and less chance of the companies doing so facing the public scrutiny suffered by First Chicago. Peppers and Rogers are not fringe thinkers, embarrassing to mainstream electronic commerce developers. In 1997 IBM was giving away a sponsored edition of *Enterprise One to One* at conferences in Europe: in 1998 Oracle, a big supplier of business software, announced a global partnership with the duo's consulting firm.[26]

Pioneers of the trading revolution are putting considerable effort into refining Customer Value Management tools that enable their computers more subtly to assess the worth of any customer. This process will become easier still as trading moves online and, once again, it favours large companies with an extensive customer base. One 1998 survey found as many as 40 or 50 per cent of retail customers are actually not profitable.[27] With online sellers no longer needing to maintain a minimum level of service the underclass are likely to find they are discreetly earmarked for expulsion by many service providers. Crucial to this ruthless new approach to marketing is the ability of those operating sales channels to compile information about their customers and trade it with other providers. 'We'll all have to get used to the fact that there will simply be less privacy' writes *Wired* magazine in their *Encyclopaedia of the New Economy*.[28] Automated marketing techniques feed on details of individual lives which are being gathered from increasingly ingenious sources. An advertisement in Britain's *Direct Marketing* magazine for March/April 1998 offers to sell a database of 'affluent home improvers'.

The firm offering the data, Glenigan Direct Marketing Solutions, has had no dealings with these householders: it has gleaned their status from 'planning applications nation-wide'. As early as 1995 a report into the future of electronic commerce warned 'it is now possible to assemble a profile of an individual that draws upon quite disparate sources of data – health care information, consumer purchases, banking habits, movies watched, travel and dining habits gleaned from credit card transactions and so on'.[29]

Means of collecting this information continue to advance, driven by the competitive advantages of new marketing methodologies. A Colorado-based company, Earthwatch Inc., has launched the first commercially accessible spy satellite. It allows marketing departments to purchase detailed photographs of homes, perhaps clocking what make of car sits on the drive or whether they would have space for a backyard swimming pool.[30] Insensitive use of personal data can undisputedly provoke hostile sentiments from consumers, *The Economist* has reported on one woman who tried to break her relationship with a supermarket chain after receiving an automatically generated letter reminding her it was time she replenished supplies of tampons.[31] Online trade bodies are aware of these concerns and have responded with groupings such as TRUSTe which allows subscribing organizations to display an award mark in return for signing up to principles that protect shoppers' privacy. A weakness here, as the trade magazine *Future Shopping* notes, is '[the] possibility that policies might change after the data was collected'.[32] It is not clear how these self-regulating schemes will evolve as electronic commerce concentrates on to interactive television channels. It may be hard for governments to rule effectively on online privacy, as information can so easily be moved around the world to offshore 'data havens' by unscrupulous operators. Once again, a GEMs system would offer a different approach, assiduously protecting its users' information within a closed network. More importantly it could remove much of the incentive to collect personal details by any other route. Buyers in GEMs would automatically find their best value deal instantly, there would be little point incurring overheads to build a relationship with them unless they expressly wished to form that bond (Box 13.1).

Box 13.1

GEMS AND USER PRIVACY

GEMs would have an unequivocal approach to confidentiality. The system invites constant inspection to demonstrate it is simply not capable of collating details of an individual user's activities or preferences. Standard contracts include a 'no unsolicited communications' clause which a seller can remove at the risk of turning away potential buyers or a buyer can remove if they want to be kept informed by a particular seller. Information about a user's trades could only be accessed with a court order. Suppose for example a distraught wife rings the control room of a future Brazilian GEMs system at 1.00 am to say she knows her spouse has booked accommodation in Rio that night and she needs to know the address because their daughter has had an accident. That may be the case, alternately she might suspect him of entertaining a mistress and be planning to go round and spoil the party. That is not a judgement, between the man's absolute right to privacy and his likely wish to be informed of a familial catastrophe, that GEMs staff would be empowered to make. If the wife wants his records on the system opened she must obtain a court order, possibly over the phone from a duty judge, which will include a PIN. This becomes the equivalent of a launch code in a missile bunker, allowing staff to open the man's record of most recent contracts which are sent blind to the judge's terminal. It would be his decision what information is revealed to the wife. A message is automatically left for the husband telling him what has happened.

The potential impact of uncoordinated electronic commerce on society

The early days of technological revolutions have often been economically intoxicating but socially damaging. Even as Britain ascended to domination of global manufacturing on the back of the Industrial Revolution, small children were learning to work 12-hour days in her factories. Philanthropists who questioned this were blankly assured that a need to remain competitive forced factory owners to extract maximum value from the families they housed. Only after the inhumanity of the revolution became inarguable were Factory Acts, limiting the age of employees, forced on grudging industrialists who collectively tended to believe their new vista of wealth creation should advance without hindrance. Some electronic trade gurus have shown themselves dangerously prone to the same view. It may yet emerge that the trading revolution will likewise add to the sum of human misery even as it delights economists and investment analysts. No-one seriously disputes that the move to an online economy will destroy jobs, for instance. Hardware supplier Cisco, one of the early giants of Net selling, has saved itself a reported $363 million a year and the need for 1000 employees by automating its order taking through a web site.[33] Its customer companies, too, save on labour costs because there is no paperwork or payment procedures. The hotly contested point is: will new avenues of work emerge to replace the retail, supply management and finance jobs now being decimated? In the short term there is little shortage of employment for computing personnel but this may only be a temporary bonus as companies switch to new technology and then settle down to years of updates by a skeleton staff. Two journalists on the German news magazine *Der Spiegel* analysed the underlying trends in developed world employment for a book and concluded that eventually 20 per cent of the workforce will suffice to keep the economy going. The remainder will be perpetually surplus to requirements.[34] Defenders of the new online economy, however, point to a sustained growth in service industries, particularly call centre operations. Assuming they are correct and this booming sector will ultimately cancel out the downsizing in other industries, what quality of employment will it offer?

Customer care in a world where companies enjoy unprecedented computing power demands a very different salesperson from the traditional ambassador for his employer. A 1998 UK report described call centres, the fastest growing employment sector in the British economy, as 'the ultimate form of industrial tyranny'.[35] Serried ranks of operators are usually expected to complete between 100 and 150 near identical calls a day with only seconds between them.[36] The operations manager of one such centre for the British Halifax Direct financial services company explains, 'there is no button pushing, the system dials and as soon as the call goes through it is routed to a free agent. This means agents can maximize the time they spend talking to customers.'[37] Dialogue is read from a computer screen which is where the intelligence of the system resides. A website for Graham Technology, one of the companies supplying call centres boasts their GT-X software analyses the result of each call as input by operators and '"learns" which scripts are most effective in terms of results and the minimum number of steps to complete the transaction'.[38] Monitoring employee productivity in this environment presents no problems; 'the tyranny of the assembly line is but a Sunday school picnic compared with the control that management can exercise in computer telephony', surmised the report's authors.[39] Rate of calls and their duration for each worker on a shift are routinely collated, the actual words spoken can be taped for later analysis. The efficiency demanded by many centres dictates that staff dare not take coffee or lunch breaks away from their desks for fear of rebuke.[40] Despite one in four British call centre operators being a university graduate, there is virtually no hope of promotion: performance is monitored for senior management by the central computer with only a handful of supervisors required.[41] Is there a danger of this conveyor belt communication being a turn off for customers? Human warmth can be made part of the script. A former call centre operator, writing to a newspaper in February 1998, attested to the tiring nature of her work, which demanded a new call be answered within a second of the old one finishing and added 'if you didn't get in the "closing salutation" you would be assigned to retraining'.[42] This new role for business computing, as day-to-day driver of the organization, with closely monitored humans carrying out its decisions, can only increase as software developments like Enterprise Resource Planning penetrate further into the market.

Despite this maximized productivity, call centre operations are expensive, which makes them vulnerable. One US survey puts the average total cost of each call at $3.21.[43] A medium-term threat to call centre jobs comes from mass migration away from the phone towards screen-based shopping through interactive television sets. Customer service need not suffer in this new environment. Programming that mimics a human dialogue when potential customers type in their individual enquiry is already well developed. E-mail a few lines to Insure Direct in the USA, for example, asking for a quote on motor cover and its computer will communicate back and forth in an individualised conversation.[44] Because the firm have shaved that $3.21 off the cost of each interaction they may well be able to offer a lower price than elsewhere.

Guaranteed Electronic Markets could offer a long-term alternative to mind-numbing and insecure work in call centres and other lowly business functions. A country with GEMs would enable its citizens effortlessly to seek their own mix of work, including time at a call centre on their own terms if they wished. Take as an instance a young woman who currently answers the phone for a financial sector employer: she may have initially been attracted to that post because of an aptitude for figures and a desire to help people. With GEMs on her side those factors would provide far wider choice. She might for instance hire herself out as a coach for schoolchildren having problems with their arithmetic, as a financial planner for local enterprises or as an expert in very particular investment vehicles whose knowledge can be bought over the phone by the hour. In each market she would be scheduled according to personal priorities, have every incentive to upgrade her qualifications and reap the rewards of a stable trading record. If pickings were lean, she could additionally enter the market for general clerical work signifying a willingness to work in call centres. Her life could be enriched in this way once politicians offered a vision for electronic commerce to run alongside the current exploitation by corporations. The point is not that governments have any inherent duty to provide richness and variety of experience for their electorates. Simply that it might soon be a vote winner to do so. It is also worth considering that the bright young woman reduced to conversations parroted from her computer screen for 40 hours a week is contributing a fraction of her economic potential to society, compared with a motivated and flexible trader spanning several markets as she responds to ever-changing local conditions.

In many sections of society people who work in call centres are regarded as the lucky ones: they have a job. The long-term unemployed are not a topic that merit much discussion at e-commerce conferences. As one round table put it, 'we don't need what they have and they can't buy what we sell'.[45] But in most developed countries these people have votes and they may not like what they see as the online marketplace begins to bite. Unable to afford the hardware for Internet or interactive TV shopping, and of little interest to sellers even if they could, they are likely to be meeting their needs from what remains of high-street retailing after it has been progressively vacated by the better off. The lingering demise of shopping centres could remove what is often the last safe community space for many. Social provision can only be restricted in an era where governments must compete with low tax regimes to entice foreign investment and keep their own companies competitive on the world stage. Realistic hopes of a job are already folklore in depressed areas of first world countries. In the UK, for example, nearly

40 per cent of the tens of thousands of 16-year-olds who leave school without significant qualifications fail to find work or further training.[46] The grey economy becomes a continued temptation for these young people, further depriving state services of tax income and increasing the fear of the lawless world beyond their front door that others perceive.

What can governments do to improve quality of life for their electorates if they decide to go with the current flow of online developments rather than offering their own vision with a GEMs style system? Few commentators dispute that multinational businesses are already becoming more powerful at the expense of national politicians. Some argue this is a good thing, because at least businesses have a sense of direction and tendency towards efficiency. But the story of the Canadian parliament's conflict with the Virginia-based Ethyl Corporation in July 1998 illustrates the fears behind the opposing view. Ethyl manufacture MMT, a fuel additive thought by some scientists to be a dangerous pollutant.[47] After a debate the Ottawa parliament voted to ban the substance in April 1997. Under the terms of NAFTA (North American Free Trade Agreement) however, Ethyl sued the government alleging unfair barriers to trade had been raised. With little chance of upholding their judgement, Canada's legislators capitulated to the corporation and agreed to pay the firm $13 million in compensation. The framework of NAFTA is similar to that of the, as yet unrealized, Multilateral Agreement on Investment or MAI which will, many believe, allow big businesses to shape a global marketplace suiting their priorities in the online age rather than the concerns of national governments. Defeated in April 1998, the MAI is scheduled for a new round of preliminary negotiations with a view to becoming international law in the future.[48]

The sum of bleak projections in this chapter may not be the outcome of a mature uncoordinated online economy. It could be that the portal model does not last and Internet shoppers find ways of traversing all sorts of sales outlets with total faith in the results. Interactive TV shoppers might then successfully demand access to the untamed Internet so they can do the same (thereby destroying the business model for an entire sector). Either the US model of industry regulation or the European belief in enforced restraint may resolve issues of privacy. And high quality jobs for the masses could emerge from a source as yet largely unforeseen. If this were to happen, GEMs could be no more than the final step on a road towards wide-open online marketplaces. If, however, the trends at the time of writing converge further, we could be heading for a two-tier online economy. The well off will eventually enjoy handy, secure and low-cost access to large suppliers who fight for their custom. An underclass, who are at best tolerated by operators of the new channels, will have to contend with poorly developed buyer–seller matching services on the Internet, in which the buyer has to beware at every stage of the transaction. In this case underpinned public markets would offer a completely alternative route.

It is possible that the voracious computerisation of capital flows, order taking and product marketing may contain the seeds of its own collapse. In *One World Ready or Not: the Manic Logic of Global Capitalism*,[49] journalist William Greider compares the new economy to a powerful runaway machine rampaging through countryside with no one at the wheel. As that machine builds momentum it is difficult to see who will enjoy any sustained advantages from its progress. Large businesses? Initially yes, but in the longer term they could see their customer bases truncated as more and more people are excluded from significant participation in economies. Company executives? But the marketplace is increasingly unstable; mergers and acquisitions often result in scant respect for valuable career histories and the pressure to deliver increasing returns can be inescapable. It is telling that personal counselling services for senior executives are mushrooming.[50] Owners of capital? In an acute irony it is often the individuals being downsized and marginalized who provide the money, through pensions and savings, with which fund managers are working so pitilessly to obtain the best return. Customers? There will be those so enamoured with falling comparative prices and immediate gratification but untroubled by the wider state of society who will welcome uncoordinated e-trade even after any pernicious effects are clear. But GEMs would also offer lower prices, across a far wider range of markets. Those who hold principles of non-government intervention higher than social conditions could start to become a minority.

Would financial companies, retailers and service providers really offload staff while targeting only well-off individuals for sales, thereby ultimately shrinking the number of people who are economically active enough to be potential customers? Could a whole industry charge into new technology with so little consideration for its wider long-term effects? It has happened before. A few decades ago equipment developed for submarine warfare allowed fishing boats to precisely locate shoals of fish, which could then be instantly scooped up in a new generation of super nets. It was pointed out at the time that once this became commonplace the biological diversity on which trawling's future rested would be compromised but individual skippers reasoned that the big picture was someone else's problem. As the previous vagaries of deep sea netting gave way to trawlers leaving port for a precise destination at which point they simply harvested a boat load of marine life and returned, governments found themselves unable to prevent an impending crisis. The problems were similar to those that will face any parliament trying to rein in e-commerce. If Iceland had successfully commanded its trawlers to stop hauling cod out of the North Atlantic those fish would simply have ended up in boats bound for Newfoundland. By 1992 the targeting and gathering efficiencies of trawling technology had laid waste to fragile food chains and left entire species commercially extinct. Governments and the industry finally agreed to implement quotas, which saw boats around the world decommissioned while communities wait for the previous diversity to re-establish itself. The comparative richness of our economic life could conceivably be demolished by paradigm-shifting technology as inexorably as was the diversity of species on our fishing grounds.

Government's response to maturing e-trade

It is the contention of this book that the future of online commerce is going to become a subject of sustained public debate sooner or later. Multinational businesses and their consultants should not be held as villains in this scenario. They exist, as firms always have, to pursue profitable opportunities as they arise. Corporations have no mandate to restrict their potential in pursuit of amorphous, off balance sheet, social objectives. It is governments who will eventually have to face the problems caused by selective new efficiencies in commerce. They could opt to constrain the technology, but national restraints risk being counterproductive in a globalised arena. Industry self-regulation would avoid the need for legislative action but, as with the world's trawler captains, it may take epoch-defining calamity to unite participants on this course. Another option would simply be for governments to accept they can do more than sit on the sidelines of the trading revolution and put a system of Guaranteed Markets in place, while leaving global business channels to go their own way. *Information Strategy* magazine, aimed at a corporate readership, examined the possibility of GEMs in February 1998 after an interview with this author. 'If any government did seek to intervene in the market in such a way there would be very loud howls of protest from some very powerful companies' they wrote in an editorial headed 'Behave or else…'. It continued: 'but what is the alternative? If governments adopt a completely *laissez-faire* approach they risk leaving themselves and a large number of their citizens completely powerless.'[51] It would be a brave parliament that began outlining a social vision for electronic commerce, but one motivated by understanding of a changed world rather than ingrained ideology. The notion of public electronic markets transcends philosophies of left or right. True, it would require fleeting government involvement in the initiatory phase but any rightist condemning the concept as left wing for that reason must attach the same label to Margaret Thatcher's Channel Tunnel project. GEMs' immediate beneficiaries would include the currently poor but they would be elevated not by handouts or centrally imposed restrictions on the well off. Instead closer equality would come from the chance to participate in what could be some of the most uncompromised free markets the world would ever have seen. Crucially, those markets would no longer be protective of big players. The broad aims of Karl Marx might be achieved by the philosophy of Adam Smith.

History suggests there is an inevitability about new technology being channelled towards maximum social benefit by policy makers. Debate can be fierce but it has a tendency to cross party lines. For example, 150 years ago an arch priest of non-government intervention, Nassau Senior, considered problems of sanitation and proposals for public water supply in Britain before writing 'with all our reverence for the principle of non-interference, we cannot doubt that in this matter it has been pushed too far'.[52] Another infrastructure scheme, universal flat rate postage, was introduced by a Whig (centre party) parliament in the UK but nurtured, and defended from attacks, by its Tory (rightist) successor, then, once it was seen to work, initiated by governments of all hues around the world. Railways, roads, telephones and broadcasting spread across the world as public infrastructure, with governing ideologies able only to speed or delay their introduction by a few years. Notable exceptions, South

Africa's resistance to the liberalising potential of television until the 1970s for instance, hardly halted that medium's otherwise relentless advance and only increased the apartheid regime's isolation. It might take only one country to successfully demonstrate the benefits of officially underpinned electronic markets before they started to spread to other nations. There are some countries in which public debate has become too calcified around unquestioned belief that government inactivity is always the preferable option for GEMs ever to be launched. Other nations could be more pragmatic.

14

How a government could instigate GEMs

The act that launched a GEMs service would need plotting in immense detail to ensure it achieved its desired effect, an outcome that can never be guaranteed. The US Telecommunications Act of 1996, for instance, was intended to open the telephony market to a wide range of sellers but instead encouraged big players to consolidate.[53] In the case of GEMs, the aim would be to shape a viable business opportunity for the winning consortium while ensuring benefits of trading technology were spread as widely as possible. Once the official protection for a potential system and its accompanying obligations had been crafted and a winning consortium selected, the goals both of parliament and the consortium would be very similar. In a democracy, both would need the new markets to grow while having every reason to continuously assert their independence from each other. Even in countries where many utilities are state run it would be undesirable for parliament to control a GEMs system: the technology has social implications that puts it on a par with broadcasting rather than water or electricity supply. Furthermore, politicians around the world have proved themselves spectacularly inept at articulating a consistent vision for large computer projects. Past evidence suggests that, once a vision is outlined, it is the private sector that should make it reality. Both sides of the pact should adhere to a fundamental principle of GEMs: taxpayers do not fund the project and no one is ever to be forced to use the system (except in the context of a professional relationship at the behest of an employer). Another absolute is that the launch not be predicated on any attempt to restrict the non-GEMs world of online commerce in any way. There would not, for instance, be a repeat of the French government's effective outlawing of Teletext to protect a nascent Minitel online service in the 1980s.

Politicians would probably be tempted to launch part of a GEMs service rather than the full system, which could unite so many powerful opponents. They might opt for a system that trades periods of work, for instance, but lacks the critical mass and software efficiencies of other sectors. That is to risk being a national also-ran if other countries move to full underpinned public electronic markets. A consortium that is looking to a future building additional countries' GEMs-style facilities would be rightly cautious of such an opportunity, particularly if they were expected to obtain a return using the 'penny post' model of radically low pricing. A parliament truly committed to the full GEMs vision would need to instigate changes that would run through to every nerve end of government. The first politicians along this road would suffer the hardest battles; once a first country had a system in operation, later entrants would at least have a map to follow. However a consortium serious about GEMs might treat the first country in which it wins a commission as a loss leader, to be allocated additional spending so the markets evolve more quickly.

What do governments have to offer a winning consortium?

The package of benefits enshrined in law for a winning consortium should include:

- ◼ 'Must carry' status with high visibility, mandated on the nation's television platforms. This would be akin to the British government's decision to award key multiplexes (channels) on its digital spectrum to the established broadcasters on the grounds that those organizations are crucial to national culture. Where a very low number channel was no longer available, GEMs would be assured of a prominently flagged position in the main programme guides.
- ◼ Contracts on the system to be legally enforced with GEMs specifically absolved from ever being judged a counterparty in any deal enacted between its users. The courts would need to uphold contracts drawn up by the system and accept its mechanism for freezing monies until resolution. Further, court officials around the country would accept disputed transactions forwarded automatically by the system and input judgement on their GEMs terminals, so that the system could apply any fines awarded.

- Pump priming of the markets. All government buying, selling and staff rostering goes through the system in its initial stages. If the prison service is buying bread, for instance, it shops first in GEMs and has to justify a decision to then buy elsewhere on grounds of better value. Hospital staff are scheduled through their individual GEMs diaries, which they can control with the same flexibility as any other user. If they do not wish to connect to the system at home, they could of course use a terminal at work.

- The system is allowed the highest levels of encryption and legal protection of users' privacy because of its near crime-free status.

- A raft of miscellaneous legislation that acknowledges the safety of trading in a GEMs environment would also be required. As the insurance function is so important to the new marketplace, for instance, the rules on who can act as an insurer might be relaxed. For example an individual with $200 to invest for a week might put it in GEMs bond and sell the cover to someone at the opposite end of the country who was hiring herself out to iron neighbours' clothes during that period. So long as she did not exceed say five bookings that could be all the cover for accidental damage to garments she would require: her trading record would automatically rank the statistical likelihood of an insurer having to pay out for her negligence. With freeing of regulations, the GEMs capital market could instantly show investors where their most profitable opportunity for a chosen level of risk was to be found across the entire spectrum of demand for money. Likewise lawyers need to be enabled to work across the board on a no-win no-fee basis (Box 14.1).

- State agencies would also need to be made ready for the system. The driver licensing authority for example would need to start issuing PINs generated by GEMs with its paperwork: it should not be a difficult process, their computer could obtain the codes through a link to the GEMs machine.

- The new system should be given stringent protection for its interface with users, just as banknotes usually have legal status above other copyrighted designs. Online services who try to confuse the public by passing themselves off as GEMs would be treated as forgers.

- Legal backing for the system's relationship with banks so it can credit and debit users' acounts. In countries without a reliable financial infrastructure the system may itself need authority to act as a bank for users.

Box 14.1

THE ROLE OF LAWYERS IN A GEMS DISPUTE:

Verifiable lawyers who chose to offer their services on GEMs could be automatically allocated cases according to their pricing formula or, if prices of many individuals and firms converge, randomizing software. They would act for groups of aggrieved purchasers. If, for instance, a trader delivering parcels is unacceptably late on his round, the senders of every package in his van can be banded together by GEMs and all their contracts passed to a legal services provider trading on the system. This would be provided for in each of their contracts for delivery although they could, of course, remove the clause. The wording would specify a level of trading record for lawyers to which complaints would be passed. If the parcel operator denied culpability, a lawyer needs to be able to take the case on without having to contact each individual counterpart to see if they were willing to pay an upfront fee.

■ One further possibility: governments might agree to use their control of taxation to tempt people on to the system. The advantages of increasing market turnover, attracting activity out of the grey economy and ease of collection could arguably offset a reduction in rates for GEMs transactions.

A winning consortium would be assured of a monopoly on this package of benefits for a specified period, perhaps fifteen years. In return they would have to comply with conditions enshrined in their tender document, designed to spread the benefits of the new marketplace as widely as possible.

What concessions might politicians extract from a winning consortium?

Government's priorities in a GEMs launch should be to ensure that full benefits of the new markets are available to anyone in the country who wishes to use them, while giving existing businesses sufficient time and information to adapt to their impact. In addition to their set-up costs for the system core, a winning consortium might find their agreement with parliament stipulated the following:

- The successful companies fund a given number and geographic spread of GEMs terminals in public places around the country. These should be efficiently used; unlike, say, web browsers, a GEMs' interface would not be a source of entertainment. Apart from browsing for purchases, most users should primarily be checking their work diaries and printing details of any contracts they had secured, a process taking minutes. (A micro-charge for printing could, of course, be deducted from their account.) One terminal in perhaps the bus station of a depressed area might service 120 people a day. Many of them could be daily users of that machine each running a range of GEMs businesses, perhaps undertaking to log on in search of assignments before a certain time every weekday morning.

- Restrictions on increases in the commission charged to users so the consortium could not abuse its position. This should not hamper potential earnings from the project: merely ensure they have to come from continued growth in usage. This, coupled with a fixed term on the agreement, could counter any tendency towards undynamic complacency in the consortium.

- A clear timetable of roll out for individual market sectors is published in advance, so the transition to GEMs trading can be predicted. An accountancy firm specialising in sports club clients, for instance, would be entitled to know when the system's market for football ticket sales with its automatic auditing would be unveiled. Policymakers might chose to enforce this timetable with fines for the consortium if it was behind schedule. The interlocking nature of GEMs markets would dictate a reasonably rapid launching order: the usefulness of a market in sheet glass for instance would be limited without an accompanying forum in which specialist transport was traded, that in turn would be dependent on active general haulage and driver hire sectors. Similarities in software requirements might also influence the order in which sectors are made available: once a market in shipping domestic goods abroad was written, perhaps with customs routines for purchasers automated, a similar market in air freight could be ready almost immediately.

- Full transparency of operation to enable constant inspection of the system.

■ The consortium might have to provide certain non commission generating facilities such as voting and perhaps local friendship matching without charge to users.

■ Although the consortium is likely to be made up of international companies running the core GEMs hardware and software, parliament could insist that the individual markets are run by franchisees who would all be nationals. (The details of a proposed GEMs franchising system that would allow for organic growth is contained in Appendix two.)

■ Additionally, government might want to tie the launch of GEMs to other online initiatives, the provision of nationwide e-mail perhaps. These might be run on the GEMs core computers using the system's networking but should be operated by other companies to avoid unjustified centralization.

■ Automatic tax collection on the system but always at individual user's discretion. The consortium might be required to pay for interface with government legacy computers that provide up-to-date information on tax rates for transactions in any given market. Once that was achieved a newly directive scale of taxation across countless sectors of the economy could be applied. Assume, for instance, policymakers had specific economic aims in the market for taxi journeys. They might perhaps drop the rate of purchase tax on off-peak bookings by a user who was registered as a schoolchild, or charge a lower percentage on journeys involving multiple pick ups or encourage trips to local high streets with reduced tax on trips from less than a mile away. To discourage drunk driving there might be a tax free hour as people are leaving bars to go home. Multiple permutations would be calculated automatically by GEMs for each booking across the market with rates varying daily if that was the wish of lawmakers. A taxi driver taking assignments through a simplified GEMs terminal on his dashboard might for instance call up end of day accounts that looked like this.

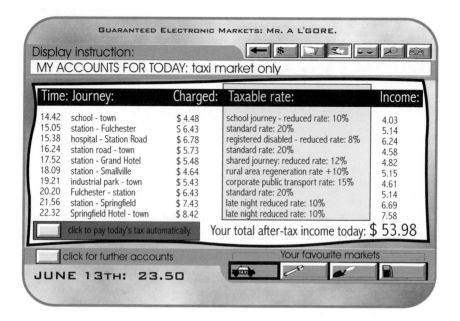

Time:	Journey:	Charged:	Taxable rate:	Income:
14.42	school - town	$ 4.48	school journey - reduced rate: 10%	4.03
15.05	station - Fulchester	S 6.43	standard rate: 20%	5.14
15.38	hospital - Station Road	$ 6.78	registered disabled - reduced rate: 8%	6.24
16.24	station road - town	$ 5.73	standard rate: 20%	4.58
17.52	station - Grand Hotel	$ 5.48	shared journey: reduced rate: 12%	4.82
18.09	station - Smallville	$ 4.64	rural area regeneration rate +10%	5.15
19.21	industrial park - town	$ 5.43	corporate public transport rate: 15%	4.61
20.20	Fulchester - station	$ 6.43	standard rate: 20%	5.14
21.56	station - Springfield	$ 7.43	late night reduced rate: 10%	6.69
22.32	Springfield Hotel - town	$ 8.42	late night reduced rate: 10%	7.58

GUARANTEED ELECTRONIC MARKETS: MR. A L'GORE.

Display instruction:

MY ACCOUNTS FOR TODAY: taxi market only

click to pay today's tax automatically.   Your total after-tax income today: $ 53.98

click for further accounts   Your favourite markets

JUNE 13TH: 23.50

The taxi operator has no need to study these accounts of course, he can simply set his basic pricing structure and tell GEMs to calculate the tax on top to arrive at a price for each assignment. Nor need he even click to release payment to an Inland Revenue account. If he wishes it could be transferred automatically through the day.

chapter

15

Opposition
to public markets

Since the dawn of commercial computing, millions of jobs have been lost to successive new technologies. The pain involved is generally regarded as an unavoidable part of progress: as one commentator told *Business Week* in 1993, when cheaper software for clerical and administrative functions was becoming widely available, 'people who don't add value are going to be in trouble'.[54] A full-scale GEMs system would be but the latest encroachment of computerization on previously established ways of doing business. A crucial difference, however, would be the status of its victims: corporations and executives rather than humble office workers. Will they accept their fate as thousands of past employees were expected to and resign themselves to irrelevance? They might not and they would have ample scope to resist. A GEMs service should not be initiated without full public debate. That would ensure the legitimacy of government involvement in a launch and, as a bonus for the consortium behind the system, heightened public awareness. During this phase the proposed system would be vulnerable to attack on several counts. Like all previous major public infrastructure projects, it would push existing technology to its limits in a leap of faith that initially may not stand up to aggressive probing. Historians would recognise the pattern. In 1845, for instance, work began on Britain's Chester to Holyhead railway with a 5-mile gap in the plans because no one knew how the plunging gorge of the Menai Straits was to be bridged. A race for solutions led finally to the invention of box girders, which could bear all required loads, even as lines leading to the gorge were being laid.[55] In the case of GEMs, it would not necessarily be the functions performed that would stretch existing know-how but the scale on which they might have to be delivered. It is worth pointing out, however, that the system could start small and grow, launching simpler markets first and leaving its equivalents to the Menai Straits problem until later. Additionally, those convinced the project was infeasible might need to be reminded that it would be the consortium, not taxpayers, who would bear the impact of failure.

Debate over Guaranteed Markets tends to invoke five often repeated arguments in opposition. Each will be considered in turn.

Points of opposition

■ **Government does not need to get involved in electronic commerce. If there is demand for a service like GEMs, market forces will ensure it emerges**

'Intelligent agent' software, which takes details of an Internet shopper's requirements and searches thousands of sites for the best price, is expected to have an increasing impact on online retailers. Many believe that consumer demand for this function will overcome currently formidable resistance from retailers and the portal sites that charge sellers for high-visibility positions. Some argue that if advanced 'shopbots' (shopping robots) become reality, and start roaming the whole gamut of web sales sites on behalf of buyers, everyone will instantly get the best possible deal and GEMs would be unnecessary. Others point to a panoply of buyer–seller matching services emerging on the Net. These consumer-orientated services often adopt the language of a wide-open market but remain restricted to favoured sellers. In the USA, for instance, 15 per cent of cars are purchased through the Net from far wider pools of vehicles than any one dealer site could offer, but services like Autobytel and Microsoft's Carpoint offer autos from mutually exclusive pools of dealerships, who pay to be listed and collectively offer only a fraction of the country's available cars at any given moment. In the UK, SCOOT allows Net users to type in their location and a service they seek, a plumber perhaps or a Pizza delivery firm, to get details of a nearby trader returned. The beginnings of an unbiased marketplace which can be freely entered? No, SCOOT earns its money on fees from the companies it lists and makes a speciality of collecting data on consumers who use its service. As their Corporate Communications Manager explained in a presentation to retailers 'once we recognise [the individual computer an enquirer is using] we can start to log their interests. If we'd seen that they'd asked about details for mortgage brokers and then for removal men – we might justifiably push offers relating to DIY. ...I'm sure that even greater possibilities will appear, to help you effectively market to your customers'.[56] Companies have little incentive to take on the gargantuan investment and uncertain prospects of growing a neutral, fully functioned electronic marketplace running on wafer-thin transaction charges: there are better short-term returns from what appears to be an open market but is actually a vehicle for client sellers.

It is worth repeating the advantages a fully enabled GEMs system would have over intelligent agents and existing services: the simplest possible market entry for sellers, authenticated trading records enabling reliable individuals and companies to selectively trade with each other, arbitration backed by frozen payment to instantly underpin any deal and interlocking markets that can pull together a personalised contractual chain at once. All this delivered not by a patchwork of software packages each with their own incompatibilities and value adding business models but in one simplified system that has been committed to user privacy, utility pricing and ever-widening ranges of sellers. Only a national parliament has the clout and legitimacy to shape an opportunity for one potentially dominant marketplace to rise from the online bedlam, then force its operators to invest in its full potential for an inclusive economy. Only government can write the laws that would underpin and promote an atomization of economic life. There are certainly those who find such a step unthinkable from the perspective of prevailing ideology: that is not the same as saying it could never work.

There is widespread recognition in electronic commerce circles that users want a simplified and convenient online marketplace. That is the force behind home shopping through interactive television, which is scheduled to deliver anything but a marketplace open to all sellers. Nevertheless, services like Open, Autobytel and SCOOT are undoubtedly useful and offer a huge improvement on old ways for consumers to meet their needs, but they should not be mistaken for the full potential of an online marketplace.

■ **A GEMs service would create an unacceptable monopoly**

The computer age has a natural tendency towards monopolies: a point made many times by Microsoft, the world's biggest company by market value, when justifying its 95 per cent share of personal computer operating system software. Everyone wants to have programming compatible with the bulk of existing users. The controversy over Microsoft as monopolist stems from the company's attempts to leverage dominance in one sector into others. Its chief technologist, Nathan Myhrvold, for instance, told the *Wall Street Journal* in 1997 that Microsoft hopes eventually to take a cut from every Internet transaction using their technology.[57] The uncoordinated marketplace does not dispel monopolies in the online world. What is more, it gives companies who achieve that position enormous market-controlling power. A GEMs operator backed by government would admittedly start with advantages no other online service could match in the country of operation but would pay for that privilege with a mass of unique obligations, annulling its potential for control. They would include an inability to extend into additional areas and the sacrifice of normal commercial secrecy to transparent accountability. All this would be enforced with pitiless inspection. Nor would GEMs be a Microsoft-style mammoth but a consortium of companies running a minimal core operation while individual franchisees oversee the marketplaces. Although united by a financial need to develop the system, it is difficult to see any ideological certainties that would bind together such a diverse group of participants. Unlike software houses, GEMs could do nothing to 'lock in' its users: there would be no cost for them to start using the system and little time required to learn its interface. Any user could disengage at any time and switch to other online channels without having to write off an investment in time or money.

The power that goes with dominance in outside industries would be denied the GEMs consortium: the economy running on their machines would be controlled, as in the outside world, by government, who could be made further accountable if they enabled GEMs' referendum capabilities. Additionally, a public market system meets the economist's test of a 'useful monopoly': someone seeking, say, a fur coat demonstrably benefits from access to one universal, dependable exchange showing a full range of second-hand and new options, rather than having to track down multiple forums and evaluating the offers therein. The indisputable advantages of having multiple suppliers from which to choose should not be confused with the more debatable benefits of being forced to hunt around a slew of marketplaces to find them.

GEMs' opponents would probably invoke images of 'big brother': one massive core computer that knows exactly what individuals are up to and when they are logging in. It is a valid fear. In 1996 San Fransisco based I/PRO was forced to abandon its plan to set up a central repository of individual's details on the Net with a view to sparing them the need to re-enter data every time they began a relationship with a company online. Centralized pre-registration through one company proved unacceptable to most users. But large computer systems harvesting information about us are now a fact of life, although the extent of the data they are allowed to reap is still being debated. At least in a GEMs system there would be stringent checking by a wide range of bodies to demonstrate that the system could not make improper use of the information it held and was unable to retain any details on a user who decided to close his account. If ever there was mass loss of faith in the system it would probably be followed by an exodus of users who would leave no trail behind. The system's power would be theoretical rather than exploitable. In the early days of broadcasting it was pointed out that the companies being licensed to transmit would have enormous power to create unfounded mass panic at will. Like GEMs operators in the case of privacy betrayal, it is something they could only ever do once and has never happened on a significant scale.

Arguments about the impact of failure in the central control room of a mature GEMs service have a firmer basis. Such disasters can happen. In late January 1990, AT&T, the USA's dominant telecommunications provider, experienced long-distance switching breakdown as a result of one logic circuit faltering in their central computer, the world's biggest. With a 9-hour break in service, the day the US phone system died is legendary among computing experts.[58] Existing large trading systems are coy about their particular failure rates although SABRE, the biggest, is known to have very occasional short periods of non-availability.[59] Prolonged gaps in service are less likely: SABRE's core computer is in a bomb-proof, concrete-lined bunker which can survive on its own air water and power for up to three days in case of above-ground holocaust. Instantaneous back ups are another route towards fail safe operation: the Reuters' 2000–2 currency market system, for instance, runs on hardware now in London Docklands that relays every deal immediately to other computers in Geneva and Singapore. Should London fail for any reason, trading can be switched seamlessly to far-away machines. Despite this, Reuters admit there has been a handful of brief gaps in the service.[60] The impact of crashed technology on a marketplace that has become reliant on electronic trading is demonstrated by the July 1998 chaos among worldwide currency dealers after Reuters's rival, the Electronic Broking Service, stalled. Non-availability led to '20 minutes of mass panic' and 'raised concerns about the widespread use of electronic matching' according to a trade newsletter.[61] It would be facile to promise GEMs could never fail or to minimise the consequences of any gap in service. But the consortium should commit itself to the array of technologies known as fault tolerant computing, which increasingly offers what professionals call nine fives reliability: full service 99.999 per cent of the time. Like SABRE, military-level security at the core should be an indisputable condition. If fears of down time became an issue, a scale of fines might be instigated, payable by the consortium for any breakdown and distributed perhaps as a few pennies to the accounts of 25 per cent of users chosen at random.

■ Big corporations are vital to national advantage

Behind the latest cheap headline about CEO compensation, this argument goes, are valuable organisations that if weakened could leave a country uncompetitive. GEMs would be a move into a new economic model, the effects of which cannot be fully predicted but which is likely to deliver new sources of international advantage, primarily efficiency of trading, a flexible workforce and cheapness of resources. The firms likely to be first hit by public electronic markets would be in service industries such as financial provision. These companies are already being rapidly transformed by computerization, from pillars of community and employment provision to amorphous computer networks overseen by a diminished cadre of executives. A GEMs system would deliver to the national economy the efficiencies these globalizing organizations currently stand to gain from moving online.

Manufacturers should feel the impact of GEMs later. In the first country in its region with GEMs they could enjoy purchasing labour, services and some materials in a very efficient marketplace, while selling under less competitive pressure elsewhere. Might they find themselves under attack at home from imports now able to go instantly to market? It would be up to government whether to erect tariff barriers but without them imports would certainly be able to go more rapidly into distribution although they could be overpriced relative to domestic production.

■ A GEMs system would be an employment killer

GEMs would probably create new work opportunities and redistribute existing work as it effectively removed transaction costs from the economy, encouraging money into more rapid circulation. The jobs it undercut would almost all be those vulnerable to computerization anyway; if GEMs was not the threat, a proprietary software package would be.

■ Citizens in a GEMs country would be restricted by shopping in a national rather than international marketplace

Internet shopping would not come to an end after a first GEMs system was launched. Users of national public markets would still want to shop globally for novelty, for needs from niche markets and for digitised products like software or music, which can come dependably from around the world as well as via GEMs sellers. More entrepreneurial Net shoppers may see a role in arbitrage between the worldwide market and GEMs and then start a home import business. Anyone can sell anything in GEMs (with the exception of legally restricted markets). A user in Saudi Arabia, for instance, who noticed a particular brand of Cuban cigars could be ordered cheaply from Havana over the Internet might purchase 10 boxes and then sell them in his country's GEM for tobacco products. He adds value to the final transaction by putting up the GEMs bond that turns a difficult-to-find, precarious Internet purchase into a solidly underpinned and very convenient deal. Because the import market has atomized, GEMs shoppers should enjoy a far wider range of foreign goods in this way.

It is sometimes argued that consumers will always want to shop in an online, branded environment. Opponents should not assume the logical corollary of this view: that GEMs' interfaces would be functional and unimaginative with uniform presentation across all sectors. It would be the ever-changing offerings of any number of sellers, mass market and exclusive, that would make the GEMs market for, say, sportswear a constant source of interest. There would, of course, be nothing to stop shoppers purchasing in whatever online forum they wished, but once they started comparing prices they would be likely to find the branded sales channel was a good place to browse and GEMs the best place to buy.

Likely tactics of the opposition

Individual corporations come and go but, as a community, big business can fight tenaciously for its future. A GEMs project, once it was taken seriously, would antagonize virtually every significant power base in a developed economy. Crucial opponents would include the established media, who might fear a diminished role for advertising in a world with pure markets available to everyone. This could make it difficult for pro-GEMs arguments to enter circulation. If the debate over merits of institution-led 'old' capitalism versus atomized 'new' capitalism were confined to rational analysis of the benefits and risks inherent in both, there would probably be a swing in public opinion towards GEMs. Recent history of localized infrastructure projects suggests intelligent debate may not be the case: distortion and emotionally loaded arguments could be used to obfuscate the true issues. When the Los Angeles Chamber of Commerce, for instance, responded to demand for comprehensive public transport with a plan for an integrated rapid transit system centred on downtown, opponents dubbed the scheme 'socialistic'. As such it was deemed unpalatable and killed. An 'astonishing defeat' according to the episode's historian.[62] Years later the city has to cope with a legacy of medical, social and planning problems following an over reliance on cars but it at least avoided the spectre of active government! Officially initiated public electronic markets would be particularly prone to this kind of emotional pigeon-holing whereby even a scheme's potential beneficiaries might be convinced of its undesirability without any exposure to reasoned discussion.

Were sustained grass roots support for government intervention to create GEMs to emerge, this kind of tactic could be employed whole-sale, as has already been the case with corporate opposition to the environmental movement. In the USA an anti-green movement first emerged with far right authors who, for example, claimed environmentalism stood for a new religion which was 'anti humanity, anti civilisation and anti technology'.[63] This coherent philosophy of attack provided the foundation for a sophisticated movement against a movement: the Wise Use organization. 'The public will never love big business. The pro-industry activist group is the answer to these problems' leader Ron Arnold told a gathering of Canadian forest industries representatives in 1988.[64] Explaining his tactics in a later newspaper interview he added that the most effective way of defeating the environmental movement is 'by taking their money and members' with another movement.[65] Wise Use appears to be an ecologically sound organization; opponents see it as nothing more than a misleading front for voracious industrialization. The growing influence enjoyed by Wise Use and its corporate supporters became clear in 1994 when the group stopped the antici-pated ratification of the United Nations agreement on biological diver-sity in the US Senate with a barrage of opposing letters, calls and faxes.[66] Similar tactics can be seen in tobacco giant Philip Morris's 'whitecoat project': the establishment of a network of scientists throughout Europe paid to cast doubt on the dangers of passive smoking while appearing independent.[67] British salt producers adopted a similar ploy to counter links between their product and stomach cancer, successfully removing salt consumption from the list of points in official health advice.[68] Anyone campaigning for underpinned public electronic markets would be wise to brace themselves for well-funded opposition claiming to represent a wide constituency and for a succes-sion of experts, only some of whom will have started with an open mind, asserting that the project is unrealistic or undesirable.

Moral panic has been productively deployed against infrastructure proposals in the past. The telephone was denounced as occultist because it brought disembodied voices into the room. Clergymen sympathetic to canal and turnpike road companies described early railway locomotives as satanic because of their propulsion by fire. One small aspect of a GEMs operation that may be inflated by opponents in search of similar hysteria is the potential it would offer to adulterers and relationship dabblers by GEMs' local friendship-building facilities. Public markets should be predicated on a conviction that elected politicians, not system managers, decide what areas of trade in a country are available to citizens. If prostitution is deemed permissible by legislators in the country of operation, for instance, there should ultimately be a GEM for sexual services, in which providers can enjoy the protection and freedom from touting for business available to any other trader on the system. However, GEMs could widen such market activity unless restricted by government, a potential boon for the proposed system's detractors. (Conversely, of course, the system may lead to increased prices in the market by making so much alternative employment available to the supply side.)

The sheer ambitiousness of the system could be another profitable area of attack, with every mistake along the consortium's learning curve given crisis coverage. If there were to come a point when opponents realized they were losing public sympathy they might shift to a campaign for a limited system, or lobby for alternative government schemes that would provide a compromise with corporate interests. Firms that currently oppose any involvement by national policy makers in the new economy might start advocating projects like Singapore's Approved Cyber Trader scheme, which bestows concessionary tax rates on companies deemed to be using electronic commerce for officially sanctioned economic ends. Full-scale acceptance of such schemes might pare down the potential abuses of electronic trading capability among big players; they would not deliver an atomized economy. Other firms might demand government issue of digital certificates to prove individual identity and increase security in the uncoordinated online marketplace. There is no reason why such schemes to help those who wish to shop outside GEMs should not be launched alongside an eventual system. The project aims to increase choice, not stifle any other form of marketplace.

Another tactic to watch for would be the pre-emptive strike. In spring 1996, for instance, the local US telecommunications companies petitioned the Federal Communications Commission demanding a ban on technology enabling Internet users to make international phone calls between computers at local rates. Few people at the time were aware the technology existed.[69] A further alarming trend for GEMs' proponents is meetings between corporate interests and governments in secrecy. The Multilateral Agreement on Investment, a set of statutes to protect international money flows, for instance, was initially negotiated in three years of almost total secrecy. Politicians could find themselves under enormous pressure to quietly acquiesce to elegantly worded agreements actually designed to prevent their citizens ever discovering the full benefits electronic markets have to offer.

The luxury of fully explaining public markets' potential may be denied to those who seek a newly inclusive capitalism. Advocates of GEMs-style systems might need to focus on communicating three simple messages: using the system would always be a matter of choice not compulsion, it would cost taxpayers nothing despite being government initiated and it would not involve restricting existing channels to market in any way. While braced for a particularly vituperative battle they could console themselves that similarly bloody conflicts, by the standards of their day, were fought before the need for mass public transport, postage and water provision became self-evident. Historically, no new technology has been indefinitely withheld from widespread public usage because of resulting damage to powerful institutions of its time. Infrastructure proposals have always won, ultimately.

16 Which countries would have most to gain from a GEMs launch?

The potential unpopularity of a raw online marketplace in the first world notwithstanding, GEMs is unlikely to be launched in a developed country. It is in 'second world' nations that the opposition to such a move by government could be most readily overcome. The possibility of GEMs in a far off country might be enthusiastically supported by investors who would bitterly contest the same project on their home ground. Unlike, say, online entertainment applications GEMs can operate with very basic displays to users and would not require substantial bandwidth or advanced technology in terminals. The personal computers with 486 processors now being piled into skips across Europe and the US and the copper wire discarded for high-density fibre optics could provide the spine for a usable, if not particularly glossy, GEMs in a developing nation. Many of these countries are propagating the awareness and technical backbone required for a GEMs service. Internet access and usage is accelerating faster in developing countries than elsewhere.[70] In China, for example, twice as much fibre optic is now being laid as in the USA, encouraging the number of Net accounts to double in the first half of 1998.[71] The Prime Minister of India (which has an existing middle class of 200 million people) has set out to reverse his country's slow take up of the Internet with a national task force designed to make the country 'an Information Technology super-power'.[72] Brazil is now committed to growth through privatization deals to create commercially driven infrastructure. With a favourable government any of these countries could achieve much from launching a first GEMs service.

It would be in a country plagued by a bandit economy that underpinned electronic markets for mass use might have the most dramatic impact. Take Russia as an example. Since the country's banks closed for a 'technical break' in August 1998 an estimated 75 per cent of transactions have been in the form of barter, even between companies. It starves the government of tax revenue, is inefficient and extremely time consuming. A Russian textile factory, for example, will routinely make 50 to 60 deals a month with suppliers of meat, footwear, jewellery, furniture and concrete blocks employing a 'hunt-and-gather' team to locate potential swaps.[73] GEMs should be able to staunch the underlying problems that created this catastrophe: state and private corruption, financial scams and capital flight. Assuming a system had been set up in August 1998 with all the inspection protocols and guarantees of democratic independence already outlined, it should have begun to stabilize the economy almost immediately. With terminals around the country provided by a foreign consortium of GEMs companies, individual Russians could have started to trade at grassroots level, selling their produce for instance with providers of delivery or storage emerging in other GEMs. Because of low computer awareness among nationals the system might have a specially simplified interface in its early days. Market consolidators could have started to buy in rural areas and supply in town with no administration or central planning required to kickstart activity.

Initially the medium for this trade would probably be GEMs' own parallel currency, sealed from big institutions and speculators and eked into supply as users increased. The system's currency exchange may then be trading in a reverse situation to that expected in a first world economy: the rouble almost valueless against a Russian equivalent of POETs (Parallel Official Economy Tokens). Low-level economic activity for ordinary people would thus be separated from the currency crisis, creating breathing space for officials. A second stage might be ensuring the nation's natural resources such as oil and metals are sold on the system with downstream processing being driven by open market efficiencies. With core exports moving solidly through the economy the Duma would then have to persuade other firms and state institutions to trade on the system, foregoing backdoor deals and crony capitalism for pure markets in which every transaction can be instantly audited if the parties are willing. As big players moved on to GEMs roubles should approach parity with parallel economy points and overtake them in value once major capital providers domestic or international began using the GEMs money markets. The mafia, which has blocked so many past attempts at reform, should find it difficult to stall this process. Core software would have been written overseas not by tainted local suppliers, inspection would be international. Big crime would be as handicapped as large service companies in an atomized economy made up of countless, ever-changing, underpinned small deals rather than dominated by large transactions. Tax collection could become immediate with infinitesimal sums transferred to government coffers as part of each sale, although any tendency towards over taxation that could price people off the system would need to be contained. Politicians would not be immune from this clean-up imposed on economic life by GEMs. Official purchasing and hiring could be made open to scrutiny, perhaps with the system proffering an 'automatically audited' symbol on official contracts to show they represented the best value purchase available at the time. More fundamentally, government would have to decide whether to submit itself to public approval by allowing GEMs voting, dependent on system penetration and take-up. If they did use the system to endorse their own legitimacy it could be the final step that brought foreign funds back into what should now be a lean and durable economy.

To see how sensationally an economy can be lifted out of total wreckage by stabilizing domestic money supply, as GEMs could do uniquely with its limited currency for users only, it is worth looking at the launch of Germany's deutschmark in 1948. In the rubble of wartime defeat, as in modern day Moscow, the black market dominated with 8 hours of an average worker's toil required just to buy an egg in the legitimate shops. Paid work was, in any case, barely available so stores remained empty as financial anarchy prevailed. The new currency, given out in allocations at Post Offices, reversed the situation immediately. As one contemporary politician who had struggled with earlier attempts to resolve the problems wrote: 'I'll never forget the impression when I walked through the city on the Monday after the currency reform and saw goods in the shop windows once again. In this unforgettable moment I realised for the first time that a stable currency and liberal economic policy belong together'.[74] A decade later the mark was one of the world's most sought after currencies. Marshall Aid money from the USA was a vital part of that process but it was stability induced by the launch of a virgin currency that allowed the benefits to filter through the economy. Now that the currency controls of 1940s Europe have been replaced by global 'hot money' flows the only way to achieve similar impact could be through a sealed system of computerized transactions, available exclusively to nationals.

The mechanism for this economic revival would have involved no financial outlay for Russia. Costs of hardware and some public access terminals would be met by a consortium wanting to launch GEMs. Would such large scale investment in a crashed economy be viable for those companies? They would be gambling on enthusiastic take up by the populace and progressive 'GEMification' of economic life, making a future flow of commissions on every transaction in a newly-hardened currency worthwhile. For a country of the size and natural resources of Russia, that could be a worthwhile prize. Once a first GEMs was launched, further systems in additional countries would cost little to develop beyond the costs of dedicated programming, such as mapping software and charges involved in recruiting franchisees and setting up hardware. Would national pride be dented by inviting a consortium inevitably featuring foreign companies to build a new economic framework? Most second world nations already pay overseas companies to print their banknotes and are finding they must turn to foreigners to computerize banks and government departments. Eastern Europe, for instance, has widely promised exclusive monopoly rights to foreigners for years to come in key areas of telecommunications. This has been judged the only way to obtain lasting investment.[75] The core software at the heart of the new system would probably be transnational in its roots but each country with GEMs should have its own core computer on national soil for security reasons. Market front ends should be run by a national franchisee each aware of the multiple local sensitivities in his area of trade (Box 16.1). Unlike the Internet, interfaces would all be in the local language(s).

If a race between countries to roll out the benefits of public electronic markets developed alongside the existing contest between companies racing to control the new infrastructure, there could be worldwide realignment. For a possible indication of the outcome it is worth looking at power plays in the financial sector, which has been both global in its competition and dependent on true electronic markets longer than any other area of trade. Countries that had little to offer but a willingness to adopt the full force of electronic markets have shown an ability to overtake centres of trading previously regarded as impregnable. An example: Frankfurt's financial futures exchange, the DTB, adopted

BOX 16.1

GEMS AND NATIONAL SENSITIVITIES

The GEMs consortium should not seek to impose one uniform marketplace on the world but develop core software that can then be amended by franchisees. Some emerging market countries have traditions of cooperative capitalism at odds with GEMs' ruthless enforcement of each deal for instance. The Chinese diaspora throughout south east Asia is marked by a willingness to seal agreements at the highest level with nothing more than a handshake. It is difficult to see how automated markets could incorporate this valuable role for trust in a society across the board but government might decide to preserve that culture perhaps by allowing unprotected deals in certain sectors. Other regional traits that would not sit easily on GEMs include Islamic banking. With strict adherence to scriptural injunctions against charging interest, predominantly Muslim countries might require more complex financial instruments in a basic loans market.

unbridled computerised markets while its London counterpart loftily opted only to move its 'open pit trading' system online at hours when their physical trading floor was closed. As successive trading contracts moved to Germany, The London International Financial Futures Exchange has spent millions trying to catch up with the cheapness and convenience which so spectacularly benefited Frankfurt.[76] There are several large countries with plentiful natural resources and a reasonably educated workforce kept low in world rankings by corruption and monetary instability. A coherent government vision for electronic markets might enable them to overtake nations mired in adherence to the online *status quo*.

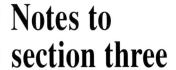

notes

Notes to
section three

1. Douglas N. Muir, *Postal Reform and the Penny Black: a New Appreciation*, The National Postal Museum, 1990, p. 46.
2. L. T. C. Rolt, *Victorian Engineering*, Penguin, 1970, p. 20.
3. D. P. Titley, *Machines, Money and Men: An Economic and Social History of Great Britain from 1700 to the 1970s*, Collins Educational, 1969, p. 80.
4. S. E. Finer, *The Life and Times of Sir Edwin Chadwick*, Barnes and Noble, 1970, p. 410.
5. David Milsted, *They Got it Wrong! The Guinness Book of Regrettable Quotations*, Guinness, 1995, p. 191.
6. Published by Harvard Business School, 1997. The quote comes from the Mc-Kenna Group web site. www.mckennagroup.com/realtime/rt/rt_primer/primmer001.html.
7. Media journalist Alfred Balk quoted in Radio Days All Over Again? Today's wannabe Web stars can learn from the past – 75 years to be exact. *Business Week,* 27 August 1998, electronic edition.
8. Portal Play, *Information Strategy*, September 1998, p. 10.
9. J. William Gurley, The Soaring Cost of E-commerce, *Fortune*, 3 August 1998, p. 165.
10. Case study 9-490-012, *People Express Airlines: Rise and Decline*, Harvard Business School, revised 14 September 1993. Quoted in Jerry Yoram Wind and Jeremy Main, *Driving Change: How the best Companies are Preparing for the 21st Century*, Kogan Page, 1998, p. 23.
11. Evan I. Schwartz, *Webonomics: Nine Essential Principals for Growing your Business on the World Wide Web*, Penguin, 1997, p. 108.
12. The examples used come from Follower of Fashion, *Ovum Update,* Ovum Consulting, January–April 1998, p. 4.
13. Increasing Customer Loyalty through Knowledge Management, conference, London, 10–11 March 1998. Presentation by Dr Michael Wolf, Executive Director, Swiss Bank Corporation.
14. The Walled Garden: Interactive digital television could offer widespread access to the Internet. But broadcasters are not keen, *Information Strategy*, October 1998, p. 9.
15. Kenneth Helps, Managing Director of Cabot Software. Phone conversation with the author 22 September 1998.
16. The Walled Garden: Interactive digital television could offer widespread access to the Internet. But broadcasters are not keen. *Information Strategy*, October 1998, p. 9.

17. Consolidation on the Internet, *Internet for Business*, September/October 1997, p. 10
18. Adam Nicholson, The view from Perch Hill, *Sunday Telegraph Magazine*, 4 October 1998, p. 78. Also Peter Hitchens, Superstores are turning our cities into ghost towns, *Express*, 28 September 1998, p. 13.
19. IMRG statement 'E-commerce and the Universal Network', part of the notes for Online Delivery '98, held 11/12 February 1998, London.
20. Martha Rogers and Stacey Riordan, Building Learning Relationships with Mass Customized Clothes, *Inside 1to1*, 16 July 1998, p. 1.
21. Currency Doubleday.
22. Don Peppers and Martha Rogers, *Enterprise One to One: Tools for Competing in the Interactive Age*, Currency Doubleday, 1997, p. 104.
23. Ibid. p. 127.
24. Ibid. p. 127.
25. Confirmed in e-mail exchange between the author and Thomas A. Kelly, Public Relations Division, First Chicago, September 1998.
26. Bob Dorf, M1to1/PRG launches global partnership with Oracle, *Inside 1to1*, 21 October 1998, p. 1.
27. 1998 survey by Mercer Management Consulting quoted in *Inside 1to1*, 15 July 1998, electronic edition.
28. *Encyclopaedia of the New Economy*, *Wired* reprint, 1998.
29. The Aspen Institute, Colorado, *The Future of Electronic Commerce*, 1995, p. 35.
30. Mike McDowall, Big Brother Brokers, *Direct Marketing*, March/April 1998, p. 38
31. Market Makers, Some of the Most Familiar Ways to Market Consumer goods are Proving to be Costly Failures, *The Economist*, 14 March 1998, p. 87.
32. Wendy Grossman, Who's Watching the Webwatchers? *Future Shopping*, September 1998, p. 12.
33. Business at Net Speed, *Business Week*, 22 June 1998, p. 72 and Online Computer Sales. Dell and Cisco: leading indicators? *Electronic Commerce Briefing*, January 1998, p. 13.
34. Hans-Peter Martin and Harald Schumann, *The Global Trap*, Zed Books, 1997.
35. David Metcalfe and Syue Fernie, Hanging on the Telephone, *Centrepiece*, 3(1). Quoted in Remote Control of the High Street, *Guardian*, 2 June 1998, p. 17.
36. The Human Answering Machines, *Guardian Jobs and Money*, 26 July 1997, p. 2.
37. Alec Maycock, operations manager of Halifax Direct quoted in It's all in the call for a little extra, *Information Week*, 10–23 December 1997, p. 62.
38. Graham Technology website www.gtnet.com. Extracted on 20 May 1998.
39. Quoted in Employees at the Mercy of Company Bugging Spree, *Daily Telegraph Connected*, 21 May 1998.
40. Paul Thompson and Chris Warhurst (eds), *Workplaces of the Future*, Macmillan Business, 1998, p. 176.
41. The Human Answering Machines, *Guardian Jobs and Money*, 26 July 1997, p. 2 and Paul Thompson and Chris Warhurst (eds) *Workplaces of the Future*, Macmillan Business, 1998, p. 128.

42.   Sarah Adamczuck of Bristol writing in the letters page of the *Guardian*, 24 February 1998.
43.   Variable Compensation Helps Keep Call Centers Buzzing, Mercer Consulting, www.mercer.com/usa, extracted 10 September 1998.
44.   Bob Dorf, The One to One Insurance Policy, *Inside 1to1*, 16 April 1998, electronic edition.
45.   David Bollier, Rapporteur, Charles M. Firestone, Program Director, *The Future of Electronic Commerce*, The Aspen Institute, Communications and Society Program, 1995, p. 41.
46.   Fine line between a role and the dole, *Times Educational Supplement,* 28 August 1998, p. 7.
47.   George Monbiot, Running on MMT, *Guardian*, 13 August 1998, p. 16.
48.   Larry Elliott, Move to revive world pact, *Guardian*, 10 September 1998.
49.   Published by Allen Lane, The Penguin Press, 1997.
50.   Simon Caulkin, Pity the poor CEO. Those share options are to die for – literally, *Observer Business News*, 23 August 1998, p. 7.
51.   Behave or else…, *Information Strategy*, February 1998, p. 13.
52.   *Report on the Sanitary Condition of the Labouring Population of Great Britain* by Edwin Chadwick 1842. From a new introduction to the report by M. W. Flinn, University of Edinburgh Press, 1965, p. 39.
53.   Robert W. McChesney, Digital Highway Robbery: where is the 'competition' the Telecommunications Act was supposed to provide? *The Nation*, 21 April 1997, electronic edition.
54.   *Business Week*, 14 June 1993. Reprinted in Caroll Pursell, *Heat,* BBC Books, 1994, p. 197.
55.   L. T. C. Rolt, *Victorian Engineering*, Penguin, 1970, p. 28.
56.   Miranda Cleverdon, Corporate Communications Manager, Scoot UK, speaking at the Non-Shop Shopping conference, London 17 September 1998. The same speech was originally to have been delivered by Marc Lynne, Internet Manager of Scoot.
57.   *The Electronic Commerce Briefing*, June 1998, electronic edition.
58.   David Brown, *Cybertrends: Chaos, Power and Accountability in the Information Age*, Viking, 1997, p. 201.
59.   Phone conversation with Peter Heath, Countrywide Public Relations, SABRE's spokesfirm in the UK, August 1998.
60.   Peter V. Thomas of Reuters Transaction Products, London, e-mail to author, 5 October 1998.
61.   Price Glitch on EBS Raises Debate over Automation, *fxweek: the global business of foreign exchange newsletter*, Waters' Treasury/Risk Group, 6 July 1998, p. 1.
62.   Mike Davis, *City of Quartz: Excavating the Future in Los Angeles*, Verso, 1990, p. 122.
63.   R. Arnold, *At the Eye of the Storm: James Watt and the Environmentalists,* Regnery Gateway, 1982, p. 248. Quoted in Andrew Rowell, *Green Backlash: Global Subversion of the Environment Movement*, Routledge, 1996, p. 10.
64.   Andrew Rowell, *Green Backlash: Global Subversion of the Environment Movement*, Routledge, 1996, p. 13.
65.   Interview with *The Toronto Star*, ibid., p. 14.
66.   Ibid., p. 30.
67.   Clare Dyer, Tobacco company set up network of sympathetic scientists, *British Medical Journal* **316**, 23 May 1998, p. 1555.

68. Marie Woolf, Food Firms Twist Science to Minimise Dangers of Salt, *Observer*, 7 June 1998, p. 15.

69. Evan I. Schwartz, *Webonomics: Nine Essential Principals for Growing your Business on the World Wide Web*, Penguin, 1997, p. 188.

70. The Internet and Poverty. Real Help or Real Hype? *Panos Briefing 28*, The Panos Institute, (TBC) 1998, p. 2.

71. Godfrey Linge (ed.) *China's New Spatial Economy*, Oxford University Press, 1997, p. 55 and China's Net Population Doubles, *The Industry Standard Intelligencer,* vl. 32, 11 September 1998, electronic edition.

72. Quoted in the National Taskforce website: http://it-taskforce.nic.in/.

73. Sharon LaFraniere, An Enemy of Russian Economic Reform: Barter, *The International Herald Tribune*, 4 September 1998, p. 1.

74. Count Otto Lambsdorff, former leader of the Liberal Free Democrats quoted in David Gow and Denis Stuanton, Arrival of euro marks end of a golden era for Germany, *Guardian,* 20 June 1998.

75. Why tortoises won't win: A slow but steady approach to modernising the telecoms sector had served the region well through the course of the 1990s. Now it is time to speed up the process, *Business Central Europe*, September 1998, p. 39.

76. Jill Treanor, Liffe turns for help to bring back glory days, *Guardian*, 8 September 1998, p. 19.

How might businesses respond to the rise of public electronic markets?

This section assumes that what many might see as a nightmare scenario for established businesses has become reality. After public debate a country has decided to launch a GEMs-style facility. It has been efficiently constructed and launched then embraced by a grateful populace who increasingly trust the system for a widening range of transactions. As usage increases the operating consortium is ploughing further funds into new software features and market-widening activity. What do large businesses do now? The GEMs project is emphatically not anti-business; any left-wing government who viewed it through such a prism would be likely to cripple their economy. GEMs' only concern is to provide a comprehensive trading platform open to any seller: consumer choice in this new marketplace then decides winners and losers.

It could be a mistake to underestimate the potential reach of such a system. Certainly, it could not compete with those providing the highest levels of personal attention at the top end of the market nor with shifty 'back of a truck' deals at the bottom. But there is a broad middle of the spectrum of transactions for which it should provide better reliability, range, convenience and price competition than other means of trading. Companies with exceptional customer relations, however, would probably not be threatened. The Italian mail order clothiers, for instance, whose selling point is that their size 40 dresses will fit a size 44 woman would be unlikely to see an exodus of customers to a GEM for womenswear, where enforced standards of truthfulness could lead to painful revelations. Other brands who are particularly cosy with their purchasers include Jack Daniels whiskey whose web site offers personalised interaction with staff and lavishly produced displays.[1] Even with the brand cheaply available in a GEM for alcoholic drinks there are likely to be customers who would prefer their buying experience wrapped up in a personal online exchange with a fellow whiskey enthusiast, rather than as a functional transaction in the public markets. The key impact of GEMs would be in removing any automatic benefits currently gained from owning trading infrastructure: the system would make that infrastructure universally available. At time of writing, for instance, Federal Express have a policy of giving their biggest customers automated shipping and invoicing facilities that, among other functions, group packages for nearby destinations together for cheaper shipment. GEMs could do this for any user in its parcel deliveries market. It would then be up to FedEx whether to input a GEMs pricing policy and accept parcels through the system, but the full infrastructure required for a parcel despatch market would now be available to anyone with a van who had cleared the verification hurdles required (Box S4.1).

Could it be worthwhile for firms to find ways of reaching the customer in places where public markets would not be on hand? Certain mobile phones in the USA, for instance, have a 'car breakdown' button that instantly connects the caller to American Automobile Association (AAA) headquarters from where a mechanic can be despatched. In the uncoordinated market for car repairs at present the simplicity of this concept has real appeal to users and allows AAA to circumvent local competition. But if GEMs flowered in the way past communications infrastructure has done it would not be long before mobile phone makers were offering handsets with instant connections to GEMs. With perhaps four programmable buttons an owner might set the first to access his GEMs account and immediately book the nearest available experienced car mechanic to his location at the time, a second for use if suddenly working late could tell GEMs 'book a high grade babysitter who I have hired previously for four hours from 6.00 p.m. today' and so on. The phone's display might then confirm transaction details. Once the new marketplace gained momentum it is likely to be futile trying to set up channels around it unless they were based on a shopping experience so rich and distinctive it outweighed the value and convenience that could have the bulk of the population seeking additional ways of connecting to GEMs.

Box S4.1

THE GEMS PARCELS MARKET

Any GEMs user could tell the system they have a package to despatch, say from Chicago to Manhattan. They would then be asked for a timeframe: clicking on 'immediate' would ensure a place on the next available flight that had space for sale on the system and the arrival of the most promptly available courier to take it to the airport, while a New York courier was lined up to await arrival. If a cheaper, more leisurely, journey was acceptable, GEMs would look for the lowest-cost departure for packages of that size and weight and ensure the deliverer whose pricing formula made them the best value for that assignment collected, possibly as part of an afternoon's worth of pick ups around the city. If cheapness was the overriding consideration travel between the cities might be by road, in which case the parcel could be carried by a one-man-and-a-truck operator who aggregated packages from couriers all over Chicago. Every provider in this market would need extensive bonding because of the security implications of their work; they would be unlikely to get it without an incontestable trading record. The system would allocate a code number to each package that shows who was responsible for it at any given time in its transit. Open to thousands of providers and with trends in demand freely available, this market should be both more responsive (because its pool of couriers and potential hubs are larger) and cheaper than any one of the existing big parcel companies.

An immediate response of many companies to a GEMs launch could be a retreat from areas of trade that were reaching commodity prices on the system towards more exotic value-added services. Once electronic markets became key to global money exchange, for instance, the big banks virtually surrendered trade in mainstream currencies to new entrants and concentrated on rarer denominations such as the Yugoslav dinar and more complex financial products that defied easy categorization for electronic trading. That would be one battleplan for a company faced with a GEMs launch. Some other suggestions follow. Most of them contradict thinking about how to succeed in an uncoordinated online marketplace.

chapter
17

Innovation becomes decisive

Constantly experiment with product range

The existing online marketplace is concentrating economic power and diminishing the variety in mainstream outlets. Under pressure from globalizing retailers, for instance, consumer goods manufacturers led by Proctor & Gamble are slashing their ranges to focus on a smaller number of key products standardized for marketing to the world.[2] Advertising and brand building would still be beneficial in a GEMs selling environment, although not crucial. However, speed to market would be so fast and demand data so freely available that the range of products available to GEMs users is likely to be constantly refreshing itself. Big companies would be foolish to respond with nothing more than a small number of unchanging lines when brand extensions or new merchandise could be painlessly tried on thousands of waiting consumers.

The following example shows how a fictitious, fast-moving consumer goods manufacturer might launch a chocolate candy bar product on GEMs. A launch process that would currently involve trade promotion, consumer awareness raising, commitment to pre-ordained production runs and a mass of distribution agreements could take the brand manager less than twenty minutes in the public markets. Assuming his employer already had an account on the system and he was authorized to input new products, his task would start in the market for confectionery distribution.

Told that he wants to launch a new product, GEMs begins with a request for basic details. Once he has finished typing it looks like this.

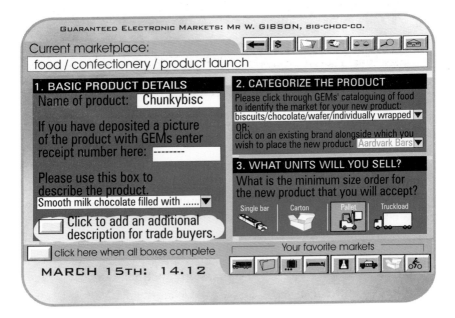

The market for confectionery sales would be available to home cookery enthusiasts with a kitchen table full of sweet cookies they wanted to sell locally that afternoon as much as food multinationals. GEMs asks for the size of units to be sold so it knows whether to proceed with a very simple list of questions for a home baker who probably would not have standardized biscuits, or a more complex formula for a major supplier. It now knows it is dealing with the latter who will only sell pallets of output, that the product is to be called 'Chunkybisc', and proceeds with questions that would be crucial for trade buyers.

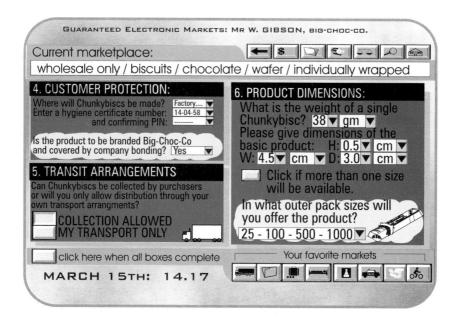

Sales in GEMs could be driven by consumer pull rather than manufacturers pushing their products through a distribution network. It is asking if their brand manager wants to limit distribution of Chunkybiscs to the company's own vehicles or whether he is willing to allow anyone who has bought a sufficient quantity of the product to arrange their own vehicle for collection. The latter keeps the price competitive because GEMs can compute a delivery price independently from a wider marketplace and construct a contractual chain with the haulier for a buyer, it is also more flexible. Some basic information is now needed so distribution through multiple operators can be arranged.

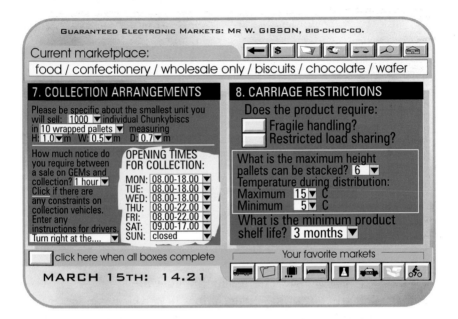

Now the system needs a pricing formula. That can factor in overall demand for chocolate bars: making Chunkybiscs expensive in a slack market for instance when only a minimum production run was likely to be sold. Or it can drop prices according to size of order, previous history with a given buyer, postal code of purchaser and so on. GEMs also needs to know parameters for supply. It could be as simple as saying there will be 2000 pallets a day available for the next four weeks but a more sophisticated service is available. The brand manager can in effect tell GEMs his variable costs knowing the system will constantly alter the price to buyers to maximize profitability. How many bars does he need to sell to make it worthwhile running the production line? Having reached that figure, does he then want to sell more competitively still? Like all individual user information on the system these details will not be available to anyone working for GEMs or released to anyone else.

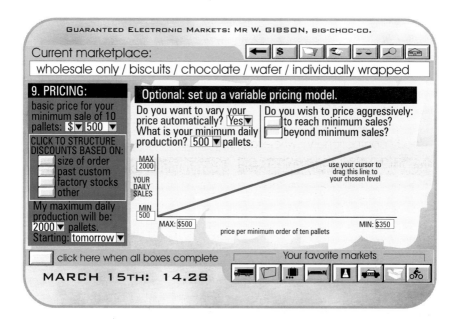

Now the brand manager is asked for consumer information: for example, what are the key ingredients, does the product contain specific substances to which some individuals are allergic, is it kosher and is it suitable for home freezing? Then GEMs asks if the product is to be made eligible for users who have boycotts in force. If this page is not filled in Chunkybiscs when re-entered on the system by wholesalers, retailers, buyers club organisers and other re-sellers will not be displayed to individual users with an applicable ban in force. It might be, for instance, that 2 per cent of regular biscuit buyers in GEMs were punishing the Nestlé food group for alleged bad practice in marketing baby milk to developing countries. The brand manager would have to decide whether to banish any trace of Nestle output from his supply chain and allow a clause in contracts with buyers to that effect or to write off that segment of the market.

GEMs could offer unparalleled marketing opportunities without compromising user privacy. It might for example offer individual users the option of accepting messages according to their consumption patterns. These would be sent blind by sellers. In this case there might be thousands of individuals around the country who purchase more than say five chocolate bars a week and have told GEMs they are happy to receive unsolicited messages so long as they contain a relevant free product offer. After studying market overview information for past take up of such offers in this sector, the brand manager might chose to activate a message to these people that tells them they qualify for a free Chunkybisc. If they click to accept it, their details are released to the company, which is then contracted to deliver a biscuit. Next time those who accept browse the chocolate bars in their GEMs grocery store Chunkybiscs would be prominently displayed, making a first purchase especially easy. With faith that his new launch is genuinely innovative and likely to have a lasting hold on consumers' affections the brand manager might select some variation of this option.

He has now provided GEMs with the essential information it needs to launch his product in the marketplace. Before offering a contract, it can provide a snapshot of the likely impact of Chunkybiscs on the confectionery market. First it feeds his product details and pricing formula into stored overview data from that sector to show how the new entrant might have performed, given demand for chocolate bars without an established brand name and price levels over past weeks. Then it uses the same data to predict immediate demand for Chunkybiscs.

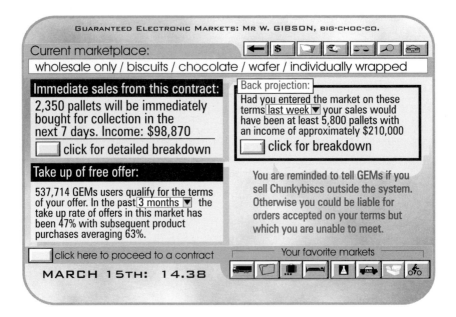

GEMs could include a facility for buyers called 'wait-and-purchase' whereby a maximum price for a given commodity is entered and the system buys automatically when the right deal becomes available. In this case there might be wholesalers or caterers on the system seeking individually wrapped chocolate bars within size, price and availability criteria met by Chunkybiscs: they would account for immediate sales within seconds of launch. Happy with these projections the brand manager clicks for a contract in which all his commitments just entered are embedded. His assurances will pass through the distribution chain to consumers. Because this leads to potentially enormous liability GEMs might have been told a more senior manager at the company has to countersign such agreements with his PIN before release.

Consider expansion into previously unthinkable sectors

With market entry and distribution this simple there should be little problem competing in new sectors. A company making paper cups, for instance, which had formerly only had relationships in the food services sector might launch disposable paper vases in the GEM for florist accessories, cautiously building up production as orders came in.

Service industry innovation might acquire a new importance

With access to the marketplace removed as a source of competitive advantage and the need (as opposed to emotional desire) for branding nullified by mechanisms that make every deal reliable, innovation is likely to become a key differentiator. The problem then becomes the speed with which a competitor could launch a me-too copy through GEMs. For manufacturers this is less of a problem. They can patent the processes and protect the descriptive trademarks behind a launch. In other sectors government could do much to encourage innovation by strengthening patent protection as they unroll an enabling act for a GEMs service. They might even allow service companies to protect their ideas from competitors for a given period.

The US government has made tentative steps in this direction already by granting patent protection to Internet service Priceline which has a distinctive way of matching buyers and sellers, initially on airline seats. This kind of protection for an idea rather than a technology could be extended. A week-long coach tour of South Africa's wine country for example is clearly not a concept that could be owned by any one travel operator but the same tour operated for the benefit of kite-flying enthusiasts with all equipment provided might be. As with existing patent law the onus could be on the pioneer to register his idea and take action against violators, but putting the laws in place would further ensure the vibrancy of the new marketplace by rewarding innovators. Financial service providers might find increasingly imaginative packages were the only way they could add value compared to the system's own loan matching. If those ideas were protected there could be even greater flexibility in the money marketplace. The cataloguing on GEMs would need to keep pace with the full diversity of offerings in each sector, the way this might grow organically is discussed in Appendix two.

18

Prepare to let go of customers

'Customer owning' would be an option, but would probably not be worthwhile

Any seller in GEMs could stipulate favoured buyers for whom he will drop prices. This could be automated so that, for instance, someone designated a member of a furniture store's loyalty programme would always have cheaper prices displayed. But they would be shown to the customer seeking a new armchair alongside those of multiple other sellers. As she narrowed her search down, by defining perhaps style of chair, pattern of material, then cost and availability with delivery charges for each option already calculated, the chances of the store being in her final selection would be increasingly slim. It would probably be more beneficial to orientate the company towards market overview information, trying to predict trends and 'own' a niche: individually tailored leather armchairs perhaps. Instead of outlining a pricing formula for one product the company specifies a rate at which it will build chairs of different sizes. These options, on as yet unbuilt items, are offered to every buyer whose requirements they match with the details sheet giving a delivery timetable and emphasizing the benefits of made-to-measure seating.

There would be little point in taking on the costs of communicating with a customer base for basic provisions. The manufacturer of Chunky-biscs in the example earlier, for instance, would harvest the names and addresses of individuals who had clicked to receive a free sample, but sending them a letter to cross-sell a second product would probably not be productive if competitors were offering easy click samples of their new creations. The same might not, however, apply to sellers of high-value items. A car maker, for instance, might offer a free test drive to

GEMs users who last bought a new vehicle on the system two years previously and were willing to take marketing messages containing an offer. (All GEMs messages would be bound by a contract so anyone originating the equivalent of unsolicited junk e-mails would be identifiable, with damaging consequences for their bond and trading record.) Car makers could follow up accepted road tests with postal or e-mail inducements to prospective purchasers but they would do so knowing several other test drives were probably only a click away. A manufacturer might instead focus on promotions made uniquely easy through GEMs contracts: lending a new model to qualified potential buyers for a week perhaps.

Expect a rise in ideological customers

A significant proportion of personal investors now opt for funds with an ideological bent. Likewise, GEMs users faced with a much wider marketplace than before might choose to complete sections in the system's user questionnaire that identify personal affiliations and allow them to be used as a means of prioritizing options in all markets. Devout Christians for instance might tell GEMs they will always favour suppliers who provenly donate to church causes and specify belief as a requirement when hiring staff on the system. An ethnic household might demand a similarly affirming political stance from sellers. This could be how emotional value is added to products in the wide-open marketplace. It might lead to a situation where, say, a shampoo production line is run one month by a firm that has genuinely positioned itself as pro-life in the abortion debate and the next by a similarly sized enterprise that meets requirements set out by pro-choice customers. There would be little point in either owning the line, it could be hired according to precise demand through GEMs, but they might be buying identical bottles to fit the machines and shipping the same ingredients. Illogical? It may be, but GEMs has no remit to iron out idiosyncrasies in consumerism.

19

Exploit the flexibility now on offer

Reassess the importance of a fixed supply chain

Order processing between manufacturers and their supplying companies was one of the first areas of business to go electronic. The now ageing technology known as Electronic Data Interchange turned *ad hoc* orders by e-mail into on-screen forms from which information could be extracted by the computer at either end for billing, transit details, stock management and so on. Later attempts to cut costs by creating more efficient supply chains led to the creation of electronic markets in which buyers were limited to large corporations whose presence made it worthwhile for sellers to invest in the software for that market. General Electric (GE), for instance, set up the Trading Process Network (TPN) through which they bought more than a billion dollars' worth of goods and services in 1997.[3] Other substantial purchasers including utility giant Con Edison now use the TPN to meet their needs. For the sellers a recurrent problem is how to integrate the demands of TPN with their in-house computer systems, so that information can flow seamlessly around the company.

The advantages GE and Con Edison gain from being big enough to set up their own marketplace in which potential suppliers must invest would be lost in a country with GEMs. Any regular purchaser, whatever their size, could personalize a template on the system listing the materials needed to keep a production line or home workshop fed. This could involve auto ordering if desired. So, for example, a chicken farmer who bought 500 additional birds on the system in the morning might find a truck load of feed from the cheapest supplier automatically arriving in the afternoon. Would purchasing in an open marketplace be preferable to buying from a small number of approved suppliers? The latter option would of course be available to GEMs users but the newly enabled capacity to shop from the entire marketplace in a few keystrokes could ensure unprecedented efficiency in supply. In the 1920s General Motors (GM) was the world's most integrated company, owning the manufacturers of 70 per cent of its automobiles' components. Despite this unique leverage on the supply chain William C. Durant, father of GM, insisted each of the owned firms sell half their output outside the company. Unable to luxuriate in assured sales the subsidiaries remained competitive on price and quality.[4] Any company with a strong trading record of supply in GEMs would have attained Durant's standards for the same reason.

GEMs could facilitate a tendering process for companies supplying non-standardized goods. Sign makers, for instance, could click through a list of specialities – stonework perhaps or three-dimensional displays – and highlight the ones in which they were interested in building a business. They would then tell the system how quickly they undertook to respond to enquiries: one working day, for instance, in a given week. (The time could be changed at will, being lengthened during busy periods, for example.) A design company that wanted say an illuminated figure constructed on behalf of a client would go to the GEM for signs and click on 'customized neon', immediately the system would specify response times to which suppliers had contractually bound themselves: perhaps a dozen firms willing to produce a quote in six hours, a further twenty to do so by the next day and so on. The buyer then types a description of the sign they want made and it is circulated to the selected suppliers who can phone or e-mail for more details before coming back with a price that, together with a newly agreed description, is sealed in a contract offered by the system.

Start rostering employees and assets on the system

There will be many companies who choose not to sell output in the new marketplace. Even so, they could use it for staff and resource management. Take for instance a house-building company. Their best workers would probably find themselves able to sell their services effortlessly in GEMs and would be the most tempted to leave an erstwhile employer. But by allowing staff to set pricing formulas and work more flexibly even while hiring themselves out elsewhere (employer confidentiality being a requirement in every contract they sign) the firm should retain at least a part share in their brightest stars. They might give GEMs a ranked list of their approved employees and ensure the best were offered periods of work first, the list could be supplemented by new recruits, for whom the system would search endlessly, who may be only willing to work on a part-time basis. It would require a different mind set for those used to pushing out weekly rosters compiled by software on a manager's desktop computer. But the flexibility in fixed costs offered could be a buffer against winds of change as the market for house purchasing moved to GEMs.

GEMs should offer users a 'shadow trading' facility whereby they can input details of an asset into the system plus a pricing formula but not enter the market. Managers can then see the worth of that item. A house builder for instance could 'shadow trade' their mobile crane on GEMs and see the pattern of bookings they would achieve if they were actually offering it on their stipulated terms. It might be in this finely tuned market that the cranes could be earning hire charges at times not required by their owner, even that they would be worth more rented out than employed on the house builder's own projects. The same could be true of production lines, distribution vehicles and fixed purpose buildings.

Be prepared for the business to erode to a core activity

However much the market atomizes there will be functions that can not be performed by individuals. A diving school, for example, that had previously employed ten instructors would probably find them migrating to GEMs where they could sell their services without over-heads and according to an ever-changing willingness to work. But those newly enfranchised instructors still need equipment for pupils: providing and maintaining it could be the school's new *raison d'être*. For some firms, information will become their new product: selling a paper-back recommendation service, for instance, rather than offering it as a marketing package with book sales. Or offering a 'we help you move' service based on local knowledge instead of selling houses.

Sellers who currently capitalize on confusion in the uncoordinated marketplace by bundling goods together for the convenience of buyers might find they were no longer adding value when all the components of an enquiry could be pieced together by the system. A camera seller for instance offering 'free' rolls of film with a particular model could find it made him uncompetitive. He would of course be able to promote the offer on his details page for that camera but the cost of films would be likely to push him down the price rankings for that model. Any user wanting a new camera and say six film rolls for next day delivery could input the two requirements in precise detail and have the two components from disparate sources with delivery priced alongside any bundled offers. However, in a widening marketplace, it may be that consumers become much more demanding about, for instance, the brand of film they require and find bundled offers too inflexible. Knowing what kind of cameras to sell and maybe offering separately bought after-sales packages would be the business focus, not inventing marketing offers.

In some sectors a supplier may even choose to abdicate the need to plan their exact offering in the market. In long-distance bus travel, for instance, most operators will select destinations and enter their seats for sale at given departure times. Travellers who require immediate confirmation of journey details would be matched with those suppliers. Other more leisurely travellers might tell GEMs something like 'book me a seat from Delhi to Agra at some point next Monday and confirm the details by Friday. Once it had 50 such commitments to purchase, the system might band them together then hire a vehicle and driver with a collective contract. They would simply be in the GEMs for coach charter, offering the best value for times and distance on the day in question.

Notes to section four

1. www.jackdaniels.com
2. P&G's Hottest New Product: P&G, *Business Week*, 5 October 1998, European Edition, p. 58.
3. Business at Net Speed, *Business Week*, 22 June 1998, p. 3.
4. Peter Drucker, The End of Command and Control, *Forbes Global Business and Finance*, 5 October 1998, p. 61.

conclusion

Electronic markets as a public utility

The world has been here before. A potent new technology is being exploited but only for restricted commercial advantage. Meanwhile, problems that it could address if made more widely available worsen. In the 1840s the technology was water pumping; the problem, epidemics caused by poor sanitation. Now electronic trading is being used primarily for new efficiencies in marketing while economies around the world become exclusive and inefficient. This is not a 'them' and 'us' argument. Just as no amount of wealth in Victorian England could create a barrier against airborne diseases that started in the poor areas so the impact of disintegrating social structures in the technological age can not be reassuringly compartmentalized.

Victorian advocates of mass water supply faced many questions about their unfamiliar concept. What rate would be charged for each cup of water? How would people who worked irregular hours store their share of water for use late at night or early in the morning? Who would be responsible for telling users when the product was safe to drink? It took some time for the sheer simplicity of the proposed service to be widely understood. Water was to make a transition from its status as a costly, laboriously collected and sparingly used resource to an abundant commodity, unthinkingly available at high quality around the clock in every home. A similar point needs to be made about Guaranteed Electronic Markets. Although indisputably complex in their inner workings, their role in a user's life would be elementary. With a few clicks on a TV remote control the service would allow individuals and companies to buy or sell anything instantly at the best possible price in a huge market-place that anyone was always free to enter on their own terms.

Despite making small units of production uniquely efficient, a GEMs system should have absolutely no ideological agenda. If automatic weapons for instance are legal in the country of operation there will be a GEM for them run by a committed franchisee with a pressing incentive to grow the market. Those who oppose guns would find the system equally useful. They would be only a few clicks away from joining a boycott of any firm in the armaments business or forming a solidly administered group to lobby for tighter gun laws. GEMs itself would be, like the World Wide Web, telephones or the money supply, simply a platform for diverse activity across a pluralist society. Its only agenda is to provide all the features of electronic trade to anyone who wants to use them. While the system would need to be built by big companies they would do so on the basis which corporations currently build our roads. Once finished a new highway is handed over for use by all drivers according to their individual priorities, not annexed for the advantage of the companies that built it.

A GEMs system would require vigilance to ensure its subservience was unwavering. It is not impossible, however, to construct a legal framework that creates profitable opportunity for electronic markets as a lowly public utility with the potentially pernicious applications of such powerful technology thoroughly eliminated. When centralised water supply was advocated, for instance, a key worry for many was the damage that an operator could inflict on an entire city with a phial of poison. Such an event has not happened during the century in which aggregated water provision has become the norm. Equally it should not be supposed that because a GEMs consortium could theoretically wield significant power it would put the opportunity for a once only megalo-maniacal act above commercial considerations and abuse that position.

Will the vision in this book become reality? Not immediately, certainly. The economic entities that dominate uncoordinated market-places will not go quietly and have multi-tentacled patronage that binds most of us to the *status quo* in some way. There is, additionally, a fear of managed change: a view that adverse social impact of new technology adopted by corporations is 'inevitable' whereas government initiation is an abhorrent interference in natural events. Faith in free markets runs deep. Paradoxically it is likely to be appropriated by organisations who, having become winners in the free market of today, are determined to stop a much freer market emerging for tomorrow.

Despite this resistance to planned transitions it is worth asking what the alternative to GEMs-style systems is. Electronic trade for corporate benefit is now on the march. Already we can see how electronic markets have made world-wide capital flows ultra-efficient. It is now often more effective to put funds into financial instruments divorced from economic reality, tradable only between bank computers, than to invest in workers, companies and communities. Money is leaching out of the tangible economy, which is overhead ridden, imprecise and unresponsive, towards a near-pure marketplace for world-wide capital. If the destabilizing impact of global money currents is to be diminished, governments face a choice. Either they band together and somehow disable the current efficiencies of capital movement or they elevate their populations' individual trading potential to the same effectiveness. GEMs should destroy a cardinal concept now underpinning the world economy: that money works most effectively for its owners when aggregated into enormous blocks. Once a public electronic markets system reached maturity it could push funds into highly efficient, rapid, atomized circulation.

Existing e-commerce companies – the firms who would logically build GEMs – are unlikely to be enthusiastic advocates of low margin, unknowing, universally provided electronic markets. They may yet repeat the fate of mainframe computer manufacturers in the 1970s and 80s. The notion of personal computers was beyond the corporate vision of these companies, run as they were by men who had devoted their lives to creating basement-sized hardware. Once PCs took off, former behemoths found themselves marooned in a backwater. New technology has always flowed towards maximized usefulness and cheapness, with little regard for the tenets of those who progressed its development. A conviction that 'the trading revolution will be decided by companies alone, governments are irrelevant' could one day seem as naïve as the view, once widely held, that the then powerful telegraph companies could stop the telephone being born. If policy makers can initiate the benefits of electronic trade for less cost and on a wider scale than private companies alone then, history suggests, that is what will ultimately happen.

appendix
one

Principles
governing GEMs

The benefits of a Guaranteed Electronic Markets system would be balanced by its potential to become the most sophisticated pervasive technology in history. In years to come there could be countless systems claiming to bring the unexpurgated advantages of electronic trade into mass public use. The following points are extracts from a lengthier attempt to define such a system that genuinely delivers the promise of this formidable technology, while protecting its users' interests and respecting a wider responsibility to society. Containment of the potential service is crucial to these principles. It should be restricted by statute to its core role: provision of automated markets, whose management have sacrificed any power they might expect to accrue from their key position.

Such a system would benefit from a mature relationship with users. Human error and occasional machine failings would be near inevitable on such a complex project. They should be promptly admitted and remedial action detailed: a politicized culture of whitewash and mis-focused recriminations would ultimately be self-defeating. Some principles that should guide a GEMs system are contradictory. On one hand it would want to give users a choice of regulatory regimes in any market, on the other it should prioritize simplicity of operation, for instance. Resolution will come down to editorial judgement based, as ever, on the balance deemed most likely to encourage market use. Ultimately faith in the system could depend on public perception of the consortium that runs it. If member companies see GEMs as a potential world-wide business opportunity, they would have every commercial incentive to see that their service adhered strictly to guidelines such as the following, where five key principles are outlined.

1. The system is programmed to automatically enforce fair trade

Each transaction is thoroughly enforced

■ Every deal in every market goes through a contract that can be amended by a seller; such amendments must be immediately obvious to a buyer. Except in the loans market, no user can be in debt to another user. Instead, payment is held in escrow by the system until such point as the contract has been clearly completed. In some cases (the decoration of a house for instance), this may entail release in tranches, as the buyer approves each stage of work according to steps laid out in the standard contract.

■ Sellers must provide proof of insurance cover to a level determined by the liabilities they could incur. These sums, held by GEMs so they are unquestioningly accessible, pay all earned interest to the company or individual who deposited them. Depositors should be able to stipulate how their bond is invested within the system's money markets, subject only to a requirement that the funds be automatically available at short notice by GEMs, in case of dispute. GEMs itself does not assess the cover required by any individual trader, that figure applies across all sellers in any given market: it is insurers who decide what it costs to find the requisite bonding. A hotel owner selling 100 rooms a night for a maximum $90 each, for instance, might have to deposit a bond of three times his room charge (the maximum likely payout to any disgruntled customer) multiplied by his number of rooms. If he has a credible trading record in related markets however this cover should be cheaply obtained from an insurer who judges him to be a worthwhile risk.

■ All GEMs are underpinned by immediately available adjudication, the steps of which are established in the contract between buyer and seller. In sensitive markets the first level of judgement if users can not agree reconciliation is the lower courts. For other sectors the system would establish panels of representatives from appropriate organizations. Judgement is funded by individual deposits and bonds. Some markets (childcare is one) require heavy regulation and verified entry requirements, others (fortune tellers for instance) will have to rely on 'best of ability' clauses in each contract.

■ GEMs tries to avoid allowing one organization to dominate adjudication in a particular marketplace, seeking instead to combine input from qualified groups who should be induced to agree on unified standards that will maximize turnover. Adjudication decisions are published openly on the system's information pages for users but identities of the parties involved might be removed.

■ The GEMs franchisee acts as a check on the power of adjudication authorities. He must see that they are acting within the broad aims of GEMs markets and building what amounts to predictable case law in judgements. If not, an alternative body has to be found: that process would be made public.

■ Franchisees must decide on the level of transparency appropriate to their market. Providers of medical services for instance might have to reveal not only their true identity but their full qualifications and professional history to prospective purchasers. Conversely neither sellers or buyers in a GEM for prostitution might be required to trade under their real names, the system alone knows who they are and would only release the information on receipt of a court order following criminal allegations.

■ The system can facilitate product recalls by allowing sellers to access their stored contracts with buyers and send a message to each. Before doing so they would have to sign a contract attesting to the genuineness of the recall. Abuse of the facility, by attempting to cross-sell under the guise of a recall for instance, would then incur sanctions.

■ The system is itself entitled to demand fair treatment from users. Any seller seeking to use GEMs simply as a means of listing their availability: displaying themselves in the electricians market for instance but then taking bookings by phone to avoid the strictures of a GEMs contract should be penalized. If they consistently list themselves but then withdraw from the market without a booking made over the system they could be warned automatically and eventually suspended. This should be explained as part of a contract with the system to be signed online by new users.

■ Provenly responsible buyers and sellers must be able to prove their status to each other.

Market conditions are structured around the needs of buyers, rather than favouring particular sellers

- The only deals enacted on the system are straightforward. There is no facility for instance to allow inertia selling where a purchase is made in a month's time if not stopped by the buyer within a fortnight.
- Customer-specific information, the extent of no-claims bonuses accumulated by a motorist for example, is owned by, and automatically verified for, the customer, who can use it to freely shop around.
- Full comparisons – cost per litre for various sizes of wine bottle for example – are always available. Where suppliers use contrasting classifications – measurement of audio amplifier power in RMS or MPC for instance – the system will convert between the two or, if that is not possible, invite sellers to input measurements in both and allow buyers to select which metric they wish to use. In a highly confusing marketplace, mobile phone tariffs perhaps, the relevant GEMs franchisee might construct a grid of options and invite sellers to input their rates in such a way that they can be fairly shown alongside competitors once a buyer has ranked her requirements. Sellers would not have to enter information for the grid but would risk losing sales by not doing so.
- The system trades in units of need, not sources of supply. Someone wanting to book a journey, for instance, could see different combinations of available rail, bus, taxi, rideshare and car hire options ranked according to their priorities.
- If a buyer's query turns up multiple sellers charging the same price all are listed but displayed according to randomizing software. Someone who wants a new copy of a widely available book delivered tomorrow, for instance, might find several hundred bookshops could meet that requirement with no price differential. In the absence of prioritizing from data in the buyer's user questionnaire (preference for local stores perhaps) all the shops will be displayed in jumbled order.
- Clear cataloguing is essential to each market. Sellers are responsible for categorizing their offering and not allowed unjustified listings for which they are penalized if reported. Someone selling places on a 'learn to fish' holiday, for instance, could justifiably offer them in markets for sports teaching, country breaks and angling holidays. Once all available places had been sold that offering would disappear from all three sectors. Conversely someone trying to list their

humorous wedding congratulations product in all sectors of the GEM for greetings cards would be stopped by the system.

■ Big companies trading on the system would have to decide whether to accumulate a corporation-wide trading record or a spectrum of records on a division by division basis. They could not switch between the two to disguise a poorly performing division.

■ Sellers are made to input a pricing formula in such a way that a straightforward price can then be calculated for each buyer's enquiry.

■ Tougher conditions are imposed on probationary traders. A driver in his early weeks, due to pick up a vehicle at a specified truckstop might have to arrive, and sign in on the location-specific terminal there, 60 minutes early so there is ample time for the software to hire another driver if the probationer does not log in.

Everything possible is done to attract wide-ranging sellers into each marketplace

■ Cumulative selling is enabled. So, for instance, a swimming pool manager could tell the system his facility would open late in the evening once a minimum of 12 buyers paid for an hour in the water. (He could also instruct it to roster one of his approved lifeguards before letting the sales go through.) Or a property developer could offer a building for conversion to flats, subject to a minimum number of apartments being pre-sold. The system will always tell prospective buyers what the required figure is, and the number of currently confirmed takers.

■ GEMs can facilitate trade in digitized products and can if desired act as their delivery medium. A company selling digital streams of music on the system, for instance, could choose between having them delivered via GEMs or from their own web site. The music could only be sold directly via GEMs once the core computer had received it and confirmed its technical suitability for playout. If this was not possible, or not desired by the seller, buyers would be sent automatically to the seller's web site on completion of their contract. Failure to receive the song would then lead to a disputes procedure. An icon would tell potential purchasers which option applied to each song.

■ The system is committed to full market information for all users. Where there is demand that is not being met in any market the extent of enquiries for the non-existent service would be freely available.

■ Sellers can keep their offerings out of certain markets. Someone selling live rabbits for instance could stipulate in the contract they are only to be purchased as a pet and not be available to rabbit farmers. Similarly, potential buyers can be defined, down to one individual if desired. Someone who had successfully hired a neighbour's car in the past, for instance, might phone them and ask if the vehicle could be made available that evening. The owner could then put the car on the market with full GEMs back-up but only one buyer listed as acceptable.

2. The system is committed to maximum usefulness

Each market must deliver the full benefits that electronic trading technology has to offer that sector

■ Guaranteed electronic markets operate no protectionism, seeking only to match each buyer with the best seller according to the purchaser's priorities at the time. They should not restrict their potential to preserve any existing or nascent structures of business or government.
■ The system itself needs constant public scrutiny to see that it is not delaying low-value markets out of fear they will cannibalize higher-value sectors. For example, management focused on the short term might be reluctant to open up a local deliveries market for the benefit of teenagers with bikes because those trades would undercut delivering by adults in cars, who charge more and therefore earn the consortium more commission. The order in which sectors are unfurled must be publicly justified.
■ Markets should cater for the smallest possible units of need so, for example, someone seeking a child's play house would be offered not only purchase options but a hire market in case they only required it for a week or less.
■ The system can offer 'soft matches' between suppliers and buyers seeking a custom-made product. It will bring together each purchaser with an array of sellers who have expressed interest in a particular category of work, then facilitate messages about requirements before binding the messages, with potential for amendment, into a contract for the final work.

- GEMs must have full indexing of products on offer and allow users a choice of ways of navigating the market categories.
- Any user could use the system to pay his household bills if he and the recipient desired.
- The system should offer users the opportunity to boycott certain sellers, or categories of sellers. However, it has a duty to see such boycotts can be 'turned off' at each user's discretion, and not remain in force through inertia long after the issue that prompted them has been resolved. A reminder of boycotts in force at perhaps three monthly intervals with buttons for ease of cancellation might be one solution.

The system is committed to simplicity of operation for users

- As each user becomes familiar with GEMs displays the number of key strokes in each transaction can be reduced, by displaying a symbol for 'standard contract not amended' against purchasing options, for instance. Buyers do not then have to call up the contract before signing. Likewise, a trading record can be expressed as a percentage, based on a standard formula that factors number of assignments, number of customers and number of complaints: this would enable easy comparison between traders.
- Ways of loading options for sale into the system must be constantly made easier. For example, the computer should be able to recognize every barcode on every product in the country of operation. Anyone wanting to sell food, books, records, clothes, toys, furnishings and so on need only find a barcode reader connected to the system to swipe in full details of their inventory, which will then be displayed on screen.
- In many sectors GEMs would need to grade its sellers so buyers can instantly select the level of service for which they are willing to pay. Wherever possible these increments should mirror existing structures for professional grades.
- All the formulae by which each market operates (grade levels, scales of fines and so on) are to be published openly.

The way options are displayed is to be constantly improved

■ Information is always presented in the most visual way possible. Sellers should be offered opportunities to individualize interactive displays; for example, cinema managers would be able to create a seating plan of their auditorium that could be used by buyers to select unsold seats for each showing. (The system would allow movie goers to click on a film title to see a map of cinemas in their area showing it, then call up available seating for each performance.)

■ Shoppers are given the widest range of criteria from which to prioritize a custom search. Someone selecting a holiday, for instance, could see available options listed in order of monthly average temperatures at destination, price, type of accommodation, precise depart and return dates, departure airports, availability of facilities selected by the buyer and so on. Once fully developed, GEMs should enable an individual to have exactly the best holiday for his personal requirements, constructed from a market of hundreds of thousands of offers.

■ Refinements should be added to each market as lessons are learned. In the pet-walking market, for instance, the franchisee might offer pet owners a chance to add a 'prone to biting' clause in each contract. That would ensure sellers were forewarned (at the risk they might charge more for such engagements) and could lessen the dog owner's liability in case of any subsequent claim.

■ Computer Aided Design software should be customized for GEMs. In the market for stairlifts, for instance, the interface would allow a buyer to construct a plan of their stairs by inputting measurements as requested. It then offers prices for that particular length and shape constructed from the pricing formulae of competing manufacturers coupled with similarly costed quotes from installers.

■ Bargain hunters should be allowed to shop with full flexibility. For instance, it should be possible to tell GEMs to book a journey 'when cheapest' in a window defined by two dates.

The system is committed to low overheads

■ Electronic markets must be cheap to be truly useful. GEMs should be fully featured but totally automated; no franchisee or member of system staff ever gets involved in an individual transaction. There must be external mechanisms to deal with trades that go awry, and provision for funding of those mechanisms within the terms of each user's acceptance into the market.

■ The behaviour of traders is regulated by the market, not by staff, but the system is set up to heavily penalize those who are found misbehaving. This involves holding its own copy of contracts for perhaps a month after each transaction. A manufacturer can make unrealistic claims, for instance, but they will be enshrined in every contract with a buyer. If one of them sues for misrepresentation and wins, the system will offer all other buyers from the previous month the chance to form a class action with an online lawyer. As ever, this is an immediate software function, not something decided on a case-by-case basis by staff. This principle – that traders' promises are not checked but they can expect competitors and consumers to challenge any dubious claims – translates into voting. Users could pose any question they like but, once the poll is complete, the fairness of the question has to be verified by an appropriate body before the result is deemed to have any validity. By asking a biased question, organizers would know their efforts will be wasted.

■ The system itself must be soundly financed with ample revenue-protection devices incorporated.

■ GEMs do not offer any function that requires human judgement on a day-to-day basis. The system can operate (if permitted) a range of lotteries, for instance. It would take in funds from users and pay out winnings, after deducting its own flat rate commission, according to a random number generator. But the system itself can not operate as a bookmaker because the setting of odds requires daily judgement; it is up to users to provide a market-making facility.

3. The system's neutrality is to be aggressively asserted

GEMs stand alone, divorced from political ideology or vested interests

■ All discussions between government and system management are on the record, posted on the system's own information pages.

■ Any decision about market operation that can be made outside the GEMs organisation – by a relevant regulatory body or by government – is resolved in that way.

■ Operating companies and staff must declare any business activity or affiliation that could give them an interest in a particular market sector; this information to be openly available to users.

■ Because of the danger of an unrepresentative elite emerging to run the system, senior staff are only allowed to work in day-to-day management for eight years (excluding a launch period); after that they can become consultants, but relinquish hands-on control. There is nothing of course to stop an individual then working on another country's GEMs-style system.

■ There are to be no favoured means of access to the system: it can be carried by any cable company, Internet provider or similar channel that can match required security standards. Nor can the system favour particular consumer technologies, including those of its consortium members. Because of its size, GEMs should accept input from all widely used types of smartcard readers for instance.

■ No outside body that is regulating a market on the system is to be allowed to use their involvement to propagate a particular ideological view of that market. In particular, the system does not pursue regulation to the point where it bars innovative 'fringe' traders from GEMs. For example, if registration of therapists was in force in the country of operation, that GEM might still allow unregistered practitioners to trade while making the distinction clear.

■ Offerings in a market can be ranked according to user choice by volume of sales, newest entries first, locality of traders and so on, but there are to be no 'GEMs recommends' selections. The system is neutral. It should, however, allow buyers to navigate its markets through templates constructed by outsiders. There might for instance be a 'Martha Stewart recommends' filter (created by an outside company who sells it to users) through which options in the home furnishing markets can be viewed.

■ A clear route for complaints about the system itself needs to be established, perhaps to an independent ombudsman who publishes findings openly. He might additionally pass on complaints to the rotating international bodies paid to inspect the system. Attempts to skew the markets or otherwise interfere with system purity should be a criminal offence.

The system has no other purpose than provision of electronic markets and immediately related functions

■ The system provides only the minimum service needed for a fully featured electronic markets operation. Additional facilities must be the preserve of competing outside suppliers. For example, many users would want to tailor their interface with GEMs as an alternative to the system's standard design. The consortium does not market a range of value-added interface options but ensures that any outside designer who wants to market software that converts the image sent by GEMs into something more distinctive can do so.

■ The GEMs brand name is not be to be applied to any other service.

■ The system knows its limitations. It is a marketplace not an information service, or a message forwarder. Any encroachment into these areas is only where required to facilitate specific trades.

■ A market in peripheral services could grow up with GEMs: digitizing traders' photographs and sending them to the central computer, for instance. Beyond ensuring that access is available to any company wanting to provide this service, the consortium should not get involved.

No one is to be coerced into using the system or deepening their level of involvement with the system

■ Management must not permit any attempt to make the use of the system mandatory. They should, for instance, actively oppose any plans to compel a user to file tax returns though GEMs.

■ GEMs are not to be used as a social order device, requiring offenders to sign on at a certain time to prove they are abiding by a curfew, for example.

■ Any user can sign off the system at any time once all their contractual obligations have expired. If their parallel economy account matches the number of points they were awarded on joining then no record is kept of their membership. If they have spent their points, minimal details are kept to ensure they do not receive a fresh supply on rejoining.

■ There is no minimum level of service for users and no 'relationship-building' attempts to increase usage. The consortium can buy poster space to advertise new features on GEMs, they cannot send messages to individuals, identified by the central computer as low users, promoting its wider benefits.

■ The system does not set out to limit access to any other online service, by stipulating monopoly carriage to cable TV companies, for instance.

■ A user can choose between having copies of contracts they sign on GEMs filed in their personal folder on the central computer (in which case they would be destroyed if the user closes his account) or downloaded to his own computer.

All adult users are treated equally

■ All sellers must submit to GEMs' verification, bonding, escrow and contract procedures, regardless of their size or trading background. This is an automated market that makes no exceptions for big brands or companies pleading exceptional reputations.

■ No one earns preferential treatment in the GEMs marketplace through spending power, frequency of use, type of business or ideological viewpoint. The only exception is emergency services; a verified doctor requiring a defibrillator, for example, would be able to click on a 'rush' icon and go ahead of any other users in a queue for available deliverers at that time.

■ Junior users must be restricted in terms of the trading responsibilities they can take on (only being able to agree a contract with a parent's PIN as counter signature, for instance) and the sectors they can access.

4. The system has responsibilities to the society in which it operates

In recognition of the importance that a mature GEMs network could acquire within the national economy, management have a special duty to run the system responsibly

■ Management should publish an online annual report focusing particularly on objectives for the following 12 months.

■ The system's own accounts must be compiled openly on its 'information about GEMs' pages so any user can see which markets are most – or least – profitable and monitor those sectors with added vigilance.

■ Despite the absolute commitment to user privacy, some sectors should track sensitive purchases: guns, pelts, rare animals or explosives for instance. These transactions will generate a data shadow enabling, say, a particular gun's ownership to be traced back for years if police gain a court order to open the records. Users must always be informed when these records are being compiled. Honest purchasers, of course, have nothing to fear from the process.

■ GEMs' technology could eventually be applied to sensitive social work, matching foster children and approved parents for initial meetings, for example. This should be provided through closed markets, only available to foster parents and social workers.

■ Provision must be made for checking traded items against a list of stolen goods, administered by the police.

■ The system could acquire a pivotal role in the nation's money supply and must be subject to publicly issued edicts from the government. In particular, there is a danger that the efficiency of the GEMs loans markets could create an unprecedented multiplier effect in cash circulation. Parliament may want to dampen this with minimum periods of borrowing.

GEMs could, eventually, become part of the checks and balances of a democratic society

■ Like a healthy press or broadcast industry, GEMs cannot afford to be cosy with government. Management must be relentless in their focus on rolling out unimpeded benefits of trading technology unless restrained by law. There are to be no backroom agreements with anyone.

- The only exception to the foregoing is at times of national emergency. GEMs recognizes its potential usefulness in a crisis, helping orderly evacuation of a city, for instance, by allocating places on trains or pick-up points for coaches, while issuing codes to residents of a particular zone who are to be allowed through road-blocks. Like the broadcasting networks, government could take over the system in a crisis: the central computer would seal personal data, wiping it rather than revealing information beyond that legitimately required in an emergency. GEMs should not bear the costs of setting up this programming which should be met from civil defence funds.
- Where the system's usefulness is restricted – by government limiting trade on GEMs that is legal in other forms, for instance – management must alert users that they are trading in a hobbled sector.
- System management must make public any information they obtain by virtue of their unique position but need not do so with information they chose to gather from sources available to all. Averaged patterns of GEMs usage through the day, for example, must be published. But should management decide to hire a polling company to assess public reaction to the system they can keep the results private because there is nothing to stop any other body conducting the same exercise.

GEMs have responsibility to existing organizational structures

- The system is not opposed to any form of doing business and will do everything – short of restricting its own potential – to accommodate existing organizations into its marketplaces.
- Brands are to have their status preserved; they should be displayed in illustrative material supplied by the maker (but not allowed to mislead in any way). Additionally, a brand owner is entitled to have pirated versions of his product range removed from the system. This would need to be done through the courts.
- GEMs would probably increase the sales of second-hand books, pre-owned movies on video and other items likely to deprive copyright holders of income. Policy makers might decide that a levy be made,

on each such sale, that is automatically transferred to the originator of the material and the system should facilitate this.

■ Charities must be able to collect donations on the system.

■ Without lowering its commitment to political neutrality, the system recognizes the desirability of according certain status to some government functions. When parliament launch a referendum on the system, for instance, it must be showcased on the voting page, not simply listed amid polls launched by ordinary users.

5. Maximum security is an overriding priority

The system has automatic protection built in for users

■ Any user who fears their communication with the system is being monitored through a tap on the phone line can make use of a room at the GEMs building which allows direct access to the core by nervous users (who may be running a sensitive political group on the system for instance).

■ Management should recognize that security is as much a human as a technical consideration. The consortium must encourage a culture of openness and recruit from all sections of society. In particular they should:

  ■ place no restrictions on staff talking to the press if they have concerns about the system's probity.

  ■ set up a 'whistleblowers' page where authenticated staff can leave indelible messages readable by any user browsing the page. This would leave the consortium open to embarrassing attack by disgruntled workers, but a vulnerable management is preferable to a potentially omnipotent system.

■ Nobody is allowed remote access to the core programming. Franchisees who want to change the layout of their market front end compile the changes remotely but then have to send them to a secure control room to be assessed for security and uploaded.

As a natural monopoly, with so much potential for difficult-to-detect interference, the system is too sensitive to be regulated by any one body

■ Tough, and increasingly ingenious, inspection is to be welcomed. The system must genuinely have nothing to hide and everything to gain from showing its willingness to be dissected by inspectors with a range of ideological viewpoints and technical experience. Money should be set aside to fund these inspections (by organizations across the political spectrum from around the world) via an independent body which publishes their findings immediately.

■ The consistent points for inspection are always verification that any user can leave the system with all personal data irrevocably destroyed at any time and that the software has triggers which will warn users automatically of any attempt to tamper with data.

■ Mechanisms that provide for independent inspectors at short notice must be set up. Management cannot alter the central code unchecked, by pleading special requirements in an emergency.

■ A GEMs consortium that has been sanctioned for monopoly of government approval must accept it has forfeited rights to normal commercial secrecy; it has no comparable competitors, while demonstrable integrity has become its most important long-term asset. Nothing can be concealed from inspection teams.

Security of individual trades is an equal priority

■ No one can use the system without an identifying password or PIN. These can be changed whenever a user believes her personal security might have been breached. Additionally users can opt for an array of passwords, insisting on an additional word for trades over a certain amount for example. Partial-access code-words can also be generated; a frequent motorist for instance might have a code-word that allowed a colleague to access his account, but only for a restricted one-off visit to book a mechanic in case of a breakdown.

■ Apart from an automatically compiled trading record, the system does not hold any file on users that they cannot control fully.

■ One party in a transaction cannot obtain any information about the other except what they have chosen to reveal.

- Information entered by a seller to flesh out a details page is their copyright and must be protected from unauthorized downloading.
- Any automatic transfer of information is flagged to the user. In the UK, for instance, anyone buying a television must by law have their details passed to the TV licensing authority. GEMs would tell buyers this was happening.
- With company accounts the user is identified by their title within the organization (that is, senior purchasing manager, Acme Corp.) not in any way that links to their personal trading account. Any sanctions are applied to the company as a whole, to avoid shifting job titles as a technique for escaping punishment.

appendix
two

A business model for initiating GEMs

Overview

This model is an attempt to outline one possible route for companies who seek to make the GEMs vision a reality. It is not a detailed business plan. As with previous launches of public infrastructure there can be no numerical evidence of final demand, but omens abound. To take one example of desire for underpinned screen trading once provided: the French futures exchange, the MATIF, experimented with online markets in April 1997. The plan was to see after a year or so if they could establish a niche alongside long-established open outcry trading by traders. Within two weeks however electronic trading had won so conclusively that the trading floor was wound down.[1]

Although a fully integrated GEMs system could only be initiated by government there might be opportunity for interested companies to propagate the potential of public markets while positioning themselves as logical first port of call for any parliament wanting to offer such a system. This demands an unusual business model: part hearts and minds campaign, part international lobbying effort and part partnership-building exercise. Many computing success stories have been born out of previously unthinkable commercial strategies. The newborn Netscape gave away its sole product without charge, to establish quick critical mass; Digital developed the AltaVista search engine with no income line in sight, motivated only by an urge to grow the Internet. Despite the uncertainty and enormous investment required to construct a GEMs core computer, however, it is worth reiterating the scale of potential return: accumulated commissions (individually small but aggregated automatically) on what could be a significant proportion of domestic transactions in the countries of operation for the period of concession.

Awkwardly for a project likely to lead to the demise of so many corporations, GEMs could only be effectively promoted by large companies. A small start-up, however ambitious, would find it hard to open doors to senior politicians and be taken seriously by their electors. Nor could it pull together the heavyweight partners required to build such a demanding system while ensuring that the vision remained true. Only a sizeable organization could withstand the resourceful, high-level, hostility public markets will inevitably attract. The corporate mind-set required for GEMs is far from the short-term, technology-driven, opportunism that pervades Silicon Valley. An authentic commitment to inspection, transparency and preserving national identities might seem laughable in the early days of such a business but if it is to succeed the final consortium would be trusted unthinkingly by millions of people around the world, many of them having little faith in their own government's rectitude. Like an airline predicated on enhanced cabin service but dispensing with safety procedures, a GEMs builder viewing their task purely in technological terms could enjoy only short-term success. Because of the unique core competencies involved, the companies that bring fully fledged public markets to the world may come from far outside the computing establishment.

What a business model must deliver

- Decentralized control to make GEMs acceptable to diverse populations.
- Long-term perspective in an industry constantly restricted to short-termism by ever-changing technical foundations.
- Public trust, even affection. There are lessons to be learned from companies like Apple Computer and Hewlett Packard that, in their formative stages, reaped considerable benefits from a positive culture of humanity when compared to unimaginatively commercial behemoths like IBM. If the relationships within the organization are

right, GEMs, with its dedication to rolling out trading advantages for the benefits of all, could have the potential to become a very popular institution in the mind of potential users and prospective employees.

■ The system needs to be prepared for a swift growth phase when, perhaps, dozens of new market sectors are being launched every week with all the attendant advantages of momentum in roll out. However, the markets being launched need to be properly thought through, intuitive to use and competently edged towards critical mass.

■ The markets offered, and features within them, should be driven by a diverse array of entrepreneurs, each believing that they can make a particular sector work and not controlled by a core staff. However, all markets have to pass GEMs' rigorous requirements for guaranteeing transactions.

■ As market usage builds, GEMs would need to remain closely in touch with the needs of users in each of its thousands of sectors. The sophistication with which buyers and sellers are matched, and the enforcement mechanisms underlying the safety of each transaction, must be constantly evolving to increase the attractiveness of each sector.

■ Enduring 'reality antennae' would be crucial. Seismic shifts in technology and customer expectations have, in the past two decades, exposed the corporate complacency of once indomitable industry giants like IBM and Apple. As a semi-protected industry, GEMs could be particularly prone to a collective mind-set that calcified the *status quo* while the outside world moved on.

Structure of the core organization

This business model assumes a board representing a consortium of three companies or more, divided into three areas of expertise.

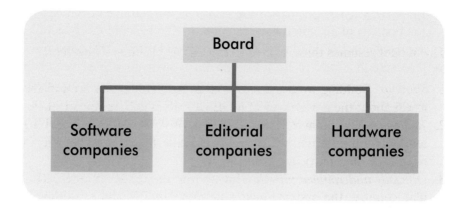

Of the three areas of expertise bought to the enterprise by these companies it is 'editorial' that would drive the business plan. Hardware requirements have past precedents to rely on: the enormous installations at the heart of long standing systems like SABRE, AMADEUS and WORLDSPAN for instance. Likewise, software provision has antecedents on which to draw (SQL databases, CGI interfaces and PDF document technology, for example). It is what can be loosely termed 'editorial' – the writing of market interfaces, liaison with outside verification bodies, political negotiation and dealing with opposition – that will break new ground and determine the system's success. Like media organizations, those who define GEMs' editorial stance will have to live with unending controversy about their decisions. This model focuses on the editorial process and assumes the technological side, although undoubtedly demanding, need not be elaborated at this point.

The editorial companies would need to be in a position to provide the following:

■ Funding
■ Willingness to allow GEMs to be a stand-alone brand with its own identity and values
■ No ideological or self-preservation restrictions on GEMs' potential
■ Understanding of concepts around governmental independence
■ Clout for consortium building and political networking
■ Willingness to engage with opposition.

A timetable for the operation

This model assumes three phases to the GEMs business. They are:

1. *Start up.* Building awareness and lobbying parliaments around the world about the advantages of a GEMs system underpinned by law.
2. *Tendering.* The point at which one or more governments is inviting tenders for a system to which they will grant the required benefits in return for their particular concessions.
3. *Officially underpinned growth.* Having won the tender in one particular country, the system must now move swiftly and smoothly to mass usage.

Each phase will now be examined in detail.

Phase 1: Start up

The key strategy for phase 1 is to position the consortium as clear market leader for phase 2. A small team is envisaged within an editorial company keen to initiate the project. They would have six distinct tasks:

1. *Launch at least one initial GEM market sector on the Web.* Big software schemes, launched from scratch, have a tendency to implode. Nine out of ten software projects overrun.[2] A small-scale web-based GEM, initially in just one sector in one country, would create a test case of how the enforcement mechanisms, even without governmental support, should ensure a free and open market. It would also give a head start in refining the core programming to drive this kind of service.

   Characteristics of trade sectors where a GEM could have maximum impact include:

   ■ Multiple buyers and sellers with high rates of Net connectivity
   ■ Requirements of both sides changing constantly
   ■ Potential users who can be cost-effectively targeted with advertising.

Possible sectors for a web-based market might be:

- Load space – a market allowing truck operators to trade space in empty and half-empty lorries already committed to a journey.
- Computer equipment
- Short-term professional services

2. *Begin building a pool of qualified people who understand the project.* Through public meetings, Internet discussion and presentations at conferences, the team aim to communicate the aims, and culture, of GEMs to qualified individuals who are encouraged to enlist on the project's web site (currently www.gems.org.uk) as potential candidates to work within the system at a later date. Ownership of this database, listing people who had engaged with the project, and understood how it needed to proceed within their particular area of expertise, could be a significant asset (compared to latecomers) once phase 2 was underway.

3. *Begin constructing the consortium.* Potential software, hardware and connectivity partners can be sounded out and given explanations of the project and its aspirations.

4. *Promote independent thinking about GEMs and their uses.* Academics, think tanks and journalists should be encouraged to explore the social applications of GEMs with any seed money offered, free of editorial control. The aim is to give any government contemplating phase 2 a range of voices and areas of knowledge that have been applied to the concept. Genuine scepticism about the project will also be useful: it emphasizes the undoubtedly real commercial risks being taken by the consortium who, perhaps, should also anticipate criticism of any financial success in later years.

5. *Spread awareness among carriage providers.* GEMs could be a killer application for digital TV. For Web users a browser button, similar to the one negotiated on British copies of Internet Explorer by BBC Online, would be an asset.

6. *Begin lobbying governments around the world.* Countries like Singapore, Sweden and Ireland who have demonstrated deep official commitment to IT projects would be logical places to start. Their small populations would limit the scale of potential return from one of these nations but technologically literate users would probably be more tolerant of the glitches that will inevitably blight a first GEMs launch. Some of the arguments that could be used in support of the project when approaching politicians or opinion formers at organiza-

tions like the International Monetary Fund are listed below. It would take only one government to fully appreciate the benefits GEMs have to offer for phase 2 to begin.

Selling GEMs to politicians

Some points to be made:

- GEMs is not about regulating or restricting electronic commerce. Instead it creates an additional track to the technology's development which companies and businesses can use if they wish. No one would ever be forced to trade on the system.
- GEMs would cost the taxpayer nothing.
- A mature GEMs system could mobilize much of the resources of a country's economy for inward investors at very short notice.
- The first country to go down this route would become a focus for international attention.
- Global 'free market' electronic commerce threatens to diminish nations' control over their own economies. GEMs gives that control back.
- GEMs can clean up an economy because each transaction is automated and contracted. A government might target tax decreases to encourage deals currently in the grey market onto the system.
- GEMs could be the 'killer application' that encourages a population to move online and further drive infrastructure and terminal development. This is particularly applicable to countries like the UK where the government has politically committed itself to digital TV.
- The notion of government awarding a protected monopoly to enable deep private investment is more common than many realize. It is, for instance, how the Channel Tunnel was built.
- Inviting GEMs into your country does not involve handing over to a foreign company: the markets would be run by franchisees, all of whom will be nationals.

Above all:

- Uniquely among commercial e-commerce schemes, the GEMs project has every incentive to extend sophisticated facilities to even the poorest in society. Public access terminals in depressed areas make business sense for the consortium because, having unlocked the economic potential of those residents, the consortium then takes a flow of commissions from their resulting activity.

Within a year of formation, the GEMs team could be nourishing a growing database of desirable potential employees who already share the culture and aspirations for the project. There should be a web of potential consortium members and governmental contacts around the world. Intellectually, the project would be underpinned by at least one operating market and a spectrum of expert thinking independent of the consortium. This would be accomplished against a backdrop of increasing public awareness of the potential of point-and-click purchasing and, if the team are competent evangelists, a growing realization of the limitations to come in an uncoordinated online marketplace versus the potential that guaranteed electronic markets have to offer.

Phase 2: Tendering

Phase 2 begins when a government announces they are committed to setting up officially underpinned, universally available, fully featured electronic markets and invites bids to construct and run the service. If phase 1 has been pursued with sufficient vigour, one consortium may be the only candidate to run such a service at this point. A focused early start to phase 1 could be a highly effective barrier to competitors. Other consortia who have not meticulously prepared the groundwork and developed the principled commitment to neutrality, national identity and ruthless inspection could find it hard to convince politicians that they are ready for an unembarrassing launch and smooth trajectory to critical mass in the new markets. Just as in the 1970s 'no-one got fired for buying IBM', in the first decades of the 21st century no politician should have any problem explaining why they entrusted their country's fledgling public electronic markets system to a well-prepared consortium.

It is important to differentiate between the character of a final GEMs service and the tone of any campaign to win a tender which would inevitably involve a high profile in the relevant country. The former should be impartial, unobtrusive and banal in its reliability. The latter could be much more spunky.

Phase 3: Officially underpinned growth

Phase 3 begins with the winning of an officially backed universal electronic markets concession anywhere in the world. The consortium should eventually confine itself to providing core functions of this system with independent franchisees running each market sector: one person franchised to launch the GEM for industrial clays, for instance, another licensed by the consortium to operate the house cleaning market. Franchisees would be responsible for drawing up the front-end screen designs for that market, while all the processing is carried out by the core computer. They earn a percentage of commission from their sector.

Why adopt this model rather than simply employing staff to oversee the markets?

■ Public trust in the system will be higher if the people running its markets are sole traders from a variety of backgrounds spread around the country with their own financial stake in the project rather than employees of one monolithic enterprise.

■ Each market must be run by someone who is constantly motivated to grow the number of buyers and sellers using that sector daily. They do this by progressively adding new sophistication to the buyer–seller matching process (in conjunction with the consortium software writers) and by promoting their particular GEM to relevant companies and individuals. There is every reason for someone who is running, say, the manufacturers' pigments GEM to remain with that sector, developing their relationships and knowledge, over many years. Employees would expect to be promoted, constantly destroying the system's knowledge base.

■ The consortium's requirement for start-up funding is lessened. Franchisees could bear the unique costs of establishing their particular market.

■ An employee-based operation would open a gap between high profile markets, which everyone wanted to run, and less desirable, low turnover, sectors. The right franchising formula, however, can financially motivate the less attractive markets on to an equal footing.

■ Franchisees act as a check on management that should keep the consortium constantly alert, avoiding complacency. Witness, for example, the recent determined response from McDonald's franchisees to the company's unpopular launch of a 55 cent burger in the USA. Employee managers would have been far more reticent.

■ A rogue franchisee is less likely than a rogue employee because of a financial stake in their particular market. They would however be harder to dismiss.

■ New markets can be added organically by entrepreneurial would-be franchisees who approach the consortium with an idea for a market that centrally directed development could not have imagined. A committed individual for instance might want to launch a GEM for 'home tea parties' allowing anyone who wished to sell places at a gathering in their home to neighbours to do so. Assuming that individual was judged sound enough to operate under the GEMs name and could find the cash to set up their market they could then attempt to establish a whole new area of trade.

How the franchising might work

GEMs' requirements of its franchisees would not be unique. The individuals must become part of a strong corporate culture, remain motivated for long-term growth in an otherwise short-term industry and use individual flair to drive their small part of a highly standardized operation. Other organizations have mastered this formula already. In his book *Behind the Arches*, author John F Love says of the company that pushed its fast food operations around the world: 'McDonald's is run neither by one man nor by executive committee. Indeed, it is not even a single company. It is a federation of hundreds of independent entrepreneurs – franchisees, suppliers and managers – united by a complex web of partnerships and creativity… a contemporary franchise system flourishing on an unparalleled scale.'[3] Eighty-five per cent of McDonald's front ends (high street outlets) worldwide are franchisee operated. Individuals running their particular sector within a government backed electronic market system would probably require greater powers of diplomacy and lateral thinking on a day-to-day basis than the manager of a fast food operation but there is much the GEMs franchising operation could learn from McDonald's. In particular:

■ franchisees are required to commit themselves for lengthy periods; 20-year contracts are the norm at McDonald's

- the company will only franchise to hands-on individuals, not companies, groups, families or absent investors
- prospective franchisees must become thoroughly immersed in the company's culture and values, starting with a period working menially in an existing outlet before graduating to one of their 'hamburger universities'.

Like McDonald's, GEMs would aim to present a very simple and uniform face to the world, one that masks a complex and evolving structure behind the scenes. The burger giant, for instance, famously imported new cattle breeds and potato varieties into Russia before opening their Moscow branches rather than endanger customers' expectations of consistency. GEMs need to be this invisibly resourceful to a mass of unattached customers who take the service completely for granted. The project should build a pool of potential franchisees who have imbibed – and contributed to – its philosophy. The roll out plan is based on these individuals each becoming completely immersed in their eventual sector, using their developing knowledge to grow that particular market. If they are properly trained, and supported, the system should be capable of unveiling, perhaps, a hundred or more new sectors a week during phase 3.

Franchisees would be overseen by a 'markets executive' who is in charge of a group of related sectors, ensuring the markets blend into each other seamlessly and consistent standards are imposed across that area as a whole. The franchisee for curtain making and fitting for instance would be supervised by the markets executive for home furnishings. Franchisees would pay no up-front fee to the consortium but might have to put a sum in bond to cover any professional negligence. Additionally they would be responsible for financing support services for their particular launch. These would include lawyers to write the contracts (within a house style), archivists to collect photographic material and data such as manufacturer's model numbers, and screen designers who translate the franchisee's vision into a GEMs-compatible display to users. The consortium should not restrict the market for these suppliers with a licensing system but encourage competing provision by setting up a GEM for those who wish to enter the market, enabling new franchisees to hire traders at the price and experience level with which they are personally comfortable.

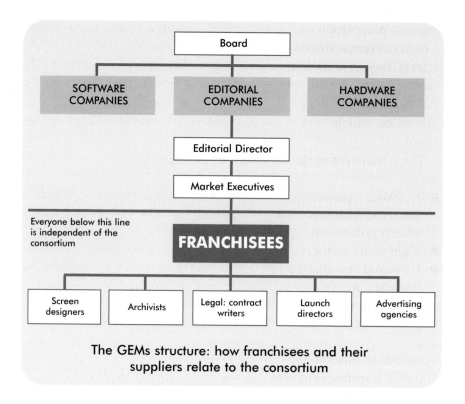

The GEMs structure: how franchisees and their
suppliers relate to the consortium

The franchisee funding formula

In pursuit of simplicity and universal value, GEMs should charge its
users a single flat rate percentage of each deal across all markets. How
are franchisees rewards calculated? They can not receive a fixed
percentage of turnover in their sector otherwise everyone would want to
run commission-rich markets like office rentals while no-one could
make a living from a low value sector such as surgical appliances.
Instead, franchisees bid for the percentage of commission they would
require to run a particular market. In a high-turnover, easy-growth,
sector like overnight accommodation the franchisee might agree that 98
per cent of commission received goes to the consortium, the remaining
2 per cent could still amount to a significant income for the individual.
On a less attractive sector, say the market for hearing aids, the
successful franchisee might have stipulated the consortium keep only
four per cent of the commission earned. The latter is still a valuable

business proposition for the core companies: 4 per cent of something is a better revenue stream than 0 per cent of nothing. The hearing aids market, though in itself not a money spinner, would help to drive GEMs further into the health service, where other sectors can reap more lucrative benefits. The price of universal, flat rate, service to users is franchisees on widely varying percentages of revenue generated by their sector.

The advantages of this funding formula are:

■ It favours pioneering, risk-bearing franchisees who can bid for attractive markets at a high percentage rate before competition among potential franchisees is fully developed
■ Tight niche sectors can still be profitable for franchisees
■ It would encourage organic growth through entrepreneurial launches, where only one person was convinced they could make a particular sector work. They would be able to negotiate a high percentage in return for the risk they undertook.

Crucial to this funding formula is the maintenance of a large pool of potential franchisees to keep bidding competitive. This should enforce a humane tendering system: if a franchisee is outbid for one sector it is worth encouraging them to go for others rather than simply rejecting them. Like McDonald's, the GEMs consortium should seek out sympathetic financial institutions who understand the business plan and will construct loans specifically for successful franchisees who do not have their own funds to invest.

The stages in rolling out a new market

Consortium management would have a sector-by-sector roll out timetable which would be published openly. Anyone could bid to run a market on that timetable or come up with a sector of their own that is not on the list of obvious GEMs markets. Potential franchisees would then be assessed by a panel of consortium staff. They would be expected to have absorbed the project's values, in the early days through attendance at public meetings or Internet discussions and as the system develops, by spending time with working franchisees.

Candidates would be assessed on:

- the percentage of commission that they wish to retain if awarded the contract
- their understanding of, and commitment to, GEMs values
- coherence of plans for harnessing core GEMs software functions for that particular market and plans for further functions they may require
- their knowledge of, and contacts in, the proposed sector
- marketing plans to target potential users of the new sector
- relevant experience running some sort of service.

Once a franchisee was selected they would be expected to hire an experienced GEMs launch director to provide assistance and, from their own funds, have to complete the following within a fixed timescale of perhaps three months:

- 'Storyboard' potential screen designs to be demonstrated in rough to potential users whose input is then used to further refine the way options are presented.
- Assess whether there is a need to offer additional regulatory options to ensure confidence in the new market. This process would not be unique to GEMs. In Britain in the 1980s for instance aerobics instructors were hampered by lack of any recognizable qualification for their skills. A group of them initiated a new certificate in teaching of exercise to music. Occasionally a GEMs franchisee might need to encourage something similar in sectors without any existing structure for sellers who wished for external assessment of their abilities.
- Hire a lawyer to draw up the standard contracts and their permissible variations for that sector within the guidelines laid down by the consortium's legal department.
- Find insurance to cover their personal liability within GEMs' terms of operation.
- Set up verification and adjudication panels that can grow organically as their market expands. By far the easiest way of doing this would be to induce an existing organisation to take on the responsibility and ensure that they are sufficiently rewarded through the price charged to potential traders for assessment. For example, the franchisee for the locksmiths sector on a UK GEMs system might ensure the Master Guild of Locksmiths set the standards for market entry

and acted as arbiter in any disputes. The principles of guaranteed electronic markets lay down ground rules for these relationships.

■ Ensure government are advised of any likely regulatory issues inherent in the new market. If planning to launch a GEM for raw meat, for instance, it would be wise to see if officials planned to restrict sales to licensed butchers on public health grounds.

■ Define the range of parameters for market overview screens covering their sector.

■ Hire an advertising agency to work on promotional materials; like the screen displays these would be within a GEMs' house style.

■ When ready, launch their market on the system. During this initial period the interface appears with a white border around the screen containing the words 'not guaranteed'. Users are warned they should take all the precautions they would in an ordinary trading environment: dealing only with sellers they will trust, not relying entirely on the GEMs contract, confirming a deal by phone if it is complex and so on. No commission is extracted from transactions at this point, the aim is to get a market going and take feedback.

■ Over following weeks the border progressively fades as turnover increases, potential loopholes are closed, user navigation is tightened and transactions become more solid. Eventually the border is removed, signifying GEMs and the franchisee now take full responsibility for the service, and the market starts to take commission.

What do franchisees do after their launch?

Once a particular market is running the launch director withdraws and the franchisee settles down to life managing that marketplace: continually looking at ways to constantly attract new buyers and sellers. Franchisees could work from home or in local office accommodation of their choice, not in a consortium building. Their consistent priorities would be to publicise their service while monitoring reaction from users and to look for new functions and categories to add to their sector. Additional software facilities, however, should be coordinated at consortium level so the core programming is not fragmented and new functions can be shared around. The franchisee for fresh vegetables, for instance, might want to give growers the option of inputting a batch of carrots for sale at a certain price while telling GEMs to automatically drop the price if they remain unsold a day later. This time-related pricing mechanism could be equally useful in, say, the periodicals sector, where sellers may want to charge a high price on the day of issue and drop it progressively in the days that follow. Once demanded by one franchisee, a new software function must then be available across the system. When considering in which order to develop functions, the core software team could prioritize the needs of markets in which the consortium retains a high commission percentage: the needs of the overnight accommodation franchisee taking precedence over those of the hearing aids market operator.

A GEMs-style market would probably encourage a far wider range of offers than the uncoordinated world where shoppers are so restricted in the range they can access. Franchisees would be responsible for encouraging new offerings, many of which could scarcely exist outside the system. They do this by providing new contract clauses to sellers who want them and displaying icons that allow higher level sellers to identify themselves from the start of a buyer's search. To take an example: some computer owners who need repairs to their machine are deterred by the way technicians unnecessarily peruse the contents of hard drives in order to establish the level of data corruption. A hardware repairer selling in GEMs who wanted to offer a 'guaranteed confidential' service, in which customer drives were assessed by another computer, and not human eyes, might start to write such a clause into contracts himself and list that facility on his details page. Others might follow his lead. The franchisee should then see that his lawyers fashion a defining paragraph for that level of service, which is made available to all sellers when they enter the market, while a 'click here if you are willing to pay extra for confidential service' facility is offered to buyers.

Another part of a GEMs' franchisee's job would be monitoring the cataloguing of their sector. The system's need to provide order for shoppers must not drive out innovative sellers who defy any existing category. Each GEM should include a 'miscellaneous' section where offers far from the mainstream could be browsed and purchased in safety. Someone who wanted to offer a horse whispering service, for instance, would probably find no GEMs section existed for their chosen profession but they would be welcome at the veterinary services/equine/miscellaneous marketplace. Here they would be asked to type in a name for their uncategorized offering, their qualifications to offer it and a pricing formula. With no intelligent questions available for people who heal sickly steeds by murmuring in their ears, GEMs would have to fall back on a standard formula for unclassified suppliers to assess the bonding required for buyer protection. It might for instance insist the seller provide a minimum five times the highest fee they planned to charge for any particular assignment and accepted judgement by the country's leading animal charity in case of dispute. Anyone who repeatedly mis-filed their offerings, trying to pointlessly input details of their horse whispering into the optical supplies marketplace perhaps would be treated in the same way as a driver who behaves badly on the roads. If they persist they are warned and finally banned: in the case of GEMs this process would be automatic and inescapable. Each franchisee would monitor their miscellaneous section in search of new market trends. If horse whisperers were proliferating, the individual running the veterinary services/equine sector would have every incentive to discuss their priorities then build them a specific marketplace.

Kickstarting the markets

It is sometimes argued that a GEMs system would be hamstrung by 'the telephone trap': once everyone is using the new system it becomes invaluable, but until that point is reached there is little incentive to join. This 'Catch 22' kept telephone usage low for several decades. Like the phone network, GEMs relies on critical mass for much of its appeal. However, GEMs would be free of many of the drags on usage experienced by pioneering telephone companies:

■ GEMs would not require users to invest in specialized hardware.
■ Much of the cultural conditioning required to appreciate the value of GEMs will be carried out by other service providers. Potential telephone users had to be educated into the notion of having a number that related to each friend or business contact and speaking to them down a wire. By the time GEMs launches, populations will have access to point and click shopping through the Internet and interactive television. The cultural leap from online purchasing to an open electronic marketplace is far less than that from meeting friends to phoning them.
■ Entering the GEMs marketplace as a buyer or seller would be free, you can see what the system has to offer for your particular needs without cost. Public kiosks would make this facility available to even the least connected household.
■ GEMs could facilitate impulse registration. Browse the system as a non-user, see something you want to buy or a niche in which you want to sell, take your passport to the Post Office (or other registration centre) and return ready to buy or sell. It costs nothing and there is no delay for installation.

■ GEMs would function as a non-trading terminal for anyone reluctant to
take a first step to selling online. A hairdresser, for instance, could type
appointments taken over the phone into a GEMs diary and have all their
records and accounts intelligently compiled by software that understood the
mechanics of their business. This would cost them nothing, but would make
it a very short step to entering a pricing formula and accepting bookings on
the system.

Even without critical mass, a GEMs system offers significant benefits when
compared to other forms of trade:

■ Neutral, watertight contracts. If hiring a plumber through the Yellow Pages
for instance it could be worth a householder telling him she wished to sign
a contract in the GEMs household services market just to put the relationship on a solid footing.
■ Verification of traders. It is very much in the interests of say, temporary
secretaries to offer themselves on the system because a reliable automatically compiled bookings record would validate future claims about levels of
experience.
■ Market overview facilities allow sellers an instant pricing guide that will be
less precise, but only marginally less useful, in a system that has not
attained critical mass.
■ The parallel economy within GEMs effectively gives users money for
nothing, but it can only be spent on the system.

GEMs would offer its users not novelty or short-term promotional benefits but
deep and sustainable trading and shopping advantages. The fledgling system
should not be reticent about spreading this message:

■ GEMs' publicity budget is probably most effectively spent at franchisee level
rather than on a national message. The franchisee for gym sessions for
instance should have the funds, and the growing web of contacts, that
enable her to have 'make your next booking through GEMs' posters put up
in changing rooms across the country. Likewise the market operator for
quarrying equipment could be advertising in the relevant trade press,
maybe with running weekly totals of the kinds of equipment available
within his sector. These targeted messages, within a house style, could be
funded in a partnership between franchisee and consortium. The aim is to
bombard a population with messages about GEMs' particular relevance to
sectors in which they personally might trade.
■ Carriage providers could have much to gain from cross promoting the
service on their existing output.
■ Inevitably the system will have a news profile as for instance the UK
National Lottery did.
■ Each franchisee is responsible for evangelizing their particular sector,
constantly selling the service's advantages to substantial buyers and sellers
in the relevant industries.

■ System management could adopt an aggressive policy of 'First Aid' – aid for the first big player in any given sector to move into GEMs selling. For instance the car hire companies might hold out against the system because they feared competition from ordinary motorists now empowered to rent out their vehicle on their own terms with total security. Management might in effect say to the biggest five companies 'the first one of you to commit to selling on GEMs alongside your existing routes to market will have the interfacing with your computer systems, that will allow you to rent out cars automatically in GEMs, paid for by us. Later entrants will have to fund their own interface or rely on staff manually updating vehicle availability in GEMs.'

How the franchisee system might develop as GEMs grew

As usage increased, two further refinements would be needed to keep franchisees motivated with clear areas of responsibility.

Half markets

If A runs the market for dental appointments and B is the franchisee for cosmetic surgery who handles the market for cosmetic dentistry appointments? This borderline sector is a 'half market', it could be established and run by either individual but the other is encouraged to increase its usage through a share in the proceeds, where a user has clicked through from that franchisee's market. Similarly, templates spanning several markets would be run by franchisees who negotiate a percentage with their counterparts running the markets covered. Someone setting up a 'wedding arrangements' page for instance would need agreements with the franchisees for bridal wear, photographers, ceremonial cars and so on, which the system would then automatically apply to income.

Market splits

As GEMs usage increased, sectors in which one person could initially oversee day-to-day operation would start requiring much more work if they are to continue growing. The overnight accommodation market, for instance, could start by providing just the basics of matching on price and location with facilities for sellers to add some rudimentary details. As usage increased it might need to become the work of three people, each supervising a higher level of technical sophistication, user liaison and publicity for the budget, mid-range or luxury sectors respectively. As growth continued there would be demand for additional segmenting, splitting budget accommodation between someone charged with group bookings and a colleague in charge of individual overnights for instance, in turn the group bookings market might then fragment between adult groups and youth and school parties, and so on. In a fully fledged system operating in a country with significant population there could be perhaps fifty people running the overnight accommodation market with responsibilities along a spectrum from luxury hotels and homes to tent pitches.

The initial franchisee who launches an overnight accommodation GEM should not be allowed to turn this predictable growth into an empire employing increasing numbers of staff who are neither motivated nor committed to their sector's long-term strengths while he enjoys an ever increasing revenue stream. Nor should one entity be allowed such influence over the country's hoteliers and accommodation providers. Once a GEMs market reaches a level in demand where it requires more than one full-time person to realize its further potential it should have to split: the original franchisee decides which part he wants to continue to run himself and offers the remainder to a pool of approved GEMs potential franchisees who bid to buy that sector. The successful bidder's whole payment goes to the initial market operator, the new one takes on the percentage of commission of the original market. This formula would encourage franchisees to grow all areas of their market: a healthy mass of buyers and sellers will earn them a higher fee than a neglected, low-turnover market when they come to sell the split franchise.

Users, needless to say, would remain unaware of this segmenting franchise structure; their interface must remain seamless. A buyer seeking overnight accommodation would simply input her desired dates, area, price range and number in the party to see her options displayed in a standardized way. However, she would realize that as the market grows the range of options increases. If booking accommodation for a school trip for instance she probably wouldn't spare a thought for what amounts to a family tree of franchisees who have split the market into ever narrower areas of responsibility over preceding months but she would notice how the software allowed her to be increasingly precise about her requirements and perhaps how new sellers had been coaxed into the market. A franchisee concentrating on this tight sector might, for example, launch an initiative through the agricultural press to attract farmers with unused, but comfortably habitable, barns for camping to rent them overnight in GEMs. Like the McDonald's model, there is a motivated individual, focused on long-term expansion, invisibly behind each part of the uniform interface.

If the system needed to contract, the split markets process would be reversed. One franchisee could buy out the sector of another and personally run both. The key principle is that each franchise is the full-time work of only one person. This structure would offer all the cultural advantages of distributed computing – individuals spread around the country thinking independently from each other, dissipation of power and so on – with all the cost savings of a centralized hardware and software operation.

The ethos of a growing organization

Ray Krok, the former salesman who built McDonald's, instilled the 'Q.V.S.' dogma into the heart of his budding empire. Just as relentless commitment to Quality, Value and Service enabled a high-standard, world-wide roll out for the burger giant, so GEMs should have a consistent ethos that pervades all levels of the organization. It too has three points:

Integrity: A franchisee running the GEMs for portable music players must not be in any financial relationship with Sony, Aiwa, Grundig or anyone else who may be selling in that sector. Nor can they themselves ever sell in the marketplace they run. Certainly there should be ongoing conversations about new products and additional software facilities to make the GEM more useful to both sides of its transactions but they are conducted openly and without favour.

Simplicity: As new functions are added to each market they must not be just bolted on to the existing interface, becoming an added complexity for users. The basic design needs to evolve so the new function is incorporated as an intuitive question. A vegetable grower putting his produce up for sale is asked 'Do you wish to drop your price automatically if these carrots are unsold within 24 hours?' and not told 'Click here to activate time related pricing mechanism'.

Growing markets: It would take considerable initiative but GEMs offer the chance to bring previously unrealized resources to market. Inducing their owners to trade would be a key task. A themed party company in Australia for instance already offers the opportunity for demolition companies to sell the chance to push the plunger on their latest job as the highlight for a birthday celebration. A GEMs franchisee running the parties market might seek to raise awareness of this possibility among building clearance companies and, if they started selling, look for some press coverage of the latest sensation in his marketplace. Despite the system's desire to be an unremarkable essential, widely taken for granted, some of its franchisees could become national figures, particularly those running sensitive areas such as the hospital beds market.

The mature organization

Collectively the GEMs consortium would not be selling hardware or software, nor would it have any stake in specific channels of distribution. Companies involved in the consortium could market their expertise gained from the project of course, but the agreement with government should forbid brand extension of whatever name the final service is given. Otherwise the consortium could leverage their officially awarded position into new areas of dominance. The consortium business plan is driven only by the need to bring ever-increasing numbers of buyers and sellers into regular usage, accessing the system through whatever technology they wish.

Sources of income

The mature system would have four revenue streams:

- Commission on transactions: the main income line.
- Float management: substantial amounts of money would be held in escrow by the system on behalf of users for known periods. This could be invested in the system's own loan markets. Float exploitation would only be available on funds held pending completion of a deal, not on insurance bonds held on behalf of sellers. The latter must pay out interest in full to the provider otherwise the system's demand for a bond would constitute a market entry cost, anathema to the GEMs vision. Purchase costs only are acceptable.
- Flat fee services: offering legal contracts and agreements for business partnerships, for instance, or for individuals wishing to join a club in the appropriate GEM.
- Value-added services: a user who wishes his details sheet to show a photograph of himself or something he is selling could get it scanned at a copyshop or on their own equipment and then sent down the line to the core computer. The user would be given a receipt number against which it could be retrieved later and added to a details page, but could be expected to pay for the facility. A photograph is not essential to start trading so these fees would not detract from GEMs' commitment to no-cost market entry.

A potential structure for the mature organization

(See chart overleaf)

Some notes on this structure

- The loans market would be too crucial to the system, and too extensive in its potential liabilities, to be handled by an individual franchisee. At least one established financial institution would need to be in charge. They would agree a percentage of flat rate commission to be retained like any other franchisee.
- The core program team would constantly look at the most basic cornerstone programming in the system. In a mature GEMs service in just one country this could be matching buyers and sellers many millions of times a day. If just one instruction set can be tightened further that soon amounts to a significant saving in processing power.

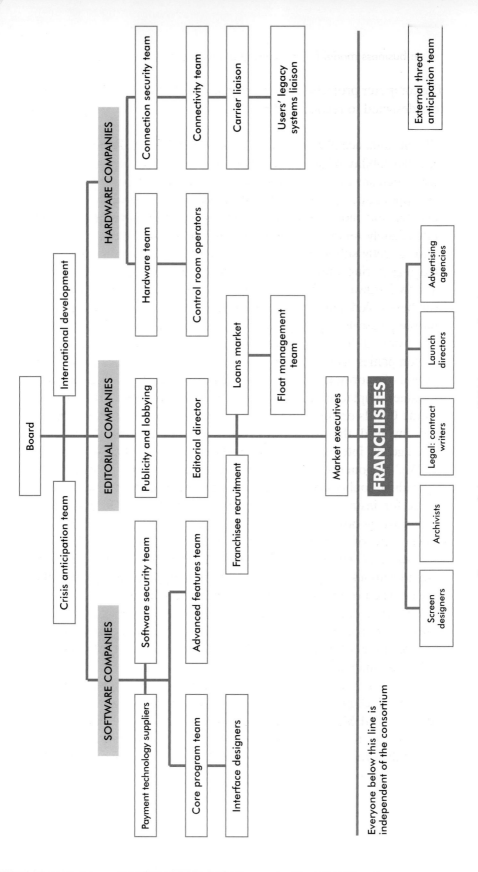

Structure of the mature GEMs organization

Board

Crisis anticipation team

International development

SOFTWARE COMPANIES

EDITORIAL COMPANIES

HARDWARE COMPANIES

Payment technology suppliers

Software security team

Core program team

Advanced features team

Interface designers

Publicity and lobbying

Editorial director

Franchisee recruitment

Loans market

Float management team

Hardware team

Control room operators

Connection security team

Connectivity team

Carrier liaison

Users' legacy systems liaison

External threat anticipation team

Market executives

FRANCHISEES

Everyone below this line is independent of the consortium

Screen designers

Archivists

Legal: contract writers

Launch directors

Advertising agencies

Big computer projects rarely go as planned. The organizational structure is designed to recognize this.

■ The prominence of a crisis anticipation team is intended to recognize the inevitability of unplanned incidents, particularly during the early days when any evidence of disarray could be most effectively exploited by opponents. The team would consider all potential sources of disaster and plot a series of responses based on core principles of immediately telling the truth publicly, compensating any users who have directly suffered a loss, swift external investigation and knowledge-gathering internal response. More importantly, they would look at how hardware, software, corruption-induced or financial disasters can be avoided and should have sufficient clout in the organization to pursue an escalating programme of preventative measures.

■ The external threat anticipation team is an attempt to avoid the fate of companies like IBM and Apple Computer who each, during a period of enormous success, lost track of changes in the market and became complacent in their own culture. This team would be funded by the GEMs organization but based well outside any of the companies involved, their only contact being a one-way flow of ideas and intelligence into the consortium. This group constantly asks how GEMs' opponents might attack the project, either politically (by spreading doubts about its honesty, or over-publicizing small problems, for instance) or competitively (could the GEMs markets in expensive goods be undercut by a start-up operation charging a lower rate of commission for example?) Analysis is fed into a rebuttal unit within the publicity team, in preparation for prompt counter-attack to possible charges from opponents, or into the board, when competitive position might be under threat.

This team is emphatically not envisioned as a remote outpost for out-of-sight and out-of-mind executives but an established route into the top layers of management. It is worth remembering that GEMs' principles mandate that no-one remain in management of the system longer than 8 years to avoid any accusations it was being run by a privileged clique. Newcomers who had spent a year thoroughly looking at GEMs from the point of view of a predator could be useful elements in this evolving view at the top, arguably more informed about the project's strengths and weaknesses than someone who had spent years soaking up the culture at headquarters.

Expanding beyond the first country

Once a GEMs system was working in one country with confident franchisees driving its further development, consortium focus could shift to
rolling out similar systems elsewhere around the world. This is when the
project's commitment to political neutrality becomes crucial. The
system must keep government in a first country of operation at arm's
length and not become associated with any one set of political values.

Despite using loosely-standardized core software, a consortium
driving GEMs forward should not seek to impose one uniform name for
the service across the world. Attempting to bulldoze a global brand
name into the heart of national economies would probably be counterproductive. Instead Russia might have its *Sistema Obshchestvennykh
Rynkov* (Public Markets System) while perhaps Brazil offers its citizens
the *Serviço Eletrônico de Comércio* (Electronic Trading Service.) Like De
La Rue, banknote printer to the world, the consortium should be
content that key opinion formers would know about the depth of their
operation while allowing national identity to take precedence over any
desire to force that message on ordinary users. The consortium would,
however, have every reason to help individual users distinguish between
a GEMs system that was being allowed to operate free from any
prospect of political interference and its counterparts in less democratic
nations. As one small part of the checks and balances around the system,
users need to know if the consortium is happy that they are operating
with all the independence they require. Otherwise the companies propagating GEMs could be seen as malleable by governments, a damaging
perception likely to arouse significant resistance to use elsewhere. The
consortium could adopt a purist stance, of course, refusing to launch a
system except where they were assured of a place among the institutions
in a democratic society, but that would cut them off from many emerging
economies. Instead, member companies could adopt a phrase such as
Guaranteed Electronic Markets as a master brand, akin to Visa or
Mastercard on credit cards issued by multiple banks, bestowed as a seal
of approval on systems operating in a healthy society. The logo might for
instance show up fleetingly in a screen corner each time a user logged on
to the system, but not in countries that insisted on government supervision extending beyond legitimate law making or where authorities
demanded access to information not available to all users.

Even in countries which would appear to be grateful for any kind of reliable markets service the consortium should actively seek to factor-in full democratic protection. A disintegrated economy in an immature democracy such as Russia might look like a chance for easy pickings by offering electronic markets without the more costly protection and inspection protocols citizens in a first world country would demand. But GEMs would be aiming to lift Russians out of their parlous conditions. Once they were more prosperous they would be likely to place the system under much greater scrutiny. A half-hearted approach to their rights at any point could then become a problem.

Would public electronic markets in different countries communicate with each other? Might a resident of Mombassa displaying his paintings on a Kenyan system find he had a purchaser in Sydney who had been browsing the artwork for sale in an Australian GEM? Could the levels of protection that define these new markets extend to cross-border trade? That will be decided by parliaments: would the Kenyan courts uphold the rights of a New South Wales art lover in an automated referral if the deal went to dispute and could not be resolved any other way? It is likely a patchwork of agreements on a sector-by-sector basis would arise over time but the countries that had a seal of approval from one of the consortia building public electronic markets would be logical partners in upholding each other's citizens' trades.

Once the core software was fully developed and easily transferable around the world smaller countries would have to decide whether they wanted to share a GEMs system with a larger neighbour or offer a diminished level of service in an exclusively national system. For instance a mature GEMs in Andorra (population 55 000) might only be cost effective with a full complement of 100 franchisees, each of them covering a huge swathe of categories. Neighbouring Spain (population 40 million) conversely could have several thousand franchisees after fragmenting areas of responsibility as the system grew. Andorrans would not necessarily be limited in the range of goods available to them in GEMs, anyone could import and sell anything on the system, but they would find marketplace management far less precise than that on the lower slopes of the Pyrenees. They may prefer to trade on the Spanish system if courts would uphold their rights and those of their contractual partners. Alternately they could lobby for a European Union-wide GEMs system which should be able to offer all member nations a phenomenal degree of sophistication and initiative in each sector.

After a number of countries had a public electronics markets system running with competing consortia demonstrating viable business models, remaining governments could be in the awkward position of justifying a decision to stay out of GEMs and deprive their populations of its benefits. Once that point was reached it could be the consortium that had been rigorous in asserting its probity and maintaining the highest standards for its master brand which became the most sought after by populations. Thus, sound business logic encourages the spread both of democracy and of atomized capitalism.

Notes

1. The twenty-first-century stock market, *Business Week,* 10 August 1998, p. 52.
2. BBC Television, *Disaster: the Millennium Time Bomb,* transmitted 9 June 1998.
3. John F. Love, *McDonald's Behind the Arches*, Bantam Books, revised edition, 1995. Quoted in McDonald's brochure *Thinking about a Franchise?* 1998.

index